Oral Poetry

To DAVID

ORAL POETRY

Its nature, significance and social context

RUTH FINNEGAN

SENIOR LECTURER IN COMPARATIVE
SOCIAL INSTITUTIONS, OPEN UNIVERSITY
AND READER IN SOCIOLOGY
UNIVERSITY OF THE SOUTH PACIFIC

CAMBRIDGE UNIVERSITY PRESS

CAMBRIDGE

LONDON · NEW YORK · MELBOURNE

Published by the Syndics of the Cambridge University Press
The Pitt Building, Trumpington Street, Cambridge CB2 IRP
Bentley House, 200 Euston Road, London NW1 2DB
32 East 57th Street, New York, NY 10022, USA
296 Beaconsfield Parade, Middle Park, Melbourne 3206, Australia

First published 1977

Library of Congress catalogue card number: 76–11077

ISBN 0 521 21316 9

Printed in Great Britain at the
University Press, Cambridge

Library of Congress Cataloguing in Publication Data
Finnegan, Ruth H
Oral poetry.
Bibliography: p.
Includes index.
1. Folk poetry – History and criticism. 2. Oral
tradition. I. Title.
PN1341.F46   398.2   76-11077
ISBN 0 521 21316 9

Contents

Plates

Preface

This book is about oral poetry – its nature and its social context and significance – treated comparatively. It considers, therefore, examples such as unwritten Tatar epics, Eskimo lyrics, Malay love songs, South African praise poems to traditional chiefs or modern personalities, Nigerian election songs, or Anglo-American ballads, old and new. It is intended not as a comprehensive survey of oral poetry throughout the world but as a general introduction to oral poetry and to the range of controversies and problems in its study. Thus the book treats much-debated questions: whether there is a distinctive form of 'oral composition'; the competing theories about oral transmission; whether there is a special 'oral style'; how far one can generalise about the 'functions' of oral poetry; how 'oral' 'oral poetry' is; whether there is such a thing as 'oral poetry' at all as a separate and distinctive category. (So the book does not begin with a neat definition of 'oral poetry' – though the subject is discussed in a preliminary way in chapter 1, section 3 – for the problem of its nature is one of the controversies followed through in the book.) In discussing these controversies, I have tried to include as much evidence as is feasible by using actual examples of oral poetry – this book is about the poetry, not about some proposed sociological model for studying it – and I hope that the book will provide a preliminary account of this fascinating but often neglected field.

It does not pretend to be a comprehensive survey of the incidence and forms of oral poetry throughout the world. It is not therefore directed to specialists, but to those students of literature or sociology who would like to have some general introduction to the controversies and findings concerning oral poetry. I hope it will be useful, for instance, to students of the sociology of literature and art, comparative literature, communication, and perhaps comparative social institutions. It may also interest those with specialisms in other subjects who want to acquaint themselves with developments in the study of oral poetry; they may be surprised to find that once-unquestioned generalisations have become matters of controversy, and that the implications of this can be far-reaching. Finally, though this book is not aimed at experts, it may be useful to those who specialise in one aspect of the subject and are not necessarily acquainted with others. In particular I hope the book may provide a broader framework for anyone embarking on the study of a particular oral literature, giving some idea of the problems likely to arise and the questions it may be useful to ask (and to know about) in approaching a given instance or tradition of oral literature.

I have not attempted to put forward one model or theory of oral literature, but have tried to discuss the controversies and interpretations in the light of the evidence as I understand it. However there are doubtless some consistent personal predilections in the way I assess the evidence. For one thing I distrust over-arching theory or large generalisations purporting to cover *all* oral poetry. This dislike arises, I think, from an examination of the evidence and an awareness of its variety, as well as from a personal distaste for sociological jargon. Secondly, though I have not wished to burden the text with many references to sociological theory, those interested in defining my own position will notice that I am more impressed by the approach of writers like Weber, Blumer or Becker to the analysis of literature and literary activity than by that of Durkheim, Parsons or Radcliffe-Brown. I regard literature as something at least partially analysable in terms of people acting and interacting and creating within accepted social conventions, rather than as an abstraction that could be juxtaposed to Society, or that could be fully analysable in terms of social function, type of society or other external 'sociological' factors.

Despite this underlying approach, the book is not primarily intended as a contribution to sociological theory nor as staking out a particular defensive position, but as an introduction to one substantive field, that of oral poetry as a social phenomenon. I hope that it will be useful in setting this topic in perspective and in encouraging others to enter or persevere in a study that is too often regarded as merely peripheral to literature and sociology.

The two conventional disciplines on which this book chiefly draws are those of literature and sociology. The main body of the book (after the two more general introductory chapters) might seem to be divided neatly between these two disciplines, since questions of composition, style and transmission tend to interest literary scholars, while the position of the poet, the function of oral poetry and the possible relations between 'literature' and 'society' concern sociologists. In practice I have found that this distinction is impossible to maintain, for no literature (above all no oral literature) can be understood without reference to social conventions, even in apparently 'literary' aspects like verbal style; nor can the social significance of literary activity be explained without remembering that what is involved is, after all, 'literature' and not just some external 'social function'. So that even those who think that only one part of the book is of obvious relevance to their own interests will find much of concern to them in other chapters.

Other disciplines have contributed too, besides literature and sociology (a term in which I include what is sometimes differentiated as social anthropology). The references at the end include works by linguists, psychologists, classical and mediaeval scholars, missionaries, Biblical scholars, specialists in Far Eastern Studies, political scientists, historians and many others. I must also mention in particular the contribution of 'folklorists', a group which I was at first suspicious of (sometimes with reason, as chapter 2 will make clear) but whose recent work, above all in America, is important: it is a pity that the overtones inherent in some earlier 'folklore' studies, and the misleading connotations of the term 'folklore' itself have led other scholars to underestimate the solid and detailed research often carried out under this admittedly unfortunate[1] term. Without this huge volume of work – much larger than most outsiders realise – this book could never have been contemplated, far less written.

Even to try to provide an *introduction* has seemed increasingly ambitious to me as I have worked on this book. Even to begin to fulfil my claim I would need several more lifetimes, world wide travel as well as unremitting labour in libraries, a whole range of skills I do not possess and, of course, unlimited linguistic ability. All the same, I have come to think that even a sketchy and inadequate introduction to the subject may serve some purpose. I have certainly learnt a great deal from trying to consider the general subject of oral poetry in a comparative way – looking not only at classical poetry, for instance, but also at modern 'folk' singing, not only at contemporary African poetry but also at the magnificent traditional poetry of Central Asia or of Polynesia. I now realise that my own earlier work on African oral literature could have been more balanced and in-formed if I had had a greater appreciation of comparative material: and I suspect the same may be true of scholars who have specialised in other areas. So, even though I am doubtful about several of the conventional generalisations about oral poetry, I have found it revealing to consider such instances in a comparative context; this has shed new light on their nature and on the arguments about them. An attempt to pull together some of the findings and controversies may be useful to others as well as myself, if only as preliminary to more detailed work. Too often the subject has suffered from a very localised viewpoint, so that just 'primitive poetry', or just historical Europe, or 'Indo-European' or American-Indian or some other single tradition has been the focus.[2] But without some regard for a comparative perspective, even the most scholarly and specialised work can be ill-founded.

The comparative approach in this book may thus serve as a general background to more specialised research. But I can only claim to have

[1] Unfortunate in my opinion, that is. The term is one I prefer to avoid, for its inherently misleading associations (see chapter 2).
[2] There have been a few magnificent exceptions (the Chadwicks' *Growth of Literature*, above all, and perhaps Bowra's *Heroic Poetry*), but these have been unusual.

written a very preliminary account and know only too well the vast range of material that I have not had time or space to refer to.[1] I emphasise this lack of comprehensiveness, not out of personal modesty, but to make clear that the book must not be thought of as an attempt at a definitive and final work.

For me one of the main findings has been how many of the confident generalisations once made about 'oral poetry' (or, for that matter about 'folk literature' or about 'primitive' or 'non-literate society') have turned out to be much less certain than they once seemed, or to have hidden overtones which, once made explicit, become questionable. Certainly in matters like the type of society in which oral poetry tends to occur, the nature of 'oral composition' or of the mode of transmission, even of the definition and differentiation of 'oral' from 'written' modes, certain patterns and commonly occurring syndromes may be detectable: but the main characteristic is complexity rather than rigidly determined uniformity.

This flexibility and variety have to be indicated by means of a relatively few examples, and not by comprehensive coverage of the field. Lack of space has often meant that I have been unable to illustrate general points as fully as I would have liked (and the quotations included are often in translation only) and the analysis is sometimes rather dry and abstract.[2] I hope however that this preliminary book, for all its limitations, will serve to introduce others to this rich field and perhaps encourage specialist scholars to take the subject far further through detailed study of particular oral poetries in their own languages.

R. F.

Milton Keynes and *Suva 1976*

---

[1] I draw attention in particular to the absence of musicological analysis. This is a specialism which I am not competent to treat, and I have in any case chosen to concentrate on the literary aspects of oral poetry and its social context. Readers should be aware of this limitation; a full account of many instances of oral poetry would have to include musicological analysis.

[2] Those interested in pursuing some of the points may find it rewarding to turn to the instances of 'oral poetry' (in translation) which I have collected up in the *Penguin Anthology of Oral Poetry* (1977) or to the world-wide anthologies edited by Willard Trask (2 vols, 1969) and Rothenberg (1969).

Acknowledgements

I am grateful to many libraries and librarians who have assisted me: in particular the libraries and staff of the British Museum, the School of Oriental and African Studies in the University of London, the Royal Anthropological Institute, the Open University (in particular their Inter-Library Loans Librarian) and, at an earlier stage, the University of Ibadan. Without the generous and expert help of these individuals and organisations the work for this book could never have been contemplated, still less completed.

I also owe a great deal to the encouragement and help of friends and colleagues, from my earlier teachers – above all E. E. Evans-Pritchard and Godfrey Lienhardt – to more recent colleagues and friendly acquaintances, whose quick enthusiasm and interest in the subject encouraged me to persevere. I am especially grateful to 'Goosh' Andrzejewski for his long-standing encouragement, to Gordon Innes, Michael Philps and the late Wilfred Whiteley for stimulating discussion of the general topic, and to Peter Burke and my mother, Agnes Finnegan, for reading and commenting on all or part of the typescript. To my husband, David Murray, I owe a special debt, not only for his overall interest and pertinent critiques, but also for not complaining when I retreated to the study, leaving him with the children and the garden and the business letters!

I thank Mrs Pam Gardner and Mrs Joy Rickson for their help with typing, and the Open University for providing some facilities for research even in the intensive developmental stages of its opening years.

Certain portions of chapter 1, section 3 and chapter 2, section 4 appeared for the first time in a slightly different form in the *Bulletin of the School of Oriental and African Studies* (vol. 37, 1974) and I am grateful for permission to re-use it here.

Publisher's Note
An acknowledgement of the author's source for each quoted poem or part poem is included, and a list of references, giving author, title and publisher in full, will be found at the end of the book. Every effort has been made to ensure the accuracy of these acknowledgements.

1

Introductory

What is man's body? It is a spark from the fire
It meets water and it is put out.
What is man's body? It is a bit of straw
It meets fire and it is burnt.
What is man's body? It is a bubble of water
Broken by the wind.

(Gond song from Central India, recorded in the 1930s when the
Gond could be described as 'one of the poorest peoples on earth'.

Elwin and Hivale, 1944, p. 255)

Many days of sorrow, many nights of woe,
Many days of sorrow, many nights of woe,
And a ball and chain, everywhere I go.

Chains on my feet, padlocks on my hands,
Chains on my feet and padlocks on my hands,
It's all on account of stealing a woman's man.

It was early this mornin' that I had my trial,
It was early this mornin' that I had my trial,
Ninety days on the county road, and the judge didn't even smile.

(Negro poem 'Chain gang blues', published in Hollo, 1964, p. 11)

A wonderful occupation
Making songs!
But all too often they
Are failures...

(From Piuvkaq's poem 'The joy of a singer', translated from the
Eskimo in Rasmussen, 1931, p. 511)

These poems, and those from similar backgrounds, are not usually studied
in courses on 'literature' or included in discussion of the sociology of
literature and art. If mentioned at all, they are likely to be placed in some
special category – like 'oral tradition', or 'folklore' or perhaps 'popular
culture'. This firmly separates it from mainstream literature as something
with its own rationale but which, while no doubt splendid in its own terms,
need not be taken into account when discussing literature proper. Equally,
such poems are rarely considered significant for the sociology of literature,

since such oral literary forms are presumed to be natural, communal and unconsidered, and relatively free from the constraints of social differentiation, of prescribed roles or socially recognised conventions – things the sociologist looks for. As a result, oral poetry has often been ignored both in literary study and (still more, perhaps) in the sociology of literature, and, generally speaking, assumed to be of merely marginal interest. It is a common assumption that it is best relegated to 'folklore' studies, or specialised ethnographies, or left to those concerned to propagate 'popular' or 'underground' culture.

And yet there is a great amount of oral poetry already recorded and still being performed, in addition to the instances documented from the past, and interest in these forms seems to be increasing. It is difficult to argue that they should be ignored as aberrant or unusual in human society, or in principle outside the normal field of established scholarly research. In practice there is everything to be gained by bringing the study of oral poetry into the mainstream of work on literature and sociology.

It is a basic contention of this book that the nature of oral poetry is such that its study falls squarely within the field of literature; it can throw light on literature 'proper' (understood as written literature) and is also part of literature as it is most generally understood. What is more, there *is* no clear-cut line between 'oral' and 'written' literature, and when one tries to differentiate between them – as has often been attempted – it becomes clear that there are constant overlaps. Contrary to earlier assumptions which classed forms like those quoted as items of 'oral tradition', 'folklore' or 'traditional formulae', there proves to be no definitive and unitary body of poetry which, being 'oral', can be clearly differentiated from written and, as it were, 'normal' poetry.

One consequence of the questioning of this assumed special and different category of oral literature is that the assumptions about oral literature which made it seem inappropriate for sociological enquiry fall to the ground. There is no reason for assuming that all oral poetry is necessarily artless, 'close to nature', shared by the whole 'tribe' or 'community' equally, and so on. In practice, and contrary to the concept of oral literature given by many romantic writers of the traditional folklore school, the normal questions in the sociology of literature can equally, and most pertinently, be asked of oral poetry. Indeed it should surely become a major task of sociological analysis to include the scrutiny of oral and literary forms within society – whether in a non-literate, or a literate and 'modern' context – and thus to help redress the impression so often gained from sociological writing of intellectual and artistic barrenness in the cultures described. People are moved not only by economic or political factors and groupings, but also by artistic ones. Whether sociology is concerned with 'meaning' (as is often claimed) or with 'play' (as Huizinga would have had it) or with the social functions of institutions, some analysis of oral literary forms within society is an important aspect of the sociologist's task.

In this area as in others, a comparative perspective can be illuminating. Within literature one can learn much, for instance, by considering Homer in the light of findings about recent Yugoslav oral epic poetry or about Eskimo or Gilbertese poets or modern blues singers. Similarly, some aspects of poetry may prove not to be peculiar to, say, Homer or Piuvkaq or 'Left Wing Gordon', or even (as suggested in some linguistic work) to 'Indo-European culture', but to be practised and performed in many areas of the world. A comparative perspective can lead to awareness of the complexity and diversity of forms throughout human culture and history, and cast doubt on some crude dichotomies used by social scientists in the past – that between 'civilised' as against 'primitive' and 'simple' society, for instance; or *Gesellschaft* opposed to *Gemeinschaft*; or 'modern' as against 'traditional' culture. This emphasis on the relevance of comparative material and on the complexity and absence of rigid uniformity in oral poetry is one recurrent theme of this book.

1 The importance of oral poetry

Oral poetry is not an odd or aberrant phenomenon in human culture, nor a fossilised survival from the far past, destined to wither away with increasing modernisation. In fact, it is of common occurrence in human society, literate as well as non-literate. It is found all over the world, past and present, from the meditative personal poetry of recent Eskimo or Maori poets, to mediaeval European and Chinese ballads, or the orally composed epics of pre-classical Greek in the first millenium B.C. One can compare the twentieth-century love lyrics of the Gond poet

> As in a pot the milk turns sour,
> As silver is debased,
> So the love I won so hardly
> Has been shattered since you have betrayed me
>
> (Hivale and Elwin, 1935, p. 128)

or

> Jump over the wall and come to me,
> And I will give you every happiness.
> I will give you fruit from my garden,
> And to drink, water of Ganges.
> Jump over the wall and come to me,
> I will give you a bed of silk,
> And to cover you a fair, fine-woven cloth,
> Only jump over the wall and all delight shall be yours.
>
> (Hivale and Elwin, 1935, p. 118)

to those of the mediaeval troubadours, the stanza, for instance, from Jaufre
Rudel's love-lyric in the twelfth century

> Love from a far-off land,
> For you all my being aches;
> I can find no remedy for it
> If I do not hear your call
> With the lure of soft love
> In an orchard or behind curtains
> With my longed-for beloved
>
> (Dronke, 1968, p. 119)

Again, one can draw parallels between the epic poetry of Homer or
mediaeval romances, and that of recent oral poets in Yugoslavia or Cyprus
or the Soviet Union. One can contrast the condensed imagery of a recent
Somali 'miniature' lyric like

> A flash of lightning does not satisfy thirst,
> What then is it to me if you just pass by?
>
> (Andrzejewski and Lewis, 1964, p. 146)

to the lengthy and high-flown praise-poem about the famous nineteenth-
century Zulu warrior Shaka, a panegyric extending to some hundreds of
lines

> Dlungwana son of Ndaba!
> Ferocious one of the Mbelebele brigade,
> Who raged among the large kraals,
> So that until dawn the huts were being turned upside-down...
>
> (Cope, 1968, p. 88)

Oral poetry is not just something of far away and long ago. In a sense
it is all around us still. Certainly in most definitions of oral poetry, one
should also include the kinds of ballads and 'folksongs' (both those dubbed
'modern' *and* 'traditional') sung widely in America or the British Isles,
American Negro verse, the popular songs transmitted by radio and television, the chanted and emotional verse of some preachers in the American
South, or even the kind of children's verse made familiar in the Opies'
collection. The British school-child's jeer

> That's the way to the zoo,
> That's the way to the zoo,
> The monkey house is nearly full
> But there's room enough for you
>
> (Opie, 1967, p. 176)

is parallel in some respects to the children's song of abuse recently recorded
in West Africa

The one who does not love me
He will become a frog
And he will jump jump jump away
He will become a monkey with one leg
And he will hop hop hop away.

(Beier and Gbadamosi, n.d.) (Yoruba)

Even well-known carols and hymns – 'Once in royal David's city', 'Away in a manger', 'There is a green hill far away' – can be regarded as oral poetry in contemporary circulation: for though they also appear in written form, they surely achieve their main impact and active circulation through ever-renewed oral means.

It is easy to overlook such oral poetry. This is a special temptation to the scholar and those committed to 'high culture' whose preconceptions all tend to direct attention towards written literature as the characteristic location of poetry. Oral forms are often just not noticed – particularly those which are near-by or contemporary. A much-quoted instance of this is the experience of Cecil Sharp, the famous collector of English 'folk songs', at the beginning of this century. He wrote:

> One of the most amazing and puzzling things about the English folk song is the way in which it has hitherto escaped the notice of the educated people resident in the country districts. When I have had the good fortune to collect some especially fine songs in a village, I have often called upon the Vicar to tell him of my success. My story has usually been received, at first, with polite incredulity, and, afterwards, when I have displayed the contents of my notebook, with amazement. Naturally, the Vicar finds it difficult to realize that the old men and women of his parish, whom he has known and seen day by day for many a long year, but whom he has never suspected of any musical leanings, should all the while have possessed, secretly treasured in their old heads, songs of such remarkable interest and loveliness.

> (Sharp, 1972 (first published 1907), p. 131)

This experience has often been repeated by collectors trying to discover and record local oral poetry, and in some countries – England is one example – the study of local contemporary oral forms is still largely unrecognised and neglected by formal university scholarship.

Oral literature produced in the past, on the other hand, has seemed more acceptable as a subject for scholarly study, provided the items have come down to us through the written tradition. So the analysis of the ultimately oral quality of Homer's *Iliad* and *Odyssey* or of the *Epic of Gilgamesh* have entered into accepted academic scholarship in a way that more recent oral art has not. Exotic examples too – the poetry produced by largely non-literate peoples in Africa or Oceania – has attracted attention as, at the least,

interesting examples of primitive literary forms, a suitable topic for anthropologists and ethnographers (even if not for literary scholars). Once
collected and transmitted in written translations to a reading public, Zulu
praise-poems or Maori lyrics seem obvious examples of oral poetry, just
the type of thing to fit one popular picture of the 'primitive unlettered
singer' – even though to the local administrator or teacher they may have
appeared of little interest, at best the artless and uninformed repetitions
of tribal culture or the crude accompaniment to tribal dancing. Similarly
the stress in 'folklore' collecting has, until recently, been on the 'old' and
'traditional', survivals from the rural past rather than contemporaneous
and urban forms, and on the products of marginal and immigrant groups,
surviving despite modern life rather than as part of it.

Much of the interest in oral forms has in the past been directed to what
was far off in space or time, or had achieved scholarly recognition in
authoritative collections of 'traditional' forms – the canonical nineteenth-
century collections of ballads by Child, for instance, rather than recently
sung versions or hillbilly songs etc. So the importance of local and contemporary forms has been continuously underplayed. It must therefore be
stressed at the outset that there is much more 'oral poetry' than is often
recognised, at least if one takes a reasonably wide definition of the term.
And it is not just a survival of past ages and stages; it is a normal part of
our modern life as well as that of more distant peoples.

For all the relative neglect of modern forms, oral poetry has interested
many scholars throughout the world, amateur and professional. This
interest has taken various forms. Under the name of 'folklore', a flourishing
movement for two centuries or so has collected and studied popular and
'folk' traditions, including poetry and song. Though it was initially directed
to rural and supposedly 'traditional' forms in Europe and America, these
being analysed largely in terms of an evolutionary and romantic model,
some folklorists are now turning more to urban and 'Third World' forms
in their studies. One recent study has treated the contemporary sermons
chanted by preachers in the American South (Rosenberg, 1970) and a
symposium of the American Folklore Society was specifically directed
towards work in the urban context (Paredes and Stekert, 1971). In addition,
collections of industrial songs (e.g. Lloyd, 1952; Korson, 1943), and so-called
'protest verse' (e.g. Greenway, 1953; Denisoff, 1966) are being recognised
as part of 'folklore study': they are instances of oral poetry, to use the
terminology preferred in this book. Classical and mediaeval scholars also
discuss 'oral poetry', in work largely stimulated by the comparative research
of Milman Parry and Albert Lord on the Homeric epics and more recent
Yugoslav heroic poetry, so influentially expounded in Lord's *The Singer of
Tales* (first published 1960). This has led to discussion of the likely 'oral
composition' of such poems as the *Iliad* and *Odyssey*, the Biblical psalms,

the *Chanson de Roland* and *Beowulf*. By now too anthropologists and linguists (particularly those trained in America) often include the study of local oral literature as part of their subject, and this is recorded in a large number of publications. Writers such as Marshall McLuhan have drawn the attention of social scientists and others to the 'oral' nature of earlier cultures and of recent developments in communication patterns in our industrial world. The current interest in oral literature is augmented by the common connection between a 'left wing' or 'progressive' stance and a concern with 'popular culture' or 'protest songs' and (in some cases) the productions of modern radio and television. When one remembers, too, the many generations of collectors and annotators in country after country – linguists, missionaries, administrators, extra-mural teachers – it becomes clear that there is a great deal of interest in and information on the subject. It may not be systematised as a formal academic discipline, but there is no shortage of basic material.

Many emotions are also involved. For some, like the traditional folklorists and earlier anthropologists, the topic is closely connected with 'tradition', with nationalist movements or with the faith in progress which expresses itself in the theory of social evolution. For others it forms part of a left-wing faith and a belief in 'popular' culture, along with a revolt against 'bourgeois art forms' or 'the establishment'. In others it goes with a romantic ideal of the noble savage and of the pure natural impulses which, it is felt, we have lost in the urban mechanical way of life today. Many of the positions taken up implicitly link with scholarly controversies about the development of society, the nature of art and communication, or various models of man.

Oral poetry and its study is a complex and emotive study, involving many often disputed assumptions. The history of some of the approaches to the subject and the preconceptions behind them are worth looking at because they show what is being implied in statements and claims about the subject. This is set out a little later, in chapter 2. The present chapter considers some more general points about the nature of 'oral poetry' and the problems of studying it.

2 Some forms of oral poetry

The term 'oral poetry' sounds fairly simple and clear-cut. This is also the impression one gets from some statements about it. 'Oral poetry' is described in one authoritative encyclopaedia article as 'poetry composed *in* oral performance by people who cannot read or write. It is synonymous with traditional and folk poetry' (Lord, 1965, p. 591). Magoun tells us confidently that 'oral poetry... is composed entirely of formulas, large and small, while lettered poetry is never formulaic' (Magoun in Nicholson, 1971, p. 190).

If one concentrates on the 'oral' element in oral poetry, many confident assertions give the impression that 'oral' is a straightforward and easily identified characteristic of certain literature. 'Oral literature' is often equated with 'oral tradition', for instance, the 'traditional' element apparently being what makes it 'oral'; this identification is implied in Lord's comment just quoted and has been explicit in the work of most folklorists in the past. General and unequivocal statements are also made about the style of 'oral poetry'. It is, for instance, 'totally formulaic' (Magoun, loc. cit.; cf. Lord, 1968a, p. 47), characterised by a special 'oral technique' and 'oral method' (Buchan, 1972, pp. 55, 58) and 'of *necessity* paratactic' (Lord, 1965, p. 592). It is often suggested that oral literature, not being written, is self-evidently the possession of non-literate peoples living in isolation from the centres of urban civilisation, or differentiated in some radical way from modern civilised society. Notopoulos claims among the 'facts of life about oral poetry' that 'the society which gives birth to oral poetry is characterized by traditional fixed ways in all aspects of its life' (Notopoulos, 1964, pp. 50, 51). The main conclusion appears to be that oral poetry is something clear and distinctive, with known characteristics and setting, and that to isolate it for study is in principle a simple matter.

The truth, however, is more complicated. When one looks in any detail at the manifold instances which have variously been termed oral poetry, it quickly becomes clear that the whole concept of 'oral poetry' is in fact a complex and variegated one. One can get round this, partially at least, by adopting a restrictive definition of 'oral poetry' – which cuts out much that most people would include under the term and that is of greatest interest to students of the subject. If one takes a fairly wide approach, it has to be admitted that the term 'oral poetry' is both a complex and a relative one. It is true that if one is *determined* to set up a single uniform model of oral poetry, it is possible to discover certain regularities (especially when one does not have a very close acquaintance with a wide range of detail). Thus it might be possible to find something in common between, on the one hand, a short and pregnant Somali *balwo* lyric

> Like a sailing ship pulled by a storm,
> I set my compass towards a place empty of people[1]

or a witty Malay *pantun* – like the one describing an opium den

> As red as a starling's his peepers,
> And he hails from the isle of Ceylon.
> On their beds round a lamp lounge the sleepers
> And pipes are the flutes that they play on
>
> (Wilkinson and Winstedt, 1957, p. 10)

---

[1] The forsaken lover compares his situation with the much-feared experience along the Somali coast when a small sailing ship is blown off course, and the sailors find themselves near an unknown desert shore, far from their familiar port. (Andrzejewski, 1967, p. 9)

– and, on the other hand, a long and effusive Zulu panegyric ode memorised by its reciter and running to several hundred lines, or the famous epics of Homer, or the great Central Asian epic of *Manas*, in one version 250,000 lines long. But whatever can be found in common, the differences of style, symbolism, performance and social background are surely as striking as any real similarities. Too ready generalisation either risks setting up mere speculation in the place of evidence or is reducible to tautologies.

A basic argument running through this book is that many of the generalisations made about oral poetry are over-simplified, and thus misleading Oral poetry can take many different forms, and occurs in many cultural situations; it does not manifest itself only in the one unitary model envisaged by some scholars.

This can be briefly illustrated by a quick initial look at a few of the various types of oral poetry known to occur throughout the world. This brings home something of the diversity of forms in which human beings have expressed their poetic imagination. At the same time it reminds us of the many parallels and overlaps with written literature. An initial survey of this kind necessarily begs the question of how 'oral poetry' should be defined and delineated – a question that must be faced later. But a preliminary survey of the field will give a general idea, in ostensive terms, of the kind of instances to be considered, and will at the same time illustrate my claim that what is commonly regarded as 'oral poetry' is by no means a clearly differentiated and unitary category.

In the brief discussion below, I have mainly adopted the terms long used in Western literary study to describe different genres. These terms form a convenient means of grouping together certain broad similarities. They can only take one so far, however; it cannot be assumed that they would be the most appropriate ones for detailed analysis of a given oral literature, or that their use in a preliminary account implies any attempt to set up a definitive typology of genres.

The first form that springs to mind – some would say the most developed form of oral poetry – is epic. In the general sense of a long narrative poem with an emphasis on the heroic, this genre has a wide distribution in time and space. The range runs from historic cases in the ancient world like the Sumerian epic of *Gilgamesh*, the Greek Homeric poems of the *Iliad* and *Odyssey*, the Indian *Mahabharata*, or the mediaeval European epics like the *Song of Roland*, to more recent cases like the Finnish *Kalevala* or the long and impressive epics recorded in Russia and the Soviet Union in the nineteenth and twentieth centuries, the 'Gesar' epic so widely found throughout Tibet, Mongolia and China, the Yugoslav heroic poems recorded in the 1930s or the story about Anggun Nan Tungga recently recorded in West Sumatra, whose recitation takes up seven or more complete nights (Phillips, 1975).

The term 'epic' is a relative one. 'Pure' epics like the *Iliad* or *Odyssey* are totally in verse, but it is also common for there to be some prose; this sometimes comes in the narrative portions, with soliloquies, conversations or purple passages in verse. In Kazakh epic, for instance, much of the basic narrative was often in prose, delivered in a kind of recitative, while the speeches of the main characters were in verse (Winner, 1958, p. 68). In the so-called 'epic tales' in the mediaeval Turkish *Book of Dede Korkut* (Sümer *et al.*, 1972, pp. xxff) the verse is only about 35 per cent of the wordage, but plays a crucial part in the emotional and poetic impact of the whole. When the amount of prose is relatively slight, it seems fair not to exclude such poems totally from the general category of epic, but this is obviously a matter of degree. Extreme cases like the early Irish *Tain Bo Cuailgne*, the Congolese *Mwindo* and *Lianja* 'epics' or possibly the West African *Sunjata* narrative,[1] with their apparently minimal use of verse, may not perhaps be regarded as satisfying the 'verse' criterion of true epic.

This list of examples gives only a few of the known cases. Epic has a very wide distribution over the world and throughout a period of several millennia. But it does not occur everywhere. Its absence in some cultures disappoints the expectation that 'epic' is a universal poetic stage in the development of society. In the usual sense of the term it seems to be uncommon in Africa and in general not to occur in aboriginal America or, to any great extent, in Oceania and Australasia. All in all, epic poetry seems to be a feature of the Old World, where it is, or has been, held in high regard and composed or performed by specific individuals of recognised poetic expertise.

The ballad is another well-known form. It has been variously defined, but is generally agreed to be a sung narrative poem, shorter than the epic and with a concentration on a single episode rather than a series of heroic acts. In this sense, it is exemplified most clearly in English and Scottish ballads like *Lord Randal, Barbara Allen* or *The bonny earl of Murray*.

The incidence of the ballad is usually held to extend from mediaeval times (when the form arguably first appears) to the present, and to cover not just the European forms but the ballads apparently taken to the New World by immigrants over the last three centuries or so: the ballad *Fair Margaret and Sweet William*, for instance, is known both in Britain (it is No. 74 in Child's classic collection) and, as in the version printed here, in the Southern Appalachian Mountains in the American South where it was one of the many ballads recorded by Cecil Sharp in his famous collecting expedition of 1916–18.

---

[1] On *Sunjata*, however, see further in chapter 3, section 4.

FAIR MARGARET AND SWEET WILLIAM

Sweet Wil - liam a-rose one _ May morn - ing And
dressed him - self in blue. Come tell to me all a -
bout that love Be - tween La-dy Mar-g'ret and you.

O I know nothing of Lady Marg'ret's love
And she knows nothing of me,
But in the morning at half-past eight
Lady Marg'ret my bride shall see.

Lady Marg'ret was sitting in her bower
    room
A-combing back her hair;
When who should she spy but Sweet
    William and his bride
As to church they did draw nigh.

Then down she threw her ivory comb,
In silk bound up her hair;
And out of the room this fair lady ran.
She was never any more seen there.

The day passed away and the night coming
    on
And the most of the men asleep,
Sweet William espied Lady Marg'ret's ghost
A-standing at his bed-feet.

The night passed away and the day coming
    on
And the most of the men awake,
Sweet William said: I am troubled in my
    head
By the dream I dreamed last night.

He rode up to Lady Marg'ret's door
And jingled at the ring;
And none so ready as her seventh born
    brother
To arise and let him in.

O is she in her kitchen room,
Or is she in her hall,
Or is she in her bower room
Among her merry maids all?

She's neither in her kitchen room,
Nor neither in her hall,
But she is in her cold, cold coffin
With her pale face towards the wall.

Pull down, pull down those winding-sheets
A-made of satin so fine.
Ten thousand times you have kissed my
    lips,
And now, love, I'll kiss thine.

Three times he kissed her snowy white
    breast,
Three times he kissed her chin;
And when he kissed her cold clay lips
His heart it broke within.

Lady Marg'ret was buried in the old
    churchyard,
Sweet William was buried close by;
And out of her there sprung a red rose
And out of him a brier.

They grew so tall and they grew so high,
They scarce could grow any higher;
And there they tied a true lover's knot,
The red rose and the brier.

(From Sharp, 1932, 1, p. 132, as reproduced in Sharp and Karpeles, 1968, p. 38)

There is clearly a cultural unity involved here, between English, Scottish
and American ballads; for though not all ballads are of the same kind,
certain common plots, phrases, formulae, and repeated choruses recur.
The interaction of orally performed with written and printed forms is also
a well-known characteristic of these poems, due to the long-established

custom of publishing them in printed broadsheet form as well as transmitting them orally.

Such ballads can thus be regarded as belonging to a common cultural
matrix in time and space, albeit a fluid and developing one. It is this
category of oral poems – an extensively recorded and studied one – that
usually forms the primary reference when 'the ballad' is spoken of. But
there are other forms sometimes called 'ballad' which do not belong to the
same cultural complex. Further work is needed to determine the exact
incidence and the possible usage of the term 'ballad'; but in a broad
definition (in the sense of a relatively short and non-heroic narrative song)
the term could be applied also to such cases as Yugoslav 'women's' poems
(Chadwick, 1940, III, p. 690), Indian forms like the Gond 'The goodwife
had twelve ploughmen', a ballad sung while weeding (Elwin and Hivale,
1944, pp. 269–75) or the mediaeval Chinese 'ballads' described by Doleželová-
Velingerová and Crump (1971). Though much depends on further research and on the terminology used, it seems again as if the most frequent
occurrence of this genre is in the Old World rather than America, Oceania
or Africa.

By contrast, panegyric odes are extremely common in both Africa and
Oceania. In these the theme is praise of rulers and other notables, with
consequent emphasis on apostrophaic ode and impressionistic evocation of
the hero's exploits rather than a chronological account of successive episodes. Perhaps one can see this form in these areas as balancing the
interest in narrative verse in the Old World (though panegyric is not
unknown there). Though an element of praise for patron or listener forms
part of many different kinds of verse, its development as a specialist and
highly valued genre is particularly marked in Africa and the Pacific. One
could mention the Hawaiian eulogies of kings and princes, or the long
Southern African praise poems, exemplified by these lines from the 300-line
praise of Joel, a Sotho chief's son:

> Lightning of the village of Mohato, you who take all and leave
>   nothing,
> If you're not the moon, you're a star;
> If you're not the sun, you're a comet.
> The child of the chief is like an elephant in spring,
> He's like a stag that bends low as it runs,
> When the cannons set the flames ablaze,
> And the fires take slowly, catch light, and blaze...
>
> (Damane and Sanders, 1974, p. 190)

Similar is the Yoruba *oriki* praise of the famous local king, the Timi of Ede,
which opens

> Huge fellow whose body fills an anthill
> You are heavily pregnant with war.
> All your body except your teeth is black.

No one can prevent the monkey
From sitting on the branch of a tree.

No one can dispute the throne with you.
No one can try to fight you...

(Beier, 1970, p. 40)

Lyric poetry, in the general sense of a (relatively) short non-narrative poem that is sung, is of extremely wide occurrence; it can probably be regarded as universal in human culture.

Though certain oral poems like epics and some panegyrics are chanted or declaimed only, sung delivery is the most common characteristic of oral poetry. Throughout this book (as in many discussions of oral literature) the term 'song' is often used interchangeably with 'poem' in the sense of a lyric, and the quickest way to suggest the scope of 'oral poetry' is to say that it largely coincides with that of the popular term 'folk song'. Lyric is thus an extremely important and wide category of oral poetry.

Poems with many diverse functions occur in this sung form; love lyrics, psalms and hymns, songs to accompany dancing and drinking, political and topical verse, war songs, initiation songs, 'spirituals', laments, work songs, lullabies, and many others. A very few examples will suggest the wide range of 'lyrics' in oral poetry. They extend, for example, from mediaeval lyrics like the thirteenth-century attack on the Church's worldliness by Philip the Chancellor of Notre Dame

Dic, Christi veritas,	Tell me, you truth of Christ,
Dic, cara raritas,	Tell me, dear rareness,
Dic, rara caritas,	Tell me, rare dearness,
Ubi nunc habitas?	Where are you now?

(quoted in Dronke, 1968, p. 56)

or the nineteenth-century Maori song of mourning by Te Heuheu Herea for his wife

MOURNING SONG FOR RANGIAHO

Many women call on me to sleep with them
But I'll have none so worthless and so wanton
There is not one like Rangiaho, so soft to feel
Like a small, black eel.
I would hold her again –
Even the wood in which she lies;
But like the slender flax stem
She slides from the first to the second heaven
The mother of my children
Gone
Blown by the wind
Like the spume of a wave
Into the eye of the void.

(Mitcalfe, 1961, p. 20)

to a recent Gond dance song from Central India

> She goes with her pot for water
> But who can tell the sorrow of her heart?
>
> (Elwin and Hivale, 1944, p. 259)

or, from Africa, a Shona drinking song

> Keep it dark!
> Don't tell your wife,
> For your wife is a log
> That is smouldering surely!
> Keep it dark!
>
> (Tracey, 1933, no. 9)

or the hard-hitting *African National Congress* song in pre-independence Zambia

> When talking about democracy
> We must teach these Europeans
> Because they do not know.
> See here in Africa they bring their clothes
> But leave democracy in Europe.
> [Refrain] Go back, go back and
>   Bring true democracy.
>
> We are no longer asleep
> We are up and about democracy
> We have known for a long time.
> We are the majority and we demand
> A majority in the Legislative Council...
>
> (Rhodes, 1962, p. 20)

In the English language alone, the range of 'lyric' is immense in style, function and setting. It covers the songs in Shakespearian drama and other Elizabethan lyrics – surely an 'oral' form in most senses of the word – and also American Negro spirituals, popular hymns and carols, favourite 'folk' and 'traditional' songs like *The foggy dew* or *Loch Lomond*, the 'rebel' as well as the 'Orange' songs of Ireland (compare, for instance, *The wearing of the green* with *The sash me father wore*), football supporters' songs, sung nursery rhymes, the compositions of Woody Guthrie, Bob Dylan and the Beatles, and even the lyrics – however ephemeral – propagated through radio, television and discs as the 'Top Twenty'. The lyrics may not be approved by particular sections of musical and literary taste, but that they are all lyrics of a kind and at least arguably 'oral' is undeniable. Their very variety and their different appeal to different types of audiences bring home the huge range in style and content as well as in time and space of the short lyric form of oral verse.

No clear-cut classification of these various forms can readily be drawn up, nor can a simple account of their detailed distribution be given.[1] But it can be said, first, that lyric forms occur constantly in descriptions of oral literatures all over the world (in this differing from epic and ballad forms); and second, that cultural groups vary in how far they make explicit distinctions between various categories of verse and how far they recognise some or all of these categories as specific genres.

Even a quick account like this shows the difficulty of arriving at simple generalisations applicable to all oral verse, or of trying to establish definitive genres on a comparative basis. Useful enough as a starting point, reliance on such genres may not be helpful in the more detailed study of local practice and terminology. Here one might have to take account of many things, some discussed in detail in later chapters: style and structure; treatment; occasion and function. One also has to accept that the whole idea of a 'genre' is relative and ambiguous, dependent on culturally-accepted canons of differentiation rather than universal criteria. Even the elementary account given so far – which would probably be fairly widely accepted as a preliminary categorisation – has drawn on a rather confused and inconsistent set of criteria (length, treatment, purpose, mode of delivery).

And many important forms have been left out in this quick survey: lengthy religious verse, like the elaborate mythological chants of traditional Polynesian religion (the Maori *Six periods of creation*, for instance, or Hawaiian *Kumulipo*) or chanted poetic sermons; dialogue verse, which can sometimes be assimilated to verse drama – ranging from Mongol 'conversation' songs (a dramatic verse form suitable for performance in traditional Mongol tents) to the fully developed form in modern Somali plays like the recently published *Shabeelnaagood. Leopard among the women* (Mumin, 1974); short verse forms – prayers, curses, street-cries and counting-out rhymes that are not sung; or the special oral poetry of African drums and horns.

Possibly enough has been said to make questionable some of the confident generalisations made about the whole category of oral poetry. Can we really continue to accept that 'oral poetry' is basically of one kind, or that it is practicable – as Milman Parry once hoped (Parry and Lord, 1954, p. 4) – to attempt to draw up 'a series of generalities applicable to all oral poetries'?

It might seem unfair that I have taken such a wide sweep in my delineation of 'oral poetry'. It might be argued that a more precise and limited definition of the term would make it possible to generalise about 'oral poetry'. On this argument, my conclusions about the heterogeneous nature of oral poetry are the inbuilt result of my taking a loose (even sloppy) definition of the key term.

The whole problem of the definition of 'oral' must indeed now be

[1] A number of summary accounts have been suggested, e.g. Greenway, 1964, chapter 2, Boswell and Reaver, 1969. See also the useful survey of 'The distribution of literary types' in Chadwick, 1940, III, pp. 706–26.

considered. The problem itself, in my view, tends to support my emphasis on diversity. This forms the topic of the section immediately following. On arguments such as I present here (and in the book generally) the reader must in the end determine whether he prefers my relatively wide interpretation of the term 'oral poetry', or the narrower definitions proposed by other theorists. In the meantime it must be pointed out that all the forms mentioned in the brief account above have indeed been claimed at one time or another to be either 'oral', or correctly characterised by one of those other terms which people often lump together with 'oral' properties: 'folk', 'traditional', 'tribal' or (in the currently fashionable sense of 'pop' and 'popular culture') 'popular': most of these being precisely the terms used when a single category of oral-folk-traditional poetry is being assumed. Even if the forms were removed which some might feel uneasy about dubbing 'oral' – modern pop songs, for instance, hymns, or lyrics which happen to be in Latin – the overall picture of diversity remains, together with a growing doubt whether the gulf between 'oral' and 'written' literature is as deep as sometimes assumed.

3   What is 'oral' in oral poetry?

Contrary to what is sometimes supposed the meaning of the term 'oral' is far from self-evident; it is a relative and often ambiguous term. Some discussion of the term is necessary at this stage, both to elucidate some of the problems, and to indicate the usage to be followed in this book.

In one sense 'oral poetry' is roughly delimited and differentiated from written poetry, and in a rough and ready way the term 'oral' is then clear enough. 'Oral' poetry essentially circulates by oral rather than written means; in contrast to written poetry, its distribution, composition or performance are by word of mouth and not through reliance on the written or printed word. In this sense it is a form of 'oral literature' – the wider term which also includes oral prose. This wider term has sometimes been disputed on the ground that it is self-contradictory if the original etymology of 'literature' (connected with *literae*, letters) is borne in mind. But the term is now so widely accepted and the instances clearly covered by the term so numerous, that it is an excess of pedantry to worry about the etymology of the word 'literature', any more that we worry about extending the term 'politics' from its original meaning of the affairs of the classical Greek *polis* to the business of the modern state. Over-concern with etymologies can only blind us to observation of the facts as they are. 'Oral literature' and 'unwritten literature' are terms useful and meaningful in describing something real, and have come to stay.

'Oral poetry' – which does not raise the same etymological problems – is a particular type of oral literature, and so has a relatively clear initial scope. Most people with an interest in the subject will recognise it as covering instances such as the orally composed and performed Yugoslav epic poems being sung in the 1930s, the English and Scottish ballads that emigrants to America took with them and sang in their new homes, the lyrics composed by unlettered poets in Hawaii or New Zealand or the Gilbert Islands, modern schoolchildren's verse or Australian Aboriginal song-cycles. In a general way, 'oral poetry', with its implied contrast with written literature, is a meaningful and useful term.

It is when one tries to analyse it and delimit it that difficulties arise. What are we to say, for instance, about some of the schoolchildren's verse that has now been written down and published? Does the fact of its having been recorded in writing make it no longer oral? Or, if this seems far-fetched, what about the situation where a child hears a parent read out one of the printed verses (or even reads it himself) and then goes back to repeat it and propagate it in his school playground? And what then about popular hymns, whether English, Zulu or Kikuyu, which may begin their lives as written forms and appear in collected hymnodies, but nevertheless circulate largely by oral means through the performances of congregations made thoroughly familiar with them? Or forms like jazz poetry, or much mediaeval verse, written expressly for oral performance and delivery? Or a poem originally composed in oral performance, but later written down, learnt by others and used in later oral recitations? Cases like these are not marginal and aberrant; they are constantly cropping up and raise problems which any student of oral poetry must recognise.

When one looks at cases of this kind, it seems that there are three main ways in which a poem may or may not be called oral and that these three do not necessarily coincide. It is important to separate them out, for analytic purposes, and to be clear which aspect is being stressed in any one account. It will emerge that different scholars have concentrated on different elements among these three, and that the resultant conclusions and apparent contradictions can sometimes be resolved by our greater clarity about which element is being emphasised.

The three ways in which a poem can most readily be called oral are in terms of (1) its composition, (2) its mode of transmission, and (3) (related to (2)) its performance. Some oral poetry is oral in all these respects, some in only one or two. It is important to be clear how oral poetry can vary in these ways, as well as about the problems involved in assessing each of these aspects of 'oral-ness'. It emerges that the 'oral' nature of oral poetry is not easy to pin down precisely.

Take, first, the aspect of composition. (This is considered in greater detail in chapter 3, where some controversies in this field are discussed.) Basically, if one relies on this criterion, a poem is 'oral' if it is composed orally, without reliance on writing. Just what 'composed orally' implies is rather complex. One form of 'oral composition' is described by Parry and Lord in their analysis of the art of Yugoslav minstrels in the 1930s. Here the poet in a sense composes his heroic epics at the actual moment of performance, relying on a known fund of conventional 'oral formulae' which he has built up from his own practice as well as from hearing other poets. Even if some of the sources for the basic plots and language include written material, this kind of oral composition-in-performance is the basic criterion, in the eyes of Lord and his followers, for considering the resultant poem 'oral'. This criterion has been accepted by many scholars, including those who find in classical poems like the Homeric epics, *Beowulf* and the *Song of Roland* the formulaic style which can be taken as a mark of this kind of 'oral composition', and hence as an indication that these poems were, in some sense, originally 'oral', even if *also* later written down and circulating over many centuries in written form.

This kind of composition-in-performance is not the only kind of oral composition. The process of composition can also be prior to, and largely separate from, the act of performance. This is the case, for instance, with many Eskimo, Somali or Gilbertese lyrics, where the poet labours for hours or even days over the composition of the poem, which is only later presented in a public performance by the poet or others (see chapter 3, section 4). In this case the poet may have others helping him from time to time during the long period of composition, and may adapt the poem in minor ways during later performance. But it is clear that the actual process of composition is analytically separable from later performance and is, in these cases, too, '*oral*'. So, if composition is to be the criterion, the poems thus composed must also be 'oral'.

Sometimes the process is more complicated, and involves oral composition both before and during performance, with subsequent modifications to later performances in the light of audience-reaction to specific portions – as with Dorrance Weir's versions of 'Take that night train to Selma' (Glassie *et al.*, 1970). In this case, or in Joe Scott's 'Plain golden band', the resultant song may also be written down and begin to circulate in print and writing as well as orally. Similarly with many of the broadside and 'street' ballads hawked around by pedlars and minstrels in eighteenth-century England: some of these originated in orally-composed country songs and then started to circulate in print as well.

The exact delimitation of 'oral composition' thus turns out to be not very easy to fix, and often to involve overlap or interaction with written forms. Indeed it is sometimes hard to draw any very clear line of principle between the kind of mental composition sometimes engaged in by a literate poet, only later committing his words to writing, and that of the Eskimo or the mediaeval Irish poet. Take the following description, for instance, of composition in the mediaeval Irish bardic schools. The pupils were required to work at their poems

> 'each by himself on his own Bed, the whole next Day in the Dark, till at a certain Hour in the Night, Lights being brought in, they committed to to writing'
>
> (Clanricarde, 1722, quoted in Williams, 1971, p. 36)

Composition in this form is reminiscent of processes found in what would normally be called 'written composition'.

'Oral composition' can therefore be a useful term that roughly conveys a general emphasis on composition without reliance on writing, but cannot provide any absolute criterion for definitively differentiating oral poetry as a single category clearly separable from written poetry.

Much the same applies to the criterion of transmission. At first sight, the characteristic of being transmitted by oral means seems a straightforward yardstick for differentiating oral from written literature. This criterion, which is usually the central one stressed by folklorists, is sometimes merely taken to imply that a given piece circulates or is actualised by oral means. This is clear and relevant enough, though if pressed it often turns out to be a relative rather than absolute property of 'oral literature', for one needs to enquire about the *degree* to which something circulates by oral rather than written means. In this sense 'oral transmission' often overlaps or even coincides with 'oral performance'.

Oral transmission is, however, often taken to imply the oral handing on of some piece over fairly long periods of time in a relatively unchanged form. Thus the Indian sacred book the *Rgveda* is said to have been orally transmitted over centuries or millennia, and it is this characteristic, besides its presumed oral composition, that leads scholars to classify it as 'oral literature'. Again many of the English and Scottish ballads that 'travelled' to America with successive waves of immigrants may have been originally composed and published in broadsheet (or printed) form; but because they were apparently preserved over the generations in certain rural areas of America through *oral transmission*, it has often seemed appropriate to classify them as 'oral' or (to use the more popular and roughly equivalent term among folklorists) as 'folk' poetry. Similarly the criterion of 'oral transmission' has been used as an implicit yardstick by anthropologists and others in deciding whether a given story or poem is worth documenting. A text apparently transmitted through a recently published book or modern school-teaching is assumed not to be properly 'oral' because it has not come to the area through long 'oral transmission'. This can be so even when the piece is in some sense originally 'orally' composed or circulating through oral performance in the locality being studied. In the same way the 'oral' nature of certain written texts – *Beowulf*, for instance – is some-times claimed to be indicated or partially indicated not so much because of oral composition or performance as because of its supposed long pre-vious transmission by 'oral tradition', depending 'for its material on oral rather than written sources' (Wright, 1957, p. 21).

The application of this criterion is therefore perforce often merely speculative. Frequently there is little or no hard information about the earlier oral history of a given piece of literature. The evidence is even harder to pin down than might be expected because of the frequent probability of oral/written interaction and the fact that informants' claims to be transmitting texts based on long word-for-word tradition have often turned out to be undependable. The criterion is thus not an easy one to use with confidence.

Its application is made all the more tricky by the romantic and evolutionist overtones of the concept of 'oral transmission': the idea of long tradition through 'folklore' and 'folk memory' from the dim primaeval mists of the infancy of the human race. These assumptions are now widely rejected by modern scholars but still tend to linger on as part of the mystique surround-ing oral literature, affecting its practitioners as well as its analysts. This makes many claims about the long 'oral transmission' of some literary piece *prima facie* suspect or at any rate only to be accepted with caution.

So this aspect too of the 'oralness' of oral poetry turns out to be relative rather than absolute ('oral transmission' can, after all, be over a long or a short period), as well as being extremely elusive and difficult to pinpoint in practice.

The third possible criterion is actualisation in performance. Compared to the criterion of transmission, this is far less speculative and much more susceptible to discussion in terms of actual evidence. After all, it is some-times possible actually to observe an oral performance taking place, and there is not the same reason as with claimed 'oral transmission' to distrust reported descriptions of such performances. In most cases, therefore, this is a relatively straightforward criterion.[1]

Even with oral performances, there can be problems. What is one to say, for instance, of the not unknown situation when one poet composes a piece for another to deliver – for instance the differentiation (at times anyway) between the mediaeval *trobador* ('composer') and *joglar* ('performer') in Europe, or the Irish *filid* ('poets') compared to the 'bards'? When both categories – composers and performers – proceed orally, there is no prob-lem. But what about the case when the composition is written, and only the delivery or performance oral? Each native operatic troupe in Malaya,

---

[1] Though not all scholars would accept it as the most significant criterion. Lord for instance, excludes 'poetry...written to be recited...What is important is not the oral performance but rather the composition *during* oral performance' (1968a, p. 5).

WHAT IS 'ORAL' IN ORAL POETRY?

for instance, 'has its own versifier to write words to well-known tunes just as it has its own clown to invent new jokes for each performance' (Wilkinson, 1924, p. 40). Written narratives apparently sometimes formed the basis of orally-performed mediaeval Chinese ballads (Doleželová-Velingerová and Crump, 1971, pp. 2, 8), and this pattern was common in classical Greece, where 'the regular method of publication was by public recitation' (Hadas, 1954, p. 50) as well as in the Middle Ages in Europe where, since 'oral delivery of popular literature was the rule rather than the exception', the works of popular writers were 'intended for oral delivery' and composed in a form suitable for performance (Crosby, 1936, pp. 110, 100). There are instances even within highly literate cultures, where plays or poems for live performances or broadcasting are written with the specific intention that they are to be performed. If oral *performance* is the central criterion, such cases must be classified as oral literature. One has to admit that in cases like these (which are not uncommon) there may be contradiction between the two criteria, composition and performance.

There is also the problem, if we press the matter of performance, of deciding just what is the oral piece: surely the actual performance, and not the text from which it was delivered, which is all we usually have a full record of? And it becomes even more difficult when we include not just items specifically written for oral delivery, but any literary items which are *in fact* performed or performable. To include these may seem to make the coverage excessively wide, yet to exclude them means we may find ourselves making assumptions about the author's intentions for a piece which it may be impossible to justify.

In addition, what is to count as 'performance'? Some cases are clear enough, but there are marginal ones. The Swahili autobiography of Tippu Tip, for instance, is characterised by Wilfred Whiteley as belonging 'partly to oral and partly to written prose...his audience seems not to have been a circle of kinsfolk or friends but rather a scribe' (Whiteley, 1964a, p. 107). This situation is not necessarily uncommon, even for poetic pieces, and much has been written about the possibility of the Homeric and other epics being 'orally dictated texts' in this sense. Again, a performance need not involve an audience – witness the extreme but definite cases of oral litera-ture being actualised by performers on their own, as, for example, by herdsmen among the Nilotes of the Sudan. But could one then call reading aloud a 'performance', or even the related process of hearing the sound of a poem in one's head while reading it? Clearly, even with the relatively straightforward criterion of performance there are likely to be marginal cases and problems about application.

Where all three criteria of oral composition, oral transmission and oral performance unambiguously apply, there is no problem. A Maori poem known to have been composed and performed by an old man and transmitted by him to his children and grandchildren without any knowledge of writing, can be called 'oral' without any qualification. But in practice most cases are not like that. Very often the criteria conflict, and these cases are common enough not to count as the odd or untypical exception. In such circumstances no one criterion or set of criteria is self-evidently 'right', for the characteristic of 'oralness' has turned out to be relative and complex. A number of possible characteristics are involved, and need not necessarily coincide. They certainly do not, jointly or severally, produce a precise and unambiguous category of 'oral poetry' clearly distinct from written forms.

Because of this relative and often ambiguous nature of 'oralness' I need make no apology for not producing a clear and precise definition of 'oral' poetry. For the relativity and ambiguity are part of the nature of the facts, and to try to conceal this by a brisk definition would only be misleading. It is only fair, however, to make clear that I take a fairly wide approach to the concept of oral poetry. I consider it unrealistic and unhelpful to confine oneself to more restrictive definitions like that of Lord, who would limit the term to poetry produced by one particular type (only) of oral composition. I have also laid more stress on the aspect of oral *performance* than do some analysts, considering that if a piece is orally performed – still more if it is mainly known to people through actualisation in performance – it must be regarded as in that sense an 'oral poem'. I have thus included in the discussion references to certain poetry (well-known hymns, for instance) which some students might exclude. I have in addition tried to make clear, when it is relevant, which aspect of 'oral-ness' I am stressing at any given point.

But, when all is said and done, the concept of 'oral-ness' must be relative, and 'oral poetry' is constantly overlapping into 'written poetry'. Therefore anyone interested in studying the facts about oral poetry rather than playing with verbal definitions or theoretical constructs has to recognise that consideration of 'oral poetry' cannot start from a precise and definitive delimitation of its subject matter from written literature. To repeat the theme that will recur throughout this book: 'oral poetry' is inevitably a relative and complex term rather than an absolute and clearly demarcated category.

The relative and ill-defined nature of oral poetry is hardly surprising when one reflects on the mixture of communication media that has long been a feature of human culture. We are accustomed to taking account of many different media in the world today: verbal and face-to-face communication in small groups, writing, print, radio, television, records or tape, to mention just some; and we have to recognise that poetry or song produced today may involve a mixture of several or all of these. It is easily understandable that it may not be confined to just 'written' or just 'oral' media but involve a mixture of both. But it is sometimes forgotten that this mixture is not a distinguishing feature of the modern industrial west. People in 'developing nations' too make use of the media of print, radio and television, and a number of instances of 'oral poetry' published recently from Africa or the Middle East were originally broadcast and listened to on transistor radios through even the remote areas of the country.

It is even more important to remember – since it seems to be more easily forgotten – that it is not just in the last generation or two that writing has gained significance as a medium for communication in the so-called 'Third World'. A degree of literacy has been a feature of human culture in most parts of the world for millennia.[1] This has rarely meant mass literacy (a fact significant for the popular circulation of *oral* literature) but has meant a measure of influence from the written word and literatures even in cultures often dubbed 'oral'. Illiterate populations in Malaysia have through the literate few had contact with the written literatures of Hinduism and Islam, and the influence of the high cultures of India and China has long pervaded huge areas of Asia, just as Latin learning and the sacred writings of Christendom have had a long effect in Europe as well as in the areas to which Christian missionaries carried their learning over several centuries. Literature in written form was not accessible to large masses of the population, but to regard the (till recently) largely illiterate peoples of Africa or the Middle East as having *no* contact with written literature till the twentieth century and existing in some ideal world of purely 'oral' and localised culture is seriously misleading.

Since literate and non-literate media have so long co-existed and interacted it is natural to find not only interaction between 'oral' and 'written' literature but many cases which involve overlap and mixture. Today, a large proportion of the world's population can read and write but the adult illiteracy rate in the world as a whole is still probably around one third. It is not surprising that poetry is propagated sometimes by oral, sometimes by written means, with no great and unsurmountable gulf between the two. Similarly in the past, when fewer were literate, we should expect 'oral poems' to be influenced by, and interact with, written forms, and indeed sometimes coincide with them.

This point is worth stressing. For though, put this way, it seems obvious, it runs counter to some presuppositions commonly held about oral literature and its incidence. In particular it raises questions about one very commonly held assumption about the incidence and nature of oral literature and oral poetry. This is that its most common context is the kind of 'primitive' communal and artless society depicted in the older stereotypes of many sociologists and folklorists. The 'traditional' rural and non-literate

---

[1] Relative exceptions are probably much of Polynesia, Aboriginal Australia, the far northern fringes of America and Asia, and some of Aboriginal America.

type of culture, it is presupposed, is the 'natural' setting for oral literature and we should take it as the reference point for 'real' oral literature. This fits with various myths about the Noble Savage or the value of the deep and unconscious springs of our being. This set of ideas has a long history in the western world and naturally it has affected our appreciation of the nature of oral literature and its probable setting. The implicit assumption that oral poetry most commonly and naturally belongs to the kind of 'primitive' society envisaged in these stereotypes goes very deep, accompanied by the idea that any other setting for oral poetry must be unusual, or perhaps 'transitional' between the two settled states of 'primitive' and non-literate on the one hand, and industrial and fully literate on the other.

Because these presuppositions go so deep, it is necessary to stress the point already made: that 'oral poetry' is not a single and simple thing. It can occur in many different kinds of setting. Oral poetry can occur in a society with partial literacy or even mass literacy, as well as in supposed 'primitive' cultures. One only needs to think of the celebrated Yugoslav oral epics, with their constant interaction over generations with printed versions; English and American ballads, which have been sung in very different geographical areas, cultures and periods; modern 'pop' songs; or the productions of Canadian lumberers or American 'folksingers' like Larry Gorman, Almeda Riddle or Woody Guthrie. The 'typical' oral poet is as likely to have some knowledge of writing as to live in the remote and purely 'oral' atmosphere envisaged in the stereotype. If one considers actually recorded and studied cases of oral poetry, its authors are really more likely than not to have had some contact with literacy.

The basic point then, is the continuity of 'oral' and 'written' literature. There is no deep gulf between the two: they shade into each other both in the present and over many centuries of historical development, and there are innumerable cases of poetry which has both 'oral' and 'written' elements. The idea of pure and uncontaminated 'oral culture' as the primary reference point for the discussion of oral poetry is a myth.

4   The 'poetry' in oral poetry

I cannot here enter into deep discussion of the question 'what is poetry?'. Apart from a couple of relatively minor points (considered below), deciding what is poetry is no more easy or difficult for oral than for written literature. Nor will I discuss what, in universal terms, is to count as 'good' poetry – the connotation sometimes attached to the English term 'poetry'. For the purposes of comparative study, what must be culture-bound judgement will as far as possible be avoided (it is perhaps not possible entirely), and the term 'poetry' used in the wide sense to cover all kinds of poetry: 'bad' and 'good'. No protracted or profound treatment, therefore, of the deeper literary or aesthetic issues need be expected here.

Some brief discussion, however, of the particular problems of delimiting poetry in oral literature is essential. These are not basic to the general aesthetic theory of the essence of poetry, but at a straightforward level can provide practical difficulties for the fieldworker and analyst.

The first and most important point is that in written literature poetry is normally *typographically* defined. There are other factors in play too, but – trivial though this may sound – it has to be accepted that in our culture, the handiest rule of thumb for deciding on whether something is poetry or prose is to look at how it is written out: whether 'as verse' or not. On the surface, this rule of thumb makes it easy for even a schoolchild to differentiate quickly between 'prose' and 'poetry'.

Obviously this particular rule will not, by definition, work for unwritten poetry. One is thus forced to look for other, apparently more 'intrinsic' characteristics by which something can be delineated as 'poetry' within *oral* literature.

The first property that springs to mind is 'rhythm' or 'metre', and this indeed is often a useful test. But much the same difficulty applies here in oral as in written poetry: the concept and manifestation of 'rhythm' is a *relative* thing, and depends partly on culturally defined perceptions; it cannot be an absolute or universally applicable criterion. Where does one draw the line, for instance, among the various 'speech modes', some more 'poetic' than others, in which the Mandinka *Sunjata* 'epic' is delivered in West Africa? Or once something is categorised as 'rhythmic prose' – some curses for instance – must we suspect a contradiction in terms and change the categorisation to 'verse'? In addition, there are some oral literary pieces which a number of observers have regarded as 'poems' in which metre or regular rhythm in the normal sense seem to be missing – and yet there seem to be other prosodic and stylistic features which replace them (see chapter 4, section 2). What we must look for is not one absolute criterion but a range of stylistic and formal attributes – features like heightened language, metaphorical expression, musical form or accompaniment, structural repetitiveness (like the recurrence of stanzas, lines or refrains), prosodic features like metre, alliteration, even perhaps parallelism. So the concept of 'poetry' turns out to be a relative one, depending on a combination of stylistic elements no *one* of which need necessarily and invariably be present.

A further aspect is the way in which a poem is, as it were, italicised, set apart from everyday life and language. This is so of any piece we would term 'literature'[1] – but especially so of a poem. In the written form we set it apart typographically, but also by its setting or the way it is performed or read aloud: whatever its rhythmic properties may be, a poem is likely (even in a literate culture) to be delivered in a manner and mood which sets it apart from everyday speech and prose utterance. This 'setting apart'

---

[1] With unwritten forms, even the delimitation of what is 'literature' becomes a problem to which there is no easy solution (see Finnegan, 1970, pp. 22ff).

through performance and context is clearly also applicable to unwritten poetry. Such factors are difficult to pin down exactly, but the ways in which a literary piece may be 'framed' or 'italicised', and so may be more suitably termed a 'poem', may include the context and setting of the performance, the mode of delivery, the audience's action, the musical attributes – not for nothing do we speak of a musical 'setting' – as well as the stylistic features already mentioned (particularly the recurrence of refrains), and in general the atmosphere of 'play' rather than 'reality', an activity set apart from 'real life'. Factors like these are inevitably both relative and elusive; partly empirically observable, they also depend on the assessment of observer and actors. But something of this sort – an assessment that a given piece is picked out and 'framed' – often enters into the classification of a particular verbal phenomenon as an instance of 'poetry'. In accepting these instances as 'poems' we should be aware of the factors likely to lie behind such assessments by ourselves or others.

Finally, there is the local classification of a piece as 'poetry'. In one sense this is the most important, but it is by no means simple. For one thing, the relatively neat formal differentiation we make in our culture between poetry and prose is not recognised everywhere. In Malay literature – to mention one instance – the distinction between prose and poetry is blurred. Wilkinson points out that 'prose' as well as 'poetry' is often chanted or sung, and 'much Malay prose-literature is in a transition stage; it contains jingling, half-rhyming and even metrical passages; it is written for a singer and not for a reciter or reader' (Wilkinson, 1924, p. 44). In some languages there is no single word that exactly covers our 'poetry', even though special terms may differentiate literary genres, some or all of which we may, following our other criteria, term types of 'poetry'. In Yoruba, for instance, there are special terms for 'praise poetry', 'hunters' poems', 'festival poetry', and so on, but no one word corresponding to 'poetry' in general, and the same is true of Gaelic verse. Furthermore, local classifications do not necessarily coincide with the line we draw between 'prose' and 'verse', but emphasise some other factor, like mode of delivery or social function and setting, so that what at first sight may look like the category equivalent to our 'poetry' may turn out to include and exclude unexpected cases. Indeed, even the English case turns out to be more complicated than it first appears. For the normally accepted coverage of 'poetry' tends to exclude certain linguistic forms which, if we take account of the factors mentioned earlier, might have been expected to count. Thus the words of Elizabethan lyrics are normally included in the category of 'poetry', but many liturgical forms or the words of more recent lyrics are excluded.

Instances of this sort remind us that while we need to take account of local classifications – and in any analysis of a *particular* poetic culture this would be an essential preliminary – these, too, may not give a clear-cut and simple guide in any comparative study of poetry, whether oral or written. For this one needs to use general comparative terms – 'poetry', 'literature' – which inevitably misrepresent some local distinctions. This difficulty is not unique to the study of poetry, for it arises in *any* kind of comparative study, even within a single culture, but it adds to the difficulty of producing any very exact delimitation of 'poetry'.

It emerges, then, that any differentiation of 'poetry' from 'prose' or, indeed of 'poetry' as a specific literary product or activity, can only be approximate. The distinction between 'poetry' and 'prose' is relative, and the whole delimitation of what is to count as 'poetry' necessarily depends not on one strictly verbal definition but on a series of factors to do with style, form, setting and local classification, not all of which are likely to coincide.

This conclusion about the relativity of 'poetry' is not unreasonable in principle. More important, it takes account of the complex realities of the practice of 'oral poetry' thoughout the world, and helps to explain why there is continuing controversy about, for instance, whether Pueblo (Zuni) narratives are 'prose' or 'poetry' (Tedlock, 1972), or how far the 'speech modes' in the West African 'epic' of *Sunjata* can be interpreted as types of poetry (Innes, 1974). It also recognises the practical difficulties of collectors and analysts of oral literature, and provides a background to frequent comments such as this:

> The distinction between prose and verse is a small one...the border-line between them is extremely difficult to ascertain and define, while the verse-technique, in so far as verse can be separated from prose, is extremely free and unmechanical. Broadly speaking, it may be said that the difference between prose and verse in Bantu literature is one of spirit rather than of form, and that such formal distinction as there is is one of degree of use rather than of quality of formal elements. Prose tends to be less emotionally charged, less moving in content and full-throated in expression than verse; and also – but only in the second place – less formal in structure, less rhythmical in movement, less metrically balanced.
>
> (Lestrade, 1937, p. 306, on Southern Bantu literature)

This complexity and relativity of 'poetry' will emerge further in later chapters. For the moment it is worth making two points.

First, it is interesting how far one is forced to take account of social and not just textual criteria in assessing whether something is to count as a 'poem' or not – social conventions about appropriate style, form or setting, socially recognised classifications at the local level. This supports another recurrent theme of this book: that poetry is not just something 'natural' and 'universal' that can be abstracted from its social setting: its very delimitation depends to a large extent on the varying social conventions that surround its performance and recognition. Its manifestation as a social phenomenon makes it a subject for both the literary scholar and the sociologist.

Second, it is worth remembering that this discussion was prompted initially by the problem of delimiting 'poetry' in oral literature. But it is worth asking how far some of the points made here might be applicable to the study of *written* poetry as well. Here too – if one wants to go beyond the 'typographical' yardstick, itself a circular one – it is a question of taking account of the same general range of factors relating to style, performance, setting, and local or contemporary classification.

5   Performance and text

Discussion of the incidence of genres, and the continuity of oral and written poetry, takes as its reference-point the *text* of oral poems: the idea that there is something that can be called 'the poem', such that one can discuss its oral or other characteristics, or how widely it and similar instances can be found throughout the world. This indeed is how the subject has commonly been approached. But the text is, of course, only one element of the essence of oral literature – a fact which emerged in the previous discussion. Oral poetry does indeed, like written literature, possess a verbal text. But in one respect it is different: a piece of oral literature, to reach its full actualisation, *must be performed.* The text alone cannot constitute the oral poem.

This *performance* aspect of oral poetry is sometimes forgotten, even though it lies at the heart of the whole concept of oral literature. It is easy to concentrate on an analysis of the verbal elements – on style and content, imagery, or perhaps transmission. All this has its importance for oral literature, of course. But one *also* needs to remember the circumstances of the performance of a piece – this is not a secondary or peripheral matter, but integral to the identity of the poem as actually realised. Differently performed, or performed at a different time or to a different audience or by a different singer, it is a different poem.

In this sense, an oral poem is an essentially ephemeral work of art, and has no existence or continuity apart from its performance. The skill and personality of the performer, the nature and reaction of the audience, the context, the purpose – these are essential aspects of the artistry and mean-ing of an oral poem. Even when there is little or no change of actual wording in a given poem between performances, the context still adds its own weight and meaning to the delivery, so that the whole occasion is unique. And in many cases, as will be seen in later chapters, there is considerable variation between performances, so that the literate model of a fixed correct version – *the* text of a given poem – does not necessarily apply.

In this respect, oral literature differs from our implicit model of written literature: the mode of communication to a silent reader, through the eye alone, from a definitive written text. Oral literature is more flexible and more dependent on its social context. For this reason, no discussion of oral poetry can afford to concentrate on the text alone, but must take account of the nature of the audience, the context of performance, the personality of the poet-performer, and the details of the performance itself.

It is only recently that much interest has been taken in these aspects, which are harder to record and analyse than the verbal texts. But there is now a growing awareness that any piece of oral poetry must, to be fully understood, be seen in its context; that it is not a separable thing but a 'communicative event' (Ben-Amos, 1972, p. 10).

If oral poetry is 'different', there is also a basic continuity. Even if the text is not the whole of an oral poem, it is one part – which it shares with written literature. It would be exaggerated to pursue the 'communication' approach to oral literature so far that the text, still a fundamental, was ignored. Even without knowledge of the social background or style of performance we can still find meaning in these lines by a Gilbertese poet:

> Even in a little thing
> (A leaf, a child's hand, a star's flicker)
> I shall find a song worth singing
> If my eyes are wide, and sleep not.
>
> Even in a laughable thing
> (Oh hark! The children are laughing!)
> There is that which fills the heart to over-flowing,
> And makes dreams wistful.
>
> Small is the life of a man
> (Not too sad, not too happy):
> I shall find my songs in a man's small life. Behold them soaring!
>
> Very low on earth are the frigate-birds hatched,
> Yet they soar as high as the sun.
>
> (Grimble, 1957, pp. 207–8)

Through all the difficulties of relativity and translation, we still recognise in this text what we term 'a poem'. The linguistic content – the text – provides the frame and focus of the piece, whatever the surrounding circumstances, and without the structuring device of poetic expression in fine and imaginative words, no amount of 'communication' or 'context' could make 'a poem'.

2

Some approaches to the study of oral poetry

The study of oral poetry can be an emotive subject, often shot through with deeply-held assumptions and value-judgements. Some grasp of the repercussions of these assumptions, theories or models is essential. Many assumptions are so much part of the unspoken premises of some writers that one constantly meets them stated as firm truth. If dogmatic speculations appear as incontrovertible facts, even in the writings of respected scholars, it is necessary to be able to set statements about oral poetry against this background of different approaches and assumptions. Otherwise it is difficult to disentangle which claims are controversial, which are attempts to build on modern empirical research, and which are plain wrong in the light of recent findings. It is often associations and connotations rather than the explicit positions which are hardest to pin down without some knowledge of the theoretical approach being taken for granted. Yet many of them have been influential in the interpretation of oral literature. It is all the more important to see what they are.

The main approaches considered in this chapter are (1) romantic and evolutionist theories (2) the Finnish historical-geographical approach (3) controversies in the sociology of literature and (4) the general sociological concept of a relationship between type of society and mode of communication (literary and other). The brief presentation of these here provides a background to discussions in later chapters of topics like oral composition, transmission, the position of poets, or the relation of poetry and society.

1 Romantic and evolutionist theories

The first group of theories has had a profound influence on the study of oral literature. They have radically affected not only scholarly analysis (particularly by evolutionist anthropologists and many folklorists) but also popular assumptions about the subject. These theories in part depend on an evolutionist approach – the idea that societies progress up through set stages with 'survivals' from earlier strata sometimes continuing in later ones. To understand the import of this, one must also bear in mind certain developments in western intellectual history.

The set of assumptions involved is closely related to certain strands in the romantic tradition in European thought in the eighteenth and nine-teenth centuries (and in some respects up to the present); and in particular its expression in the romantic nationalism of the nineteenth century. 'Romanticism' is a wide term with a plethora of variegated meanings. I cannot embark on a detailed account here. But it is possible to point to an identifiable tradition of central significance for the study of oral poetry. This is the emphasis on the spontaneous expressive quality of art and the artist, beginning around the middle of the eighteenth century and fostered by the rise of 'nationalism' in the nineteenth. This intellectual tradition has had a deep influence on enduring assumptions about the nature of 'oral literature' specifically (often under the name of 'folklore') and about the nature of society/ies more generally.

A central strand in romanticism is the stress on the expressive, emotional side of art and the genius of the artist himself. This is unlike previous approaches to the analysis of art which tended to stress its relation with audience and patron. The poet is now seen as the vehicle for spontaneous emotion which bubbles up through him in the form of a poem. The description of poetry in terms of passion, emotion, 'inspiration', 'uttering forth' and expressiveness, is common among nineteenth-century Romantic writers, and typified by Wordsworth's famous description of poetry as 'the spontaneous overflow of powerful feelings' (*Preface to lyrical ballads*, in Smith, 1905, p. 15).

Allied to this is the common idea of poetry as natural and instinctive. 'Nature' is opposed to 'art', so that the truest poetry is essentially spon-taneous, artless and natural. As M. H. Abrams sums it up, this is closely connected with 'the general romantic use of spontaneity, sincerity, and integral unity of thought and feeling as the essential criteria of poetry, in place of their neo-classic counterparts: judgment, truth, and the appro-priateness with which diction is matched to the speaker, the subject matter, and the literary kind' (Abrams, 1958, p. 102).

This approach has parallels in more wide-ranging theories about the nature of man and society. Rousseau, often regarded as one of the pre-cursors of Romanticism, presents man as of natural and spontaneous goodness, untrammelled by the constraining non-natural bonds of society – 'Man is born free, and everywhere he is in chains' – and in his educational writings he advocates a kind of 'return to nature'. The interest in literary expressiveness adds a further dimension to general enthusiasm among many eighteenth-century writers for a return to the state of nature and the abolition of 'society'. 'Nature' as opposed to 'art' has its parallels in the idea of 'nature' (or the natural individual) as opposed to 'society'. As Lovejoy put it, 'nature' was supposed to consist in 'those expressions of human nature which are most spontaneous, unpremeditated, untouched by reflection or design, and free from the bondage of social convention'

(Lovejoy, 1948, p. 238). In the romantic interpretations these attitudes to untrammelled, untamed 'nature' were applied to the theory of poetry so that in aesthetic terms too, the 'natural' or 'simple' came to be prized above 'art':

> What are the lays of artful Addison,
> Coldly correct, to Shakespeare's warblings wild?[1]

In the Romantic view, the quintessence of emotional expression and natural spontaneity is found in 'primitive' language and culture. Poetry originates in primaeval expressions of emotion which are by nature expressed in rhythmic and figurative form. Further, 'unlettered' folk as well as far-off 'primitive' peoples are thought to represent the essence of the natural and instinctive poetic expression so valued by romantic writers. When Wordsworth wants to illustrate the 'primary laws of our nature' through poetry he chooses

> humble and rustic life...because, in that condition, the essential passions of the heart...are less under restraint, and speak a plainer and more emphatic language; because in that condition of life our elementary feelings co-exist in a state of greater simplicity...because the manners of rural life germinate from those elementary feelings ...and, lastly, because in that condition the passions of men are incorporated with the beautiful and permanent forms of nature.
>
> (Wordsworth in Smith, 1905, p. 14)

Similarly, much eighteenth-century theorising about the origins of language and poetry stressed their fundamentally instinctive and natural qualities. Art first developed in 'savage Life, where untaught Nature rules', as John Brown summed it up in his *Dissertation on the Rise...of Poetry and Music* in 1763 (p. 27). The same sort of view is repeated by Gummere over a century later. Poetry was first found in 'that aboriginal wildness, that ecstasy of the horde, first utterance of unaccommodated man...from this dancing throng came emotion and rhythm, the raw material of poetry' (Gummere, 1897, reprinted in Leach and Coffin, 1961, p. 29), and 'if we could catch a glimpse of primitive conditions, we should find poetry entirely ruled by the mechanical, the spontaneous, the unreflecting element' (ibid., p. 28). His general view, expressed in typically romantic terms, was that the first origins of poetry in primitive cultures were 'communal' and characterised by 'the lack of individuality, the homogenous mental state of any primitive throng, the absence of deliberation and thought, the immediate relation of emotion to expression, the accompanying leap or step of the dance under conditions of communal exhilaration' (ibid., p. 27).

---

[1] From Joseph Warton's *The Enthusiast* (1740), a poem often quoted as the first clear manifestation of Romanticism.

The concept of Nature as the prime force in 'primitive', 'unlettered' poetry was sometimes taken so far as to imply an organic and even 'vegetable' theory of poetic genesis. True literature – above all 'primitive literature' – grew up of itself without conscious deliberation or individual volition, an idea given further force by the German romantic philosophers. Schlegel, for instance, opposes mechanical form – external and accidental – to innate 'organic form' which 'unfolds itself from within, and reaches its determination simultaneously with the fullest development of the seed...In the fine arts, just as in the province of nature – the supreme artist – all genuine forms are "organic"' (A. W. Schlegel, *Viennese lectures on dramatic art and literature*, published 1809–11, quoted in Abrams, 1958, p. 213). This botanical imagery, with its overtones of non-conscious automatic growth, is frequently applied to unwritten literature, from Baissac's description of a Mauritian story as 'cette fleur spontanée du génie de l'enfance' (Baissac, 1888, p. vii), or Fletcher's description of American Indian songs as 'near to nature...untrammelled by the intellectual control of schools ...like the wild flowers that have not yet come under the transforming hand of the gardener' (Fletcher, 1900, p. ix) to John Lomax's suggestion that cowboy songs 'have sprung up as has the grass on the plains' (quoted in Wilgus, 1959, p. 80), or Bronson's more recent characterisation of folk song: 'as natural as wildflowers' (Bronson, 1969, p. 202).

This attitude to the 'natural' products of 'primitive' and 'unlettered' people, and to the 'folk', the 'peasants', and 'the common people' generally, often involved a sentimental and glamorising admiration. This received further encouragement from another frequent characteristic of Romanticism: a dissatisfaction with the current state of the world and a deep yearning for something other – 'for the remote, the unusual, the unattainable...it loves the past because it can no longer partake of the past; it loves the future because it can never arrive at the future' (Anderson and Warnock, 1967, pp. 269–70).

Correspondingly, speculation about the primitive origins of poetry and language in 'nature', and the view of poetry as originally and ideally an instinctive, artless outburst of feeling, involves not just a theory about origins but a romanticising glorification of the 'natural', the 'primitive', and the 'emotional', and a reaching out to a supposed lost world in the past when man and his emotional expressions were free, integrated and natural.

This romantic approach did more than affect the analysis of oral literature as part of the general climate of opinion within which it was first closely studied. It also had an intimate connection with the rise of what was then called 'folklore' study (which normally at least *included* what is now termed 'oral literature' and was sometimes identified primarily with it). For one element in Romanticism has had direct influence on the development of studies of oral literature: the emergence of the romantic nationalism of the nineteenth and (to some extent) twentieth centuries.

The outburst of nationalism in Europe following the French Revolution and Napoleonic Wars has often been remarked as one of the strands in Romanticism. Along with this went an emphasis on local origins and languages, accompanied by an enthusiasm for the collection of 'folklore' in various senses – what would now be called 'oral literature' (ballads, folk songs, stories) as well as 'traditional' dances and vernacular languages and 'customs'. The political and ideological implications of this return to 'origins' are obvious, and the appeal was all the more forceful because of the Romantic stress on the significance of the 'other' and the 'lost', and the virtue of 'unlettered' and 'natural' folk both now and in the past.

The connection between the interest in folklore and the tenets of Romanticism may not be altogether clear. Indeed there are contradictions – not surprisingly – within the complex group of attitudes known as Romanticism. But the key strands in the approach to national and 'folk' literature are, first, the view of the artless spontaneity of such literature, and, second, the yearning for another, more organic and natural world from the analyst's own. Hence that concept of literature among our ancestors, among contemporary 'primitive' peoples, and among unlettered and peasant 'folk' generally as arising spontaneously and without conscious volition on the part of those involved: a 'natural growth'. It springs up of itself from deep, mysterious roots which can be traced far back in the history and inner depths of mankind. This sort of 'folklore' – national epics, ballads, folk songs, local stories – seemed to mark a continuity with the longed-for lost, other world or organic and emotional unity, so that here contact could be made with the natural and primaeval depths, as distinct from the externally-imposed, mechanical and rationalist forms of the contemporary world.

In this complex of attitudes the idea of tradition plays a central role. For if such folk ways develop of their own accord and, as it were, naturally, without deliberate art, their continued existence and 'tradit-ing' through the generations without conscious acts of choice or even understanding by the traditors seems to follow. Thus one has the paradox – often noted – that the movement which laid such stress on the *individual* artist and his freedom should also be led to such deep belief in, and romantic respect for, 'tradition' and 'the collective'. For all the apparent contradiction, the feeling that through folk popular art one could reach back to the lost period of natural spontaneous literary utterance as well as to the deep and natural springs of national identity was basic to the romantic attitude, and received extra force through ideological and nationalist references to 'tradition'. It became accepted that there was a clear and valid distinction between learned, consciously composed literature and the kind of poems which –

like the sources of the Finnish *Kalevala* – 'belong to a period of spontaneous epic production...popular or national...Poetry which gave rise to them is natural, spontaneous, collective, impersonal, popular: hence national in its origins and its developments' (Comparetti, 1898, p. v). In the romantic approach the concept of tradition through the generations in relatively unchanging form plays a vital part.

This is the background against which 'folklore' as a specialist study first began, around the middle of the nineteenth century. Clearly, there had been interest in the materials of folklore before that – for example, the publication of Grimm's *Household Tales*, Keightley's *The Fairy Mythology* or Scott's *Ministrelsy of the Scottish Border* earlier in the century – but the emergence of 'folklore' as a named discipline is usually dated precisely to 1846, when William Thoms wrote a letter to *The Athenaeum* proposing a new name for what had hitherto been called 'Popular Antiquities' or 'Popular Literature':

> Your pages have so often given evidence of the interest which you take in what we in England designate as Popular Antiquities, or Popular Literature (though by-the-bye it is more a Lore than a Literature, and would be most aptly described by a good Saxon compound, Folklore, – *the Lore of the People*) – that I am not without hopes of enlisting your aid in garnering the few ears which are remaining, scattered over that field from which our forefathers might have gathered a goodly crop.
>
> (Thoms, 1846, p. 862)

He goes on to give examples of what he intends, suggesting that readers should note or send to *The Athenaeum* 'some record of old Time – some recollection of a now neglected custom – some fading legend, local tradition, or fragmentary ballad!'.

Thom's suggestions were taken up with enthusiasm, and 'folklore' study and collection attracted wide interest throughout the century and later, fostered by romantic and nationalist attitudes to 'traditional lore', and the nostalgic belief that it was dying out and must be recorded before it was lost for ever. 'Fast-perishing relics' was a common phrase and the accepted initial definition of 'folklore' was 'study of survivals'. G. L. Gomme, for example, an important figure in the development of the subject, describes 'the science of folk-lore' as 'the science which treats of the survivals of archaic beliefs and customs in modern ages' (Gomme, 1885, p. 14) and similar remarks stressing the age, lengthy survival and 'traditional' nature of the objects of folklore study recur through the nineteenth century. Later, the anthropologist J. G. Frazer made the same assumptions when he spoke of survivals of 'the old modes of life and thought': 'Such survivals are included under the head of folklore, which, in the broadest sense of the word, may be said to embrace the whole body of a people's traditionary beliefs and customs, so far as these appear to be due to the collective action of the multitude and cannot be traced to the individual influence of great men' (Frazer, 1918, 1, p. vii).

Through the study of folklore, then, it was possible to reach back to the 'age-old' survivals that had been handed down from the 'dim before-time' by 'oral tradition', and thus to the 'far-back ages' when man was artless, natural and unbound by the artificial constraints of external mechanical society. Through this study, too, minority or despised groups could seek their supposed or claimed national roots; so the collecting of 'folklore' and 'oral tradition' went along with the upsurge of national feeling in the smaller European countries in the nineteenth century. We can see a similar process in the twentieth-century assertions of national identity: like the sponsorship of the Irish Folklore Institute and Irish Folklore Commission by the Irish government in the period following the establishment of the Irish Republic, or the emphasis on *Négritude* and the return to 'our ancestral wisdom and folkways' by some African politicians.

The approach to oral literature which connects it with the development of 'folklore' in the romantic and nationalist context is so dominant that as soon as one uses the term 'unwritten' or 'oral' or 'folk' literature, the whole series of assumptions crystallised in the term 'folklore'[1] may rush into the mind. The various elements of the romantic interpretation are immediately evoked, and it is easy to take them as given and proved rather than the inheritance of one particular complex of ideas about the (wished-for) nature of society.

The common identification of 'oral literature' with 'oral tradition' thus becomes more comprehensible. 'Oral literature' (often assumed in this approach to be interchangeable with 'folk art', 'folk literature' etc.) is seen as arising in a spontaneous way and handed down, relatively unchanged, through unconscious 'oral tradition' into which conscious choice, judgement and 'art' do not enter.

These themes recur remarkably often in discussion of unwritten literature in this century as well. The supposed natural and artless quality is often emphasised. Fijian narrative poetry, for instance, is 'totally unreflective, totally childlike' (Leonard in Quain, 1942, p. vii), folk songs have 'evolved unconsciously' (Karpeles, 1973, p. 19) and the poetry of the ancient Germanic tribes of which some of the oldest remnants were, it is assumed, preserved and written down centuries later, 'did not belong to the realm of conscious artistic creation' (Rose, 1961, p. 5). An eminent authority can sum up 'folk-song as it existed in the past' as 'an instinctive

---

[1] 'Folklore' does not exactly coincide with the term 'oral literature'. Whatever the controversies about its exact meaning, all scholars, it seems, agree that it includes (most of) what could be termed 'oral literature' and the majority would probably see oral literature as comprising a major part of 'folklore'. (For further discussion of the controversies over the exact delimitation of the field of folklore see essays in Dundes, 1965.)

expression of the free artistic impulse in man, as natural as wildflowers'
(Bronson, 1969, p. 202). Cecil Sharp's famous encounter with the gardener's
song 'Seeds of Love' showed him, his colleague Maud Karpeles writes, 'the
real significance of the folk-song tradition. It revealed to him the existence
of a world of natural musical expression to which everyone, no matter how
humble nor how exalted, could lay claim by virtue of his common humanity'
(Karpeles, 1973, p. 94). Similarly with ballads, whose study was part of the
whole development of romanticism: they can be regarded as 'non-art',
created by 'the folk' rather than individuals and characterised by a 'lack
of self-conscious formulations' ('The non-art of the ballad', *TLS*, 1971),
while 'folksong' is 'the product of the spontaneous and intuitive exercise
of untrained faculties' and 'the folk-singer, being un-selfconscious and
unsophisticated and bound by no prejudice or musical etiquette, is
absolutely free in his rhythmical figures' (Vaughan Williams, 1934, p. 42).
The same contrast between the natural quality of 'primitive' thought and
the trained and conscious forms of civilised thinking crops up again in
Lévi-Strauss's opposition of *la pensée sauvage* to *la pensée cultivée et domes-
tiquée*. It is a commonplace for writers on oral poetry under the title of
'folksongs' to claim, as in Karpeles's *An Introduction to English Folk Song*,
that the folk-song tradition is most noticeable among people 'living close
to nature' (1973, p. 13). Again, the materials of 'folklore' (which includes
'folk literature') are said to constitute 'the mythopoeic, philosophic, and
esthetic mental world of nonliterate...or close-to-nature folk everywhere'
(Bayard, 1953, p. 9). Elsewhere 'folklore' is said to be 'a precipitate of
the scientific and cultural lag of centuries and millennia of human
experience...deeply entrenched in the racial unconscious...Beauty [these
primitive patterns] have because they were formed slowly close to nature
herself, and reflect her symmetry and simplicity...the poetic wisdom of
the childhood of the race' (Potter, 1949, p. 401).

The communal and 'folk' element in unwritten ('folk') literature is also
still commonly invoked as self-evident (even by those who reject more
extreme theories of the communal origin of all such material). Folklore in
general is 'essentially a communal product' (Kurath, 1949, p. 401) and the
art (including literature) of primitive societies is 'essentially communal'
(Kettle, 1970, p. 13), just as Polynesian myths and legends are 'composite
productions of the whole tribe' (Andersen, 1928, p. 44), while ballads are
'the voice of the people in the deepest sense in which that phrase can have
meaning' (Hendron in Leach and Coffin, 1961, p. 10).

Intimately connected with the idea of the spontaneous and communal
nature of unwritten literature is its continuing interpretation as oral tradition, as having been handed down over the ages. 'Folk-memory' is used
to 'explain' the postulated continuity of some 'oral tradition' over many
generations. For example, the 'Daura legend' among the Hausa is ex-

plained as 'the crystallisation in the folk-memory of the peaceful union of the Berbers and Sudanese in the eleventh century which produced the Hausa peoples' (Johnston, 1966, p. 113). In other cases oral tradition in more or less unchanged form is taken for granted as a natural and collective process, not needing further elaboration. Contemporary Ewe poems are described as 'folk songs' or 'traditional songs', and 'known' to be 'almost as old as the Ewe people themselves' (Adali-Mortty in Beier, 1967, pp. 3–4), Hausa tales 'lead right back into the mists of a remote past' (Johnston, 1966, p. xlix) and the Wolof oral narratives told by Amadou Koumba draw 'from his memory' tales 'that his grandfather's grandfather had learned from his grandfather' (Diop, 1966, p. xxiii). This sort of assumption is extrapolated into historical spculations about earlier oral literature. Some of the oldest epics in Persian literature are claimed to have been 'handed down by men orally for some fifteen-hundred years' (Boyce in Lang, 1971, p. 101), while the Gilgamesh poems, which were written down by the second millennium B.C. 'probably existed in much the same form many centuries earlier' (Sandars, 1971, p. 8). The assumed identity between 'oral literature' and 'oral tradition' comes out neatly in the indexes of many books where items of oral literature are jointly indexed under the general category of 'oral tradition'.

Once the word 'folk' comes in too – as it does so readily in forms like 'folk songs', 'folk poetry' or 'folk literature' – 'tradition' is taken for granted as of cental importance. Admittedly, there are controversies about the exact meaning of 'folklore', and many different suggested definitions: but in one survey of usages as recent as 1961 (Utley, 1961) the most common single characteristic was still 'tradition' and 'traditional'. Here are some typical phrases from definitions of folklore by a series of authorities in the much-used Funk and Wagnalls *Standard Dictionary of Folklore, Mythology, and Legend* (Leach, 1949, re-issued 1972): 'the science of traditional popular beliefs, tales, superstitions, rhymes...essentially a communal product, handed down from generation to generation' (G. P. Kurath); 'traditional creations of peoples, primitive and civilized' (J. Balys); 'popular and traditional knowledge...has very deep roots...a true and direct expression of the mind of "primitive" man' (A. M. Espinosa); while for the leading folklorist Stith Thompson, 'the common idea present in all folklore is that of tradition, something handed down from one person to another and preserved either by memory or practice rather than written record' (all quotations taken from entry under 'Folklore' in Leach, 1949, pp. 398ff). A similar emphasis is clear in S. P. Bayard's conclusion that 'one point upon which folklorists can safely be said to agree is that folklore is "traditional"' (Bayard, 1953, p. 5). When oral or unwritten literature is, as so often assumed, just another way of saying 'folk literature', i.e. a species of 'folklore', it is small wonder that one essential characteristic of oral literature is assumed without question to be its 'traditional' quality.

The tone in which the assumed spontaneous, communal and 'traditional' nature of unwritten literature is expressed is still often that of the romantic and glamorised evocation of a far-off world, in keeping with the typical romantic yearning for the mysterious, organic and harmonious past. The words used are often emotive, and one often gains an impression that oral literature – 'oral tradition' – somehow takes place in a primaeval, natural context, where 'the wisdom of our ancestors' can be found and where natural emotions and expressiveness have free play, unlike the mechanical artificial bonds of our modern industrial world. 'Oral tradition' enshrines 'Immemorial values and attitudes' and can help us to fight the 'waves of mechanization and depersonalization that threaten our life and thinking today', as one folklore expert put it recently (*The Times*, 1971). Again an African writer speaks of 'our rich, luxuriant folklore, whose roots strike deep into the earth…an incorporeal treasure…[which] has fed the mind through centuries, just as the parcel of inaccessible earth procures nourishment to the body' (Dadie, 1964, pp. 203, 207). Writers on various forms of oral literature constantly make direct and indirect reference to the supposed 'homogeneous', 'unsophisticated', 'communal', 'co-operative' characteristics of the sort of culture where oral tradition or folk art 'must have' existed or 'would naturally' or actually 'did' thrive. 'Folklore', as one authority sums it up, is the product of 'a homogeneous unsophisticated people, tied together not only by common physical bonds, but also by emotional ones which colour their every expression' (MacE. Leach on 'Folklore' in M. Leach, 1949).

Besides the glamourising approach, there is also the dismissive one (often paradoxically combined with the romantic view), based on the premiss that 'oral poetry' or 'folksong' are not really suitable for sociological or even literary analysis. On the extreme view, 'folklore' or 'traditional poetry' is a 'survival' from an earlier stage, a fossil preserved by unchanging tradition, not a part of functioning contemporary society or affected by conscious and individual actors. Even the less extreme view still tends to envisage oral poetry (under its categorisation as 'folk literature' or similar terms) as communal and 'traditional', unaffected by ordinary social conventions and differentiation. This relates to the whole idea that such literature represents 'nature' rather than 'society'. Thus one consequence of the romantic interpretation was that those who embarked on consistent research on aspects of oral poetry – A. L. Lloyd, for instance – have tended not to receive recognition as serious scholars, while sociologists and literary scholars were in general encouraged to avoid oral poetry as a subject of academic study.

The whole romantic (and in places evolutionist) approach is pertinent to the subject of this book. Although much of the writing which adopts this approach refers to prose, poetry is often mentioned. The idea goes very deep that what is often described as 'folk poetry' or 'folk song' has come down through long 'tradition', and that it essentially belongs to the rural, natural and communal context so stressed by the romantic folklorist.

As will already be evident, this approach is questioned in this book. Much of the detailed argument must be left to later discussion of, for example, the nature of transmission (chapter 5), of composition (chapter 3), the question of 'individual' as against 'communal' creativity (chapter 6), the functions and context of oral poetry (chapters 7 and 8) or the whole susceptibility of the subject to sociological and literary analysis (passim). For the moment, two general points can be made about this approach (or set of approaches).

It is illuminating, in the first place, to set the assumptions involved against the historical background and intellectual movement in which they were formulated. This brings home that these are indeed *assumptions*, related to particular historical currents, and do not necessarily arise from solid empirical evidence. These assumptions should be regarded as at least open to *question*, and in principle testable by the findings of empirical research.

The other point is that folklorists too are now beginning to question some of these assumptions. In American folklore, for instance, there has been an increasing interest in urban and contemporary forms, in individuals' varying styles, or in the change of function of a particular literary piece over time; there is a growing acceptance that these things are important and relevant to folklorists, who have also questioned some of the traditional assumptions. A recent influential statement by Ben-Amos, for instance, raises pertinent questions about the ideas of 'communality' and 'tradition' (1972, pp. 7–8). He suggests that the framework of preconceptions held by folklorists in the past has interfered with the understanding of the subject: 'These attempts to reconcile romantic with empirical approaches actually have held back scientific research in the field and are partially responsible for the fact that, while other disciplines that emerged during the nineteenth century have made headway, folklore is still suffering growing pains' (1972, p. 9). When to this is added the growing interest by a number of sociologists and folklorists in modern 'popular culture' and the 'mass media' – topics which partially overlap with contemporary oral poetry – it can be seen that the romantic approach, still deeply influential, is at least in part being questioned, even rejected, by some who, a generation ago, could have been expected to have been its strongest exponents.

I have thought it worth while to treat the background to this approach in more detail than the others because of its profound and continuing influence on the whole study of oral literature. It is part of the widely accepted stock of 'what everyone knows' about oral literature. And until one recognises that these assumptions *are* assumptions belonging to one particular approach and are not as yet necessarily proved it is difficult to carry out any empirical study without potentially misleading preconceptions.

2   The 'historical-geographical' school

A second approach that has been very influential in the study of oral literature is the so-called 'historical-geographical' school. This approach first became pre-eminent in Scandinavia (hence its frequent description as the 'Finnish' school); it was later taken up by American folklorists and now has a widespread influence. It has concentrated particularly on oral prose narratives – usually termed 'folktales' in this school – but the repercussions of the method, together with its implicit assumptions, have affected the approach to oral literature generally (again under the title of 'folk literature').

Scholars of this school take some particular literary item – most often a story – and try to trace its exact historical and geographical origins, then plot its journeys from place to place. Their interest is in reconstructing the earlier 'life history of the tale', working back to the first local forms, hence to the ultimate archetype from which, it is argued, these local variants all derive, in much the same way as later manuscript forms of a written piece can be traced back to an original manuscript archetype. For example, one particular plot – the 'root motif' – which tells how a crocodile was misled into releasing his hold on a potential victim's foot when told it was a root, has been traced from its African and American variants back through Europe and finally to India (Mofokeng, 1955, pp. 123ff). Similarly 'the star husband tale' – the marriage of two girls to the stars followed by a successful escape – has been studied in its many variants over a wide area in the United States and Southern Canada with its origin postulated as somewhere in the Central Plains (Stith Thompson, in Dundes, 1965, pp. 414ff).

To aid the process of recognising the 'same' tale in its various guises at different places and times, folklorists of this school have laid great emphasis on developing systems of classification. Plots, motifs and episodes have been classified and labelled, so that any given item can be isolated, identified and followed by a systematic mapping of its occurrences, and hence the eventual tracing of its origins. In this way all the variants of a tale can be collected and divided into their various components, so that finally the 'life history' of that particular tale can be established. The most monumental of the systems of classification is Stith Thompson's massive *Motif Index of Folk Literature* (6 volumes, 1955–8), but the general interest in classification and typologies runs through all the work of this school, and beyond. Any collection of tales was deemed incomplete – in fact not even to have started on the process of analysis – if it did not include references to the relevant types in Thompson's *Motif Index*, and, where possible, comparative material on occurrences of the same types elsewhere.

This approach to the study of 'folk literature' is perhaps a method rather than a theoretical construct involving a set of explanatory assumptions. But in practice it has acquired a number of implicit assumptions about the nature of oral narrative and a general emphasis on certain aspects of literature. These have washed off onto the study of oral literature more generally (including oral poetry).

The first characteristic is the emphasis on the *content* of literature. Plots, episodes and motifs are assumed to provide the substance of literature, with the implicit conclusion that these constitute the literary piece involved, what essentially defines it. No account is taken of factors like performance, occasion for delivery, social context or function or, indeed, the varying meanings that the same words may have for different audiences. For the historical-geographical analysts the content as defined and classified in standard typologies is what matters and what gives the essential reality of the piece: 'subjective' characteristics like local meaning or social context are, for their purposes, irrelevant.

To play down the social context and mode of performance of oral literature is to give a very truncated picture of its nature and essence. Even with written literature, to ignore the social background and public to which it is addressed gives a misleading view of its significance. And with oral literature, the import of a particular piece can scarcely be discovered from the textual content alone, without some attention to the occasion, audience, local meaning, individual touches by the performer at the moment of delivery, and so on. The concept, furthermore, of the diffusion of particular plots and motifs throughout the world is often stated in such a way that the active force seems to be the motifs and texts themselves rather than the performers or audiences of the oral works in question. The creative role of local poets or the effect of a participating audience in helping to mould a traditional motif into a new and unique literary act is played down in favour of an almost botanical concentration on the collection and classification of 'types' and their distribution. Thus the active part played by *local* participants in a given oral literature tends to be overlooked.

The method is clearly more difficult to apply to poetic than prose texts, for with poetry it is harder to argue that the essence of the piece lies in the subject-matter – in certain 'motifs', say – and that the language in which this is expressed and the style the poet chooses are of secondary importance. A few folklorists have tried to pursue a version of the historical-geographical method with 'folk songs', and have attempted to reconstruct the travels of particular poems. Hugh Tracey, for instance, (in Dundes, 1965) tries to trace an old Negro lullaby sung in Georgia in the United States to Zambezia a century earlier, while Archie Taylor (1931) finds that the song *Sven i Rosengård* came originally from the song *Edward* which travelled from Britain to Scandinavia; and questions have often been pursued about the origins and travels of European and American ballads (e.g. Brewster, 1953, Wilgus, 1959).

The general notion that content and its transmission are of the first import has often led to an underestimate of the significance of style or of the personal contribution of the individual poet. But by and large this method has not often been applied *directly* to the analysis of poetry, so that the massive collecting of texts inspired by this approach has tended to pass poetry by. This is one reason for the widespread impression that unwritten folk literature consists mainly of prose narratives – 'folk tales' – and has little place for poetry.

The historical and geographical folklorists have always stressed the existence of large numbers of variants – the 'same' plot or episode is expressed in varying words in a way typical of the transmission of a tale through 'oral tradition'. But even so, the emphasis on general textual content to the exclusion of social context reminds one of the exclusive emphasis on the *text* in some literary criticism. The idea that having got 'the text' one then has the essence of the piece one wishes to study, and that other considerations are at best secondary and perhaps wholly irrelevant has had a great influence on the study of oral literature. It has meant that, until recently, investigators have felt largely satisfied with recording text after text, while including nothing on detailed social background, personality of the composer and performer, methods of reward, nature of audiences and so on – all the questions which would normally arise in the sociology of literature. Once the assumption is made that 'the text is the thing', these other questions fade into insignificance.

It will be clear that assumptions associated with this school have had great influence on the analysis of oral literatures and that some of them are controversial. They have been questioned by sociologists generally (perhaps particularly by the British school of functionalist anthropologists), and also in a number of analyses of particular instances of oral literature. A. B. Lord, for instance, in his classic work *The Singer of Tales* (1968a, first published 1960) has made plain the importance of the creative act by performer-composer in Yugoslav oral epic, and has argued that the concept of *the* correct or original text is inapplicable to oral poetry, where each performance produces a unique and individual poetic creation (this is described further in chapter 3). Similarly recent research in America has uncovered the complex interplay in 'folk poetry' and 'folk song' between 'tradition' on the one hand and the individual creator, local audience and social context on the other (e.g. Stekert, 1965, Wolf, 1967, Glassie *et al.* 1970, Abrahams, 1970a). And the interest in performance by some recent

American folklorists, with their view of folklore as 'a communicative event' involving social interaction has explicitly involved both a rejection of the 'Finnish' school of folklore – 'It is becoming trite to criticise the much-criticised Finnish method; but there is no doubt that part of our troubles may be traced to it' says Paredes (Paredes and Bauman, 1972, p. ix) – and a questioning of the importance of the concepts of 'oral transmission' and 'oral tradition' (Ben-Amos, 1972, p. 13). All in all, there is much to query in the approach of the historical-geographical school, but some knowledge of its influence is necessary for an understanding and assessment of the often unspoken assumptions in many authoritative publications.

3   Sociological approaches and the sociology of literature

So far the approaches discussed tend to be regarded as part of the development of 'folklore' – ones which would be familiar to every folklorist but are usually felt to be beyond the scope of the social scientist. But there are also approaches and controversies normally accepted as central to the sociology of literature but which are, in turn, often ignored by folklorists.

One question for sociologists of literature has long been: just what role does literature play in society? Does it reflect the current culture and social order with more or less directness? And if it does, is this reflection selective, or does it cover 'the whole' of society? Or does literature go beyond a passive role like 'reflection' and play an active part in the working of society?

These questions point to aspects neglected in the previous approaches. In the work of some analysts, the reflecting role of literature is taken for granted (that of the Chadwicks, for instance – see chapter 8 below). Others stress the active and functional aspect of literature. Several have described how literature can play a part in the maintenance of social control or the socialisation of children through the 'lessons' it teaches. Similarly poems like hymns, secret society songs, or initiation verse can be shown to contribute to the solidarity and self-awareness of certain groups and hence, often, to a maintenance of the *status quo*. This aspect is brought out by functionalist writers – anthropologists like Malinowski or Radcliffe-Brown and their followers – and, in a different way, by the Marxist critics who have pointed out that literature can function as a 'tool of the ruling class', propagating its ideas and interpretations. In reply, other analysts have pointed to the part literature often plays in social and intellectual change. This used to be a common view of authors: they take the lead in cultural progress, and formulate new ideals and deeper insights. More recently the detailed role of particular literatures and their manifestations has been much discussed. Marxists see literature as a potential weapon in 'the class struggle' – hence their interest in 'popular literature', 'the people's songs' and so on. Others point out how, say, political songs can make an impact during an election campaign, how satirical writings can undermine, even topple, established authority; or how new ideas and policies can be consciously propagated through popular literary forms. From the point of view of the social scientist, literature is a *social* and not just a private phenomenon, far less a 'natural' and quasi-botanical one, and it is therefore subject to the kind of investigation relevant in the analysis of any social institution. That this involves controversy is certain, but it is controversy about the kinds of social-scientific questions often ignored in the other approaches.

In much work on oral literature it has seemed easy to overlook such controversies, and to take one or other answer for granted as the only possible one, as if the wider controversies about literature as a social phenomenon do not apply in this field. Thus a number of writers (including some sociologists and social anthropologists) have taken it for granted that oral literature can best be analysed in functional terms. It is then interpreted as primarily either reflective or else as upholding the *status quo*, a role which British functionalist anthropologists particularly emphasised. The aesthetic and 'play' element tended to be brushed aside as irrelevant to proper sociological analysis, and the study of the *detailed* functions of particular literary pieces and genres – potentially heterogeneous and changing – neglected in favour of one monolithic generalised theory about the expected function of oral literature. Another common conclusion concerns the 'democratic' nature of oral literature: it is assumed to be the possession of 'the people as a whole'. This assumption is particularly strong when the term 'folk literature' is used (as it often is). It seems to be implied in the term itself that it 'belongs to all the people', is 'the wisdom of the people, the people's knowledge' (Sokolov on 'folklore', 1950, p. 3) or (of 'folk music' or 'folk song'), that it is 'a democratic art in the true sense of the word' (Karpeles, 1973, p. 11) and so on.

Yet to any selfconscious sociologist of literature, these points about detailed functions and the extensiveness of distribution of particular literatures or genres are all questions at issue. The answers given by the researcher may depend partly on the general theoretical position he takes up on such issues – though such a position needs to be a conscious choice between possible alternatives rather than mere unconscious assumption. Even more, it must depend on the results of empirical investigation into the facts of a given literature. Sometimes a wide range of disparate and changing functions can be detected and the examples studied may or may not lend support to the established order. And contrary to the preconceptions of many folklorists, certain items which they would classify as 'folk literature' turn out to be closely identified with one particular group (perhaps a powerful monopolistic élite of trained poets) and only in a very extended sense to be a possession of 'the society' or 'the folk' at large, or a spontaneous and necessarily un-self-interested product of the people as a whole.

These questions are given further discussion later, particularly in chapters 7 and 8. The point to notice here is that they *are* questions and have to be treated as such.

4 Two 'ideal types' of society and poetry

The final approach to be considered here has been implicit at several points earlier. This is the approach basic to much classic sociological theory, in which two models or types of society are postulated, standing in contrast to one another. This is explicitly formulated in the writings of Durkheim and has been echoed by other theorists since. On the one hand, there is the model of 'primitive' or 'non-industrial' society: small-scale and homogeneous, conformist, 'oral' rather than literate, communal, dominated by religious and traditional norms and the ties of ascribed 'kinship'; unselfconscious, and probably more 'organic' and 'close to nature' than ourselves – or at any rate untouched by the mechanisation and advanced technology of our society. Opposed to this is the model of modern industrial society – secular and rational; heterogeneous; dominated by the written word and oriented towards achievement and individual development; and at the same time highly mechanised and specialised, typically bound together by artificial rather than 'natural' and 'organic' links.

The opposition of these two models has, in various forms, run through the writings of sociologists and anthropologists for a century or so, from the classic expositions of Durkheim or Tönnies to those of Parsons, Merton or Redfield. It is a dichotomy between two basically differing types of society that has had profound influence in sociological writing and has coloured the attitude of sociologists both in their construction of theories about society and in their assessment of the institutions existing in the so-called 'primitive' type.

The repercussions of this basic dichotomy have influenced the interpretation of the role of oral literature by both sociologists and folklorists. It is not logically *necessary*, even accepting the two models at their face value, that oral literary forms should occur only in the 'primitive' type of society. But the assumption is easily made, and once it is made the supposed characteristics of the society wash over onto the whole assessment of oral literature. Generalisations like that of Notopoulos become plausible: 'the society which gives birth to oral poetry is characterized by traditional fixed ways in all aspects of its life' (1964, p. 51), or Hendron's characterisation of the typical 'folk singer': 'he lives in a rural or isolated region which shuts him off from prolonged schooling and contact with industrialized urban civilization' (in Leach and Coffin, 1961, p. 7).

In such statements, the 'primitive' context is seen as the most common and, as it were, 'natural' context for oral poetry. Like the society in which it occurs, oral poetry can be assumed without further inquiry to be unselfconscious, communally rather than individually oriented, and pro- duced in a homogeneous setting with little or no specialisation by poets or audiences. Similarly, oral poetry in such societies can be assumed to be 'natural' and artless, arising from spontaneous emotion rather than cons- cious art. Furthermore, oral literary forms occurring in other contexts, in societies with partial or mass literacy, can be assumed to be not the 'natural' form, but an aberrant and unusual type. This can be ignored as untypical or explained away as merely 'transitional', perhaps a 'survival' from the 'primitive' oral type of society, its 'natural' setting.

Not all sociologists would take this extreme line, and when the assump- tions involved are stated *explicitly* would be likely to question them. But this set of assumptions implicitly underlies the attitude of many sociologists to oral literature and helps to explain why many have thought it not worth studying. While the emphasis in sociological theory on these two opposing models of society continues and is reinforced in elementary textbooks and university teaching, this implicit assessment of the nature and setting of oral literature is likely to remain influential.

When these assumptions are brought into the open, it is clear that they are questionable. In the present context, they can be tested on two main fronts: first, the postulation of the 'primitive' or 'oral' type of society as the primary setting for oral literature; and second, the general validity of these two contrasting models of society.

Anyone looking at the research on oral literature, and the various collections of texts now available will find that the typical 'primitive' society is *not* necessarily the most common setting. It is not in fact more 'normal' for oral literature to be practised in such society.

This comes out in ways that make the point more than a definitional one about how widely one uses the term 'oral'; and this throws new light on the distribution of unwritten literature.

First, most of the examples of oral literature which we possess and analyse have not been collected from pure 'primitive' cultures. In practice it is rare for collectors and recorders to operate except in conditions that to some extent run counter to the extreme 'primitive' society. True, there are rare and partial exceptions, but by and large our recorded examples of oral literature in so-called 'primitive' cultures could never have been made in the first place without the use of writing and/or some penetration by foreign observers, and without the presence of at least some administra- tive, missionary, or educational services. We are so ready to picture our oral items as coming from some 'uncontaminated' and 'primitive' oral stage of culture, that we ignore the conditions in which our examples were for the most part actually recorded: written down by schoolboys for their missionary teachers, painfully dictated by oral practitioners prepared to spend time with foreign researchers or to travel to an urban and scholarly centre, or observed by visitors complete with back-up apparatus and train of hangers-on. This is not to denigrate the methods or achievements of early or recent collectors. But to pretend that most collections were made in a pure and primitive type of culture is simply untrue.

It can, of course, be retorted that the conditions in which oral pieces have recently been collected are merely contingent, and nothing to do with the *real* nature of oral literature which is presumed to have existed for millennia in the 'pure primitive state' before writing was invented, and for even longer in areas of non-literacy before recent penetration by European literate traditions. This is true. But for detailed scholarly investigations we can scarcely afford to spend over-long on speculation about what must or might have been so in the past. We have to analyse the examples of oral literature we do have access to, either directly or in texts or recordings. One has to face the unromantic truth that few or none of these are directly recorded from the extreme type of primitive culture envisaged in the common dichotomy.

There is in any case great variety among indigenous cultures themselves. Certainly there are wide areas in which (until fairly recently) people had basically no contact with the written word: Polynesia for instance, the interior of New Guinea, the Australian aborigines, or many of the American Indian groups. But a large number of the cultures most readily classed as 'primitive' lived at least on the edges of a literate tradition. It is easy to overlook this, but one need only cite the influence of China, with its learned civilisation, over vast areas of Asia; the effects of Arabic learning and the religion of 'the Book' in many parts of Africa; or the impact of Roman and Christian learning on oral and vernacular forms in mediaeval Europe. It has to be accepted that a number of the cultures normally classified as primitive have had generations or centuries of contact with literacy, and that the examples of oral literature we study are as likely to come from a culture of this kind as from one traditionally untouched by any experience of literacy.

Apart from differences in the degree of contact with literacy, societies can also be grouped according to the degree of specialisation in literary activity. In some there is very little – thus fulfilling assumptions about the undifferentiated 'primitive' type of society so far as literature is concerned. But in others there is a definite tradition of literary and intellectual special-isation. In such cultures there may be a conscious learned tradition in which literary specialists deliberately train new recruits into their acquired skills – the poetic training in Ruanda in Central Africa, for instance (Kagame, 1951, chapter 9), the Maori 'school of learning' (Best, 1923), the Uzbek singer-teachers (Chadwick and Zhirmunsky, 1969, p. 330) and perhaps the early Irish poetic schools (Chadwick, 1932, pp. 603ff). These often involve careful control over recruitment and, sometimes, monopoly over particular types of literary productions. They are far from the unconscious and undifferentiated kind of culture assumed as *the* characteristic context for oral literature. This is not a matter of the odd exceptional case; a large proportion of recorded oral literature – for instance the vast corpus of oral epic poetry from Central Asia – comes from this kind of context.

One can also question the whole formulation of these two contrasting types, as put forward in classic sociological theory. Either as empirical generalisations, or as abstract 'models', these two postulated 'types' of society surely now need a critical re-assessment. Do societies of the kinds postulated actually exist, and if so how widely? And if the types represent conceptual models only, are these illuminating or misleading ones? The study of oral literature can lead to doubts of their validity and usefulness. These doubts have been expressed by other sociologists in more general terms. Lemert puts it well in the context of one particular implication of this typology.

> It is theoretically conceivable that there are, or have been societies in which values learned in childhood, taught as a pattern, and reinforced by structured controls, served to predict the bulk of the everyday behavior of members and to account for the prevailing conformity to norms. However, it is easier to describe the model than it is to discover societies which make a good fit with the model... It is safe to say that separatism, federation, tenuous accommodation, and perhaps open structuring, are at least as characteristic of known societies of the world as the unified kind of ideal social structure based on value consensus which impressed Durkheim, Parsons, and Merton.
>
> (Lemert, 1967, p. 7)

Add to this the increasing knowledge we have gained from the work of anthropologists and others about the diversity of forms that 'non-industrial' and 'Third World' societies can take, and it becomes an issue to be faced whether sociologists should not now radically rethink the basic dichotomy between models of society on which so much earlier writing was based. It is a real question whether they have not become more misleading than illuminating.

With this in mind, it is interesting to hark back to the earlier discussion about romanticism and the assumptions of romantic thought in the nineteenth century. It is worth remembering that much of the classical sociological theory which has so influenced later generations was formed in this period. It too bears the impress of precisely the same kinds of assumption. It is not difficult to detect the same romantic evocation of the natural and

3

organic 'state of nature', untrammelled by the mechanical and artificial bonds of today, in the models produced in scholarly writings of the time. This is evident in many of the classic formulations of what has been termed 'the sociological tradition' (Nisbet, 1970). There is Tönnies's *Gemeinschaft* with its collective 'harmony' based on 'folkways' and 'folk culture' and rooted in 'imagination', in contrast to the rational arbitrary nature of *Gesellschaft*, based on 'thinking' and liable to lead to 'the doom of culture' unless one can revivify the 'scattered seeds – and again bring forth the essence and idea of Gemeinschaft'; Durkheim's societies with low division of labour and emphasis on the collective as against those which are more 'rational' and where 'tradition has lost its sway'; or the Marxist view of the simple, unchanging and communal nature of pre-capitalist society in contrast to the exploitation involved in 'civilisation' with the increasing division of labour. In these great dichotomies between different types of society postulated by the classic social theorists and most often perpetuated today under the terms of 'traditional' as opposed to 'modern', one can see the continuation of the romantic tradition, accompanied by some of its emotive associations.

Tracing intellectual antecedents and congeners is not in itself an indication that certain formulations are wrong. But it does remind us of the need to ask ourselves whether certain generalisations (in this case about types of society) formulated at a particular time and place and in a certain cultural context are necessarily and universally valid, however many respectable followers have repeated and transmitted them since. Certainly, so far as the study of oral poetry is concerned a close look at the assumptions involved is very much overdue.

I have not tried to give a comprehensive account of the many different theoretical positions taken up in the study of literature. Even the briefest historical survey of these would have had to consider many not mentioned here – like the psychological interpretations based on Jung and Freud, 'communication studies' and semiology, 'structuralism', the whole 'Parry-Lord' school (discussed further in chapter 3), the various controversies within 'literary criticism' and so on. Again a full account would have to mention the many excellent studies of oral literature carried out in the nineteenth century and earlier this century (like the Chadwicks' monumental work, research in Eastern Europe, and collections and analysis by scholars and amateurs all over the world). Rather than trying to provide such a summary (which can to some extent be found elsewhere e.g. Bascom, 1954, Dorson, 1963, Andrzejewski and Innes, 1972, Wilgus, 1959, Jacobs, 1966, Greenway, 1964, chapter 8; also Finnegan, 1974b), my aim has been to elucidate certain themes underlying the approaches to oral literature that are persistently influential yet often unrecognised. Because of this they can impede understanding and research by implying that assumption is fact.

Once these assumptions are explicitly recognised as such, they can become useful stimuli rather than hindrances to future research.

This preliminary discussion suggests that we are more ignorant of some of the general processes involved in oral literature and its social contexts than many confident early assumptions allow; and in particular that the kinds of generalisations which suggest that all 'oral poetry' necessarily belongs to one single 'type' rather than including many diverse manifestations can prove to be misleading rather than helpful.

3
Composition

How is oral poetry composed? Does the performer memorise a given text? Does he improvise in the heat of the moment? Does the poet rely basically on formulae learnt beforehand but combined in different ways on different occasions? Or is there no one single mode of oral composition?

These and similar questions have exercised many scholars and have caused much controversy. Because the nature of composition and the controversies concerned with it are fundamental to the study of oral poetry, it is appropriate to begin the substantive account in this book of the various facets of oral poetry by considering the processes and problems of composition.

1 *Is memorisation the key factor?*

On the face of it, memorisation would appear to be the correct description of what is involved. It seems that a singer or reciter going fluently through the delivery of a piece must surely have memorised it from already existing words, and that the piece is fully formed before he starts, only needing to be called to mind at the appropriate moment. The familiar model of a child learning off a poem or song and then performing it from memory at a competition or concert seems one that could reasonably be extended to cover the general relationship of the performer of oral poetry to the process of composition. He is repeating from memory a piece which has been composed *prior* to the performance, either by himself or, more likely, by others, perhaps years or generations earlier.

This interpretation is frequently used. It looks like a common sense view. In addition, it gains apparent support from the 'folk theories' of oral tradition discussed in chapter 2. If 'oral tradition' can be seen as something which grew communally and spontaneously or was inherited by its current bearers over a period of many years (or even centuries) then all the present-day oral poet has to do is to learn and remember this tradition. Even statements which avoid the extreme view of oral literature as a 'fossil survival' or 'archaic relic' from the past still give the impression that the contemporary performer does little more than passively receive and pass on material already formed. For example, if it is true that the Old Iranian epic was 'handed down by men orally for some fifteen-hundred years' (Boyce in Lang, 1971, p. 101), that Eskimo literature was transmitted down from 'days of yore' (Thalbitzer, 1923, p. 117) or that Ewe poems in West Africa are 'almost as old as the Ewe people themselves' (Adali-Mortty in Beier, 1967, p. 3) then the present-day oral 'poet' need have little if anything to do with composition. Statements like this are widespread, and basically envisage the performer as a recipient of the oral tradition: his role is merely to memorise and deliver to contemporary audiences. As one analyst sums up this approach (in the context of the ballad), 'Memorization...is the basic vehicle of oral tradition' (Friedman, 1961, p. 114).

This view gains support from the statements of some local poets. Wakarpa, the old blind bard who recited *Kutune Shirka*, the famous Ainu epic about the Golden Sea Otter, 'insisted', according to Arthur Waley, that 'he had merely repeated the epic as he had learnt it' (Waley, 1951, p. 236). Similarly, Parry and Lord recorded statements by Yugoslav singers of oral heroic poems in the 1930s that they could repeat exactly the same song that they had heard from another singer, 'word for word, and line for line' (Lord, 1968a, pp. 27–8); and a Somali reciter often makes it clear to his audiences that the poem he is delivering was composed not by himself but by another named poet (Andrzejewski and Lewis, 1964, p. 46). Here, it seems, is definite evidence that the current performer is proceeding primarily by memorising an already formed text.

This view of memorisation and recall is still widespread. But as a scholarly theory about the basic process of oral composition it is now under fire from many scholars, and in specialist circles analyses in terms of 'memorisation' have become unpopular.

The critique has proceeded on three main fronts. First, there are the general doubts now held about the 'folk theories' of age-old oral tradition etc.; second, the growing awareness of the significance of *current* performance, and the effect of the audience and the context on the process of composition on a particular occasion – an awareness consolidated through our increased grasp of variability in oral transmission due to the extensive use of the tape-recorder; and third, a series of detailed empirical studies of actual oral composition allied to a wide comparative approach, resulting in the work of scholars such as Parry and Lord and the 'oral-formulaic' school of analysis inspired by their work.

The romantic background was discussed in the last chapter and doubts about the general validity of the underlying assumptions were raised there. The transmission of oral literature is taken up further in chapter 5. So beyond saying summarily that there is now much evidence leading us to doubt older assumptions that oral literature was naturally and inevitably formed through age-old transmission in unchanging form over generations, I will not pursue this particular line. The general emphasis on the active role of poet and audience in the examples and analyses discussed here in the context of composition, itself tends to undermine the plausibility of many romantic assumptions. More however needs to be said about the other two aspects.

First, one has to consider the effect which the situation may have on the performance. It is a striking characteristic of many performances of oral literature that the performer is affected both by his audience and by the occasion. These can affect his poem, sometimes radically, to an extent where one is forced to speak of *composition* by the poet/performer rather than memorisation, with minor variations, of a piece composed by others.

One aspect which can be affected by the nature and reactions of the audience is the length of the piece. Radlov's account of the case of the Kirghiz singer of heroic poetry is often quoted:

> The minstrel, however, understands very well when he is to desist from his song. If the slightest signs of weariness show themselves, he tries once more to arouse attention by a struggle after the loftiest effects, and then, after calling forth a storm of applause, suddenly to break off his poem. It is marvellous how the minstrel knows his public. I have myself witnessed how one of the sultans, during a song, sprang up suddenly and tore his silk overcoat from his shoulders, and flung it, cheering as he did so, as a present to the minstrel.

> (Radlov, *Proben*, v, p. xix, translated in Chadwick, III, 1940, p. 185)

As Radlov says, the minstrel 'knows how to represent one and the same picture in a few short strokes. He can depict it more fully, or he can go into a very detailed description with epic fulness.' (Ibid., p. 182).

It is not just the length of the Kirghiz minstrel's song that is affected by his audience and situation.

> Since the minstrel wants to obtain the sympathy of the crowd, by which he is to gain not only fame, but also other advantages, he tries to colour his song according to the listeners who are surrounding him. If he is not directly asked to sing a definite episode, he begins his song with a prelude which will direct his audience into the sphere of his thoughts. By a most subtle art, and allusions to the most distinguished persons in the circle of listeners, he knows how to enlist the sympathy of his audience before he passes on to the song proper. If he sees by the cheers of his listeners that he has obtained full attention, he either proceeds straight to the business, or produces a brief picture of certain events leading up to the episode which is to be sung, and then passes on to the business. The song does not proceed at a level pace. The sympathy of the hearers always spurs the minstrel to new efforts of strength, and it is by this sympathy that he knows how to adapt the song exactly to the temper of his circle of listeners. If rich and distinguished Kirghiz are present, he knows how to introduce panegyrics very skilfully on their families, and to sing of such episodes as he thinks will arouse the sympathy of

distinguished people. If his listeners are only poor people, he is not ashamed to introduce venomous remarks regarding the pretensions of the distinguished and the rich, and actually in the greater abundance according as he is gaining the assent of his listerners.

(ibid., pp. 184–5)

However much the Kirghiz minstrel has learnt from other poets – whether 'handed down by tradition' or not – it is clear how far he himself takes part in the process of composition in the performance. It is impossible to describe his poems, as actually delivered, solely in terms of 'memorisation'.

The Kirghiz possibly lay more stress on improvisation in their heroic poems, with correspondingly less on memorisation, than some other peoples. But this receptivity to the expectations of the audience and the demands of the occasion is widely documented for oral poetry. The Xhosa *imbongi* (praise singer) in South Africa is often fired to compose and declaim by some event which he observes: he responds to the situation, not to a memorised or long-deliberated text. This is how the *imbongi* Nelso Mabunu describes the process

Some people think perhaps an *imbongi* sits down and studies. That is not the thing: it's an inspiration. When you see something, you know, it's like a preacher in church when he preaches the gospel, you feel touched, then you feel like saying some words yourself, you know – that's an inspiration. It's nothing else and it can be nothing else. You can judge a recitation, you know, done by school children, I mean by a school child, something that he has learnt and he'll recite. But singing, you know, praises for a chief or anything, it's an inspiration.

(Opland, 1974, pp. 8–9)

Again the free-lance Hausa praise singer of Northern Nigeria inclines his praise poems to the needs of his own pocket as well as the circumstances of his temporary patron. The wandering singer arrives at a village and carefully finds out the names of leading personages in the area. Then he takes up his stand in a conspicuous place, and produces a praise song to the individual he has decided to apostrophise. It is punctuated by frequent demands for gifts. If he gets what he wants, he announces the amount and sings his thanks in further praise. But if he does not, his delivery becomes harsher and the song becomes interlaced with innuendo about the 'patron's' birth and status. Sooner or later the victim gives in, and buys the singer's silence with a cash payment or valuable gift (Smith, 1957). Here too, the skill with which the singer adapts his song to the circumstances cannot be explained solely in terms of memorisation.

Similar instances abound, from the adaptations of traditional themes to the circumstances of the moment by Akan dirge singers in West Africa (Nketia, 1955, chapter 4, especially pp. 66ff), to the attempts of a folk preacher in the American south to arouse a bored audience by breaking into a rhythmic passage of the 'Four Horsemen' – a theme unrelated to the original subject of the sermon (Rosenberg, 1970, pp. 68f) – or the compositions of the American Negro singer 'Left Wing Gordon': 'Wing's blues were mixed and of wonderful proportions. He could sing almost any number of blues, fairly representative of the published type with, of course, the typical additions, variations, and adaptations to time and occasion' (Odum and Johnson, 1926, p. 211). East European scholars, with their studies of the Russian *byliny* from the nineteenth century and earlier, were among the first to emphasise the creative role of the poet as an aspect of performance, and the improvisatory rather than memorising element of oral poetry. As the Chadwicks sum it up 'on the whole we must regard the free variety, which allows more or less scope for improvisation, as the normal form of oral tradition, and strict memorisation as exceptional' (Chadwick, 1940, III, p. 868).

The use of the tape-recorder to provide accessible copies of a large number of renderings has made us more aware of variability in detail. Up to a point, such variability has long been recognised. Child's classic collection set an example by giving differing versions of each of the 300 or so ballads he prints. *Mary Hamilton* appears in at least fifteen different variants, and *Barbara Allen* in three (to which can be added a dozen or more collected by Sharp in the Southern Appalachians early this century (1932, I, pp. 183ff)). The same is true with the famous ballads of Mrs Brown of Falkland in North East Scotland at the end of the eighteenth century, accepted as classic renderings. She produced two versions of *The lass of Roch Royal*, in 1783 and 1800 respectively, which differ enough to make it clear that re-creation rather than exact reproduction was involved (see Bronson, 1969, pp. 69ff). From these and other examples collected by earlier folklorists, linguists and others, it became clear that variability of detailed text is common in oral tradition – in what is usually termed 'folklore'.

This in itself weakens the memorisation theory. Variability has sometimes been accommodated in the theory and explained in terms of faulty memorisation. So variability *could* be seen as resulting from misremembered versions of some forgotten original. And indeed it is reasonable to attribute some variants to the fact that singers may have forgotten musical or verbal phrases and filled the gaps as best they could; and this is supported by the likelihood that literary pieces get distorted over time or space. The words and tunes of ballads 'could not possibly remain unaltered, considering the fallibility of human memory, which plays as many tricks with the unlettered singers of folk-songs as it does with the rest of us' writes Gerould (1932, p. 163), just as 'any composition travelling from mouth to mouth, from generation to generation, from country to country is bound to suffer from a certain amount of verbal corruption and degeneration' (Coffin, 1950, p. 3).

In general however, the widespread existence of variants *prima facie* sheds doubt on the concept of exact memorisation as the key factor in oral composition: even the early collector Sharp, who recorded only in writing, rejects the idea that variants are 'corruptions in varying degree of one original' (1972, p. 14, first published 1907). But the implausibility of attributing variability largely to faulty memory has been much increased by use of the tape-recorder. This has helped to show that variability is not just a feature of lengthy oral transmission through time and space but is inherent both in different renderings of one literary piece within the same group and period and even in texts by the same person delivered at no great interval in time. In such cases, memorisation of basic themes or plots is involved, but a generalised explanation of the oral poetry in terms of particular texts exactly memorised does not easily fit the abundant variability demonstrated in tape-recorded (as well as dictated) texts. When one adds this general evidence of variability to the specific cases mentioned earlier, showing the creative role of the poet responding to the audience and occasion, it becomes extremely difficult to continue to hold the theory that memorisation is the sole factor at work. Clearly there are many occasions when the performer takes a hand in the process of composition.

How much freedom the composer-performer has is not always clear in the published accounts. The degree of 'composition' as against 'memorisation' probably differs both between different cultures, and between different genres in the same culture, and between poets. The Chadwicks, for instance, contrasted the emphasis on memorisation among the Turkomans with the 'high development of extempore composition' of the Kirghiz (Chadwick, III, 1940, p. 184), and the amount of strict memorisation involved in the ritualistic poetry of an established religion is likely to be more than in a light-hearted topical song.

Even within one genre, there may be more, or less, improvisation. There is an instructive contrast between different kinds of work songs among Texas prisoners. The songs which accompany critically-timed tasks, such as a team of men cutting down a tree, give little scope for change or development in the singing, though 'one can interject names in formulaic lines – names of guards, fellow-workers, people one has known or heard of, and so forth – and there are chorus lines and repeats that give the singer time to think up another verse' (Jackson, 1972, p. 34). But songs for less rigorously timed group-work like cotton picking or sugarcane cutting give more opportunities for solo songs and for lyrical and ornamental development by the leader (ibid., p. 33).

Individual poets differ in the emphasis they lay on memorisation as against creation. In the study of American oral forms, it has become common to distinguish between 'passive' and 'active' traditors – those who largely reproduce what they have heard, having memorised it as best they can, and those who actively participate in composition or recomposition.

In the *nyatiti* lament-songs of the East African Luo, too, there are different degrees of personal creativity by the singer, depending less on external situation than on the ability of the singer. Some perform from a relatively fixed repertoire – or from a set of basic structures, which, once learnt, can be modified to suit the circumstances of the funeral to which the singer has been summoned: he adds an 'uncle here and a grandfather there, together with any knowledge he may possess of the attributes of the deceased'. But a gifted Luo singer creates a more individual and developed song, particularly when he is emotionally involved. His artistry is appreciated by his listeners. 'The skill and beauty with which the musician is able to improvise at such moments is a measure of his musical and poetic stature' (Anyumba, 1964, pp. 189–90).

These variations between cultures, genres and poets are in themselves interesting (see also chapter 5, where the topic is related to transmission and distribution). But the important issue is the extent of this variation. The blanket term 'memorisation' is too general to cover the manifold ways in which poets may proceeed in different contexts. And 'memorisation' is not always the most appropriate description for the process of performance/composition observed in the instances mentioned here, and many similar ones that have been observed.

To these doubts have been added the theories and findings of the 'oral-formulaic' school, initially concerned with analysis of 'formulaic' language in the Homeric epics, supplemented by research on comparable forms in twentieth-century Yugoslav oral poetry, and now influential in the whole study of oral composition.

2   Composition-in-performance and the oral-formulaic theory

There had long been controversy over the composition of the Homeric poems, the *Iliad* and *Odyssey*. The main battle was between the 'unitarians' who posited a single author, and the 'separatists' who held that the poems were a composite construction of different lays and/or strata. There had always been difficulties about either position. How could one decide questions about the composition of poems written down in Greece two and half millennia ago and perhaps composed much earlier? How explain the composition of such long poems (the *Iliad* 15,000 lines, the *Odyssey* 12,000 – surely too long to be memorised?) in an age when most people were illiterate? And what was the best explanation of the recurrent lines and phrases, some repeated many times throughout the poem?

Against this background, analysis of the 'formulaic' nature of Homer's style and its possible relationship to the *oral* composition of epic poetry was developed. Its initial exponents in the West were Milman Parry and his pupil Albert Lord – hence its designation as the 'Parry–Lord theory' although the foundations had in fact been laid by earlier writers like Murko on Yugoslav oral poetry and a number of Russian studies.

Milman Parry was an American classical scholar who became interested in the formulaic phrases in the Homeric epithets, on which he published his study of *L'Epithète traditionelle dans Homère* (Paris, 1928). He noticed, like others before him, the apparently formulaic nature of recurrent descriptions of many of the people in the poems: 'swift-footed Achilles', 'many-counselled Odysseus', 'glorious Hector', 'grey-eyed Athene', and so on. These formulaic epithets, which to a modern reader may appear an irritating repetition or a not very meaningful trick of 'epic style', can also be seen as playing a significant part in the composition of the poem. For these various epithets fit exactly the constraints of the hexameter metre in which the poems are composed: 'Achilles, son of Peleus' (Πηληιάδεω Ἀχιλῆος) exactly fills the second part of a line. These 'Homeric epithets' are often combined with other formulaic phrases – repeated word-groups – which have the right metrical qualities to fit the first part of the line. So a whole line can be rapidly and easily constructed by the oral poet, built from a ready-made diction. On other occasions, other combinations are possible from similar metrical units, to give the necessary sense. Thus 'in composing [the poet] will do no more than put together for his needs phrases which he has often heard or used himself, and which, grouping themselves in accordance with a fixed pattern of thought, come naturally to make the sentence and the verse' (Parry, 1930, p. 77).

This principle can be taken further. A single hexameter line is a relatively independent unit which usually coincides with a sentence or fairly self-contained phrase. Whole lines can thus be repeated in this 'formulaic' way, and this happens in the Homeric epics. Of all the lines in the *Iliad* and *Odyssey* about one third recur at least once (some many times). The extent of this device is usually illustrated from Parry's analysis of the first ten lines of the *Odyssey* where epithets, phrases or lines which recur elsewhere are underlined (a solid line where the formula re-appears unchanged elsewhere, a broken line where *similar* phrases occur).

Ἄνδρά μοι ἔννεπε Μοῦσα πολύτροπον ὃς μάλα πολλὰ
πλάγχθη ἐπεὶ Τροίης ἱερὸν πτολίεθρον ἔπερσε·
πολλῶν δ' ἀνθρώπων ἴδεν ἄστεα καὶ νόον ἔγνω,
πολλὰ δ' ὅ γ' ἐν πόντωι πάθεν ἄλγεα ὃν κατὰ θυμόν
ἀρνύμενος ἥν τε ψυχὴν καὶ νόστον ἑταίρων.
ἀλλ' οὐδ' ὣς ἑτάρους ἐρρύσατο ἱέμενός περ·
αὐτῶν γὰρ σφετέρηισιν ἀτασθαλίηισιν ὄλοντο
νήπιοι οἳ κατὰ βοῦς Ὑπερίονος Ἠελίοιο
ἤσθιον· αὐτὰρ ὁ τοῖσιν ἀφείλετο νόστιμον ἦμαρ.
τῶν ἁμόθεν γε θεὰ θύγατερ Διὸς εἰπὲ καὶ ἡμῖν.

(Parry, 1930, p. 120)

Sing in me, Muse, and through me tell the story
of that man skilled in all ways of contending,
the wanderer, harried for years on end,
after he plundered the stronghold
on the proud height of Troy.
                                    He saw the townlands
and learned the minds of many distant men,
and weathered many bitter nights and days
in his deep heart at sea, while he fought only
to save his life, to bring his shipmates home.
But not by will nor valour could he save them,
for their own recklessness destroyed them all –
children and fools, they killed and feasted on
the cattle of Lord Hêlios, the Sun,
and he who moves all day through heaven
took from their eyes the dawn of their return.
Of these adventures, Muse, daughter of Zeus,
tell us in our time, lift the great song again.

(trans. R. Fitzgerald, 1965, p. 13)

It can be deduced that the amount of repetition is very great in total, and 'formulaic' thus came to seem the most important characterisation of Homer's style.

The repetitions and the use of the 'Homeric epithet' had often been noticed before. But Parry took the further step of using this formulaic style to prove that the Homeric poems were *orally* composed. It was the need of the oral poet, he argued, for fluent and uninterrupted delivery throughout a lengthy performance that made the formulaic style both necessary and suitable. The poet had a store of ready-made diction already tailored to suit the metrical constraints of the hexameter line. By manipulating formulaic elements from this story – the 'building blocks' – he could construct a poem based on traditional material which was still his own unique and personal composition. The poet had at his disposal this series of traditional patterns built up over the years (so there was something in the theory of multiple authorship), but he was not passively dominated by them: he *used* them to create his own poems as he performed them.

Having come to this conclusion about the composition of the *Iliad* and *Odyssey* Parry took the imaginative step of going outside classical studies proper to try to find proof that his interpretation of them as *oral* compositions was correct. He turned to the study of Yugoslav epics, and in the 1930s, accompanied by his pupil and collaborator A. B. Lord, he collected and studied many oral heroic poems then being composed and performed by oral singers in Yugoslavia. These studies were to provide apparently irrefutable proof of Parry's findings. Yugoslav oral bards composed on the same principles.

Here is a description of the process taken from the classic product of this research, A. B. Lord's *The Singer of Tales* (1968a, first published in 1960). Lord starts from the striking fact that Yugoslav bards can perform long epics of thousands of lines (Parry recorded several with over 10,000 lines) and, with only short pauses for rest, can do this with uninterrupted fluency and remarkable speed – often at the rate of ten to twenty ten-syllable lines a minute. How does he do this?

> 'Since, as we shall see', writes Lord 'he has not memorized his song, we must conclude either that he is a phenomenal virtuoso or that he has a special technique of composition outside our own field of experience. We must rule out the first of these alternatives because there are too many singers; so many geniuses simply cannot appear in a single generation...The answer of course lies in...the special technique of composition which makes rapid composing in performance possible'
>
> (Lord, 1968a, p. 17)

This special technique involves building on repeated formulae, 'ready-made phrases' which the singer knows and can use without hesitation to fit the metrical requirements of his line.

Take the following passage, quoted by Lord from one of Parry's recordings. The phrases found more than once in the perusal of about 12,000 lines from the same singer (Salih Ugljanin) are underlined

	Jalah reče,/zasede đogata;	With 'By Allah' she mounted her horse;
790	Đogatu se/konju zamoljila:	790 She implored the white horse:
	'Davur, dogo,/krilo sokolovo!	'Hail, whitey, falcon's wing!
	Četa ti je/o zanatu bila;	Raiding has been your work;
	Vazda je Mujo/četom četovao.	Ever has Mujo raided.
	Vodi mene/do grada Kajniđe!	Lead me to the city of Kajnida!
795	Ne znam dadu/ka Kajnidi gradu.'	795 I know not the road to the city of Kajnida.'
	Hajvan beše,/zborit' ne mogaše,	It was a beast and could not talk,
	Tek mu svašta/šturak umijaše.	But the steed knew many things.
	Ode gljedat'/redom po planini.	He looked over the mountains
	Uze dadu/ka Kajniđi gradu,	And took the road to the city of Kajnida,
800	Pa silježe/planinama redom,	800 And crossed one range after another,

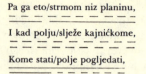

Pa ga eto/strmom niz planinu,	Until lo he rushed down the mountain,
I kad polju/slježe kajnićkome,	And when he descended to the plain of Kajnida,
Kome stati/polje pogljedati,	Were anyone to look out over the plain,

(Lord, 1968a, p. 46)

Lord comments:

> From the chart we can see at a glance the number of repeated phrases that without any hesitation can be called 'formulas'. These phrases we know by demonstration that the singer has come in time to use regularly. Even within the limited number of lines used in the experiment, that is, 12,000, one quarter of the whole lines in the sample and one half of the half lines are formulas. It is most significant that there is no line or part of a line that did not fit into some formulaic pattern. In certain instances the pattern was a very common one and there was no difficulty in proving the formulaic character of the phrase. In a few instances the evidence was not so abundant, but it was still sufficient to make one feel certain that the phrase in question was formulaic. A number of the formulaic expressions could very easily have been classified as formulas, had we relaxed our established principles and standards. For example, *davur dogo* in line 791 misses being a formula because the evidence lists only *davur sturan* and *davur doro*. But *dogo*, *sturan*, and *doro* are all terms for horses. We could thus have easily increased the number of formulas.
>
> Had we gone beyond 12,000 lines, the number of formulas would have continued to mount, and had we included material from other singers it would have increased still further, until it became clear that almost all, if not all, the lines in the sample passage were formulas and that they consisted of half lines which were also formulas. In other words, the manner of learning described earlier leads the singer to make and remake phrases, the same phrases, over and over again whenever he needs them. The formulas in oral narrative style are not limited to a comparatively few epic "tags", but are in reality all pervasive. There is nothing in the poem that is not formulaic.
>
> (Lord, 1968a, p. 47)

Yet it also becomes obvious that a formulaic style need not mean lack of flexibility in the poet. He can select what he wishes from the common stock of formulae, and can choose slightly different terms that fit his metre (for example any of several two-syllabled words for 'horse') and vary the details. Here are some linked but distinguishable alternatives used by the different singers named.

SALIH UGLJANIN

Jalah reče, zasede dogata.
'By Allah,' she said, she mounted the white horse.

Sulejman Fortić
Jalah reče, posede dogina. 'By Allah,' he said, he mounted the white horse.

Jalah reče, posede hajvana. 'By Allah,' he said, he mounted the animal.

Đemail Zogić
Jalah reče, sede na dorina. 'By Allah,' he said, he mounted the brown horse.

Jalah reče, posede hajvana. 'By Allah,' he said, he mounted the animal.

Sulejman Makić
I to reče, posede dorata. And he said this, he mounted the brown horse.

Alija Fjuljanin
A to reče, zasede hajvana. And he said this, he mounted the animal.

(Lord, 1968a, p. 48)

If one formulaic phrase filling the second part of the line is a variant of 'mounted his/her horse' etc., the singer can construct the first part of the line as the demands of his story and his art require. He can construct all the following lines, for instance, on the same basic pattern.

Svi konjici konje zasedoše. All the horsemen mounted their horses.

A svatovi konje zasedoše. And the wedding guests mounted their horses.

Ta put hajduk šajku zasednuo. Then the hajduk mounted his mare.

A Mujo svoga pojaše dogata. And Mujo mounted his white horse.

Jalah Suka sede na menzila. With a cry to Allah, Suka mounted his post horse.

(ibid., p. 51)

From these patterns, the singer can derive the lines he needs for a particular context as he simultaneously composes and performs. As Lord explains it, the singer is doing more than 'merely juggling set phrases'. He employs them because they are useful and serve the needs of the moment, and he is free to adjust them as and when he wishes. 'In making his lines the singer is not bound by the formula. The formulaic technique was developed to serve him as a craftsman, not to enslave him' (ibid., p. 54).

The formulaic quality of Yugoslav epic style is not confined to units within a line, or forming whole lines. For the singer has to compose a series of lines, one after the other. 'The need for the "next" line is upon him even before he utters the final syllable of a line' (ibid., p. 54). So the singer builds patterns of sequences of lines added to each other in a series of parallel sentences. There is little 'enjambement' (or necessary run-over of sense from line to line): of 2,400 lines analysed, 44.5 per cent had no enjambement, 40.6 per cent 'unperiodic enjambement' (i.e. the sense was complete at the end of the line but the sentence continued), and only 14.9 per cent necessary enjambement. This 'adding style' makes the singer's task easier, and is so obviously a useful device in simultaneous oral performance and composition that Lord claims it generally as 'a characteristic of oral composition' and 'one of the easiest touchstones to apply in testing the orality of a poem' (ibid., p. 54). This 'adding style' is well illustrated by the rapid, almost staccato style of this sequence:

Kud god *skita* za Aliju *pita.*	Wherever he went, he asked for Alija.
Kazaše ga u gradu Kajnidu.	They said he was in the city of Kajnida.
Kad tatarin pod Kajnidu *dode,*	When the messenger came to Kajnida,
Pa eto ga uz čaršiju *prode,*	He passed along the main street,
Pa *prilazi* novom bazdrdanu,	Then he approached the new shopkeeper,
Te upita za Alino dvore.	And he asked for Alija's court.
Bazdrdan mu dvore *ukazao.*	The shopkeeper pointed out the court to him.
Kad tatarin na kapiju *dode,*	When the messenger came to the gate,
Pa *zadrma* halkom na vratima.	He beat with the knocker on the door.
Zveknu halka a *jeknu* kapija.	The knocker rang and the gate resounded.

(quoted Lord, 1968a, pp. 54–5)

A more leisurely description may interrupt the rapid course of the narrative, where the apparently simple 'adding style' has an impressive cumulative effect.

Tevabije *brže* u podrume;	The retainers went quickly to the stable;
Izniješe takum na dogata,	They brought forth the trappings on the white horse,
Vas u srmi i u čisto zlato,	All in silver and in pure gold.
Pa konjičko *preturu* oruže,	Then they placed on the weapons for fighting from horseback,
S obe strane dvije puške male	On each side two small pistols
Sa dva grla a zrna četiri.	With two barrels which take four bullets.
Preložu hi surom mededinom,	Over them they placed a brown bearskin,
Da mu rosa ne kvari oruže.	That the dew might not rust the arms.
Pa *preložu* pulu abrahiju;	Then they placed on a blanket with sequins;
Zlatna pera biju niz dogata.	Its golden tassels beat against the white horse's flank.
Vezlje su je četiri robinje	Four slave girls had woven it
U Dubrovnik za četir' godine.	In Dubrovnik for four years.
Pa *udriše* dema nemačkoga.	Then they put a German bit into the horse's mouth.
Ej! Stasa doga, žešće bit' ne more!	The white horse stood there, he could not have been prouder or fiercer!

(ibid., p. 55)

As well as formulaic phrases and sequences, the bard has in his repertoire a number of set themes which he can draw on to form the structure of his poem. There are stock episodes (some of them familiar from other epic poetry) like the gathering of an assembly or of wedding guests, a journey, writing a letter, and so on. The wording of the episode varies from singer to singer, and so does the way in which they are joined together, or combined with other themes. But these stock episodes, as well as wider themes and plots, like rescues, returns or captures of cities, are all there as a traditional resource on which the poet can draw to construct his own poem.

The oral Yugoslav poet, therefore, can base his composition on these known patterns of phrases, lines and themes, without necessarily restricting himself to them. Through this technique of composition he is able to carry on the simultaneous performance and composition essential in his art. There is no set text which he has to learn – so that memorisation in the sense of word-for-word recall is not involved; instead he learns the poetic vocabulary and structure appropriate for heroic poetry in the way a child learns a language: it is the basic resource and medium within which and with which he composes.

One of the most significant points to emerge from the study of Yugoslav oral poets is the absence of a fixed text – the primary text or archetype so often sought for in classical studies. 'In a sense', writes Lord, 'each performance is "an" original, if not "the" original. The truth of the matter is that our concept of "the original", of "the song", simply makes no sense in oral tradition' (ibid., p. 101). There is no correct text, no idea that one version is more 'authentic' than another: each performance is a unique and original creation with its own validity.

This is so even when the poet claims to be singing 'the same' poem as one he had heard, or to be repeating a poem in exactly the same form as he sang it before. In practice, the words and detailed sequences are likely to be different, even between separate performances by the same poet. This came home forcibly to the researchers in Yugoslavia who had hoped to overcome the difficulties of recording in writing the rapidly-delivered text by filling in parts they had missed in one performance from later renderings. This proved to be impossible, for the variations between performances were too great (see Lord, 1968a, p. 149).

So the 'formulaic style', far from being an inducement to passive receptivity by the singer, provides him with the opportunity to make each performance unique and his own. This comes out clearly in the comparisons of poems by different poets on the same basic theme. As part of their research, Lord and Parry recorded experiments involving the direct transmission of 'the same' poem from one poet to another (Lord, 1968a, pp. 102ff). In 'The wedding of Relja of Pazar' the basic story remained much the same in the hands of a second poet, but a number of details were omitted, some speeches were expanded and so was the marriage theme at the end. In another case the talented singer Avdo Mededović followed a performance by another poet, Mumin Vlahovljak, with his own rendering of the 'same' poem. He expanded the poem to nearly three times the previous length (2,294 to 6,313 lines), which in itself meant many changes and elaborations. There are also new episodes and changes in the order of events, and the whole is suffused with the insights and sensitivity of Avdo

Mededović himself, a poet whom Lord considers outstanding among the Yugoslav singers he recorded.

The oral poet in Yugoslavia is always the 'author' of the epic he performs, by virtue of his simultaneous performance/composition. In this sense, each epic has a single author. But in another sense, there is also a multiplicity of authors: all those who contributed to building up the traditional patterns, the store of formulae and themes which the oral singer has at his disposal (ibid., pp. 101–2).

This in essence is the famous Parry–Lord theory: it shows how oral composition is possible during performance itself through the poet's reliance on formulaic style and themes. We now understand how long oral poems can be produced without the poet having to rely on rote memory. The theory also cut through much controversy about the authorship of Homer by demonstrating that, like Yugoslav poetry, Homeric epics were *oral* compositions using a comparable 'oral-formulaic' technique.

It would be hard to overestimate the importance of this approach. It has had a deep influence on Homeric studies; though not all scholars accept the theory *in toto*, few can ignore it, and many works have appeared which, in various ways, apply the approach to analysis of the Homeric epics (e.g. Kirk, 1965, Notopoulos, 1964, Nagler, 1967). Some puzzles and controversies remain – like the problem of how the *Iliad* and *Odyssey* were finally committed to writing – but the idea that oral composition was in some way involved in the creation of the epics is now widely accepted.

But the influence of this approach reaches far beyond Homeric studies. Lord claims in the Foreword to *The Singer of Tales* that Homer in a large sense 'represents all singers of tales from time immemorial and unrecorded to the present. Our book is about these other singers as well'. Indeed the extension of his findings beyond the Yugoslav and Homeric cases was clearly intended by Parry at the outset. He wrote explicitly that his purpose was to

> obtain evidence on the basis of which could be drawn a series of generalities applicable to all oral poetries; which would allow me, in the case of a poetry for which there was not enough evidence outside the poems themselves of the way in which they were made, to say whether that poetry was oral or not...A method is here involved, that which consists in *defining the characteristics of oral style*.

(Parry and Lord, 1954, p. 4)

It is not surprising that his approach has been more widely extended, and that many scholars have tried to apply a similar oral-formulaic analysis to texts of all kinds, from Old Testament poetry, *Beowulf*, or mediaeval European epic to recent compositions like modern Greek ballads, Gaelic poetry or the formulaic intoned sermons of the Southern States of America. One or two illustrations will demonstrate the ways in which the theory has been developed.

One application has been to Old English poetry: in particular to the Anglo-Saxon epic *Beowulf* (composed in England around the eighth century). It has been noticed for many years that elements of the style were repetitive, but Magoun now tried to demonstrate that in its formulaic character it resembled 'oral poetry', which 'it may safely be said, is composed entirely of formulas, large and small' (Magoun in Nicholson, 1971, p. 190). He illustrates this by, among other things, a chart of the opening lines of *Beowulf* in which 'word-groups' which appear elsewhere in *Beowulf* or other Anglo-Saxon poems unchanged are marked with solid underlining, while formulaic phrases (appearing in similar but not identical forms elsewhere) have broken underlinings.

Hwæt, wé Gár-Dena   on géar-dagum

þéod-cyninga   þrymm gefrugnon,

hú þá æðelingas   ellen fremedon.

Oft Scield Scéafing   sceaðena

  þréatum,

5 manigum mægðum   medu-setla

  oftéah,

egesode Eorle,   siþþan ærest wearþ

féasceaft funden; hé þæs frófre gebád,

wéox under wolcnum,   weorþ-

  myndum þáh.

oþ-þæt him æghwelć   ymbsittendra

10 ofer hran-ráde   híeran scolde,

gamban gieldan;   þæt wæs gód

  cyning!

(Magoun in Nicholson, 1971, pp. 216–17)

Attend!
We have heard of the thriving of the throne of Denmark,
how the folk-kings flourished in former days,
how those royal athelings earned that glory.

Was it not *Scyld Shefing* that shook the halls, took mead-benches, taught encroaching foes to fear him – who, found in childhood, lacked clothing? Yet he lived and prospered, grew in strength and stature under the heavens
until the clans settled in the sea-coasts neighbouring
over the whale-road all must obey him and give tribute. That was a king!

(translated M. Alexander, 1973, p. 51)

A number of the episodes can also be seen as set pieces and so 'formulaic' – like the banquet, the voyage, the funeral, the battle and so on. The overall result has been an increasing interest in *Beowulf* as an 'oral composition' – as evidenced, it is argued, by its 'oral-formulaic' style – and a rejection of older theories that it is a fixed written document assimilated to the models of the literary works of contemporaneous Latin Christianity.

A similar analysis has been made of the oral-formulaic style of the *Song of Roland*, the Old French epic perhaps composed around the eleventh century A.D. In this epic, the decasyllabic line divides into two main sections or hemistiches (the first of four, the second of six syllables). These hemistiches form the main formulaic units. Phrases like *Li reis Marsilie, dist li emperere Carles* which fit a hemistich and are substantially repeated can be counted as recurrent formulae and form the basis for the poet's original composition. It has been calculated that something like 35.2 per cent of *Roland* is 'formulaic' (Duggan, 1973, p. 34), or, taking the first hemistiches only, over 50 per cent (Nichols, 1961, p. 20). This is perhaps considerably less than the 80 or 90 per cent claimed for the Homeric poems, but enough in the view of many analysts to establish *Roland* as 'oral-formulaic' in style and composition.

This 'oral' style does not cramp the poet's individual genius. Though formulae are fairly evenly distributed through the poems, they are more frequent in the universally acclaimed purple passages, and can be used by the poet to convey subtle shades of character and feeling (Duggan, 1973, chapter 5). In addition, there are larger formulaic units, in the sense of set themes and episodes, like the many councils in *Roland* and the recurrent stages within the council episodes (Nichols, 1961), which again the poet uses as a vehicle for his composition.

Similar analyses have now been made of a good deal of poetry. There have been a few studies of recently-recorded oral poetry, like the Yugoslav epics; but for the most part scholars have concentrated on poetry which has come down to us in written texts: other early Greek poetry (e.g. Notopoulos, 1960), the Hittite epic (McNeill, 1963), early Tamil heroic poetry (Kailasapathy, 1968), mediaeval English, French and German poetry (usefully surveyed in Curschmann, 1961), English and Scottish ballads (Jones, 1961, Buchan, 1972), and early Hebrew poetry as found in poetic passages like the *Psalms*, the *Song of Solomon* and elsewhere in the Old Testament (Whallon, 1969, Culley, 1967).

Since these are all texts about whose composition and performance in the distant past we have little direct information, the emphasis has often been on the deductions about these aspects that, it is claimed, can be drawn from 'the oral-formulaic style'. Some scholars have been so impressed by the insights of the Parry–Lord approach that they have taken anything which can arguably be dubbed an 'oral-formulaic' style as proof that 'oral composition' was involved. Thus Magoun, writing of Anglo-Saxon poetry, claims an 'oral-formulaic style' as the 'touchstone' for differentiating 'oral' and 'lettered' poetry (Magoun in Nicholson, 1971, p. 194), while Nichols's interest in analysing formulaic diction and enjambement in *The Song of Roland* was 'in order to demonstrate the textual characteristics which argue its oral rather than literary character' (Nichols, 1961, p. 9). This interest in laying bare the oral character and origin of a given text has also been a preoccupation in most oral-formulaic analyses of the Homeric epics.

Thus since the initial writings of Murko and Milman Parry in the 1920s and 1930s, the 'oral-formulaic' approach has become an established school which must be taken account of by the analyst of much classical and mediaeval literature in Europe and Asia, as well as of oral poetry else-where. It has affected the work of scholars in classics, mediaeval and Biblical studies, and work in linguistics, literature, anthropology and history. It has introduced a comparative perspective into many specialist areas, so that 'oral poetry' is no longer a special phenomenon, to be looked for among far-off and exotic 'primitives', but a concept central to the pursuit of a number of traditional disciplines concerned with the development of civilisation over several thousand years.

3 How valid is the oral-formulaic theory?

No-one who has read *The Singer of Tales* – surely one of the classics in the study of oral literature – can fail to be profoundly influenced by its findings and insights. It is no longer possible to argue that the *only* way to explain lengthy oral poems is in terms of memorisation by the performer. This in itself cuts through a number of problems, with the Homeric (and other) epic poems and also with English and Scottish ballads where 'the common-places...freed the singer from memorization' (Jones, 1961, p. 105). Equally important is the emphasis on the lack of a fixed and 'correct' version of the text in oral literature. The model of written literature with its emphasis on *the* text, *the* original and correct version, has for long bedevilled study of oral literature, and led researchers into unfruitful and misleading questions in an attempt to impose a similar model on *oral* literature. Others besides Lord and Parry had pointed this out (in particular earlier scholars from Russia and Eastern Europe) but, for English-speaking readers, no one has conveyed the original aspect of *each* unique performance by a poet as convincingly as Lord in *The Singer of Tales*. The point has had a profound effect on analysts of oral literature. So has the account of the relationship between tradition and originality in oral composition: of the way the oral poet makes use of traditional patterns to express his individual and original insights. As another scholar has put it, 'all is traditional on the generative level, all unique on the level of performance' (Nagler, 1967, p. 311), and the old polarity between 'tradition' and 'originality' no longer means direct contradiction.

But there are also drawbacks and difficulties. Some of these have caused controversy within the 'oral-formulaic school', which now encompasses differences of opinion and varying wings of thought.

First, there is the problem of how far an 'oral-formulaic style' is indeed a sign of 'oral composition'. Some earlier analysts like Parry, Lord and Magoun claimed that it was an indisputable sign, and they have been followed by recent scholars such as Duggan and Kailasapathy. As recently as 1968 Lord was claiming that 'A pattern of 50 to 60 per cent formula or formulaic, with 10 to perhaps 25 per cent straight formula, indicates clearly literary or written composition. I am still convinced that it is possible to determine orality by quantitative formulaic analysis, by the study of formula density' (Lord, 1968b, p. 24). This idea has come under fire in recent studies. As Benson has demonstrated, a heavily formulaic style is characteristic not just of the Old English 'oral' epic of *Beowulf* but also of some *written* compositions in Old English, including Old English translations from Latin originals (Benson, 1966). If the style proves *Beowulf* to be 'oral', how can one explain its use in written composition? Benson concludes 'To prove that an Old English poem is formulaic is only to prove that it is an Old English poem, and to show that such work has a high or low percentage of formulas reveals nothing about whether or not it is a literate composition, though it may tell us something about the skill with which a particular poet uses the tradition' (Benson, 1966, p. 336).

Similar points have been made for other literatures. One recent example comes from research on Xhosa and Zulu oral poetry in South Africa. Opland has pointed to the formulaic style of 'traditional' Xhosa oral poetry and the way the Xhosa *imbongi* can 'compose metrical poems on the spur of the moment in praise of anything that inspires him, and in order to do this he relies on formulas' (Opland, 1971, p. 172). Opland has recorded a number of examples, and can testify from personal observation to their oral composition and performance. So far, this looks like a typical instance of 'oral composition using formulae'. But some of these Xhosa poets have also produced *written* versions of their poems – and these are equally characterised by a 'formulaic' style. This applies to a number of Bantu poets in South Africa, Zulu as well as Xhosa. Opland writes

> Literate Bantu poets are using the traditional praise songs as a basis for their poetry. The Zulu poet B. W. Vilakazi writes of his poetry that he passed through a period of imitating European models, but subsequently returned to traditional forms. Having grown up in the Zulu tradition he expressed himself most easily in a manner that was part of his cultural identity. Colleagues of mine in the Department of African Languages at the University of Cape Town have written praise poems on the highway traffic, and on the Apollo moon landing. Their poetry conforms metrically and stylistically to the traditional praise poems sung by the *imbongi*. It seems reasonable, therefore, that literate Anglo-Saxon monks could have written formulaic poetry. (Opland, 1971, p. 177)

A 'formulaic' style is not therefore inevitably a proof of 'oral composition'. Theorists have now to accept that since there can be both an 'oral' and a 'literary' use of formulae one cannot necessarily discriminate between 'oral' and 'written' on the basis of a 'formulaic' style alone. In other words, the excitement attendant on the discoveries about the 'oral-formulaic style' led some scholars to an extreme application of its findings. Now that a certain reaction has set in against the more extreme claims, it has become clear that while the kind of diction found in Homeric or Yugoslav epics is a suitable, even likely, style for oral composition, it is not an infallible sign of it.

There is the further difficulty – less often stressed by exponents of this school – that the meaning of 'oral composition' is by no means always clear. Scholar after scholar has demonstrated an 'oral-formulaic' style in his chosen texts and taken this as a sign (whether tentative or definite) of 'oral composition'. The model is often the Yugoslav singer's oral composition described by Lord; in other cases it is left unclear, and the term even seems to take on a mystical aura of its own. But there are in fact different kinds of 'oral composition'. Some is almost entirely oral, in the way that many Yugoslav singers composed/performed; but some may be based more or less directly on a written text (and this happens more often than is sometimes remembered with Yugoslav poetry) but is nevertheless recited orally. Other poems may be composed with oral performance as the aim, or composed without the initial use of writing for later written publication, or be specially dictated to a literate assistant – and so on. Which of these forms is involved is seldom explained in many analyses which deduce 'oral composition' from the style of the texts they have studied. What is needed in these cases is more discrimination of the exact meaning and application of the term 'oral composition' – except that often it is *because* there is little or no direct evidence about the process of composition that the analyst argues from the 'oral-formulaic' style.

A second difficulty about the general approach is the exact definition of a 'formula'. Here the doubts are not so much about the excessive claims of the approach, but about the method of analysis. Certain frequently repeated Homeric epithets like 'grey-eyed Athene' or 'rosy-fingered dawn' may seem obvious cases of 'formulaic units', but it is a large extension when the term is used to cover *any* group of words 'regularly employed under the same metrical conditions to represent a given essential idea' (as Parry had it) or a phrase repeated only once or twice but intuitively regarded by the analyst as somehow 'formulaic'. Even if 'repetition' is taken as basic in defining a 'formula', there are differences between analysts as to whether the repetition is, for instance, of metrical, syntactic or semantic elements, differences also about how long a 'formula' can or must be (see Watts, 1969, esp. chapter 3).

What do these various groupings have in common? Clearly there are in some sense recurrent patterns, a continuing structure within which the oral poet – or indeed *any* poet – composes. But to use the term 'formula' in an apparently exact sense, and to rely on it as the basis for a complex edifice of theory and supposedly empirical findings gives a misleading impression of precision. Does it really add to our understanding of the style or process of composition in a given piece to name certain repeated patterns of words, sounds or meanings as 'formulae'? Or to suggest that the characteristic of oral style is that such formulae are 'all-pervasive' (as in Lord, 1968a, p. 47)? Or to propound tautologous definitions of the formula as, for instance, 'a group of words, one half-line in length, which shows evidence of being the direct product of a formulaic system' (Fry, 1967, p. 204)? Reading would-be scientific and rigorous analyses based on this concept of the formula, one is tempted to apply more widely the critique H. L. Rogers made of the oral-formulaic approach to Old English poetry: 'The term 'formula' becomes a portmanteau, enclosing within its ample capacity many different, and often undefined, sorts of lexical, morphological and syntactic similarities... One is forced to suspect that the growing dogmatism about the oral-formulaic character of Old English poetry owes more to faith and presumed psychological insight than to reason' (Rogers, 1966, p. 102).

Without any exact or agreed definition of 'the formula' it is difficult to rely on the statistical analyses used either to demonstrate an 'oral-formulaic' style in a particular poem, or to compare percentages of 'formularity' across different kinds of poetry. Where the unit of measurement is unclear, such comparisons seem worth little. Further doubts have also been thrown on the kind of statistical conclusions that Parry and others derived from their analyses of the Homeric poems. Their data may at first look convincing (laying aside, that is, the fundamental point about the delimitation of 'formula' or 'formulaic system'). But as a recent analysis (Russo, 1976) has demonstrated, their apparently solid conclusions were raised on a remarkably small statistical base. The opening lines of the *Iliad* and *Odyssey* have been analysed and measured several times, leading to a claim of 'between 80 and 90 per cent formulaic content'; so have a very few other short passages. Otherwise no overall analysis has been completed, nor any systematic sampling undertaken. After all, the style of preludes is not necessarily representative of the style of the whole.

A more representative sampling might result in lower figures for 'formulaic content' than the 90 per cent usually cited. Indeed the analysis by Russo (1976) suggests that more rigorous sampling might not support the higher claims for formulaic content in Homer and that the overall level of formularity, so far as it can be measured at all, may turn out to be more like that assumed as typical of literary texts. It appears, therefore, that the search for a scientific and precise measure of oral as against written composition may turn out to be a fruitless one.

These are mostly detailed controversies within the oral-formulaic school. The basic insights remain stimulating and fruitful, and the demonstration that the oral bard composes with and within traditional patterns of various kinds will stand as a landmark in the study of oral literature. Provided that the more ambitious claims of some exponents are treated with caution, the Lord–Parry school provides a body of work which cannot be ignored by any student of comparative oral literature.

4 Prior composition, memorisation and performance

The demonstration that rote-memory need not be important in oral poetry has sometimes misled students of the subject (myself included) to assume that it is *never* important. Parry and Lord did not go so far as this, but their works can be read as implying it: 'No graver mistake could be made', writes Parry, 'than to think the art of the singer calls only for memory...the oral poem even in the mouth of the same singer is ever in a state of change; and it is the same when his poetry is sung by others' (Parry, 1932, pp. 14–15), and 'Oral...does not mean merely oral presentation...what is important is not the oral performance but rather the composition *during* oral performance' (Lord, 1968a, p. 5). Lord also goes out of his way to lay down a restrictive definition of 'oral poetry' which excludes the possibility of memorisation, when he asserts that texts which are preserved word-for-word 'could not be *oral* in any except the most literal sense' (ibid., p. 280), and defines 'oral poetry' as 'poetry composed *in* oral performance' (Lord, 1965, p. 591).

But memorisation and near-word-for-word reproduction sometimes *are* important in oral literature. We cannot ignore the possibility or define away its occurrence as not really involving oral poetry or as constituting an odd and perverse exception. It is true that one needs to be cautious of statements that a piece has been 'repeated exactly' on a different occasions or 'handed down word for word' through a time: often, statements like this rest on no evidence beyond the dubious assumptions about 'age-old tradition' or 'folk memories' discussed in the last chapter, or the interesting but often untrustworthy or ambiguous claims of the bards themselves. But the caution necessary in assessing undemonstrated statements of this kind – even when allied to the kinds of expectations we now hold about oral literature as a result of the Parry–Lord research – must not prevent us from noting instances of exact reproduction when clear evidence is provided.

Some examples can illustrate this particular process. In these cases composition and performance are separated.

The first is the case of Somali poetry. In Somalia, in the Horn of Africa, oral poetry is a highly developed art. It has been extensively studied, both in its modern phase where radio and tapes as well as face-to-face delivery are employed, and in its earlier development. It includes many different genres (described in Andrzejewski and Lewis, 1964), from lengthy *gabay* poems, sometimes of several hundred lines, to the short one- or two-line compressed *balwo* lyrics.

Poetic composition is a prized and much-discussed art among the Somali, who have been described as 'a nation of bards', and an admired poet can become widely known. A Somali poem always arouses interest and discussion and attracts criticism if it is considered mediocre. Because they are aware of this, 'Somali poets rarely perform their work until composition is completely finished in private' (Johnson, 1971, p. 28) and 'spend many hours, sometimes even days, composing their works' before they perform them (Andrzejewski and Lewis, 1964, p. 45). A poet's compositions, furthermore, become his own property, under his own name, and another poet reciting them has to acknowledge from whom he has learnt them. A good poet has an entourage of admirers some of whom learn his poems by heart and recite them. Others hear these recitations and memorise the poems they consider sufficiently beautiful and important. Andrzejewski and Lewis show that it is indeed memorisation rather than simultaneous composition/performance that is involved here.

> While we may admire Somali poets for achieving worthwhile results in the very difficult medium of Somali prosody, we are no less impressed by feats of memory on the part of the poetry reciters, some of whom are poets themselves. Unaided by writing they learn long poems by heart and some have repertoires which are too great to be exhausted even by several evenings of continuous recitation. Moreover, some of them are endowed with such powers of memory that they can learn a poem by heart after hearing it only once, which is quite astonishing, even allowing for the fact that poems are chanted very slowly, and important lines are sometimes repeated. The reciters are not only capable of acquiring a wide repertoire but can store it in their memories for many years, sometimes for their lifetime. We have met poets who at a ripe age could still remember many poems which they learnt in their early youth.
>
> In the nomadic interior whole villages move from place to place and there is constant traffic between villages, grazing camps, and towns. Poems spread very quickly over wide areas and in recent times motor transport and the radio have further accelerated the speed with which they are disseminated.
>
> A poem passes from mouth to mouth. Between a young Somali who listens today to a poem composed fifty years ago, five hundred miles away, and its first audience there is a long chain of reciters who passed it one to another. It is only natural that in this process of transmission some distortion occurs, but comparison of different versions of the same poem usually shows a surprisingly high degree of fidelity to the original. This is due to a large extent to the formal rigidity of Somali poetry: if one word is substitued for another, for instance, it must still keep to the rules of alliteration, thus limiting very considerably the number of possible changes. The general trend of the poem, on the other hand, inhibits the omission or transposition of lines.
>
> Another factor also plays an important role: the audience who listen to the poem would soon detect any gross departure from the style of the particular poet; moreover, among the audience there are often people who already know by heart the particular poem, having learnt it from another source. Heated disputes sometimes arise be-

tween a reciter and his audience concerning the purity of his version. It may even happen that the authorship of a poem is questioned by the audience, who carefully listen to the introductory phrases in which the reciter gives the name of the poet, and, if he is dead, says a prayer formula for his soul.

(Andrzejewski and Lewis, 1964, pp. 45–6)

In this case, then, memorisation is indeed involved, and the concept of a 'correct' version is locally recognised. This is not what one would expect if one relied mainly on the analogy of Yugoslav singers or the analyses of the oral-formulaic school. Somali poetic composition shows that there are other modes of composition in oral poetry.

Equally instructive is Gordon Innes's research into Mandinka griots' narrations (1973, 1974). He found a fascinating blend of stability and change, with both memorisation and fluidity involved.

These narrations are complicated, so far as style and genre are concerned, for a blend of 'speech', 'recitation' and 'song modes' are used in delivery (Innes, 1974, pp. 15ff). On the face of it, only the recitation and song modes seem to qualify as 'poetry', and the so-called 'Sunjata epic' would be largely prose since most of the narrative is in the 'speech mode'. But it is a marginal case, for even the speech mode in these narrations has to fit the musical accompaniment which is usually built on a two-, four- or eight-bar phrase, characterised by a distinctive melodic, tonal or rhythmic structure (King in Innes, 1974, p. 18). In these respects, then, even the speech mode has constraints we associate with poetic composition. It is thus not irrelevant to include here some account of composition in the various versions of this 'epic' as providing a partial parallel to Yugoslav epic composition.

At first sight, the different versions of the 'Sunjata epic' throughout the Manding area of West Africa seem to offer an exact instance of the blend of composition and performance familiar in Lord's writings. It concerns the exploits of the great hero Sunjata who established himself as king of Manding and Susu in the thirteenth century. Many versions of the story are extant even in the small area of the Gambia alone. As Innes writes, 'From these and from published versions from elsewhere in the Manding area one almost has the impression that the Sunjata legend consists of a repertoire of various motifs, incidents, themes (call them what you will), and that each griot makes a selection which he strings together into a coherent narrative' (Innes, 1973, p. 105). He goes on to show that this initial impression is wrong, for it suggests greater fluidity than is the case.

Innes made a detailed comparison of a number of versions. One set was recorded by two brothers, Banna and Dembo Kanute, both regarded as outstanding performers. They had learnt their craft from their father, assisted (in the case of Banna) by Dembo, his elder brother. Innes notes

the differences in their versions. Starting presumably from the same repertoire, their performances differed in the ground covered in two major
incidents, and in a number of details. This is the sort of fluidity one would
expect from the comparative Yugoslav material. Furthermore there are
indications that each brother adapted his version to the situation in which
he performed – when leading persons present in the audience, for instance,
could trace their descent from figures in the Sunjata story.

But when Innes came to a detailed comparison between two versions by
the same griot – Bamba Suso – a different picture emerged. Bamba was one
of the leading griots in the Gambia, with extensive historical knowledge.
In his seventies, two recordings were made of his version of the Sunjata
story, one for Radio Gambia, another at Brikama to an audience which
included Innes himself. The most striking point to emerge from a comparison of the two is their close similarity, in places amounting to word-
for-word repetition. Here are two passages quoted by Innes to illustrate
the point

(1)

| | RADIO GAMBIA |
| BRIKAMA VERSION | VERSION |

Sunjata had been a cripple from birth and when the time came for him
and the other boys of his own age to undergo circumcision and training,
he was still unable to walk, so the smiths made stout iron crutches for him.
This passage opens at the point where Sunjata tried to lift himself up by
means of these crutches.

Biring a ye wolu muta, wolu bee katita.	**A ye wolu muta, i bee katita.**
When he had taken hold of them, they all broke.	He took hold of them, they all broke.
I ko, 'Sunjata dung si wuli nyaadi?'	
People asked, 'How will Sunjata get up?'	
A fango ko i ye, 'Ali n naa kili;	**Sunjata fango ko i ye ko,**
He said to them, 'Call my mother;	Sunjata said to them,
Ning dingo boita, a naa le kara a wulindi.'	**'Ning dingo boita, a naa le kara a wulindi;**
When a child has fallen, it is his mother who picks him up.'	'When a child has fallen, it is his mother who picks him up;
	Ali n naa kili.'
	Call my mother.'
Biring a baama naata,	**Sukulung Konte naata,**
When his mother came.	Sukulung Konte came,
A ye a bulo laa a baama sanyo kang,	**A ye a bulo laa a sanyo to,**
He laid his hand upon his mother's shoulder,	He laid his hand on her shoulder,
A wulita a loota.	**A wulita a loota.**
He arose and stood up.	He arose and stood up.
Jalolu ka a fo wo le la, i ko,	**Jalolu kara a fo wo le la ko,**
It is from that that the griots say,	It is from that that the griots say,
'Jata wulita,' i ko, 'Manding Jata wulita,	**'Jata wulita,' i ko, 'Manding Jata wulita,**
'The Lion has arisen,' they say, 'The Lion of Manding has arisen,	'The Lion has arisen,' they say, 'The Lion of Manding has arisen,
Feng baa wulita.'	**Feng baa wulita.'**
The mighty one has arisen.'	The mighty one has arisen.'

(2)

BRIKAMA VERSION

A loota a baama kunto a ko a ye,
He stood by his mother's head and said to her,

Ni a ye a tara m be Manding mansaya la,
If I am to be king of Manding,
Janning fano be ke la bii ye faa.
Before dawn breaks today, may you be dead.
Ni a ye a tara n te Manding mansaya la,
If I am not to be king of Manding,
Ye tu kuuranding,
May you remain ill,
Kaatu n te i kuurang to tu la jang.
Because I will not leave you here in sickness.

Janning fano be ke la,
Before dawn broke,
Sakulung Konte faata.
Sukulung Konte died.

A ko a be Sukulung Konte baade la.
Sunjata said that he would bury Sukulung Konte.
Faring Burema Tunkara ko a ye,
Faring Burema Tunkara told him,
'I te a baade la
'You will not bury her
Fo ye a baade dula sang.'
Unless you buy her burial plot.'
A ko a ye, 'M be a sang na nyaadi?'
Sunjata asked, 'How shall I buy it?'
A ko, 'I si minkallolu bula nyo la,
He said, 'You must put earrings together,
Ye doo laa a fongo to,
And lay one on her forehead,
Ye doo laa a sing-kono-nding kumba to,
And lay another on her big toe,
Ye a sumang banko to;
And measure it on the ground;
A kanyanta dameng i si jee sing,
And you must dig the corresponding length,
I si i baama baade jee.'
And you must bury your mother there.'

(Innes, 1973, pp. 115–16)

RADIO GAMBIA VERSION

A naata loo a baama kunto,
He came and stood by his mother's head,

A ko a ye, 'N naa, ye n kili Manding mansaya la.
He said to her, 'Mother, they have called me to the kingship of Manding.

Bari ni a ye a tara n te mansaya la,
But if I am not to be king,
Ye tu kuuranding,
May you remain ill,
Kaatu n te i kuurang to tu la jang,
Because I will not leave you here in sickness.
Bari ni a ye a tara me be Manding mansaya la,
But if I am to be king of Manding,
Ye faa janning fano be ke la.'
May you die before dawn breaks.'
Janning fano be ke la,
Before dawn broke
Sukulung Konte faata.
Sukulung Konte died.
I taata fo Faring Burema Tunkara ye,
They went and told Faring Burema Tunkara,
I ko a ye, 'Sukulung Konte faata de.'
They told him, 'Sukulung Konte is dead.'

A ko, 'Ali a fo Sunjata ye,
He said, 'Tell Sunjata
A te a baama baade la
He will not bury his mother
Fo a ye a baade dula sang.'
Unless he buys her burial plot.'
A ko, 'M be a sang na nyaadi?'
Sunjata asked, 'How shall I buy it?'
A ko, 'I si sano dung nyo daa la,
He said, 'You must put gold together,
Ye doo laa a fongo to,
And lay one on her forehead,
Ye doo laa a singo to;
And lay another on her leg;

Wo kanyanta banko dameng fee,
The corresponding length of ground

I si jee sing i si i naa baade jee.'
You must dig, and you must bury your mother there.'

In these extracts, there is certainly not word-for-word *identity* throughout. But there is much more verbal and line-for-line repetition than one
might expect from the Yugoslav analogy. It is also clear that to some extent
memorisation *is* involved here; at the very least it would be misleading to
insist that 'original composition' played a large part in the performance.
The model of simultaneous composition/performance must here be modified: much of the 'composing' must have preceded the performance – to a
greater extent than in the composition/performance of the Yugoslav Avdo
Mededović or the Kirghiz bards described by Radlov. One cannot, then,
assume that the composition/performance process so well illustrated in the
case of Eastern European singers by Lord and others is *always* characteristic
of oral composition. Much (though not necessarily all) of the composing
may take place *before* the moment of performance.

Hence the need for more careful and detailed research on the respective
parts played by composition, memorisation and performance both in particular situations, and also by different individual singers – even by the same
singers at different times. On the Mandinka evidence, Innes sums up his
findings as follows

> At first sight the two pieces of evidence presented here seem to
> contradict each other. The evidence from the Kanute brothers shows
> that in the course of his professional career a griot's version of the
> Sunjata legend may undergo considerable change. The evidence
> from Bamba, on the other hand, shows that a griot's version may
> remain remarkably stable, both in content and language, over a
> period of time. Different interpretations of this evidence are no doubt
> possible, but, taken along with other evidence, it suggests to me a
> pattern of life in which a griot in his younger days travels extensively,
> listens to other griots and borrows selectively from them, repeatedly
> modifying his own version until eventually he arrives at a version
> which seems to him the most satisfying. With repetition, this version
> will become more or less fixed, and even the words will tend to become
> fixed to some extent. But even this version will of course vary from
> performance to performance, depending upon such factors as who
> happens to be present and in whose honour the performance is being
> given.
>
> (Innes, 1973, p. 118)

Many of the recorded cases where memorisation predominates rather
than the composition-in-performance characteristic of the Yugoslav model,
derive from lyric and shorter forms of poetry. Lengthy epic poetic narrations, lasting over several hours or nights of performance, are naturally
likely to fit the model of composition-in-performance given by Parry and
Lord. Yet Somali poems, it must be recalled, can extend to several hundreds
of lines and involve at least some element of narration, while the lengthy
Mandinka 'epic' is partly in 'poetry' in its recited and sung portions and
arguably has poetic elements even in the more prosaic 'spoken' parts.

There are some relatively long quasi-narrative forms where memorisation and exact recollection are sometimes more important than creativity
in performance. In western culture some ballad singers are in this category.
They can be classified as 'passive traditors' of memorised words, aiming
both in practice and in their own accounts at the exact reproduction of what
they have heard from others. That this is not the only way in which ballads
are transmitted and performed is well known (see also chapter 5 below),
but it is nevertheless one accepted mode for the transmission of ballads and
other oral poetry in the west. Some authorities go so far as to claim that,
with few exceptions, the norm for the European-American folk performer
is repetition (Glassie, 1970, p. 32) and suggest that this contrasts with the
variability of the Afro-American tradition. But there are a number of other
African examples where memorisation is important. The long panegyric
poems of Ruanda and South Africa are often cited as outstanding examples
of oral poetry. They commonly run to hundreds of lines and have an
element of narrative, though the main emphasis is on praise. Yet in Ruanda
there was often memorisation of received versions of the praise poems, with
minimal variation in performance, and the original composers were remembered by name (Kagame, 1951). And for the Zulu a recent study states
categorically that the specialist praise singers attached to the courts were
concerned more with 'performance' than 'composition': the singer 'has to
memorise [the praises of the chief and ancestors] so perfectly that on
occasions of tribal importance they pour forth in a continuous stream or
torrent. Although he may vary the order of the sections or stanzas of the
praise-poem, he may not vary the praises themselves. He commits them
to memory as he hears them, even if they are meaningless to him' (Cope,
1968, pp. 27–8).

It is therefore clear that a single model of the relation of composition to
performance will not cover all cases – perhaps not even all cases of narrative
poetry. To accept uncritically Lord's dictum that what is important in oral
poetry is 'the composition *during* oral performance' would blind us to the
differing ways in which the elements of composition, memorisation and
performance may be in play in, or before, the delivery of a specific oral
poem.

Once the possibility of prior composition followed by memorisation is
conceded it becomes obvious that there are many cases. Many work songs
are of this kind. To be sure, they often provide an inventive and skilled
leader with the opportunity for improvisation and elaboration that gives
play to his originality. But often the work involved is so demanding or the
choral element so strong – for instance in some of the Texas prison work
songs discussed in Jackson (1972) – that for the most part the words are
merely repeated from memory: and yet they are surely still 'oral poetry'.
The same goes for many Irish popular songs, Christian hymns, liturgical
poetry, or genealogical verse – all of which have some element of 'oral-ness'

about them. In performance they are all subject at times to variation and adaptation – and perhaps it is this *opportunity* rather than actual variation that is 'typical' of oral compositions. But it must be accepted that in many performances songs are not in practice much changed: the performance is from memory. The naive model of a child learning by heart in order to recite is after all not *always* misleading.

To admit the possibility of memorisation in oral literature is not, however, to go back to the idea of passive reception from memorised 'tradition'. The prior composition involved is not infrequently known to be by named and individual poets, consciously labouring over the difficult task of constructing the words (and sometimes music) of their poetry.

There are many recorded cases of oral poetry where its creation does not fit either of the two extreme cases – improvisation at the moment of performance or blind acceptance of 'tradition' – but is due to long deliberation by the individual poet *before* the performance. This is particularly the case with shorter, more lyrical poetry, rather than the narrative poems mainly stressed by the oral-formulaic school. Though Lord asserts at one point that he is only concerned with *narrative* poets, it is easy to come away with the impression that all oral poetry is subsumed under the same general rubric, and that 'oral composition' is only oral if it takes place at the moment of performance. This impression is reinforced by Lord's generalised definition of 'oral poetry' in his encyclopaedia article on the topic – 'poetry composed *in* oral performance' (1965, p. 591) – and by the many analyses in 'oral-formulaic' terms of lyrical and ballad poetry as well as epic. Since this impression that *all* oral poetry is composed on the Yugoslav model is not correct it is worth illustrating the process of deliberate composition prior to performance with some further examples.

Eskimo poetry provides an excellent instance. Long and careful consideration is given to the composition of the words of many Eskimo poems before their performance, and the Eskimo are extremely articulate about the problems and delights of composition; indeed it is a constant preoccupation of many of the poems. Here the poet Piuvkaq compares the difficulties of fishing with those of poetic composition

> ...Why, I wonder
> My song-to-be that I wish to use
> My song-to-be that I wish to put together
> I wonder why it will not come to me?
> At Sioraq it was, at a fishing hole in the ice,
> A little trout I could feel on the line
> And then it was gone,
> I stood jigging
> But why is that so difficult, I wonder?...

> (Rasmussen, 1931, pp. 517–18)

The Eskimo combine their awareness of the deliberate and conscious struggle involved in 'putting together words into a song' with the concept of poetic inspiration. One of the outstanding Eskimo poets was Orpingalik, who used to call his songs his 'comrades in solitude' and 'his breath'. He described some of the processes of composition to Rasmussen in these terms

> Songs are thoughts, sung out with the breath when people are moved by great forces and ordinary speech no longer suffices.
> Man is moved just like the ice floe sailing here and there out in the current. His thoughts are driven by a flowing force when he feels joy, when he feels fear, when he feels sorrow. Thoughts can wash over him like a flood, making his breath come in gasps and his heart throb. Something, like an abatement in the weather, will keep him thawed up. And then it will happen that we, who always think we are small, will feel still smaller. And we will fear to use his words. When the words we want to use shoot up of themselves – we get a new song.
>
> (Rasmussen, 1931, p. 321)

The same emphasis on inspiration and waiting for the right words to be born is given in an Alaskan Eskimo's description of how one must wait in silence and 'stillness' for the poems to come. Then 'they take shape in the minds of men and rise up like bubbles from the depths of the sea, bubbles that seek the air to burst in the light' (quoted in Freuchen, 1962, pp. 280–1). This process is quite unlike composition in the heat of performance such as we associate with Yugoslav epic singers; for this waiting for inspiration is expected to take place, not at the moment of public performance, but in the dark, in deep silence, as an act of artistic concentration. Walking about outside in solitude is another common occasion for Eskimo poetic composition. Rasmussen describes how great pains are taken to put the words together skilfully so that 'there is melody in them, while at the same time they are pertinent in expression', and how 'a man who wants to compose a song may long walk to and fro in some solitary place, arranging his words while humming a melody which he also has to make up himself' (Rasmussen, 1931, p. 320).

Perhaps the most vivid expression of the combination of hard work and of heightened emotive perceptiveness inherent in Eskimo poetic composition is the Eskimo poet Sadlaqé's account of trying to compose a song

> Once when I was quite young, I wished to sing a song about my village, and one winter evening when the moon was shining, I was walking back and forth to put words together that could fit into a tune I was humming. Beautiful words I found, words that should tell my friends about the greatness of the mountains and everything else that I enjoyed every time I came outside and opened my eyes. I walked, and I continued walking over the frozen snow, and I was

so busy with my thoughts that I forgot where I was. Suddenly, I stood still and lifted my head up, and looked: In front of me was the huge mountain of my settlement, greater and steeper than I had ever seen it. It was almost as if it grew slowly out of the earth and began to lean out over me, deadly dangerous and menacing. And I heard a voice from the air that cried out: 'Little human! The echo of your words has reached me! Do you really think that I can be comprehended in your song?'

(Freuchen, 1962, pp. 279–80)

Improvisation or adaptation in the moment of performance is not completely unknown in Eskimo poetry – witness for instance the special song an old woman sang to welcome the visiting Rasmussen. But the emphasis seems to be on deliberate and studied composition, with recognised personal ownership of particular songs.

Another clear instance of self-conscious and painstaking composition separated from the act of performance is documented for oral poets in the Gilbert Islands of the Southern Pacific. This Gilbertese love song gives a first impression of apparent spontaneity:

How deep are my thoughts as I sit on the point of land
Thinking of her tonight,
Her feet are luminous over dark ways,
Even as the moon stepping between clouds,
Her shoulders shine like Kaama in the South[1]
Her hands, in the sitting dance,
Trouble my eyes as the flicker of stars;
And at the lifting of her eyes to mine I am abashed,
I, who have looked undaunted into the sun.

(Grimble, 1957, p. 202)

But such a poem rests on a long process of deliberate composition. Grimble has described how when a Gilbertese poet 'feels the divine spark of inspiration once more stirring within him', he leaves the village and goes off to some lonely place where he can do the initial work on his composition alone: 'This is his "house of song", wherein he will sit in travail with the poem that is yet unborn. All the next night he squats there, bolt upright, facing east, while the song quickens within him'. Next morning he returns to the village to collect a group of friends to help him. It is their job to criticise and assess the poem – 'to interrupt, criticize, interject suggestions, applaud, or howl down, according to their taste. Very often they do howl him down, too, for they are themselves poets. On the other hand, if the poem, in their opinion, shows beauty they are indefatigable in abetting its perfection'. They spend the whole day with the poet, working with him on his 'rough draft' – 'searching for the right word, the balance, the music

[1] Southern Cross.

that will convert it into a finished work of art' (Grimble, 1957, pp. 204-5). After a day spent in this joint process, the friends leave and the poet is left on his own once more. 'He remains alone again – probably for several days – to reflect upon their advice, accept, reject, accommodate, improve, as his genius dictates. The responsibility for the completed poem will be entirely his' (Grimble, 1957, p. 205).

The result of this long-drawn out process of oral composition is that the poem as finally produced has been worked and re-worked over many days. This process results, in Arthur Grimble's words, in 'clear-cut gems of diction, polished and repolished with loving care, according to the canons of a technique as exacting as it is beautiful' (p. 200). The Gilbertese, he holds, are 'consummate poets' who, 'sincerely convinced of beauty, enlisted every artifice of balance, form and rhythm to express it worthily. The island poet thrills as subtly as our own to the exquisite values of words, labouring as patiently after the perfect epithet' (Grimble, 1957, p. 200).

There are many other documented examples of deliberate and protracted composition, divorced from the act of performance. Ila and Tonga women in Zambia make personal songs where the owner, working out the words and tune of the song, 'sings it in her heart' until it is time to stand up and sing it in public (Jones, 1943, pp. 11–12). There is a Ruanda custom of memorising praise poems by other named poets, whose prior composition is recognised (Kagame, 1951). The Dinka use an expert to make up a song to their requirements, for later performance by the 'owner' rather than the composer (Deng, 1973, p. 85). The Pueblo poet puts much preparatory work into composing a new song for an approaching festival:

> Yellow butterflies,
> Over the blossoming virgin corn,
> With pollen-painted faces
> Chase one another in brilliant throng...
> (Curtis, 1907, p. 484)

Mediaeval Gaelic court poets composed their poems orally in a darkened room. When the poem was complete it was recited or chanted to the chief not by the poet but by a bard who, according to a near-contemporary source, 'got it well by heart, and now pronounc'd it orderly' (Knott and Murphy, 1967, p. 64).

Where, as in the Gaelic case, there is a distinction between poets (responsible for composition) and reciters (responsible for performance) the situation is self-evidently unlike the Yugoslav model where 'singing, performing, composing are facets of the same act' (Lord, 1968a, p. 13). The distinction is known in other poetic traditions; compare the one sometimes made between the mediaeval European *trobador* (composer) and *joglar* (performer), the Ruanda and Somali poets, as opposed to reciters

(Johnson, 1971, p. 29), or the Dinka expert composer who is sometimes distinct from the performers of his poem (Deng, 1973, p. 85).

Where writing enters in – and (see chapter 1) it is hard to draw a strict line excluding it – possible variations in modes of composition become even more complex. There are cases of prior composition with *some* reliance on writing which is then used, in varying degrees, as an aid to memory for later oral performance. Both written narratives and brief notes were sometimes used by mediaeval Chinese ballad singers (Doleželová-Velingerová and Crump, 1971, pp. 2, 8), and texts of Irish street songs or handwritten 'ballets' of English, Scottish and American ballads have often formed one basis for later oral performance. All these can play some part in the process of composing 'oral poetry'.

The situation is made even more complex – and the possibility of a single generalisation about the nature of 'oral composition' the more remote – because of differences between 'cultures' or poetic traditions in the wide sense, and also between individual composers and differing genres within one poetic culture. American collectors have grown accustomed to working with the distinction between 'active' and 'passive' singer, and a number of studies have been devoted to the differing styles and creativity of individual composers. As early as 1908 Percy Grainger was discussing the 'Impress of personality on traditional singing', and more recently Wolf has related the amount and nature of creativity in ballads to the differing personalities of singers (Wolf, 1967). Innes's research into the stability and change in Mandinka griots' narrations is another case in point.

It is also well known that in many poetic traditions some genres are recognised as less innovative and creative – with more emphasis on memorisation, less on composition – whereas in others there can be a high degree of creativity by the individual poet. Among the Zulu, for instance, the praise poems of long-dead chiefs were fixed in form, and their recitation depended on memorisation and repetition; but some more recent praise poems 'uttered on the spur of the moment by an *imbongi* inspired by the presence of his chief or eager to incite his audience to loyalty for the chief bear the individual stamp of the singer' (Opland, 1971, p. 172): here composition-in-performance is the expected form. Another variation is found among the Dinka. There some types of song have to be composed in a short time – for instance, initiation and 'cathartic' songs – and it is common for an expert to compose rapidly while his listeners help by memorising the song for him, the composer himself often being unable to remember it when he has finished. With songs where less haste is necessary, as with ox songs, that help is not needed and the 'composers create at leisure' (Deng, 1973, p. 85).

More than one person may be involved in composition. I refer here to something over and above the effect that audiences can have on the performing poet – as described by Radlov for Kirghiz minstrels – or even beyond the help that friends and colleagues of a poet can provide, as in the Gilbertese instance. There are cases where two or more people seem to be clearly credited with, and hold the responsibility for, the composition of a particular piece. Emeneau describes how in Toda poetry there are different ways in which a song can be composed and performed.

> Solo composition is only one of the manners of delivery, and perhaps not the commonest. It must be obvious that with all details of composition closely dictated by the technique, duet and choral delivery is always possible. All the performers will have a good knowledge of the technique and will know what is being sung about. The first unit, even the first syllable of the first unit that is uttered by the chief performer almost always gives a certain clue to the limited possibilities of the two-dimensional structures that he intends to use; a quick intelligence on the part of his accompanists does the rest. In the dances there is usually a chief composer assisted by one companion; they shout in unison. If a song is being sung, the composer whistles the tune first, and those who sing with him can then accompany him in unison, or he may sing the first half of each two-dimensional structure and a single accompanist may sing the other half antiphonally, or a large group may likewise split up to perform antiphonally. My impression is that group performances are preferred to solo work.
>
> (Emeneau, 1964, p. 336)

Similar co-operation and interaction between two authors can be seen in a number of dialogue songs,[1] or the kind of poetic duels which can be interpreted as resulting in a single poetic composition, produced jointly by two composers. Larger groups too can be involved. If we leave on one side general theories about the 'public' or the 'folk' gradually affecting a composition over time, there is still evidence that a number of people sometimes take an active part in the composition of a piece. Ben-Amos mentions that song composers from Benin in Midwestern Nigeria explained that 'they often composed a song alone, but that the group of singers to whom they belonged reworked it afterwards until everybody was pleased' (Ben-Amos, 1972, p. 7). A more rigorous system is reported for Hawaiian oral poetry.

> A single poet working alone might produce the panegyric, but for the longer and more important songs of occasion a group got together, the theme was proposed and either submitted to a single composer or required line by line from each member of the group. In this way each line as it was composed was offered for criticism lest any ominous allusion creep in to mar the whole by bringing disaster

---

[1] These are not all necessarily by two authors; in some poetic traditions it is merely one of the accepted genres in which a single author can present his compositions.

upon the person celebrated, and as it was perfected it was committed
to memory by the entire group, thus insuring it against loss. Protective
criticism, therefore, and exact transmission were secured by group
composition.

(Beckwith, 1919, p. 28)

Evidence of this kind of joint authorship is not very clear-cut. But we
do have to consider dual or multiple authorship as one possible variable
in a study of the processes of oral composition.

It becomes clear that if we scrutinise the concept of 'oral composition'
in the light of the comparative empirical evidence it turns out not to be
one single and unique process as is often implied by scholars of the
oral-formulaic school. The Yugoslav evidence about the process of
composition-in-performance can be a useful analogy in cases where (as with
Kirghiz epic) the processes of composition and performance are closely
fused – but there are cases in which the analogy is not relevant, and we
cannot assume in advance that it will *necessarily* apply in a given case.

The processes of composition, memorisation and performance in oral
poetry turn out to be more complex than was once supposed. We can no
longer accept Lord's definitive generalisation about composition in oral
poetry – that 'with oral poetry we are dealing with a particular and distinctive process in which oral learning, oral composition, and oral transmission
almost merge; they seem to be different facets of the same process' (Lord,
1968a, p. 5). The reality is more interesting than any monolithic theory.
There turn out to be different combinations of the processes of composition, memorisation and performance, with differing relationships between
them according to cultural traditions, genres and individual poets. There
are several ways – and not just *one* determined way suitable for 'the oral
mind' – in which human beings can engage in the complex processes of
poetic composition.

5 Conclusion

So the relationship between composition, memorisation and performance
in oral poetry is more open than the definitive-sounding term 'oral
composition' seems to imply. The 'oral-formulaic' style of composition (as
depicted in *The Singer of Tales* and similar work) is not a sufficient indication
for concluding that a given work is 'oral', nor a necessary condition for
the creation of 'oral poetry'.

Yet Lord's insistence on moving away from the concept of a *written* model
has illuminated and stimulated all studies of oral poetry; for showing this
and for indirectly conveying to western readers the approaches of earlier
Russian scholars on the poetic creativity of oral performers there is much

to thank the oral-formulaic school. Even if the definition of 'formula' has been both too vague and too inflexible and limited to cover other formative constraints on, and opportunities of, an oral composer – some are discussed in the next chapter – it is in large measure due to the proponents of the term that we can now grasp so much better how an oral poet is both constrained and free in his composition, representing at once 'old' and 'new', 'tradition' and 'originality'. We can understand more fully how the modern improvising composer in the west can stress that he both engages in free improvisation and at the same time works within an accepted background, or appreciate the ending of the mediaeval Chinese singer's rendering of 'The ballad of the hidden dragon':

> I was asked to make a new tale from the old.
> For this worthy, intelligent assembly
> I was happy to unfold
> The story of Liu Chih-yüan
> From the beginning to the end
> And with absolutely nothing left untold.

(Doleželová-Velingerová and Crump, 1971, p. 113)

4

Style and performance

1   The relevance of style and performance

The discussion of composition has made clear that the oral poet has both constraints and opportunities, but that the range of factors encompassed in terms like 'formulaic expression' do not cover all the conventional elements involved either in the process of composition or the completed poem. This chapter discusses further factors pertaining to style and delivery. This will deepen the understanding of the nature and characteristics of oral poetry (and some of the controversies about them) and extend our sense of the oral poet's opportunities.

The chapter treats aspects of oral poetry which – as far as verbal style is concerned – have been taken as of central importance to the literary scholar, but not to the sociologist. 'Performance', on the other hand, where studied at all, has seemed significant primarily to those interested in the *social context* of literature. But I deliberately treat style and performance together here, holding that this is essential. With *oral* poetry, the distinction between the two is not a clear one, and it is impossible to appreciate either fully without some understanding of the other. I suggest that the overlap between performance and style in oral literature is such that anyone interested in one has much to learn from the other. Contrary to what might be supposed, furthermore, the study of style, as well as of performance, is relevant to sociological study, because it turns on the social conventions by which a structured human activity (in this case verbal art) is shaped. In art there is much to interest the sociologist in the socially recognised conventions that both constrain and express human imagination and artistic action. Questions of style and performance form part of the customary background of artistic convention which helps to make art possible. As Howard Becker points out, people who produce a work of art do not decide things afresh each time, but

> rely on earlier agreements now become customary, agreements that
> have become part of the conventional way of doing things in that art.
> Artistic conventions cover all the decisions that must be made with
> respect to works produced in a given art world, even though a
> particular convention may be revised for a given work. Thus, con-

88

ventions dictate the materials to be used, as when musicians agree to base their music on the notes contained in a set of modes, or on the diatonic, pentatonic or chromatic scales with their associated harmonies. Conventions dictate the abstractions to be used to convey particular ideas or experiences, as when painters use the laws of perspective to convey the illusion of three dimensions or photographers use black, white and shades of gray to convey the interplay of light and color. Conventions dictate the form in which materials and abstractions will be combined, as in the musical use of the sonata form or the poetic use of the sonnet. Conventions suggest the appropriate dimensions of a work, the proper length for a musical or dramatic event, the proper size and shape of a painting or sculpture.

(Becker, 1974, p. 771)

The whole sphere of art – of artistic impulse and performance, and of what Huizinga termed 'play' – is clearly one significant part of human culture; and within this, literature is one broad domain. Sociologists cannot ignore the ways in which these impulses and performances are mediated and constrained by social convention, on the assumption that such topics belong exclusively to literary scholars.

Socially recognised conventions apply to oral as much as to written art, and are a part of accepted *stylistic* conventions as well as more obviously 'sociological' aspects, like social function or the economic position of poets. The older prejudices (described in chapter 2) according to which *oral* poetry is composed by 'primitive folk' who are free and 'close to nature', untrammelled in their artistic creation by socially recognised rules or accepted artistic conventions, are unsupported. Here too, conventions accepted by audience and poet alike, about formal structure, range of genres, appropriate mode of delivery or verbal style, play an essential part in poetic activity.

The social nature of style can throw light on wider questions, like those of the relation of 'tradition' and innovation, of individual and society, and on the processes of socialisation and 'social action'. It is a topic which quickly leads one to a consideration of social conventions, often with political and economic overtones.

One of the qualities of literature is that it is in some way 'set apart' from common speech or writing. This applies above all to poetry, where style and structure are a kind of end in themselves as well as a signal to the audience of the type of communication intended.

Every culture has recognised conventions for its forms of poetic expression. Some of these relate to the occasion, the audience, performer or purpose. Among the most fundamental of these conventions are those pertaining to the verbal style of the piece (or genre) and, in the case of *oral* literature, to the mode of performance.

If we look comparatively at the varying forms of poetic expression in different periods and cultures, we are struck by the apparently infinite variability of these conventions, and also by the underlying patterns that, in differing combinations, recur again and again. Some of these are identified in this chapter and some recurrent patterns sketched. This discussion throws light on the question of whether there really is a special 'oral' style (and if so what it consists in), and also the question whether the dreamlike unconscious element sometimes attributed to unwritten literature is indeed a real characteristic.

The most marked feature of poetry is surely repetition. Forms and genres are recognised because they are repeated. The collocations of line or stanza or refrain are based on their repeated recurrence; metre, rhythm or stylistic features like alliteration or parallelism are also based on repeated patterns of sound, syntax or meaning. In its widest sense, repetition is part of all poetry. This is the general background against which the prosodic and other features of oral poetry must be seen. It has also been taken by some scholars as constituting one of the differentiating characteristics of oral as distinct from written literature (see pp. 127ff).

2 Prosodic systems

Against this general background of recurrences, some more specific stylistic features can be discerned in oral poetry. I begin with those which oral poetry shares with written poetry.

The prosodic system is perhaps the feature which most immediately gives form to a poem. We tend to think of this mainly in terms of *metre*, because of the influence of Greek and Roman models. Certainly metre does constitute one aspect. But as soon as one analyses the ways in which verse can be structured, one has to extend prosody to cover alliteration, assonance, rhyme, tonal repetition or even parallelism. It becomes clear that what in some languages or poetic cultures is achieved by a metre based on quantity is in others achieved by, say, alliteration; one can compare quantity in the Homeric hexameter with the elaboration of alliteration in Old English poetry (*Beowulf* for instance), assonance in the Old French epic, or the parallelism and word pairs of the Hebrew poetry in the Bible. For a full understanding of the prosodic characteristics of any poetic tradition one has to look beyond the mere counting of beats, syllables or quantities – the traditional model of a 'metre' – and look to a range of other factors which may perform a comparable function.

In discussing prosody it is impossible to get away from the notion of 'rhythm'. This is a much discussed term, and several definitions and approaches have been proposed.

Some analyse rhythm as a physiological process which underlies both poetry and many of the activities of men. Jousse, for instance, in a basically biological analysis, sees rhythm, dancing and singing as based on instinctive manifestations of 'le rythme vital' (Jousse, 1925, p. 232 etc.). This indeed fits the common view that the roots of literature are discoverable in biological functions – particularly 'primitive' literature, which would ultimately be analysable in *physical* and instinctual rather than cultural terms.

It is a tempting idea: it provides an apparently universal scientific basis for what would otherwise be an elusive phenomenon, and helps to give meaning to a nearly universal property of literature. But it is difficult to accept this rather simple theory. First, and foremost, it explains 'literature' away in terms of the kind of biological reduction that any serious student will find merely irrelevant. More directly, if it is taken as an 'explanation' of literature it does not easily fit the facts. For the concept of 'rhythm' is not a physical but a cultural and relative one. What seems like pleasing or uplifting rhythm to one group is nothing of the sort to another. Hence the common disagreement between generations in Western Europe about what is 'really' rhythmic, or the way a beginner has to *learn* to feel the – to the initiate – wildly exciting or stirring rhythm of the dochmiac metre in classical Greek tragedy, or the uplifting dynamic stress, with its overtones of nobility and eulogy, of Zulu panegyric poetry. In other words *cultural* factors help to determine what is appreciated as 'rhythmic' in any given group or period: it is not purely physical.

The same general point applies to music. Some suggest that rhythm is primary – the first musical element to appear. If so, there is something fundamental and irreducible about, say, drumming on its own. It seems an attractive proposition. But the evidence lies against it. The musicologist Bruno Nettl points out in his book *Music in Primitive Culture* that it is only in complex musical cultures (like Negro Africa) that rhythmic manifestations appear on their own – i.e. percussion without melody. In 'the simplest musical styles, like those of the Vedda...and the Fuegians' there are no solo drums and no solo percussive music (1956, p. 62). As Nettl makes clear, rhythm may be basic to music, but that does not make it a straightforward and uniform or *physically* defined phenomenon; in practice rhythmic forms are extremely varied in 'primitive music' throughout the world (1956, p. 76).

Still, even if a reductionist or biologically-based explanation will not hold up, the concept of rhythm, with all its subjectivities, does seem basic in poetry. It may be difficult to define precisely – Nettl's 'movement in time' (1956, p. 61) is perhaps as good a working definition as any – but it is in practice one of the main touchstones[1] by which we define and analyse *poetic* form. As one recent authority put it 'The simplest, most fundamental, and

---

[1] Not the only one, however. See the discussion in chapter 1 on the problem of delimiting 'prose' as against 'verse'.

most widespread feature of poetry is rhythmic structure' (Edmonson, 1971, p. 90).

This applies as much to oral as to written poetry – perhaps more so. For it is clear that much oral poetry is directly associated with rhythmic movement. Work-songs are a particularly clear example. These are found all over the world, accompanying and lightening monotonous and rhythmic work. There are songs to accompany threshing, hoeing, mining, chipping rust off a ship's side, grinding, pounding, rocking a baby, marching, paddling a canoe, launching a boat, pulling trucks, and innumerable other activities. Many children's songs, too, are of this kind – songs to go with skipping, ball-bouncing, counting out, action games and so on. Dance songs can be put in the same category. Here too the words and music are closely associated with rhythmic movements of the body, and the conjunction between the two forms part of the artistry of the whole. Indeed dance and work songs are closely allied; for the rhythm and art of the song can induce a dancing movement in the midst of work. One can see this even in uniformed troops marching to regimental songs, or West African Limba farmers hoeing in the rice seed up the slopes of their steep hillside farm, where the long line of workers structure their back-breaking labour with dancing steps that fit the rhythm both of song and work.

Cases like these illustrate once more the *cultural* aspect of rhythm. So far as the mere physical movements of hoeing go, there is no need for the song, and even less for the dancing embellishments. But the culturally defined rhythm of the songs and music help to define and decorate the physical movements, rather than being fully structured *by* them. This is even clearer in sung lyrics, like revivalist hymns or many modern pop songs, where the singers make movements in time to the rhythm of the song: swaying, twisting, clapping, or beating time. The rhythmic movements are accepted by current convention rather than dictated by universal physiological or material requirements.

In some oral poetry, the physical accompaniment to the rhythm is less marked. Oral performance of any piece tends to produce some movement, which is likely to chime in with the rhythm. But formalised rhythmic movement going with an oral poem may be only intermittent or partial in relation to the intrinsic rhythm of the piece itself. A lyric with chorus refrain may have clapping in the chorus only, or certain beats only may be emphasised, as in the recitation of *Kutune Shirka*, the Ainu epic, by the blind poet Wakarpa who used a stick to emphasise the dual stress in each line (Waley, 1951, p. 235).

In some oral forms, it has not been found possible to analyse the rhythm in terms of 'metre' in the strict sense. This may be due merely to inadequate study as yet, or (more likely) because the familiar metrical canons central to some kinds of verse are elsewhere replaced by other less readily recog-

nised prosodic features. But even where strict metre has not been discovered, it is striking how often observers have commented on the
'rhythmic' nature of the utterance – and this can be taken to be subjectively
felt by performers and listeners in the culture involved.

In other cases, rhythm can be analysed in more precise metrical terms.
There are many combinations and variations possible, but the three basic
principles – common to both written and unwritten literature – are quantity, stress and syllable. The Homeric hexameter is a metre based on
quantity – like other classical poetry – while early English poetry like *Beowulf* is based on stress (in this case allied to alliteration); stress and quantity
metres are a characteristic feature of many European literatures. In the
east, by contrast, *syllable* counting is a common basis for metrical forms. One
finds it, for instance, in Japanese court poetry, Toda songs, Malay and
Balinese verse, and in much of the poetry of China, Mongolia and Korea;
Semitic languages in general are also hospitable to syllabic verse (Edmonson, 1971, pp. 118ff). But there is no complete fit between type of metre
on the one hand and language group or geographical area on the other.
Many languages have a history of changing metrical form; there can also
be variations within a geographical area: the Ainu of Japan rely on stress
rather than the syllabic metres of poetry in Japanese, and among Russian
epic poems the Kazakh is syllabic while the Ob Ugrian relies on a strict metre
based on stress.

These various metres give structure to the verse in which they occur by
a type of verbal utterance based on sound patterning. But it is not only
through rhythmic repetition that this structuring can take place, it is also
produced by alternative (or sometimes additional) means like alliteration,
assonance, rhyme or various types of parallelism.

Alliteration is found in the Old English epic *Beowulf* where in metrical
terms it reinforces the stress-pattern. Of the four stresses in each line the
first and/or the second alliterates with the third, while the fourth must be
different. This pattern is conveyed in Michael Alexander's verse translation
which tries to reproduce the effect in modern English verse; the stressed
syllables are italicised.

> [The poet]
> Whose *tongue gave gold* to the *lang*uage
> Of the *trea*sured *re*pertory, *wrought* a *new* lay
> *Made* in the *measure*. The *man struck* up,
> *Found* the *phrase, framed rightly*
> The *deed* of *Beowulf*...
> (Alexander, 1966, p. 18)

It is not always realised that this device is also used with effect in oral
poetry. Its use can be extremely complex and impose fierce contraints on

the poet. Somali classical oral verse is one striking example of this, where, even in poems of a hundred or more lines, the same alliteration must be strictly observed throughout, with each hemistich of the poem having to contain at least one word beginning with a chosen consonant or a vowel. That the alliteration is both deliberate and binding is made clear in Andrzejewski and Lewis's study (1964, pp. 42–3):

> The rules of alliteration are very rigid in the sense that only identical initial consonants are regarded as alliterative (*higaadsan*) with one another and no substitution by similar sounds is admissible. All initial vowels count as alliterative with each other, and again this principle is most stricly observed.
>
> The same alliteration is maintained throughout the whole poem. If, for example, the alliterative sound of a poem is the consonant *g*, in every hemistich there is one word beginning with *g*. A poem of one hundred lines (two hundred hemistichs) will therefore contain two hundred words beginning with *g*. Similarly, if the alliterative sound is a vowel, in every hemistich there is one word beginning with a vowel.
>
> The two passages below illustrate these principles; the first alliterates in *g* and the second in a vowel.
>
> 1 *Dhaachaan ka gabangaabsaday e   waygu geliseen e*
> 2 *Gooddiga Ban Cawl buu fakhrigu   geed ku leeyahay e*
> 3 *Gaajada huggeedii miyaa   galabta i saaray?*
>
> 1 I lately sought this plight for myself and you put me into it,
> 2 On the edge of the 'Awl Plain, poverty has a tree (to sit under),
> 3 Have the garments of hunger been put on me this evening?
>
> 1 *Afkaagan wanaagsan*
> 2 *Udgoonkiisiyo araggaan*
> 3 *Ubachaay, u oolaa.*
>
> 1 (It is because of) your fine mouth,
> 2 Its scent and sight,
> 3 That I postpone my journey, oh Flower!
>
> The rules of alliteration also include certain restrictions on the type of words which can be used: they must be words with readily assignable meanings, such as nouns, numerals, proper names, or verbs. Prepositional particles, conjunctions, or emphasis and concord particles such as *baa* or *waa* are not regarded as suitable for alliteration and any one using them is considered as falling short of the standards required of a poet.

Clearly, alliteration is one of the main defining features of Somali classical poetry. In other poetic traditions alliteration may add to the force of a piece or genre without being subject to such rigorous patterning – it is a feature of Kazakh epic for instance (along with assonance) and in

Mongolian oral poetry. Where the patterning is systematic in some way, alliteration can fulfil something of the same function as rhyme. As Phill-potts points out in her discussion of Icelandic Edda and Saga (1931, p. 33) the ear waits attentive for the coming alliteration, and then rests satisfied, in basically the same way as it waits for the final rhyme in rhyming couplets.

Assonance is perhaps less systematically developed as a central constraint on the poet. But it can add an important element of sound repetition to poetry, and sometimes (in the absence of strict metre) is the main stylistic device. It is found in Old French epic like *The Song of Roland*, and is important in American Indian poetry. In Pima songs, for instance, Barnes describes how the musical quality of assonance helps to give unity to line and poem, with emphasis on series of open vowel sounds (Barnes, 1921, pp. 49–50).

Full end-assonance or rhyme, however, is a relatively common pattern in some areas. Sometimes this is said to be a characteristic of the language rather than calculated poetic contrivance. The rhyming vowel-endings of lines in Polynesian poetry are usually treated as rhyme proper, but some, like Greenway, consider it merely accidental – a random and auto-matic result of linguistic structure (Greenway, 1964, p. 122). In other cases it is highly mannered and unquestionably due to deliberate art. Edmonson cites the case of Burmese poetry where rhyme is extremely common and successive lines are sometimes completely assonated, as in

Ta ko dè pa
Ma so bè hma
A ngo thè hla
(Edmonson, 1971, p. 116)

Greenway (1964, p. 122) suggests that rhyme is rare in 'primitive litera-ture' (as he defines it). This is disputable. Certainly if one follows him in rejecting the end assonance in the rich and extensive corpus of Polynesian poetry as a true example of rhyme, this cuts down the field considerably. But one can also find many instances of rhyme as an occasional poetic device in such poetry as Kazakh epic (Winner, 1958, p. 69) or the Turkish poetry in *The Book of Dede Korkut* (Sümer *et al.*, 1972, p. xxi). In Fijian heroic poetry – to take an instance outside Eurasia – the double-vowel rhymes at the end of each line are deliberately achieved by the use of a series of proper names and adjectives. This is a form of assonance which sets definite constraints for the poet and leads him to choose one epithet rather than another. Quain writes

The requirements of rhyme supply a motive for the constant repeti-tion of a series of proper names. Names can be qualified by adding the adjective *kula*, 'red' or 'bloody', or *dua*, 'single' or 'superlative', without confusing their identity. Thus Village-of-the Distance (*Koro-ni-Yawa*) of Song III becomes Village-of-the-Red-Distance (*Koro-ni-Yawa-Kula*) in songs that require a U-A rhyme. In the section of Song III which shifts to a U-A rhyme, it is interesting that Tip-of-the-Single-Feather becomes the protagonist; Tip-of-the-Feather (*Vuso-ni-Lawe*) is a difficult rhyme, but Tip-of-the-Single-Feather (*Vuso-ni-Lawe-Dua*) is congenial to a U-A rhyme.

(Quain, 1942, p. 15)

But it is probably among oral literatures in close contact with writing that full vowel and consonant rhyme is most significant. It occurs in late Latin songs, modern English nursery rhymes and the rhymes of the troubadours, British ballads, Malay *pantun* quatrains, and Irish political songs. It is also used in a complicated way in mediaeval Chinese ballads like 'The ballad of the hidden dragon' where a series of 'suites' is divided by prose sections, with the poetry in each suite containing the same rhyme through-out, and clearly differentiated from other suites both by a different musical mode and a different rhyme (Doleželová-Velingerová and Crump, 1971, p. 4).

Here again one has to look to cultural rather than purely external criteria. Anyone who has tried to compare poetry from different traditions (even as close as English and French) knows that what is accepted as 'rhyme' by one ear may seem very remote from it to another. Much research needs to be carried out on *local* appreciations of devices like assonance and rhyme. Until that is done it may be impossible to fix on criteria by which to decide, for example, whether Polynesian patterns of sound repetition at the ends of lines are true examples of rhyme.

Tone repetition (sometimes called tone rhyme) is another sphere in which the outside observer will find difficulty in assessing how far it is a deliberate poetic device. In languages where the *tone* of a syllable is significant in defining its meaning (Chinese, for example, or Yoruba in West Africa) this feature too may be used as a structuring device in poetry – oral particularly. There are cases where this has been claimed.

In Yoruba poems the structure is sometimes provided not by strict metrical constraints or by rhyme, but by tonal patterns: one Yoruba scholar claims 'Tone is of the essence of Yoruba poetry' (Laṣebikan, 1955). In Yoruba hunting chants (*ijala*) line-ends and caesuras are marked by tonal assonance, and this also occurs 'in the repetition of some significant words and in the identicalness of tone sequences associated with some crucial words in the chant' (Babalọla, 1966, p. 389). Contrast between tones at the ends of two consecutive rhythm-segments is also used to 'make a strong impression on the listener's ears...[and] to increase the richness of the music of the ijala lines by adding to the element of variety in successive rhythm-segments' (ibid., p. 389).

Babalọla quotes the following example to illustrate his point about tonal assonance and contrast

O ṣe é! ./
Yẹru Ọkín | Olọfa Mọjọ̀. \/,.\
Ọlalọmi mi ni ọ́ làre | mo diju ng tó la 'ṣu. \.,/..
Ọkan o gbọdọ jù'kan l' Ọfà. .\
B'ọkan jù'kan | b'ọkan jù'kan | nwọn ni ọba ní kó wọn róro. \\,\/,/.
Ọba o ko iran anmi ri | ni lee Lalọmi. ./,./
Ija pẹurẹu | abẹ òwu | ti nwọn jà l' Ọfà. \/,\/,.\
Loju u Lalọmi | ṣoju uru uwa ii náà ni. ./,\.
Ọ́ ṣ' ojú ebè l' Ọfà. /\
O ṣ' oju u poro 'nú oko. /..
O ṣ' oju agbelẹyaràrá. \/
Ọ́ ṣ' ojú u láporubukánúoko | tí jẹ́ àgùnmọ̀nà l' Ọfà. /..,.\

(/ represents the high tone; . represents the mid tone; \ represents the low tone.)

(English translation:
Thank you!
Citizen of town with sandy street frequented by ọ̀kin birds.
King of Ọfa, the Handsome One.
My dear Ọlalọmi is the successful cutter in the traditional
    blindfold longitudinal slicing of sacrificial yam tuber.
Both slices must be of equal size at Ọfa.
If one slice was bigger than the other,
If one slice was bigger than the other,
It is said that the king would imprison and starve the
    unsuccessful cutter and his relatives.
The king at no time imprisoned any of my relations in Ọlalọmi's
    lineage.
The protracted fight under cotton plants which was fought at
    Ọfa
Was in the presence of Ọlalọmi and people of my age.
Soil heaps on the farm witnessed it.
The furrows on the farm witnessed it.
The black-eyed-bean plants witnessed it,
The groundnut plants witnessed it and likewise the maize plants
    at Ọfa.)

Tonal assonance at segment-ends is indicated here...it is worth noting that the tone sequence pattern low+low, which occurs only once at a segment-end, is repeated in the 'jù 'kàn' of line 4, 'ìjà' of line 7, and 'àgùn-mọ̀nà of line 12. Similarly, the tone-sequence pattern high+low occurring only once at a segment-end is repeated in 'Ọlọ́fà', 'náà', 'l' Ọfà', and 'agbélẹ̀...'.

The list of tones which occur at segment-ends is as follows and it clearly shows that tonal contrast is prevalent between successive pairs: high, high, low, mid, mid, low, low, high, mid, high, high, high, high, low, mid, mid, low, mid, high, mid, low. Here there are only seven instances of two consecutive rhythm-segments ending on the same tone, out of a total of twenty-one segments.

(Babalọla, 1966, p. 391)

The outsider may wonder how far these are deliberate tonal patterns, and how far fortuitous. When both assonance *and* contrast are analysed as significant, it is easy to read meaning into what may be random. More research is needed on this topic: even in Yoruba few detailed analyses have been made as yet. But when at least two native Yoruba scholars insist that these patterns *are* heard as significant by the poets and audiences involved, one must take the claim seriously. The Yoruba language is certainly intensely tonal; the *tone* of a word plays as important a part as its phonetic definition. This has led to the development of 'drum poetry' – where the verbal message is conveyed by the rhythms and changing *tones* of the drums.

The possibility receives support from the use of tone in oral literature elsewhere. Among African languages, there is possibly tonal rhyme in Efik, Ganda and perhaps Luba poetry, as well as tonal correspondence in some riddles and balanced proverbs, which helps to give them something of the air of poetry (Finnegan, 1970, p. 71). Elsewhere tone has been mentioned as significant in Burmese and Thai verse (Edmonson, 1971, p. 115), in classical Greek poetry (Stanford, 1967) and in Kazakh epic (Winner, 1958, p. 69). In some (but not all) classical Chinese poetry there are fixed end rhymes based on tones, even though most modern song composition proceeds independently of tone (Chang, 1956, pp. 54, 58).

Parallelism is another important structural device in oral poetry. It consists basically of a type of repetition (usually a binary pattern) in which one element is changed, the other – usually the syntactic frame itself – remaining constant.

> A day of darkness and of gloominess,
> A day of clouds and of thick darkness
>
> (Joel, 2: 2)

can stand as one well-known example where the changed element is fairly close to the original in pattern. In

> He hath filled me with bitterness,
> He hath made me drunken with wormwood
>
> (Lamentations, 3: 15)

or

> For love is strong as death;
> Jealousy is cruel as the grave
>
> (Song of Songs, 8: 6)

the parallelism is through repetition of *meaning* (sometimes reiterated, sometimes antithetical) using different terms (the common form in Old Testament poetry).

In some cases parallelism is one of the most important prosodic elements. It is the main formal characteristic of Old Testament poetry, comparable to Homeric metre, Old English alliteration, and Old French assonance (Whallon, 1969, pp. 140ff). Modern Toda songs from South India provide another interesting case. They lack rhyme, accent, quantity or alliteration and are based on an extremely simple three-syllable metrical unit. But

> from this simple beginning, however, there is built up a complicated structure on principles other than metrical. Sentences consist of from one sung unit to as many as five or six or even seven, with a possibility of quite complicated syntax. But, one very striking feature of the structure, no such sentence may be uttered without being paired with another sentence exactly parallel to it in syntactic structure and in number of units
>
> (Emeneau, 1964, p. 334)

This can be seen in the following extract from a Toda song about the hot dry season:

> The days of one year have elapsed,/ The days of six months have elapsed.//
> The murderous dry season has come./ The murderous kite has whistled its whistle.//
> The frost has lain on the ground like fruit./ The fruit has yielded water on the ground.//
> The sun has become hot as it has not been hot before./ The dry wind has increased as it has not increased before.//
> The sun has become hot on the head./ The dust has burned on the feet.//
> Dust has risen on one side./ Smoke has risen on one side.//...
> ...When will it become the beautiful season of showers?/ When will the beautiful dew fall?//
> When will rain fall in the black sky?/ When will thunder thunder in the clear sky?//
> When will god's lightning flash? [When will it be (like the shaman who) takes god's sword?]¹
> When will the thunder thunder in the dry season?/ When will the lightning flash on the mountains?//
>
> (Emeneau, 1971, pp. 590–1)

Similarly in Navaho poetry there is no metre in a strict sense, but the stylistic patterning of the stanzas into which the songs are normally divided is strictly based on parallelism:

¹ The translator comments that this phrase is required by the poetic technique though apparently irrelevant to the sense.

> From my head earthly beauty
> From my feet earthly beauty
> Below me earthly beauty
> Above me earthly beauty
> Around me all earthly beauty

> (Walton, 1930, pp. 105–6)

E. L. Walton concludes, on the evidence of her analysis of about 150 Navaho poems

> Parallelism in its simpler forms is always present, with occasionally a drift towards some elaboration according to traditional methods. Antithetical or incremental parallelism builds the stanza, and stanza after stanza is patterned according to the accepted formulae. Narrative may wrench the exact balance, but is reduced to some similar balance. Indeed Navajo song composition is very like the old Navajo blankets where the line of color on one end balanced the line, usually of the same color, on the other end.

> (Walton, 1930, p. 118)

Parallelism also plays an important prosodic role in the lengthy panegyric poetry of some Southern African peoples, such as the Zulu, Xhoso and Sotho. Here the poetic form is probably based partly on a type of loose stress rhythm allied to certain melodic requirements in performance, but is also very dependent on the use of parallelism of words or meaning (the former also connected with the development of alliteration and assonance). For example, in Zulu praises there are many instances of 'perfect parallelisms' like the lines about Ndaba

> Who when he lay down was the size of rivers,
> Who when he got up was the size of mountains

> **(Obeyalala wangangemimfula,
> Obeyavuka wangangezintaba.)**

and also of parallelism by linking, where the last element in one line starts the next. Shaka is praised as

> He who armed in the forest, who is like a madman,
> The mad man who is in full view of men.

> **(UMahlom' ehlathini onjengohlanya,
> Uhlanya olusemehlwen' amadoda.)**

There is also the special usage of a kind of 'noun–verb parallelism' (where the noun that starts the first line is a derivative of the verb that makes the linking in the second line) and of what has been called 'negative–positive parallelism' when the verb of the first line is the negative of the verb making the linking in the second:

Shaka did not raid herds of cattle,
He raided herds of buck

**(UShaka ubengadl' imihlambi yankomo,
Ubedl' imihlambi yezinyamazane.)**

or

He who attempted the ocean without crossing it,
It was crossed by swallows and white people.

**(Owalokoth' ulwandle engaluweli,
Lwaluwelwa zinkonjane nabelungu.)**

(Examples from Cope, 1968, pp. 41–4)

Southern Bantu praise poetry uses this device constantly, as well as variations on direct parallelism such as chiasmus (cross parallelism), deliberate change of word-order in the second of three parallel lines, and the practice of linking (or chain parallelism) by which a phrase at the end of a line is taken up and repeated in the first half of the next line.

Even where the parallelism is not one of the regularly recurring features of the prosodic structure, it may still be a significant element in poetic form. In Turkic oral epic syntactic parallelism plays an important role in the structure of the versification (Chadwick and Zhirmunsky, 1969, pp. 334–5), while in Ob Ugrian songs, parallelism appears in the form of lines repeated with one or two words (usually epithets) changed (Cushing, 1970). Parallelism also appears in Polynesian poetry. In poems from the Pacific island of Mangareva parallelism takes at least three special forms: the repetition of a verse with the name of the character or the object changed; a refrain after each verse; or a question and answer pattern, the first verse asking the name of someone's wife, the second replying in similar form with the name (Buck, 1938, pp. 384–5). Given these instances it is difficult to accept Greenway's assertion that 'conscious parallelism is a rare thing in the least sophisticated literatures' (1964, p. 120) – if by 'least sophisticated' he means (as it seems) literatures without long contact with written Eurasian forms. One could list numerous instances from different kinds of oral literature: Mongolian and Fijian poetry (Bawden, 1977, and Quain, 1942, pp. 15–16), the *Rgveda* (Gonda, 1959, pp. 46ff), Old English, Malay, Christian liturgy – but the device is so widespread that it scarcely needs further exemplification. One last instance must suffice: an Acholi love song from Uganda

Lut kot go cwara	*Lightning, strike my husband*
Lut kot go cwara,	Lightning, strike my husband,
Go cwara,	Strike my husband,
Wekka meya;	Leave my lover;
Ee, wekka meya;	Ee, leave my lover,
Twolli tong cwara,	Snake, bite my husband,
Tong cwara,	Bite my husband,
Wekka meya;	Leave my lover,
Ee, wekka meya:	Ee, leave my lover.

Nen ka woto,	See him walking,
Nenno mitta;	How beautifully he walks;
Neno ka myelo,	See him dancing,
Nenno mitta;	How beautifully he dances;
Neno ka bunyu,	See him smiling,
Nenno mitta;	How beautifully he smiles;
Iwinyo ka kutu bila,	Listen to the tune of his horn,
Winynyo mitta;	How beautifully it sounds;
Iwinyo ka loko,	Listen to him speaking,
Winyo mitta;	How beautifully he speaks,
Nen ka ucu,	See him performing the mock-fight,
Nenno mitta;	How beautifully he does it;
Nenno meya,	The sight of my lover
Nenno mitta.	Is most pleasing.
Lut kot go cwara,	Lightning, strike my husband,
Go cwara,	Strike my husband,
Wekka meya;	Leave my lover;
Ee, wekka meya.	Ee, leave my lover.

(p'Bitek, 1974, p. 57)

3 Repetition, style and structure

Parallelism can be discussed as a category on its own – and in a sense this is necessary in a comparative study of the prosodic systems of oral poetry – but it cannot be divorced from the wider subject of repetition generally. It is, after all, one type of repetition, and the forms discussed so far could equally well have been classed under that head – as could the tonal and rhythmic repetitions already mentioned under the general heading of prosody. But besides the general patterning through repetition that underlies most of the devices discussed already, there are some forms of repetition that should be specifically mentioned.

Verbal repetition can be at a number of levels, from the repetition of syllables to that of whole verses and lengthy passages. (This section is not concerned with the repetition of motifs, ideas or incidents in different words, but with verbal repetition as a poetic device within a single piece.)

Reduplication of syllables sometimes occurs as a metre-filler – in Fijian heroic poetry for instance (Quain, 1942, p. 14) – but even this minor device can have poetic effect in oral performance. The same goes for reduplication in Ob Ugrian poetry when the repetition of the root-word in such phrases as 'The five-stringed stringed instrument' or 'The landing place of my landing-placed village' is part of the accepted poetic language (Cushing, 1970). Then there is the repetition – familiar in written poetry – of one or more key words throughout a poem, of parallel phrases carried on from line to line, or of single lines which are repeated throughout a poem. One well-known American Indian example can illustrate this latter form, the Navaho *Song of the Horse*

> How joyous his neigh!
>   Lo, the Turquoise Horse of Johano-ai,
>   How joyous his neigh,

There on precious hides outspread standeth he;
    How joyous his neigh,
There on tips of fair fresh flowers feedeth he;
    How joyous his neigh,
There of mingled waters holy drinketh he;
    How joyous his neigh,
There he spurneth dust of glittering grains;
    How joyous his neigh,
There in mist of sacred pollen hidden, all hidden he;
    How joyous his neigh,
There his offspring many grow and thrive for evermore;
    How joyous his neigh!

(Curtis, 1907, p. 362)

The antiphonal forms of much religious liturgy or leader/response lyrics are based on this same pattern. In some African lyrics it is common for the cantor to introduce variations in the text or melody of his phrase (A), while the balancing responsive phrase (B) sung by the chorus remains the same (Nketia, 1962, p. 29). This type of repetition can be quite complex, for the basic principle can be extended into a sequential pattern with A and B repeated at different levels – resulting, say in a form of AB A′B′. The resulting unit (now of four sentences, or even six, or eight or more) can then be subject to yet further repetitions, sometimes embroidered by the cantor in his sections. The use of a formalised refrain – often but not always allotted to a chorus – is clearly an extension of this same principle of repetition; it is found throughout the world, from Irish political verse to Gond love lyrics, Navaho songs or Eskimo poems.

Patterns of repetition can provide structure and coherence to an oral poem – a necessary aspect in a medium as ephemeral as the spoken or sung word – but need not lead to monotony. Repetition in itself can lead to variation both in the intervening non-repeated units, and – very effectively – in strategic variation within the repeated element itself. This variation and development through the use of repetition is a widely used device in oral poetry. Here is a familiar illustration, the song composed by Frank Beddo to express his grief and helplessness, as a child, on seeing Jeff Buckner lynched in Texas.

They hanged Jeff Buckner from a sycamore tree,
And I was there, and I was there.
He went to his death so silently,
And I was there, but I never said a word.

They put him in a wagon with a rope around his neck,
And I was there, and I was there.
They pulled away the wagon and his neck it did break,
And I was there, but I never said a word.

Jeff Buckner's face was as black as coal,
And I was there, and I was there.
But white as snow alongside of my soul,
For I was there, but I never said a word.

They nailed King Jesus to an iron-bolted tree,
And I was there, and you were there.
And meek as a lamb to the slaughter went he,
And we were there, but we never said a word.

(From People's Songs Library, quoted in Greenway, 1953, p. 114)

The whole concept of a stanza is based on the principle of repetition. This is particularly striking when verbal as well as metrical parallelism is involved. In some poetic cultures this is developed to a high degree. Take this corn-grinding song, for instance, from the Pueblo Indians of New Mexico, where the Pueblo interest in the four cardinal points of the compass dominates the form of the poem.

This way from the North
Comes the cloud,
Very blue,
And inside the cloud is the blue corn.
     How beautiful the cloud
     Bringing corn of blue color!

This way from the West
Comes the cloud
Very yellow,
And inside the cloud is the yellow corn.
     How beautiful the cloud
     Bringing corn of yellow color!

This way from the South
Comes the cloud
Very red,
And inside the cloud is the red corn.
     How beautiful the cloud
     Bringing corn of red color!

This way from the East
Comes the cloud,
Very white,
And inside the cloud is the white corn.
     How beautiful the cloud
     Bringing corn of white color!

How beautiful the clouds
From the North and the West
From the South and the East
Bringing corn of all colors!

(Barnes, 1925, pp. 60–1)

Many forms of oral poetry make use to some degree of the same principle of parallelism in consecutive stanzas, a literary device which can build up successive layers of insight and meaning around the central theme and manifest a unity as well as an opportunity for development in the poem itself. It is well known, for example, in English and Scottish ballads. Here the unfolding of a story often involves repetition of a theme with slight variations, 'thereby', as Karpeles puts it, 'creating a feeling of tension, and gradually leading to the denouement' (Karpeles, 1973, p. 41). This type of parallelism is often known as 'incremental repetition' and is well illustrated in the famous ballad of *Lord Randal*.

'O where ha you been, Lord Randal, my son?
And where ha you been, my handsome young man?'
'I ha been at the greenwood; mother, mak my bed soon,
For I'm wearied wi hunting, and fain wad lie down.'

'An wha met ye there, Lord Randal, my son?
An wha met you there, my handsome young man?'
'O I met wi my true-love; mother, mak my bed soon,
For I'm wearied wi hunting, and fain wad lie down.'

'And what did she give you, Lord Randal, my son?
Amd what did she give you, my handsome young man?'
'Eels fried in a pan; mother, make my bed soon,
For I'm wearied wi huntin, and fain wad lie down.'

'An wha gat your leavins, Lord Randal, my son?
And wha gat your leavins, my handsome young man?'
'My hawks and my hounds; mother, mak my bed soon,
For I'm wearied wi huntin, and fain wad lie down.'

'And what becam of them, Lord Randal, my son?
And what becam of them, my handsome young man?'
'They stretched their legs out and died; mother, mak my bed
    soon,
For I'm wearied wi huntin, and fain wad lie down.'

'O I fear you are poisoned, Lord Randal, my son!
I fear you are poisoned, my handsome young man!'
'O yes, I am poisoned; mother, mak my bed soon,
For I'm sick at the heart, and I fain wad lie down.'

'What d'ye leave to your mother, Lord Randal, my son?
What d'ye leave to your mother, my handsome young man?'
'Four and twenty milk kye; mother, mak my bed soon,
For I'm sick at the heart, and I fain wad lie down.'

'What d'ye leave to your sister, Lord Randal, my son?
What d'ye leave to your sister, my handsome young man?'
'My gold and my silver; mother, mak my bed soon,
For I'm sick at the heart, an I fain wad lie down.'

'What d'ye leave to your brother, Lord Randal, my son?
What d'ye leave to your brother, my handsome young man?'
'My houses and my lands; mother, mak my bed soon,
For I'm sick at the heart, and I fain wad lie down.'

'What d'ye leave to your true-love, Lord Randal, my son?
What d'ye leave to your true-love, my handsome young man?'
'I leave her hell and fire; mother, mak my bed soon,
For I'm sick at the heart, and I fain wad lie down.'

(*The Faber Book of Ballads*, ed. Hodgart, 1971, pp. 34–6)

The principle of parallelism is often used in music, where it gives scope both for unity *and* for variation. The parallel occurrence in music does not make the device any less suitable or effective in verbal art – after all, much oral poetry has important musical characteristics in performance.

This general question of 'repetition' leads to the issue of structure in the larger sense, where we leave the internal style of a poem and its detailed prosodic systems. It needs to be asked how far, for instance, single poems are seen as distinct from each other in oral culture, how far stanzas are separate units or sub-units, and whether there is a sense in which one can speak of, say, 'song-cycles' or complete epics.

In cultures with a written tradition this is no great problem. By the artifice of reproducing what we classify as poetry in a particular printed form, 'as verse', and heading it with a title, we make our intentions clear; it is in a sense a typographical definition. Differentiation is more of a problem with an oral poem. In practice this is usually concealed, for the collector or translator of oral poetry commonly reproduces it for his literate public in lines, verses and so on, with a heading at the top – precisely as an indication that he *does* classify it as poetry. But the line-endings and other features are not necessarily rendered in the original performance – and how you reproduce a particular oral poem is a matter of degree and of judgement, not an absolute one. Even in a culture with a written tradition, as well as an oral one, there can be ambiguity. Which layout of this well known Irish song 'The Foggy Dew' is 'correct'? The short-line version runs:

As down the glen, one Easter morn,
To a city fair rode I,
There armed lines of marching men,
In squadrons passed me by;

In the longer-line version (here completing verse 1) in which Irish songs are also often printed, it runs:

No pipes did hum nor battle drum did sound its dread tattoo,
But the Angelus bell o'er the Liffey swell rang out in the Foggy
   Dew.

The answer must surely be that both represent the verbal structure, and that any decision between the two must depend on analysis of local canons of delivery and/or of given performance; and even then, the written representation can only be a relatively useful device for indicating certain elements of structure and of content – a matter of degree, not of absolute correctness.

This general point is often overlooked, and collected texts assumed to possess a more definitive shape than is justified. It needs to be emphasised that units like 'lines', 'verses', 'stanzas' – even 'poems' and 'cycles' are relative, and not always already defined for us by the material itself. Furthermore, collectors do not always explain the principles on which they have decided to reproduce the material in a given form. Some do – and then one can be clear what is intended by each unit and appreciate why it is being differentiated. In the magnificent Arnhem Land *Djanggawul* song cycle, for instance, R. M. Berndt makes it clear that 'the arrangement into lines conforms to the pauses made by the Aborigines themselves when singing or reciting' (1952, p. 62). This is probably a commonly-used criterion. In other cases, musical cadences or alliterative or rhythmic deliveries are used as a signal for marking the ends of lines. Similarly parallelisms of meaning and verbal form are often employed as criteria for differentiating a verse or stanza; the occurrence of a refrain is also a commonly invoked marker. But, however sensible and unavoidable such differentiations are in practice, it must be repeated that they are relative only.

The same applies to the discrimination of 'one poem'. It has to be remembered that oral poems do not normally have titles; and that in the common instances when poems are delivered by their authors (more particularly if there is an element of improvisation), the start and finish may not always be clearly delineated beforehand or even in the actual performance. Thus it is often not self-evident whether particular units of verse should be counted as several poems, consecutive stanzas in one complete poem, or as parts of a song cycle.

Development over time may also be relevant, because genres are not necessarily fixed for ever in an oral any more than a written context. One clear example is that of the development of the genre *heello* in modern Somali poetry. This grew out of the brief lyric (the *balwo*) which was itself initiated around 1945, and quickly became popular with the Somali youth and the urban population. The *balwo* is an extremely short lyric – often only two lines of text – dealing largely with love and characterised by condensed and cryptic imagery: the type of poem that has been called 'miniature'. After some years, the practice emerged of linking together a number of *balwo* to make up one long series – in a sense one poem. This gradually became the *heello*, which is now established as a long poem marked by repetition and the use of refrains. It still deals mainly with love, but there is also a stress on new political themes like anti-colonialism, or Pan-Somalism. We can thus observe the rise of a new genre. In this case it owed its development to a number of specific factors, among them the new political climate and the method of payment by length in radio performance – this being an increasingly important medium for Somali oral poetry (Johnson, 1971). But similar developments of new out of old forms are likely to have taken place in many areas (even if rarely as well documented) and show how the boundaries which apparently divide one unit from another may be fluid and changing. There are other well-known examples in the gradual development of the mediaeval troubadour lyrics or the probable change-over from couplet to quatrain-form in Scottish ballads (Buchan, 1972, pp. 167–70). The clear-cut and fixed impression given by printed versions of such poetry may therefore be misleading, and for exact information about the structure and artistic unity of a short poem, a song-cycle, or even an epic, one has to go beyond typographical conventions and ask questions about actual performance or local evaluation, history, and classification[1].

Provided one remembers this fundamental relativity, it is possible to go on to make general points about the varying structure of oral poems. If one takes the 'line' as one unit (if a relative one), it becomes clear that some oral poems are built up on a system of couplets like the Somali *heello* sequences of two-line units, or the couplets so typical of Aboriginal Aranda songs in Central Australia (Strehlow, 1971). Others are based on triplets or triads, as in some mediaeval European lyrics and mystery plays, much of the famous Hawaiian creation chant *The Kumulipo*, or well-known liturgical forms like

> Kyrie eleison
> Christe eleison
> Kyrie eleison

Four-line verse is a popular form in many areas. It can be illustrated by the well-known Malay *pantun*, where the structure is particularly complex and demanding. In this the first and third line rhyme terminally and internally, and so do the second and fourth, as indicated in the following rendering (the correspondences italicised)

> The *fate* of a *dove* is to *fly*,
> It *flies* to its *nest* on the *knoll*;
> The *gate* of true *love* is the *eye*,
> The *prize* of its *quest* is the *soul*
>
> (Wilkinson, 1924, p. 50)

(Even with this precisely defined form, however, the edges can be a little blurred, for linked series of *pantun* verses exist – raising the question

---

[1] For a useful discussion of this topic see Rothenberg 1969, pp. xx–xxi.

whether these are one poem or many – and refrains may be repeated, so that an actual performance may give a very different impression from the neat four-line verse printed on a page.)

Couplet, triplet, quatrain and so on sometimes form complete poems on their own (perhaps particularly the last) but are also commonly conjoined to form longer pieces, sometimes directly, sometimes linked together or interlaced with refrain or repetition. There are also longer units – like the (apparently) typical eight-line verses of many Irish or Irish-influenced songs, as well as a great many poems not obviously structured on precise multiples of lines, like some Eskimo or Hawaiian poems. Clearly many different variations and combinations of these units are possible, including the fairly common prosimetric or *chante fable* form in which prose alternates with verse. Longer series also occur, as in the Australian Aborigine song cycles – sometimes, as in Arnhem Land, extending to several hundred songs in a single cycle – and the longer epic poems.

Perhaps the most striking result of any review of the forms of oral poetry is the variety revealed. A relatively few basic principles of prosodic and structural patterning provide an almost infinitely wide range of development in different culturally defined modes.

4 Language and diction

It is apparently common for the language of certain genres of poetry to be somewhat removed from that of everyday speech, both in vocabulary and syntax. In extreme cases, a completely different language from the vernacular is employed, like the accepted use of Mandingo by certain West African minstrels even when singing to speakers of other languages, or Latin as the vehicle of liturgical and other poetry in Europe. In others a highly conventional or stereotyped form of language is held suitable for poetry, like the 'learned language' and archaism of some early Irish poets (Knott and Murphy, 1966, pp. 65–7, Williams, 1971, pp. 37–8) or the 'bardic language' of early Tamil itinerant minstrels (Kailasapathy, 1968, pp. 183–4). More often it involves relatively small conventional changes from ordinary language, and these apply more to some genres than to others (like children's verse for instance).

This change from or elaboration of everyday speech can be related to the constraints of prosodic and structural patterns. In Mangarevan songs and chants, for instance, there is some 'poetic licence' in grammatical usage and syllable length in order to meet the rhythmical demands, and 'words are used figuratively to avoid an extra word or words that would spoil the rhythm of the song'; there is also a specialised vocabulary different from that of prose (Buck, 1938, pp. 385–6). In Fijian heroic poetry special epithets and names are used to fit the constraints of vowel assonance at line ends, and syllables are reduplicated to fit the rhythm; there is even the situation where the poet chooses 'words which he alone understands...to fit his rhythms' (Quain, 1942, p. 16). Similarly in American Indian poetry the poet supplements ordinary vocabulary to secure a desired sound effect, often of vowel assonance, and has poetic licence to make changes by the reduplication of syllables to fit the rhythm and by the use of affixes, elisions or substitutions of sounds (Barnes, 1922, pp. 40, 50). The Tibetan poet can count a final *i* or a diphthongal *u* as syllabic or not depending on which is useful for the metre (Edmonson, 1971, p. 113); and, as has often been pointed out, the famous 'Homeric epithets' serve the function of metre fillers.

It would be a mistake, however, to explain special poetic language *solely* as a result of the pressure of formal requirements. There is also a sense in which special linguistic forms produce a specific effect, by helping to set a frame around a poem, to put it in italics as it were, and to remove it from ordinary life and language.

C. S. Lewis neatly illustrates this in discussing the dual need in 'primary epic' (e.g. the Homeric epics) of a language which is both *familiar* in the sense of being expected, but at the same time not 'colloquial or commonplace'.

> What is the point of having a poet, inspired by the Muse, if he tells the stories just as you or I would have told them? It will be seen that these two demands, taken together, absolutely necessitate a Poetic Diction; that is, a language which is familiar because it is used in every part of a poem, but unfamiliar because it is not used outside poetry. A parallel, from a different sphere, would be turkey and plum pudding on Christmas day; no one is surprised at the menu, but everyone recognises that it is not *ordinary* fare. Another parallel would be the language of a liturgy. Regular church-goers are not surprised by the service – indeed, they know a good deal of it by rote; but it is a language apart. Epic diction, Christmas fare, and the liturgy are all examples of ritual – that is, of something set deliberately apart from daily usage, but wholly familiar within its own sphere.
>
> (Lewis, 1942, pp. 20–1)

In varying forms and degrees, something of this ritual element – familiar yet special – can be found in the language of many poetic genres. Perhaps it is the more important with oral poetry in that the separation from everyday activity must inevitably rely on means other than the interposition of writing.

The literary effectiveness of these special poetic dictions can be manifested in a number of ways. The complex praise names and praise lines of much panegyric poetry – a highly specialised form of diction – give one effective example. The vocabulary used may carry its related imagery, and be felt by poet and audience to convey special depth and meaning. The Eskimo shamans present us with a striking instance of this in their séance language which puts 'a whole new set of images at their disposal' which they can exploit in poetic composition (Freuchen, 1962, p. 277). Similar, if less extreme, instances are not difficult to find – the special use of language by Fijian poet-seers who were thought to have personal rapport with the ancestors from whom they received the words of their songs direct (Quain, 1942, p. 8); or the colourful and effective epithets for heroes which lend additional glamour and dignity to so much heroic verse.

A literary language may have political as well as prosodic implications; for poets set apart from others by rank or elaborate training, like early Irish court poets or the Maori and Ruanda specialists, will not hesitate to cling to their privileged ability to manipulate a special poetic language, removed from that of the common people. This is a consideration by no means confined (as is sometimes assumed) to those literate or urban cultures where we are accustomed to inveigh against mystification by intellectuals, or to the attempted monopoly over learning by Latin, Arabic or Chinese scholars in earlier periods. Here again, as so often, one needs to look beyond the technical and even the purely literary properties of poetry to its social background and political associations.

Special linguistic forms in oral poetry are frequently dubbed 'archaic'. In so far as it is part of the poetic culture that a certain vocabulary or syntax is accepted as suitable for poetry this language may certainly be called 'archaic', if this merely means accepted into poetic tradition. Whether these forms are always 'older' is more doubtful. Often there is no evidence either way. But one needs to be wary of statements by the poets themselves, for whom the claim to have links with 'the past' or 'the ancestors' may fulfil an important social or religious function rather than representing exact linguistic history. When Velema, the Fijian poet, introduces a currently unknown word and claims to have got it directly from communing with the ancestors, is this necessarily to be regarded as an 'archaism'? or rather a new word constructed by Velema on accepted (and thus 'old') patterns to fit his poetic requirements? Certainly this seems to be the case with the specialised Eskimo séance language where the unusual word-combinations and images are long-established yet constantly developed and renewed (Freuchen, 1962, p. 277). Whatever the exact truth, it is clear that the once-held model of 'oral tradition' as necessarily involving the preservation of older strata of language and culture has to be rejected (and *this* implication at least of 'archaism' rejected with it) in favour of a view of poetic conventions where certain established forms fit the *currently accepted* view of the literary language appropriate to particular genres. Poetic selection and development is involved rather than passive acceptance of earlier forms.

The use of imagery and symbolic language in oral poetry cannot here be described in its full complexity; but it is worth giving a few examples to illustrate its variety and remove any notion that oral poetry is either all deeply symbolic or, by contrast, purely superficial and without deeper meaning conveyed through figurative expression.

One of the best known instances of figurative language in western literature is the famous 'Homeric simile' which occurs in the *Odyssey* and *Iliad*. This is how Lattimore translates Homer's evocation of the noise and crash of a battle:

> As when rivers in winter spate running down from the mountains
> Throw together at the meeting of streams the weight of their
>   water
> Out of the great springs behind in the hollow stream-bed,
> And far away in the mountains the shepherd hears their thunder;
> Such, from the coming together of men, was the shock and the
>   shouting.
>
> (*Iliad*, IV, 452–6, trans R. Lattimore, 1951, p. 125)

These marvellous and carefully contrived similes are in one way unique to Homer. But there are parallels in epic elsewhere. Many of these are illustrated in Bowra's discussion of the simile in heroic poetry (Bowra, 1966, pp. 266ff). The Kara-Kirghiz heroic poet conveys Alaman Bet's ferocity and speed:

> He flashed like a whirlwind,
> He made the light of noon like night,
> He made summer into winter,
> And with a thick veil
> He covered the empty steppe
>
> (Quoted in Bowra, 1966, p. 273)

or, by an apt comparison, he gives a vivid impression of the huge size of the warriors of Manas

> As the grass of the wormwood on the steppe
> Passes beyond the sandy wastes,
> As on the other side the grass
> Passes into the waving blue...
>
> (Bowra, 1966, p. 276)

It is not just in epic that elaborate similes occur. Take the poet's description of Griffith in the Sotho panegyric poem devoted to his praises:

> He was like the moon that appears o'er snowy mountains,
> He was like the stars of the morning when they appear,
> Appearing at Makholo, in the mountains,
> Appearing at Kokobe, at 'Malifatjana,
> A rosy dawn that vies with the Pleiades.
>
> (Damane and Sanders, 1974, p. 28)

Other instances too of a shorter and less elaborate nature abound. Something flies 'like the swiftly flying raindrops' in one Ob Ugrian song (Cushing, 1970), a Zuni poem speaks of the blossoming summer clouds in the sky as 'like shimmering flowers' (Curtis, 1907, p. 432), in a Toda song 'You danced as the white moth dances at the lamp niche' (Emeneau, 1966, p. 340), while in Yugoslav poems warriors are 'like burning coals' or 'mountain wolf-packs' and their horses race 'like a star across the cloudless heavens' (Bowra, 1966, p. 268).

Metaphor seems to be even more common than explicit simile.[1] Here again there are many possibilities. Sometimes it is merely a case of metaphorical overtones more explicit in some words than in others, or built up into the stylised 'kennings' familiar from Anglo-Saxon poetry (where the sea is expressed as 'the whale's-road' or 'the gannet's bath', a king as a 'gold-friend' or 'shield of the fighting-men'). Sometimes it is a matter of recurrent metaphors introduced from time to time within a poem as a whole, often based on accepted figurative expressions in the poetic culture. Or consider the last stanza in a recent oral poem by a Somali attacking 'the colonialists'. After a fairly descriptive if emotive account of their deeds so far, the poet Cabdullaahi Quarshe concludes:

> The point on which I end,
> And on which I would terminate my discourse,
> And what I mean by it,
> I will reveal to you:
> The birds which are flying
> And gliding about above
> Will some day tire
> And descend to earth
> (Johnson, 1971, p. 164)

The poet is figuratively predicting the downfall of the colonial powers and their expulsion from Africa.

In oral as in written poetry it is not uncommon for a whole poem to be centred on one sustained metaphor, which gives unity and depth of meaning to the poem. The Gond love poem from Central India addressed to a girl carrying water draws its effectiveness both from the common Gond image of a girl being at her most attractive when balancing the heavy water-pot on her head coming from the well and on the recurrent metaphors of water and thirst

> *Water Girl*
> O Water-girl! with tinkling anklets
> That sounded under the dark mango tree
> O water-girl! your pot of bronze
> Is shining in the setting sun
> Your lips are dry and thirsty as my heart

---

[1] In so far as these can be distinguished.

> O water-girl! with swaying hips
> Go to bring water from the lonely well
> Fear not the dark, I'll go with you
> My heart is thirsty, water-girl.
>
> (Elwin and Hivale, 1944, p. 132)

Perhaps less familiar is the use of metaphor to make personal allusions in actual performance. In the poetic contests held by the Polynesian Tongans before their chiefs in the nineteenth century, much use was made of complicated and insulting metaphors laden with two or three layers of meaning (Luomala, 1955, p. 33).

Some oral poems make their effect without much apparent reliance on figurative language, just through the beauty of evocative description, allied to pleasing formal structure. But in many, metaphorical expression is of the essence, whether one takes the brief one- or two-line miniature *balwo* lyrics of the Somali where the condensed and deeply figurative language must be interpreted by the listener (Andrzejewski, 1967), or the Malay four-line *pantun* where the metaphorical unity of the poem is evinced by the way – as one analyst put it – 'the first pair of lines should represent a poetic thought with its beauty veiled, while the second pair should give the same thought in all its unveiled beauty' (Wilkinson, 1924, p. 51):

> If there's no wick within the lamp,
> To light it toil is thrown away;
> And what reck I of loving looks,
> Except as fuel for love's play.
>
> (Wilkinson and Winstedt, 1957, p. 20)

Perhaps the most striking and elaborate use of metaphor is to be found in Polynesian poetry, where a poem often moves on two levels, the overt one perhaps a description of nature (often attractive in its own right so that many students are content to stop there), the inner one conveying some hidden meaning of love, or insult, or historical claim. The Hawaiian poem *The Kona Sea* appears to be an evocative description of the sea and its coasts – a piece of 'nature poetry' – and in a sense this is true; but it also conveys a hidden meaning of envy and abuse

> Leaf of lehua and noni-tint, the Kona sea,
> Iridescent saffron and red,
> Changeable watered red, peculiar to Kona;
> Red are the uplands, Alaea;
> Ah, 'tis the flame-red stainéd robes of women
> Much tossed by caress or desire.
> The weed-tangled water-way shines like a rope of pearls,
> Dew-pearls that droop the coco leaf,
> The hair of the trees, their long locks –
> Lo, they wilt in the heat of Kailua the deep...
>
> (Emerson, 1909, p. 76)

Besides metaphor, sustained or occasional, other figures can also be found. Personification of the heavenly bodies, especially the sun, moon or morning star, is important in American Indian poetry (Barnes, 1922, p. 47), and in a different way is often a prominent feature in praise poetry. In Southern Bantu panegyric, the hero is often depicted as an animal, thus conveying to the audience his fierceness and bravery. He is a lion, a vulture, a buffalo, a spotted hyena, an untamed bull, or a bird of prey baring its teeth as it swoops in to the attack. Or he is personified as thunder, or the sky, or a storm, or hail riding on horseback. One Sotho hero's military successes are presented as

> The whirlwind caused people to stumble
> The people were swept by the downpour of spears
> The heavy rain of summer, a storm
>
> (Mofokeng, 1945, p. 129)

Another's refusal to submit is likened to an obstinate animal,

> The black and white cow that's rebellious!
> Weave it a rope, it's broken it,
> Its milkers are still lamenting...
>
> (Damane and Sanders, 1974, p. 117)

Hyperbole is also sometimes used (it too appears in Southern Bantu panegyric for instance) and in some poetic traditions irony, often combined with wry humour and understatement, is a common poetic device. This is particularly noticeable in Eskimo poetry where frequent ironic self-depreciation by the poet perhaps represents a simultaneous awareness of man's helplessness before the great world of nature, and his ultimate self-reliance and power as an individual. Even as he composes and sings the Eskimo poet may be ironically commenting on that act:

> ...Perhaps – well.
> My tongue merely joins words
> Into a little song.
> A little mouth,
> Curling downwards at the corners,
> Like a bent twig
> For a kayak rib!
>
> (Rasmussen, 1932, p. 132)

Allusion is not the same as figurative language (and should perhaps be treated under the head of special poetic diction), but it has comparable effects. Which genres and occasions are suitable for a high degree of allusion and which not seems to be culturally defined. It is very common for praise poetry and official ceremonial poetry to be liberally sprinkled with allusions – to historical events, to the glorious lineage of the rulers and officials, to their great deeds, or to the places they or their ancestors travelled through in ancient times. One finds this kind of elaboration in many areas of the world, from the African Yoruba *oriki* or Zulu *izibongo* to the Polynesian praises of their rulers or the learned allusions of the early Irish poets.

Allusion can aid in building up a whole complex of symbolism running through a lengthy poem or group of poems. This is evident in the elaborately symbolic Australian Aboriginal song cycles of Arnhem Land. These are conceived on a vast scale, and, in co-ordination with a whole series of supporting myths allied to social groups and institutions, present a kind of re-enactment through song of the deeds and journeyings of the mythical ancestors in the primaeval 'Dream-time' of the creation of the land and of the natural species and social institutions of the world today. Lines like

> They see the well water rising and bubbling, splashing and
>   murmuring
> Soft cry of the parakeets, cocking their heads from side to side,
>   gently twittering!
> Drying their red breast feathers, like feathered pendants, like
>   nestlings
> They cry into the rays of the sun, watching the sun sinking...
>
>   (Berndt, 1952, p. 170)

have rich overtones connecting with secret rituals, sacred emblems, the divisions of the natural and social world, and the creative actions of the great ancestors of mythical times.

In appreciating these songs – or the symbolism of any foreign poetry – some knowledge of the locally accepted symbolic associations of words and objects is essential. There may be some symbols which have universal reference. But for the most part, local symbolism – whether it is to do with colours, numbers, places, phenomena of the natural world, or social forms – is culturally defined, so that a large part of appreciating the poetry of a foreign people must lie in learning its accepted range of symbols. Again, there is little difference of principle here between written and oral verse.

Another aspect to explore is the mode of expression in oral poetry; whether, for instance, the poem is presented in the third person, as an address to another person or object, a soliloquy in the first person, or a dialogue, and so on. Some writers on the subject suggest that one (or another) of these is the appropriate oral mode, but all occur. Which of them is appropriate to which genre and occasion may be differently defined in different cultures.

Those who think of oral poetry as necessarily communal and non-individual may be surprised to find how much poetry is presented in the first person. In heroic narratives the action is commonly in the third person, but it is also sometimes presented as if the singer/poet was himself the hero, as in Ob Ugrian heroic songs (Cushing, 1970), or in the Ainu epic which is related in the first person (Waley, 1951). The form may use alternate modes, as in Tungus epic in which direct speech is sung in the first person with the connecting third person narrative merely spoken (Hatto, 1970, p. 13). In the *Odyssey* there is the ingenious combination of the hero presenting his own deeds in autobiographical form in one section of the epic, with the rest in the third person narrative, a device also used in recent Yugoslav epic (Lord, 1968a, p. 122). The first person is also used to great effect in the fairly common genre of self-praises (Malay poems, or African panegyrics by Ibo, Sotho and Ankole) as well as in briefer personal poetry. Eskimo poems above all represent a reflective and personal search by the poet in which he explains the difficulties of composition or his own doubts or sufferings

> ...My thought ended in nothing.
> It was like a line
> That all runs out.
>
> Would I ever, I wondered
> Have firm ground to stand on?
> Magic words I mumbled all the way
>
> (Rasmussen, 1932, p. 133)

Poems of address are also common. Panegyric and love poetry are obviously appropriate for second person usage, as are prayers and hymns where the whole poem may be centred round an address to a spirit or deity invoking its presence or help.

> O Kane of the time of overturning,
> Overturn the bright sea-waves
> The high-arching sea-waves...
> ...O Kane send us fish
>
> (Hawaiian. Malo, 1903, p. 207)

The second person form in poetry is familiar enough in written literature, though oral delivery adds peculiar effectiveness to the exploitation of this mode.

Equally, the use of dialogue has much greater effect in oral than in written verse. It is often highly developed. For instance, Mongolian 'conversation songs' developed in the narrow confines of the Mongol tent, where several performers sometimes took part, 'acting' as they sat by facial expression and gestures; at other times all the parts were played by one performer (Bawden, 1977). Again, actual or supposed dialogues between lovers or spouses are a common form for poetic expression. One also meets dialogue in religious and ceremonial contexts – liturgical exchanges between priest and congregation, for instance, or the query/response forms of esoteric groups like the Hawaiian hula dancers. Poetic contests (discussed further in chapter 5, section 3) provide another occasion for the development of poetic dialogue and can reach heights of poetic wit, imagery and inventiveness not easily accessible in written literature.

Direct address to the audience is again peculiarly appropriate to oral literature. It is surprising that it does not occur more often. There are instances like the Yoruba *ijala* chanter's injunction

> Silence! Attention, please! All chattering must stop now
> (Babalọla, 1966, p. 58)

and the common pattern in which a poet introduces into his song a request to his patron(s) for a reward. But much oral poetry – at least as recorded – seems to dispense with such forms of address, which being implied in the whole occasion and the accepted set of expectations may not need to be introduced explicitly into the words of the poem.

5   Performance

The discussion of diction has imperceptibly led from the question of style to that of performance. This aspect is always important in oral literature. It is an element in all oral art, and some of the controversies about style can only be fully understood by reference to performance.

The main means of performance of oral poetry are through the singing, intoning, and spoken voice. It may sometimes appear that most oral poetry is sung. Certainly the singing voice is a very common medium. The impression is also due to the fact that most quotations and anthologies are naturally biased towards the shorter lyrical forms – and these are often sung, in various musical modes. Poems like the Malay *pantun*, Irish patriotic verse, Gond love lyrics, Limba work songs, mediaeval European lyrics and others are indeed sung in fully musical form, often with complex instrumental accompaniment.

But a recitative type of delivery is also common. It is not always easy to interpret remarks by commentators that such and such a piece was 'intoned' or 'chanted' or some such phrase; and more precise descriptions or categorisations are needed. But it is useful to make a general distinction between fully sung forms and the more recitative type, which often seems appropriate for longer pieces where there is interest in the *verbal* rather than the musical content. Examples of the recitative rather than sung form include, for instance, Ainu epic, Akan dirges in Ghana, many *oriki* (praise) and *ijala* (hunting) poems among the Yoruba, chanted sermons in the American South and elsewhere, as well as recitative in classical oratorio or opera which provides a similar contrast with the more melodic arias and choruses. Other cases shade into these – like the chanting of Yugoslav or Modern Cypriot Greek epics – where the melodic element is more marked than in, say, Ainu epic, but which do not have the dominant musical emphasis characteristic among shorter sung lyrics. In such cases there is often some minimal musical accompaniment, usually a stringed instrument like the Yugoslav *gusle*, Homeric lyre, or the orchestra designed to accompany Hausa praises of rulers in Northern Nigeria.

Spoken verse is possibly less frequent, because the heightened delivery common in the performance of any sort of poetry already sets the diction somewhat apart from ordinary speech tones, so that one is constantly using terms like 'intoning' and 'chanting' rather than 'speaking'. But there are some cases where the term 'spoken verse' is more apt than 'chant'. For example, Xhosa panegyric verse can best be described as 'spoken' rather than 'sung' or 'chanted', even though the delivery is definitely 'heightened' compared to ordinary speech; and much the same could be said of many prayers, verses or some items of children's verse.

These three basic modes – sung, chanted and spoken – do not exhaust the possibilities. For one thing some genres of oral literature employ a combination of several of these – a combination given clear definition and meaning by the fact that it is performed aloud. The so-called *chante fable* or prosimetric form is one widespread example of this. Here prose narrative alternates in varying proportions with poetic sung passages; it occurs throughout the Old World. It is found in Chinese literature, in Kazakh epic or in Western European examples like the thirteenth-century *Aucassin et Nicolette*. The degree of versification varies. The mediaeval Chinese *Ballad of the Hidden Dragon* is a particularly sophisticated form, for the musical and rhythmic canons for the poetic form are elaborate and rigorous and have to be mixed in a prescribed manner (Doleželová-Velingerová, 1971). In other instances – like the mediaeval Turkish *Tale of Dede Korkut* – the poetic side is less developed, about two-thirds of the total being in prose, while the Irish *Táin Bó Cúailnge* really reaches the margins of this form, for the prose narrative is predominant and the amount of verse minimal.

There are other variations on the basic principles of delivery. Some genres involve a recitative delivery by a soloist, followed by a sung response by a chorus, as happens in some Ghanaian songs (Nketia, 1962, p. 31); or a sung lyric may be interrupted by several spoken or intoned lines – a regular form in many American popular songs.

One additional mode of poetic performance should be mentioned. This is delivery through drums and similar instruments. Though unfamiliar to most western readers, the remarkable form of literature known as 'drum poetry' is widespread in the tropical forests of Africa (and sometimes elsewhere). In the 'drum literature' of Africa, the instruments do not act as a musical accompaniment to a verbal text, nor do they communicate through a pre-arranged code. Rather, the drum is used to transmit the actual *words* of the poem. Many African languages are highly tonal, so that

tones are as significant as the other prosodic features of the words. The
tone patterns can be directly reproduced on a two- or three-toned drum;
so can the rhythmic patterns. Hence the drumming represents the spoken
utterances in a way intelligible to the listeners, and heard as actual words
and groups of words.

Tonal and rhythmic patterns in themselves would not be enough for full
intelligibility, for many words in any language have the same patterns. But
there are devices in the 'drum language' to overcome ambiguity. This is
partly achieved through having conventional occasions and subjects for
drum communication. The most important device is the stereotyped
phrases used in drum language. These are often longer than the corresponding terms of everyday speech, and this extra length in itself leads
to greater identifiability and uniqueness in terms of the tonal and
rhythmical patterning.

Some of the drum phrases have a poetic ring already removed in
imagery and expression from everyday language. Thus – to take the drum
language of the Kele people in the Congo – the conventional drum phrase
for 'rain' is 'the bad spirit son of spitting cobra and sunshine', for 'money'
'the pieces of metal which arrange palavers', for 'white man' 'red as copper,
spirit from the forest' or 'he enslaves the people, enslaves the people who
remain in the land'. When a message is being sent in drum language, the
tones of these longer phrases are transmitted and understood by recipients
many miles distant through the forests (Carrington, 1949).

The same principle is used in the creation and performance of poetry.
In the West African forest there are panegyrics, historical poems, dirges
and extended poetic proverbs, all commonly performed on the drums. In
one Akan example, from Ghana, the chief is saluted and ushered to his
seat in a panegyric poem performed solely in drum language, on the famous
Akan 'talking drums'

> Chief, you are about to sit down,
> Sit down, great one.
> Sit down, gracious one.
> Chief, you have plenty of seating space.
> Like the great branch, you have spread all over this place.
> Let us crouch before him with swords of state.
> Ruler, the mention of whose name causes great stir,
> Chief, you are like the moon about to emerge.
> Noble ruler to whom we are indebted,
> You are like the moon:
> Your appearance disperses famine.
>
> (Nketia, 1963, p. 147)

Similar instances run to many pages of text when transliterated into the
normal verbal form; and drum poetry is clearly a recognised and valued

genre of poetry with its own conventions in many of the great traditional states of West Africa.

The form is not confined to Africa, though this seems to be its area of greatest development, with the tonal element being predominant. It is also found in parts of the Far East and Oceania, in New Guinea and Indonesia, as well as among some American Indian peoples, with varying combinations of rhythm, stress and tone.

The same principle of transmission can be used by other instruments: so long as an instrument can conventionally represent different tones it can 'speak' the words of a tonal language; even a mono-tone instrument like a gong can convey messages by use of stress and rhythm. Other instruments too are used to convey verbal utterances, such as whistles, horns, bells and flutes. This instrumental mode must be included in any list of the media of poetry, and 'drum poetry' mentioned as one real, if remarkable, category of oral poetry. (For further references see Stern, 1957, Finnegan, 1970, chapter 17.)

In considering 'style' in particular genres of oral poetry, one must take account of the stylistic features of actual performance. Less research has been carried out on this aspect of oral poetry than on the text – perhaps because it is more elusive and in a sense ephemeral – but it seems clear that while an individual performer can exploit and develop the given opportunities according to his ability, there are, often, recognised ways in which particular genres should be delivered, and he is expected in general to conform. This is clear in the case of Yoruba poetic genres; Beier explains that 'Anybody familiar with Yoruba poetry can identify a hunter, a masquerader, or an Ifa priest singing, merely by listening to the style of singing, or quite regardless of the words he is using' (Beier, 1970, p. 25). Similar patterns are noticeable in the tearful sobbing delivery expected of the Akan singer of dirges, the husky and jerky voice in which Tatar heroic poems like *Gold Khan* or *Blood-Marksman* were delivered (Cohn, 1946, p. 11), the even and uninterrupted delivery obligatory in Hawaiian genealogical chants (Beckwith, 1951, p. 35), the special 'growl like a hungry lion' with which Hawaiian hula singers could represent 'the underground passions of the soul' (Emerson, 1909, p. 90), or the forms of voice production thought appropriate for, say, 'folksongs', hillbilly songs or different types of recitations in modern western oral poetry. Though purely musical aspects cannot be pursued here, it must be remembered that specified musical forms and instrumental accompaniment are sometimes a recognised part of the delivery of oral verse.

'Performance' in oral literature has till recently received less attention than the element which oral poetry more closely shares with *written* poetry – the text. But performance can play a crucial part in the actual realisation of this poetry *as literature*: for its full form is more than meaningful words on a piece of paper or in the poet's mind. This is recognised even in traditions where writing has an accepted role. In Greek classical literature, as Stanford has made clear, 'the poetic meaning in the fullest sense often depends [partly]...on the sound of the words' and 'those sounds reach deep into the creative process of the author and into the unconscious mind of the hearer' (1967, pp. 4, 7). In Vedic literature, the remarkable transmission of the *Rgveda* over many centuries was not primarily the preservation of a visually apprehended text, but the correct *performance* of something *heard*: there was great emphasis on the correct pronunciation and recitation. Even in recent western culture – accepted as 'literate' – the element of performance has more significance than is allowed in conservative academic contexts. In any type of oral literature it must be regarded as an essential element of the form.

The nature and reactions of the audience itself must also be remembered. It needs to be borne in mind that the recognised style of delivery may include formal or informal participation by the audience. The act of performance as a whole can comprise not just the solo poet's declamation, but formal rejoinders from one or more of the audience (church liturgy is one obvious example, but there are others); there is also often a specified chorus part, or recognised patterns of interjections, clapping, or even dancing by the audience. Here we may seem to have passed beyond the 'style' of a particular piece or genre of poetry to more extraneous and accidental accompaniments. But this participation by the audience forms a recognised aspect of the whole occasion of the performance – part of the accepted stylistic conventions – and is integral to the artistic style of a given oral poem; it is a pity that so many bare texts have appeared which give no information on such aspects. Though clearly not present in all cases, audience participation may play a far greater part in oral poetry than is indicated in most published texts.

Besides the general conventions about overall mode of delivery – like the spoken, sung or instrumental modes – or the type of audience participation thought suitable, there are often detailed conventions that affect the style of performance and the opportunities open to a performer as he delivers the poem.

For instance, some oral poetry is expected to be delivered very fast. This is so in a number of Southern Bantu praise poems. Grant describes a well-known Zulu praiser whom he heard in the 1920s: the poet worked himself up to a high pitch of fervour with his face lifted up, shaking his shield and stick violently. As he got more and more excited his voice became louder, his gestures more dramatic, and he leaped in the air while praises poured from his lips – till at last he stopped, exhausted. Again, Cook describes the recitation of Swazi praise poems (*izibongo*)

The praises were not recited in an ordinary voice, but were called out at the top of the voice in as rapid a manner as possible. Indeed, so rapidly are these *izibongo* called out that, from habit, those who know them are unable to say them slowly, and to write them down entails countless repetitions. Anyone who is not thoroughly familiar with a *sibongo* cannot possibly understand it, and even to a Swazi it is impossible to understand it the first time he hears it.

(Cook, 1931, pp. 183–4)

Something of the same rapidity applies in Yugoslav oral epic poetry. In Lord and Parry's recording of the famous Avdo Mededović, his words are poured out with amazing speed and fluency, and Lord estimates that this is not unusual, for Yugoslav bards often sing 'at the rate of from ten to twenty ten-syllable lines a minute' (Lord, 1968a, p. 17).

By contrast, other kinds of oral poetry may be delivered much more slowly. The famous Malay *pantun* is an example. Ingenious, witty and highly compressed, the genre makes great demands of understanding and un-ravelling from its audience and might seem an obviously *written* form, depending essentially on the lengthy and selfconscious reflection said to be typical of the appreciation of written literature. And yet it has developed as an oral form. The puzzle is largely resolved when one discovers that the *pantun* is sung very slowly, with a refrain, and that the form as delivered is precisely suited to an oral rather than a written mode. As Wilkinson, one of the great authorities on Malay literature, writes

To an English reader the quatrains seem overcrowded with meaning; they force him continually to stop and think. But the *pantun* is not intended to be read. Slowly sung, with a long chorus or refrain after each line, it gains in merit by occupying the mind during the chorus instead of being dismissed as too transparent in its meaning. A verse, written to be read and to carry its meaning on its surface, would not stand the test of *pantun*-singing; it would make the chorus intolerably monotonous. This fact again makes it difficult to reproduce the attractiveness of the Malay quatrain through the medium of a foreign language and in the plain black-and-white of a printed page.

(Wilkinson, 1924, p. 53)

Much the same applies to the even more compressed Somali *balwo*, a two-line poem of the 'miniature' genre characterised by obscure language and condensed imagery. These too were commonly delivered slowly, so that the audience had time to take them in. The poems were also short enough to be memorised, so that the very complexity of the metaphorical expression would make it all the more effective in repeated performances on different occasions to an increasingly appreciative audience.

The emotional *rapport* built up by the performer with his audience can also play an important part. With a *written* piece stylistic conventions and meaning must be assessed on the basis of the verbal text. But with oral poetry it makes a real difference whether a poem is normally delivered in, say, a remote and uplifted style, as of a seer receiving his words direct from divine inspiration and aware of his spiritual source rather than his temporal audience; or as part of a gay and festive occasion, when the mood of delivery is likely to match that of the audience; or in an atmosphere of mourning, when the grief-laden emotion of the performer forms an expected quality of his performance and his poem. The text alone does not necessarily indicate this. Sotho praise poems, for instance, are obviously in high-flown and evocative language, but it is only from a description of their actual delivery and reception that one realises the full impact of the praiser's words:

> Listening to his exalted language, with its pulsating rhythms and its evocation of a glorious past, many of his followers would weep with emotion; and when at last he had stabbed the ground with his spear, there would be deafening shouts and whistles from the men, and long, trilling ululations from the women.

(Damane and Sanders, 1974, pp. 26–7)

Again, merely categorising a particular form as a 'sermon', or analysing its textual content, may give no clue to the conditions of actual delivery. This may be in an atmosphere of revivalist fervour, with intense audience participation, where some composer/performers are peculiarly effective, but all can be expected to achieve something of this impact and to satisfy (and play on) audience expectations – an atmosphere vividly conveyed in Rosenberg's study of chanted sermons in the American South (1970).

The amount of dramatisation expected is another thing that collectors rarely tell us about, though it may radically affect the realisation of oral poetry in ways which, in *written* literature, would have to be achieved through the verbal text alone. Some poems are cast in dialogue form, with more than one performer, and this characteristic might seem part of the formal structure. But a comparable effect can be obtained by the actual form of delivery, with dramatic characterisation created by one accomplished performer; indeed certain poems, like the Mongol 'conversation songs' can appear in either form. The nature of the performer's characterisation, too, can affect what the poem itself conveys. A convention that, whatever the detailed wording, the adventures of heroes in a narrative poem should be portrayed in a style that brings them close to everyday humanity is obviously different from one in which – as in some recent Yugoslav oral epics – the atmosphere is that of a remote but glorious past and the heroes shown through the poet's uplifted delivery as beyond ordinary mortals. Such differences may not emerge from the verbal text, yet clearly affect its impact and poetic nature.

Beyond the conventions of performance appropriate to particular genres, one also needs to ask what opportunities are open to individual performers. To quote Becker again

> Though standardized, conventions are seldom rigid and unchanging. They do not specify an inviolate set of rules everyone must refer to in settling questions of what to do. Even where the directions seem quite specific, they leave much unsettled which gets resolved by reference to customary modes of interpretation on the one hand and by negotiation on the other.
>
> (Becker, 1974, p. 771)

In some respects it is the accepted conventions which sometimes allow – even encourage – a certain freedom in the performer. There may be latitude over the verbal structuring of the piece during performance to the extent that 'improvisation' or 'original composition' within established conventions become more appropriate terms than the re-rendering or a variant of a known piece. This extreme is most often reached in the longer narrative poems, where composition-in-performance has been especially noted. But conventional variation in performance takes other forms too. Even in that part of the Anglo-American tradition of oral poetry where stress tends to be laid rather on exact repetition than on verbal originality, individual interpretation in *performance* has often been commented on. This is partly *musical* variation – often forgotten in the concentration on verbal texts – but it is also often accepted that a performer can inflect the message or atmosphere of a poem by his own dramatisation, speed, singing style, pauses, rhythmic movement, gestures, facial expression and so on. This individual style can obviously impart a unique quality to the poem as actually delivered, even where performer and audience both stress the importance of 'tradition' in their articulate accounts of what is involved. The well-known American ballad singer Almeda Riddle always emphasised that her songs were 'old' and 'authentic', a claim accepted by professional folklorists. But she added in performance much that was her own. This was partly verbal – as she said 'It's scarcely ever, if you sing a song from memory, that you'll sing it exactly word for word each time' – but she also used musical variations to bring out the meaning of the story, so that the slightly changing tune matched the changing speech as she moved from stanza to stanza (Abrahams, 1970, pp. 117, 162). Such individual contributions may be both accepted and valued by audiences, but are not always explicit in the local views of poetic creativity and performance. Abrahams and Foss sum up their discussion in *Anglo-American Folksong Style* by concluding that 'In many cases, these variables will exist below the threshold of perception for both the singer and his audience; that is, he may not be conscious of his variance. The extent of variation possible without the singer's awareness seems fairly high' (Abrahams and Foss, 1968, p. 14).

It is important to remember these potentialities in trying to draw conclusions about the style of any piece of oral poetry from its written text.
With *oral* poetry, qualities like emotional atmosphere, dramatic suspense,
characterisation, or the effective build-up through repeated units which
are identical and monotonous in the verbal text but not in delivery – these
can be conveyed not just in the *words* but in their performance. So
performers (and composers not themselves performers of their own poetry)
have access to a dimension in oral poetry in which they can call on individual
interpretation both within accepted conventions and, on occasion, in trying
out how far the local audience will accept innovation.

To ignore this dimension is to ignore a large part of style at the same
time as its poetic and individual quality. Paredes perhaps exaggerates the
difference between written and what he calls 'folk' literature, but makes
a real point about the importance of performance when he writes

> Here of course is a fundamental difference between folk and sophis-
> ticated literature. Folk literature is always a vehicle for the performer,
> who supplies a feeling of immediacy – of passion and power –
> through his own performance. This is another reason why folk
> literature has never felt the need for the striking or the original. It
> is when written literature gets farther and farther away from the
> spoken word that we must invent devices to hold the reader's atten-
> tion, to excite his emotions and his imagination, all with those little
> black marks upon a piece of paper. In fiction we move toward new
> narrative techniques, seeking to gain the sense of immediacy that was
> lost when the written word took the place of the living narrator, who
> acted as well as narrated...In sophisticated poetry...the tendency
> is toward more and more subtle and individualized modes of expres-
> sion once poetry has ceased to be performance and has become an
> act of private communication between poet and reader. In folk
> poetry, not only does the performer have the task of bringing the
> 'part' assigned him to temporary life, but he can re-create the text
> at will. In the end, it is the performer who is the poet – for the brief
> moment that he performs.
>
> (Paredes, 1964, p. 225)

6 Is there a special oral style?

Is there a special style peculiar to *oral* literature (in this instance, to oral
poetry)? Some scholars think there is. One idea relates to the claimed
'dreamlike' or 'unconscious' style of oral literature. Other suggestions
concern the formal properties of style, in particular the characteristic of
repetition.

First, then, is oral poetry characterised by a deeply symbolic style, produced in some unconscious and dreamlike way by the oral artist? In any
obvious sense, the answer must surely be no. Symbolism is often important

in oral poetry, but it takes different forms and is handled in different ways in different genres and cultures. Its treatment is neither uniform across the various forms of oral art nor is it in essence distinct from uses of symbolism in written literature. It cannot be fully subsumed or explained under large headings like 'Freudian symbols', 'Jungian archetypes' or 'binary structures'; such concepts, even if illuminating in some cases, cannot encompass the vast variety, the ingenuity and the imaginative artistry of oral art as a whole – at least not without stretching the terms so far that they lose all explanatory or heuristic value.

The idea that oral artists, unlike users of written media, compose 'unconsciously', may seem to have more truth. Certainly, one mark of oral poetry is that it is ephemeral and cannot involve the long-considered composition and drastic revision, blue pencil in hand, possible for the composer of written verse. This means that inconsistencies may not be ironed out in revision in an oral poem. This oral background is often given as the explanation for apparent mistakes in, say, the *Iliad* where 'Homer nodded' and represented as still alive a hero who had been killed earlier in the epic. Again, well-known epithets are sometimes applied automatically to inappropriate objects in a way which, *perhaps*, the literate poet might have modified in revision. Thus the stock epithet 'holy' is applied to Russia even by a Turkish Sultan planning an attack on it (Bowra, 1966, p. 239); and a Gaelic oral poem has the self-contradictory description 'brown-haired girl of the fair hair' – self-contradictory, that is, to the reflective *reader* (Ross, 1959, p. 3). Similar instances of inconsistent names and actions or minor contradictions often occur in oral verse, and might have been eliminated at the revision stage in a written work (see e.g. Lord, 1968a, pp. 94–5, 103).

But this can be over-stressed. As we saw in the last chapter, long-considered and deliberate composition before the moment of performance certainly occurs in some instances of oral poetry. It is hard to see the Somali poet's handling of the alliterative rigours of his medium or the Gilbertese poet's wrestling with the demands of exact and beautiful wording as a type of 'unconscious' composition. Certainly the further implications sometimes inherent in this approach – the idea of the 'typical' oral artist as 'primaeval' and 'natural' man, who acts unconsciously and through 'nature' rather than art – are highly questionable (see chapter 2 above). The related idea that some oral art is merely 'traditional' in the sense of coming unchanged from the primaeval past and handed on automatically to passive recipients of the tradition, I have queried already. (See also chapter 5 on transmission.)

Generalisations in terms of formal style look more promising. Here the main characteristic emphasised by analysts is *repetition* in its various manifestations.

Some scholars unequivocally regard repetition (including parallelism and formulaic expression) as characteristic of oral literature. Sometimes it is even the yardstick by which oral can definitively be distinguished from written literature. Boas put the argument in broad terms: 'The investigation of primitive narrative as well as of poetry proves that repetition, particularly rhythmic repetition, is a fundamental trait.' He went on to include parallelism as well, in the sense of 'rhythmic repetition of the same or similar elements' (Boas, 1925, pp. 329, 332). Similar points have been made by a number of scholars, most recently in the article by Bennison Gray on 'Repetition in oral literature', explicitly following up and refining Boas's comments. Gray asserts that 'repetition is prevalent in folk and primitive literatures because these are both oral literatures and repetition is a direct consequence of their oral nature' (Gray, 1971, p. 290). The same general line has been taken by many writers, from the recent analysis of Anglo-American folksong style by Abrahams and Foss (1968, e.g. pp. 10–11, 65) to the earlier influential writing of the Danish folklorist Olrik who saw *Repetition* as one of the primary 'epic laws' which determine the style of oral literature.

One particular type of repetition, parallelism, has also come in for much attention, and this too has seemed to be typical of unwritten forms and (sometimes) of the kind of culture assumed to go with such forms. Gonda, for instance, regards parallelisms as characteristic of 'archaic and "primitive" symmetrical compositions' (1959, p. 49), and others have taken extensive parallelism as a sign of oral rather than written composition (see e.g. discussion in Whallon, 1969, chapter 5). 'The habit', writes Buchan in the context of Scottish ballads, 'of thinking in balances, antitheses, appositions and parallelisms is intrinsic to the oral mind' (Buchan, 1972, p. 88).

The 'oral-formulaic school' also have made authoritative-sounding pronouncements about differences in style between oral and written compositions. Here it is only necessary to recall that a highly 'formulaic' style – consisting, that is, solely or largely of repeated 'formulae' – is thought typical of *oral* style, indeed the yardstick by which one can differentiate the radically different modes of oral from written composition, as in Magoun's much-cited assertions: 'Oral poetry, it may safely be said, is composed entirely of formulae, large or small, while lettered poetry is never formulaic' and 'The characteristic feature of all orally composed poetry is its totally formulaic character' (Magoun in Nicholson, 1971, p. 190).

This kind of statement is often assumed to embody unquestioned conclusions about the style of all oral literature. Indeed the truth of Parry's 'unanswerable and unassailable proof that Iliad and Odyssey belong to the class of oral literatures', because of their use of repeated formulae, has been claimed as absolute: to abide 'almost as surely as Euclid's demonstrations abide' (Carpenter, 1958, p. 6).

Repetition in some form *is* a characteristic of oral
of phrases, lines or verses; the use of parallelisms;
these are common in oral poetry. Analysing this kind
previous approach in terms of a supposed 'dreamlik
relatively straightforward proceeding; and the import
is borne out by a plenitude of comments and examples fr
students of oral literature all over the world.

The emphasis on repetition in oral literature makes s
too. *Oral* poetry – like anything transmitted through an or   ..edium – is
necessarily ephemeral. Once said, it cannot, for that performance anyway,
be recaptured. Repetition has real point in such circumstances: it makes
it easier for the audience to grasp what has been said and gives the speaker/
singer confidence that it has understood the message he is trying to communicate. This advantage is well known to those who have taught through
the permanent medium of the written word on the one hand, and the
ephemeral media of radio and television on the other. In the second case,
as with oral literature and orally-delivered lectures (or sermons), more
repetition is necessary to ensure that comprehension is complete. Similar
comments have been made about compositions in mediaeval Europe intended for oral delivery. Crosby explains how repetition is a basic feature
of such compositions. She points to the constant repetitions of words,
phrases, situations, and ideas, and to the use of repeated introductory
phrases, commonplaces and linking passages. 'The mediaeval listeners
could not glance back a few pages if they lost track of the story for a moment.
They must then have been grateful for the often recurring lines that told
them just what had happened and what was coming next' (Crosby, 1936,
p. 107). Similar points have been made for much oral epic poetry, or for
modern 'folksong' which, unlike written literature, cannot be reflected on
at leisure: 'The oral creator or performer...is obliged to use expression
which is immediately understandable because of the oral nature of his
presentation and the limitations which this places upon his audience...Oral
composition will gravitate towards conventional expression and repetitive expression because they are more immediately understandable and
retainable' (Abrahams and Foss, 1968, p. 10).

From the point of view of audience-participation too, repetition can be
important. In antiphonal forms, refrains, choruses or the direct repetition
of a leader's lines, repetition offers an opportunity for an audience to take
part with ease in the act of performance, to a degree not possible without
some measure of repetition.

Finally, there is the question of composition. As Lord and Parry have
shown, a stock of 'ready made formulae' at the disposal of the oral poet
makes his simultaneous composition-in-performance feasible. Without

pause for thought, he can produce a rapid and fluent perfor-
relying on his stock of repeated formulae, rather than on word-
or-word memorisation or long-drawn-out deliberation.

It is therefore not surprising that repetition is so widely reported – and
that it may be more extensive than is realised: just because the same degree
of repetition would be tedious and inappropriate in *written* form, the
amount of repetition in actual performance may not be fully represented
in many written texts which purport to record it.

All this is probably true, and pertinent to the question of oral style. But
to go on to take the occurrence, or a specific proportion, of repetition as
a touchstone for differentiating between 'oral' and 'written' styles is not
so easy. The hope for a precise generalisation about the nature of oral style
of the kind that Magoun, Parry and others have envisaged is, in my
opinion, bound to be disappointed.

First, the concept of repetition is itself too wide. When one considers its
many manifestations it turns out often to mean little more than recurrent
patterns. If one tries to make it more precise (as in the repetition of
incidents only, or *particular* types of stylistic repetition) the theory loses its
apparent universality and thus its appeal. The frequent recurrence of
'formulae' – or their appearance in measurable numbers – used to be taken
as a sufficient condition for calling a composition 'oral'; but 'formulaic'
literary style is equally possible in written literature. (And even that assumes
that one can define and count 'formulae' precisely in the first place.)
Similarly, composition in relatively independent and separate lines, with
little enjambement, *may* be a feature of some oral art. But it does not seem
to be confined to it, and seems to be a property identifiable in some kinds
of oral art but not all; moreover it is difficult to decide on the exact line
divisions in some oral poetry.

The same general point applies to arguments in terms of parallelism or
of the paratactic juxtaposition and duplication of incidents. So far as the
presentation of incidents goes – the aspect much stressed by Olrik and by
Gray (1971) – this seems to be relevant for prose narrative and perhaps for
narrative poetry, rather than for oral poetry generally. Parallelism seems
at first sight a more useful criterion. Certainly the feature is of wide
occurrence, and is also appropriate to oral communication. But whether
this makes it a distinctive sign of oral performance or oral composition
is more doubtful – even allowing for abstract speculations about 'binary
structures' or *la pensée sauvage*. There are, after all, clear literary effects in
parallelism which apply to written as well as oral verse. Whallon put this
well in his discussion of parallelism in Old Testament poetry; he refuses
to explain it primarily in utilitarian terms: its use for antiphonal singing
by massed choirs or as an aid to memory. Instead he sees its development
as essentially 'for its own impressive elegance' (Whallon, 1969, p. 153).

This is perhaps the main point. Repetition – whether as parallelism, or in phrases called 'formulae' – has great *literary* and aesthetic effect. The recurrent familiar ring of the Homeric epithet is more than a useful device aiding the poet to compose or the audience to translate a message: it is a beautiful and evocative element in Homeric poetry, the more so for its repeated recurrence. The use of repetition in oral poetry is not just a utilitarian tool, but something which lies at the heart of all poetry. It is one of the main criteria by which we tend to distinguish poetry from prose, in both familiar and unfamiliar cultural traditions. It may well be that repetition gives peculiar pleasure and artistic effectiveness in *oral* poetry, but it is a common device of poetic expression. The 'aesthetics of regularity' can be found in all poetry, oral as well as written.

So it is hard to envisage any precise formulation by which this basic constituent of poetry can be used as a yardstick specifically to differentiate 'oral' style. In so far as it is particularly stressed in oral poetry, one can only describe this additional emphasis in general and impressionistic terms. When one tries to make it precise (or quantifiable) the plausibility of the theory vanishes. The concept of repetition does not subsume *all* oral poetry in style or content – except in a sense so wide that the concept becomes meaningless – nor is it excluded in written poetry. (Indeed, even the additional effectiveness given to repetition in oral poetry by performance may not be as clear a difference as at first appears; for even in our highly literate culture, there are strong oral overtones of performance and auditory expression in 'written' poetry.) Even the admitted effectiveness of repetition in the oral situation must not be exaggerated: it is not universal in the sense of being essential to comprehension. Other means can be used to cope with the ephemeral nature of the oral medium, like the slow delivery of difficult and compressed poetry or the process of memorisation and reflection on known pieces. And for that matter a piece may not be *intended* to be immediately or universally comprehensible.

For some writers the appeal of this theory of the primary and special significance of repetition in oral art lies in the overtones with which it is endowed. It is worth mentioning these briefly, if only to make them explicit.

'Repetition' is sometimes seen as part of the primaeval nature of 'primitive man' – the supposed typical bearer of the oral tradition. According to Gonda (1959) primitive man is fundamentally archaising, averse to change, dependent on the constant re-enactment and repetition of old rituals. This comes out in the ritualistic repetition characteristic of his literature, of which the most natural and primaeval form is as spells and charms – where repetition has magical import. Not all writers take as explicit a line as Gonda, but similar overtones are felt in many comments about the power of tradition, the unchanging nature of 'folk poetry', or the supposed childish (and therefore (sic) 'primitive') liking for repetition. Notopoulos is clear, in his discussion of the 'facts of life about oral poetry', that 'the society which gives birth to oral poetry is characterized by traditional fixed ways in all aspects of its life' (Notopoulos, 1964, pp. 50, 51). It is against this assumed background that 'repetition' is sometimes interpreted. It is seen as one of the 'epic laws of folk narrative' (Olrik, trans. 1965), while 'devices of elemental repetition' are discovered by Leonard in the Gilgamesh epic and Fijian heroic poetry alike (in Quain, 1942, p. vii), and Abrahams and Foss in their recent book on Anglo-American folksong style can link repetition in oral literature with the generalization that 'folk society and folk art do not accept, reflect, or value change' (Abrahams and Foss, 1968, p. 11).

Apparent support is lent to theories about repetition in oral poetry by assumptions of this sort. It is therefore worth reiterating the point made earlier, that there is little evidence that oral poetry always or even most typically occurs in the 'changeless' 'tradition-bound' context often implied, and that if the theory about the significance of repetition is to be proved valid it must rely on exact research rather than assumptions of this kind.

The exact significance of repetition in oral poetry is not, therefore, clear. In general, it certainly does appear – on a rather impressionistic and often ambiguous basis – to be extremely common, probably for the commonsense reasons often suggested, and this is an interesting aspect of oral style. But any more precise theory must be based on further research – and even then is likely to elucidate specific and limited patterns, and not to support a generalisation pertaining to *all* oral literature.

This may be a disappointment to those eager for large generalisations or abstract models applicable across a very wide field; but it is not surprising. If the line between oral and written cannot be drawn with any precision, why should there be two distinct styles, differentiated by a single crucial feature? A written piece is often successfully turned into an oral one in the sense that it can be read and declaimed and owe some of its circulation to oral means. This is surely true of much of the better known written poetry in English. Similarly, some oral verse has been written down and now appeals to a literate audience through the printed page – lacking every aspect of performance, admittedly, and thus different from its original realisation, but still not posing any insuperable barrier or unmistakeable signal by its verbal style to the reader.

In any case, it would be surprising if any one generalisation about style were to be valid for all the different genres of oral poetry. On the contrary, it is clear from a study of the style of oral (as of written) poetry that it is *variety* of stylistic features that differentiates genres from each other both within and between cultures. One would not expect one single feature of style to characterise official ceremonial poetry, children's impromptu rhymes, a condensed love lyric, a genealogical poem or a work song – still less a single feature that would distinguish all these from their written counterparts.

The reality is far more interesting than if there were one special oral style. In differing cultures and among individual composers and performers there is a wide range of different stylistic possibilities that provide both constraints and opportunities for clothing the human imagination in what are recognised as beautiful and appropriate poetic forms. Any poet operates with a set of agreed local conventions within which he can operate, communicate with his audience, and even, on occasion, innovate. But he is not rigidly programmed to follow one universal form of 'oral style'.

7 Conclusion

A number of patterns in oral poetry have been enumerated in this chapter – prosodic, stylistic, structural and those concerning delivery and performance. This list is not complete, but can serve as an indication of the wide variety of features which in a given culture help to delimit particular genres of poetry.

Awareness of these patterns throws additional light on the questions about composition discussed in the last chapter. For an oral composer is not just affected by the factors usually mentioned under the head of 'oral composition': – the various 'formulae' of phrase, theme or incident, with, perhaps, the influence of audience or occasion. His performance is also shaped by the stylistic and performative aspects discussed in this chapter. These are both constraints and opportunities: he is bound by recognised patterns of prosody, style, structure and so on, but also has them as tools at his disposal, providing an opportunity to produce his own unique composition; he can even, at times, modify them according to his individual genius.

To discuss oral composition without taking account of these stylistic constraints and opportunities, and to concentrate merely on 'oral-formulaic' analysis, is to miss much of what is important in shaping the compositions of individual poets, or of recognised genres.

The search for one touchstone of 'oral style' thus turns out to be fruitless. But in conclusion I emphasise again the importance of *performance* in oral art. This, if anything, is what distinguishes it from written forms, and it is here, *as well as* in the bare text, that one must look for the stylistic characteristics of a genre of poem or an individual poet's art. It is also in the aspect of performance, in addition to the textual and content factors, that one can find the constraints and opportunities according to which an individual poet produces his compositions and his audience appreciates them.

5

Transmission, distribution and publication

The question of how oral literature reaches its patrons can never be a mere secondary matter; for its very existence depends on its realisation through verbal delivery. Certain forms can perhaps be said to be retained purely in someone's mind, through memorisation, but there must be some opportunity for him to pass this on through verbal recitation: otherwise the piece loses its existence and dies with him. This is not the case with written literature where a piece may remain in existence in written form over long periods of time and be rediscovered generations or centuries later. With written literature we can therefore partially divorce discussion of composition and content from the details of how it is/was transmitted and reached its various audiences. With unwritten literature these questions are central topics, intimately related to composition, content and authorship.

There is a further reason why the 'transmission' of oral literature needs special consideration. This is the crucial part this concept plays in the studies of many scholars concerned with oral literature, in particular the 'folklorists'. For them 'oral transmission' is not only the central focus of much of their interest, but is often taken to be the most important defining characteristic of 'folk literature'. Unless it undergoes at some point the process of verbal handing on through oral transmission a poem will not qualify as 'folk poetry' (see e.g. Boswell and Reaver, 1969, chapter 1; Dundes, 1965, p. 1ff; Utley in Dundes, 1965, pp. 8ff; Dorson, 1972, pp. 17 and 19). Some folklorists admit that this narrow definition must surely exclude some varieties of 'oral literature' (recently composed poems, for instance, which even if 'oral' in their composition and performance do not 'sink into tradition' or 'pass into general oral currency'). But the folklorists' delimitation of 'literature orally transmitted' is often assumed to cover the whole field of oral literature – or anyway the main field of interest to the scholar – and this aspect thus demands attention. The concept of 'oral transmission' is therefore inevitably of central importance.

Apart from the theoretical reasons for an interest in transmission and distribution, one is forced to notice such questions because of some of the striking facts discovered about the travels and distribution of some oral poetry. Far from only having an ephemeral and local existence through particular performances to a personal audience, certain oral forms are found in continuing and relatively unchanged existence over vast areas of the world and through long periods of time; and since the literature is oral, it has seemed reasonable to suppose that the prime vehicle for this transmission is, equally, oral.

Before entering into the various controversies about the nature and significance of oral transmission, it may be helpful to consider briefly some well-known instances of apparently lengthy oral transmission over space and time. These instances will be referred to later in the chapter in the context of the various theories and controversies that surround the subject of 'oral transmission'.

1 Oral transmission over space and time: some striking cases

Perhaps the most striking and well documented cases are the stories so often termed 'folktales', that crop up throughout the centuries and throughout the continents in near-identical form – so far as plot and motif go.[1] For many of these tales 'life-histories' of their transmission have been traced, and there is massive documentation of the occurrence of basic plots and motifs (notably in Thompson, 1955–8).

Less evidence of this kind has been collected for oral poetry – understandably more resistant to the kind of measurement and delimitation that is (arguably) possible for the content of prose stories. But there are still some remarkable instances of wide and lengthy transmission.

One example is that of the Gésar epic cycle. This tells the tale of Gésar or Kesar, the king of a legendary land named Glin. It is known in Central Asia, throughout Tibet, Mongolia and parts of China. The basic incidents of this long epic are the same throughout this vast area and apparently date back several centuries at least (Stein, 1959).

The Vedic literature of India provides an even more striking example of lengthy transmission. The *Rgveda* itself is said to have been composed around 1500–1000 B.C. and to have been handed down by oral tradition for centuries. The religious and liturgical nature of the text has, it seems, made verbal memorisation imperative, and it is claimed that even if all written versions were to be lost 'a great portion of it could be recalled out of the memory of the scholars and reciters' (Winternitz, I, 1927, p. 34) and 'the text could be restored at once with complete accuracy' (Chadwick, II, 1936, p. 463). This, if true, clearly represents an extraordinary emphasis on memory in Indian culture – for the *Rgveda* runs to about 40,000 lines (it consists of 10 books including in all over 1,000 hymns) – and would comprise a most remarkable instance of lengthy oral transmission over space and time.

[1] In what sense this makes them identical as *literature* is another question. For a critique of this 'historical-geographical' approach to the study of stories, see Finnegan, 1970, pp. 320ff.

If there is inevitably some speculation about the early history of the Vedic transmission, the evidence on certain more recent cases is much more solid. Here the best documented case is that of the transmission of certain English and Scottish ballads to America and Australia. The time involved is shorter than that claimed for the Vedic instance – centuries rather than millennia – but the facts are striking enough. Over a period of up to 300 years, popular ballads were handed on from generation to generation from the period when they were first brought out by immigrants from the British Isles, to the date in the twentieth century when they were noted and recorded by collectors. Some of the ballads arrived with later waves of immigrants and had a shorter (apparently) independent existence, but a number go back to the date when European immigrants first began to settle in America.

One of the best-known ballads is *Barbara Allen.* Here are two versions, the first, from a British source, dating back to at least the first half of the eighteenth century, and represented in Child's classic collection of *The English and Scottish Popular Ballads* (no. 84). The second is one of the many variants collected by Sharp in the Appalachian Mountains of the American South in the early twentieth century, apparently derived from the first settlers in the area over many generations of oral tradition.

BRITISH, EIGHTEENTH CENTURY

1 In Scarlet Town, where I was bound,
   There was a fair maid dwelling,
   Whom I had chosen to be my own,
   And her name it was Barbara Allen.

2 All in the merry month of May,
   When green leaves they was springing,
   This young man on his death-bed lay,
   For the love of Barbara Allen.

3 He sent his man unto her then,
   To the town where she was dwelling:
   'You must come to my master dear,
   If your name be Barbara Allen.

4 'For death is printed in his face,
   And sorrow's in him dwelling,
   And you must come to my master dear,
   If your name be Barbara Allen.'

5 'If death be printed in his face,
   And sorrow's in him dwelling,
   Then little better shall he be
   For bonny Barbara Allen.'

6 So slowly, slowly she got up,
   And so slowly she came to him.
   And all she said when she came there,
   Young man, I think you are a dying.

AMERICAN, TWENTIETH CENTURY

1 All in the month, the month of May,
   The green buds they were swelling,
   They swelled till all pretty birds chose their mates
   And Barbary her Sweet William.

2 He sent a letter through the town
   To Barbary Allen's dwelling,
   Saying: Here's a young man sick and he sends for you,
   For you to come and see him.

3 She walked in, she walked in,
   She placed her eyes upon him.
   The very first word that she said to him:
   Young man, I think you're dying.

4 I know I'm sick and very sick,
   And sorrow it is dwelling with me.
   No better, no better I never will be
   Until I get Barbary Allen.

5 I know you're sick and very sick,
   And sorrow it is dwelling with you.
   No better, no better you never will be,
   For you'll never get Barbary Allen.

7 He turned his face unto her then:
'If you be Barbara Allen,
My dear,' said he, 'come pitty me,
As on my death-bed I am lying.'

8 'If on your death-bed you be lying,
What is that to Barbara Allen?
I cannot keep you from [your] death;
So farewell,' said Barbara Allen.

9 He turnd his face unto the wall,
And death came creeping to him:
'Then adieu, adieu, and adieu to all,
And adieu to Barbara Allen!'

10 And as she was walking on a day,
She heard the bell a ringing,
And it did seem to ring to her
'Unworthy Barbara Allen.'

11 She turnd herself round about,
And she spy'd the corps a coming:
'Lay down, lay down the corps of clay,
That I may look upon him.'

12 And all the while she looked on,
So loudly she lay laughing,
While all her friends cry'd [out] amain,
'Unworthy Barbara Allen!'

13 When he was dead, and laid in grave,
Then death came creeping to she:
'O mother, mother, make my bed,
For his death hath quite undone me.'

14 'A hard-hearted creature that I was,
To slight one that lovd me so dearly:
I wish I had been more kinder to him,
The time of his life when he was near me.'

15 So this maid she then did dye,
And desired to be buried by him,
And repented her self before she dy'd,
That ever she did deny him.

(Child, 1957, II, pp. 277–8)

6 He turned his pale face to the wall,
He burst out a-crying,
Saying: Adieu, adieu to the ladies all around,
Farewell to Barbary Allen.

7 Don't you remember last Saturday night
When I were at your tavern,
You swang you treated the ladies all around,
You slighted Barbary Allen.

8 She rode, she rode a mile from town
The small birds they were singing,
They sung so loud, they sung so swift,
Hard-hearted Barbary Allen.

9 She looked East, she looked West,
She saw the cold corpse coming,
Saying: Lay him down on this cold ground
And let me look upon him.

10 The more she looked the more she mourned
Till she burst out a-crying,
Saying: I could have saved this young man's life
If I'd a-tried my true endeavour.

11 O mother, O mother, O fix my bed,
Go fix it long and narrow.
Sweet William he died for me to-day,
And I'll die for him tomorrow.

12 O father, O father, go dig my grave,
Go dig it deep and narrow.
Sweet William he died for me to-day,
AndI'll die for him tomorrow.

13 They buried Sweet William in the old churchyard
And Barbary close by the side of him.
At the head of Sweet William's grave
there sprung a red rose
And Barbary Allen's was a briar.

14 They grew, they grew to the top of the church
And they could not grow any higher.
They leaned and tied in a true lover's knot
And the rose hanged on to the briar.

(Sharp, 1932, I, pp. 188–9)

The likenesses in the two versions are impressive indeed. Sharp describes the isolation of the Appalachian Mountain region, and its consequent reliance on the culture brought with them by the early settlers from Britain

> The region is from its inaccessibility a very secluded one...Indeed, so remote and shut off from outside influence were, until quite recently, these sequestered mountain valleys that the inhabitants have for a hundred years or more been completely isolated and cut off from all traffic with the rest of the world. Their speech is English,

not American, and, from the number of expressions they use which
have long been obsolete elsewhere, and the old-fashioned way in
which they pronounce many of their words, it is clear that they are
talking the language of a past day, though exactly what period I am
not competent to decide

(Sharp, 1932, 1, p. xxii)

The local people were, Sharp argues, dependent for their knowledge of
the ballads on long oral transmission: on what their 'British forefathers
brought with them from their native country and has since survived by oral
tradition' (p. xxviii).

A case like this provides such a striking instance of long transmission that
it is tempting to take its apparent course as a model for the transmission
of all oral literature. This has been a common reaction among some
folklorists. Instances of the longevity of ballads *within* England too have
been claimed as further evidence. Thus Sharp, on 'the amazing accuracy
of the memories of folk singers'

A blind man, one Mr Henry Larcombe, also from Haselbury-
Plucknett, sang me a Robin Hood ballad. The words consisted of
eleven verses. These proved to be almost word for word the same
as the corresponding stanzas of a much longer black-letter broadside
preserved in the Bodleian Library.

The words of the ballad have since been reproduced in other books,
e.g., in Evans' *Old Ballads*, but, so far as I am aware, they have never
been printed on a 'ballet' or stall copy, or in any form that could
conceivably have reached the country singers. I cannot but conclude,
therefore, that Mr Larcombe's version, accurate as it was, had been
preserved solely by oral tradition for upwards of two hundred years.

It would be easy to multiply instances of this kind without going
beyond my own experience; but these are sufficient for our purpose.
The accuracy of the oral record is a fact, though, I admit, a very
astonishing one.

(Sharp, 1972, pp. 22–3)

This view of the 'amazing accuracy' of the oral record fits certain
widely-held views about the nature and transmission of oral poetry generally. Thus it can be asserted that 'traditional ballads' like *Lord Randal* or
Chevy Chase have been transmitted in such a way that through them we have
contact with 'the product of the pre-literate rural community living in an
atmosphere of beliefs and rituals of immemorial antiquity' (Pinto and
Rodway, 1965, p. 20), some of them transmitting beliefs 'which must have
grown from pre-Christian religion' (Hodgart, 1971, p. 15). Similar comments, often with no evidence given, are made about instances from all over
the world. The texts of Ob-Ugrian epics and songs, for instance, 'have been
transmitted orally for centuries' (Austerlitz, 1958, p. 9), Eskimo literature
in Western Greenland was 'orally handed down from "days of yore"'

(Thalbitzer, 1923, p. 117), and Indian 'folksongs' 'have roots...[in] the depths of the past' (Arya, 1961, p. 48); one ingenious account of the well-known rhyme 'Eeny, meeny, miny, mo' even derives it 'from Druid days when victims were taken across the Menai Strait to the island of Mona for sacrifice' (Boswell and Reaver, 1969, p. 72). For earlier periods too it has seemed reasonable to scholars to extrapolate from what they consider firm assumptions and make statements that, for instance, the oldest Icelandic poetry 'must have lived orally in Iceland for generations before it was written down' (Turville-Petre, 1953, p. 7) or that the Gilgamesh poems written down by the second millennium B.C. 'probably existed in much the same form many centuries earlier' (Sandars, 1971, p. 8).

A picture seems therefore to emerge of lengthy unchanging transmission over wide areas and/or through long periods of time as the expected mode of oral transmission. And the comparative evidence from the more recent ballad case seems to make it reasonable to assume this model for the earlier cases too, even where there is no direct evidence.

2 Inert tradition, memorisation or re-creation?

Evidence of lengthy transmission through space and time thus seems solid and straightforward, in cases like Anglo-American ballads or Vedic literature, and we seem to have arrived at an empirically tested generalisation about the nature of transmission.

But it is by no means certain that long transmission on the model of these instances applies to all cases of oral literature. It is important to ask whether other means of transmission and distribution are found. How far can a model based on the ballads and the *Rgveda* be extrapolated? And is it the correct one even for *these* cases in the light of modern scholarship?

The whole topic of transmission is in fact more controversial than at first appears. Some of the different theories that have emerged will be surveyed briefly here. The approaches that need to be considered are (1) the 'romantic view' about the long transmission of oral poetry from far-back 'communal' origins; (2) the theory of oral transmission as essentially memorisation; and (3) the theory of transmission as a process of re-creation, an approach which overlaps with the oral-formulaic theory. (Discussion here must be brief; further details can be found in the references given, especially in Wilgus, 1959 and McMillan, 1964).

First, there is the extreme romantic approach which has had great influence in the whole field of oral literature and, in particular, in approaches to the transmission of ballads. This is exemplified, for instance, in the writings of Gummere.

In this view – discussed in its historical context in chapter 2 – near word-for-word transmission over long periods (even centuries or milliennia) is both possible and normal, and takes place by 'pure' oral tradition, uncontaminated by influence or interference from written or printed forms. Hendron's portrait of the ballad singer and 'folk singer' has been echoed in many similar accounts: one who 'lives in a rural and isolated region which shuts him off from prolonged schooling and contact with industrialized urban civilization, so that his cultural training is oral rather than visual' (Hendron in Leach and Coffin, 1961, p. 7). The origin of ballads and other 'folklore' is envisaged as communal rather than individual, and the text or song is passed on from generation to generation in a 'state of mental sleep-walking' as Bronson puts it (1969, p. 73). This type of transmission is the natural and normal process in 'folk' or oral literature generally.

There are several strands in this still popular view: the idea of communal origin; of independence of written transmission; of word-for-word reproduction; and of memorisation as the operative factor. These need to be treated separately.

The idea of communal composition has already been questioned in chapter 2; it should also be clear from the account of composition in chapter 3 that – except in a restricted sense – the concept is seldom accurate or helpful. This strand need not be further discussed. The question of the assumed independence of oral from written transmission will be taken up in section 4 on '"Oral transmission" and writing', as will the validity of generalisations about *the* process of oral transmission, to be discussed at the end of this section. It may be said at once that there are reasons to doubt these assumptions of the romantic approach.

The concept of exact oral tradition from the long distant past is commonly held, implicit rather than explicitly argued, in much popular – and even scholarly – writing about ballads, 'folksong' and oral literature. It is sometimes supported by evocative terms like 'folk memory' or 'immemorial tradition', and by the view of ballads and other instances of 'folklore' as survivals or fossils which have come down to us from a distant past rather than instances of a living poetry.

As soon as one looks hard at the notion of exact verbal reproduction over long periods of time, it becomes clear that there is little evidence for it. Even with the Anglo-American ballad quoted earlier, it can be seen that the two texts of *Barbara Allen*, though close, are not verbally identical. The same goes for the sixteen versions of the ballad recorded in the Appalachian Mountains by Sharp, or the three versions of the 'traditional words' printed by Child. It is true that identical versions *do* exist – particularly when there is a printed copy to which, from time to time, orally transmitted ballads can be referred – and that word-perfect reproduction may often be the ideal held by singers. But, apart perhaps from the *Rgveda*, instances of identical transmission without the aid of writing over a long period are not easy to find, and it is the variability rather than the verbal identity of orally transmitted pieces that is most commonly noted. There are now few specialists, even among folklorists, who would argue that exact verbal transmission through oral tradition over long periods of time is typical of oral literature. The emphasis now and for some time in the past has been on 'variants', the differing verbal forms in which what is in some sense 'the same' basic piece or plot is expressed.

If the theory of exact verbal reproduction no longer commands support, that of memorisation as the basic process might still be acceptable. For memory can falter, and it is theoretically possible to account for variants in terms of faulty memorisation and degeneration. The emphasis on memorisation forms one strand of the extreme romantic view; but it also forms the basis of a theory of oral transmission not *necessarily* tied to other romantic assumptions and demands discussion in these terms also.

The theory goes back a long way, as does the corollary that texts are thus subject to degeneration due to imperfect remembering. Oral transmission is therefore, in this view, predominantly a deteriorating process. One influential statement of this theory – applied particularly to the British ballad – was in Sir Walter Scott's introduction to his classic collection, first published in 1802, of *Minstrelsy of the Scottish Borders*. He points out that 'recited or written copies of these ballads' sometimes disagree with each other and comments

> Such discrepancies must very frequently occur, whenever poetry is preserved by oral tradition; for the reciter, making it a uniform principle to proceed at all hazards, is very often, when his memory fails him, apt to substitute large portions from some other tale ...Some arrangement was also occasionally necessary to recover the rhyme, which was often, by the ignorance of the reciters, transposed or thrown into the middle of the line. With these freedoms, which were essentially necessary to remove obvious corruptions, and fit the ballads for the press, the editor presents them to the public.
>
> (Scott, 1802, I, pp. cii–ciii)

In his 'Introductory remarks on popular poetry', which he added in the 1833 edition, he develops this theory even more clearly

> Another cause of the flatness and insipidity, which is the great imperfection of ballad poetry, is to be ascribed less to the compositions in their original state, when rehearsed by their *authors*, than to the ignorance and errors of the reciters or transcribers, by whom they have been transmitted to us.
>
> The more popular the composition of an ancient poet, or *Maker*, became, the greater chance there was of its being corrupted; for a poem transmitted through a number of reciters, like a book reprinted in a multitude of editions, incurs the risk of impertinent interpolations from the conceit of one rehearser, unintelligible blunders from the stupidity of another, and omissions equally to be regretted, from the want of memory in a third.
>
> (Scott, ed. Henderson, 1902, I, pp. 9–10)

This theory has remained in circulation ever since, and – as McMillan shows (1964) – has recent adherents. It was widely held at the beginning of this century and was thus summed up by John Robert Moore in 1916:

> There are certain factors at work in the mind of the singer to destroy or to sustain his memory of the ballads. In the first place, there is a natural tendency to oblivescence, by which things of a year ago tend to make way for things of the present moment. Again, changes take place in the meaning or pronunciation of words, thereby obscuring the singer's memory. Similarly, words which lack associative signifi-cance are likely to drop out and be replaced by something else, especially in the case of proper names and obsolete words. Lastly, the memory of the singer is weakened by the loss of one accompanying feature of the ballad, as the dance, the tune, or the background of the story, or by the loss of a sympathetic audience or of the custom of singing... The ballad-singers are unable to create anything equal to the songs which they have received...
>
> (Moore, 1916, pp. 387, 389, quoted in McMillan, 1964, p. 301)

The theory of oral transmission as predominantly a degenerative process, with its key factor as memorisation is easy to question. Some of the factors which make memorisation as the central process look implausible have been discussed in chapter 3, in the context of composition. These are the effect on performance of occasion and audience, the creative role of the poet, and the finding of the oral-formulaic school, in Yugoslavia and elsewhere, that composition-in-performance is often involved. The present tendency among ballad scholars is to reject memorisation-with-degeneration – as the sole process at work – and to stress the element of 'recreation' in oral transmission discussed below.

Nevertheless, there is something to be said for the memorisation theory and it is over-extreme to reject it out of hand (under the influence of the oral-formulaic school, for instance). There are cases in which memorisation *does* seem to be one central process involved in transmission. It is obviously likely to play an important part where composer and reciter are not the same person, as with some Somali and early Irish poetry (and other cases mentioned in chapter 3, pp. 83–4). It also enters in – though over a shorter time span – where a poet memorises the words he had himself created in a process of prior composition, or in joint performances by a number of people.

This comes out particularly clearly in work on Anglo-American ballads. It has been suggested that here is a cultural tradition where, in contrast to Afro-American culture, there is relatively greater emphasis on memor-isation and exact reproduction, and less on re-creation and improvisation (Abrahams and Foss, 1964, p. 12). Moreover in any tradition there will be some individuals who are primarily uncreative in verbal terms and, so far as they take part in the transmission of actual texts, tend to pass on forms in much the shape they received them – though perhaps in an imperfect form due to imperfect remembering. Even in the Anglo-American tradition not all singers are of this kind, and it is easy to instance creative and original poets. But in considering the processes of transmission and distribution it would be misleading to focus only on the creative composers, and neglect the more ordinary 'traditors'.

It is relevant to recall the research on 'remembering' carried out over fifty years ago by F. C. Bartlett in his psychological experiments 'on the reproduction of folk stories'. He discovered that both where individuals after an interval reproduced a story they had been told and where the stories were passed along a chain of participants there were many changes, to such an extent that the original was often drastically altered, or even entirely transformed by the end. Incidents in the story were often changed by being turned into something familiar, and then rationalised to make sense of the new versions where omissions produced in the transmission had made the existing version nonsensical or unfamiliar; or particular words, phrases or events which 'stood out for the teller' persisted while other elements dropped out (Bartlett, 1920, reprinted in Dundes, 1965). This process will be recognised by anyone who has played the 'whispering game' at parties, where the first in a long line has to whisper a memorised sentence to the next player, and so on down the line. The final sentence is often very far from the initial one – a neat illustration of the changes that can occur in at least one type of oral transmission.

So it is plausible that variants and changes in Anglo-American ballads can be attributed to faulty memory, mishearing or misunderstanding by singers who might otherwise have transmitted the song exactly as they heard it. The church in *Lord Lovel*, for instance, is often St Pancras, and it is reasonable to suppose that this may have been the original wording: but it also appears as St Pancreas, Pancry, Pancridge, Panthry, Pankers, Patrick, Bankers, Peter, Varney, Vincent, Rebecca, King Patsybells and others (Coffin, 1950, p. 3). Consider also what happened to the (presumably) original refrain 'Savory (or Parsley), sage, rosemary and thyme'. This has been changed by ballad singers who did not understand or fully learn the refrain to a number of different variants:

> Save rosemary and thyme.
> Rosemary in time.
> Every rose grows merry in time.
> Rose de Marian Time.
> Rozz marrow and time.
> May every rose bloom merry in time.
> Let every rose grow merry and fine.
> Every leaf grows many a time.

Sing Ivy leaf, Sweet William and thyme.
Every rose grows bonny in time.
Every globe grows merry in time.
Green grows the merry antine.
Whilst every grove rings with a merry antine.
So sav'ry was said, come marry in time.

(cited in Abrahams and Foss, 1968, p. 18)

Other processes of change have been identified by folklorists who have studied memorisation in the oral transmission of the Anglo-American ballad tradition (see especially Abrahams and Foss, 1968); these may well have parallels elsewhere. One is rationalisation: when part of a song is misunderstood or forgotten, the result can be gibberish, and the singer may then try to turn the resultant nonsense into sense, as in the rationalisations of the refrains just mentioned. Again, large portions of an oral poem – as distinct from the smaller verbal elements just mentioned – can be mis-heard or forgotten, and here it is often what is regarded by particular singers as the 'emotional core' of a poem that is remembered, and the rest to some degree forgotten.

While it is, by now, hard to accept memorisation and forgetting as *the* key factors in oral transmission, the processes just mentioned are obviously important in certain circumstances and it would be misleading to ignore them. Lord's dictum that oral poetry is never memorised, or Hodgart's claim that 'every singer is both a transmitter of tradition and an original composer' (Hodgart, 1971, p. 14) go beyond the evidence.

But re-creation and re-composition theories now take the foreground in discussions of oral transmission. This approach too dates back some way. In 1904, Kittredge put it clearly in his introduction to the Child ballads

> As it [the ballad] passes from singer to singer it is changing unceas-ingly. Old stanzas are dropped and new ones are added; rhymes are altered; the names of the characters are varied; portions of other ballads work their way in; the catastrophe may be transformed completely. Finally, if the tradition continues for two or three cen-turies, as it frequently does continue, the whole linguistic complexion of the piece may be so modified with the development of the language in which it is composed, that the original author would not recognize his work if he heard it recited. Taken collectively, these processes of oral tradition amount to a second act of composition, of an inextri-cably complicated character, in which many persons share (some consciously, others without knowing it), which extends over many generations and much geographical space, and which may be as efficient a cause of the ballad in question as the original creative act of the individual author.
>
> (quoted in McMillan, 1964, p. 302)

Gerould too emphasised that 'variation cannot possibly be due to lapses of memory only' (1932, p. 184). He points out that many singers have been unable to resist the impulse to make alterations even though their memories have been extremely accurate...

I see no reason why we may not believe that some of the verbal variants, which we regard as worthy of admiration, may not be the work of persons with an instinct for playing with rhythmic patterns in words, of Miltons who though inglorious have not been content to remain mute. Such an individual would make changes unconsciously because he could not resist the impulse to experiment.

(Gerould, 1932, p. 187)

To emphasise this re-creative aspect is not to suggest creation from *nothing*. Rather – as in the oral-formulaic approach – there is a stock-in-trade of themes, plots, phrases and stanzas on which the ballad singer (or other poet) can draw, and through which he can impose more – or less – originality on his composition. There are, for example, many stock phrases and episodes which occur and recur throughout the ballads, and seem not to belong to particular ballads but to form a traditional pool at the ballad singer's disposal. Thus the same refrains appear in a number of different ballads, and as Coffin puts it 'names, phrases, lines, clichés, whole stanzas and motifs wander from song to song when the dramatic situations are approximately similar' (Coffin, 1950, p. 5). Fair Ellen or Fair Eleanor can be the heroine of almost any song and Lord Barnard, Barbara (Allen), Sweet William, and Lady Margaret are always coming in as names for ballad characters. Stock phrases and episodes are very widespread. Coffin gives some instances

A person who goes on a journey dresses in red and green or gold and white (see Child 73, 99, 243, and others); a man receiving a letter smiles at the first line and weeps at the next (see Child 58, 65, 84, 208, 209); roses and briars grow from lover's graves (see Child 7, 73, 74, 75, 76, 84, 85); a person tirls the pin at a door, and no one is so ready as the King, etc. to let him in (see Child 7, 53, 73, 74, 81); a story begins with people playing ball (see Child 20, 49, 81, 95, 155); etc. These and many similar and soon recognizable lines crop up in every part of the country and appear in almost any song with the proper story situations.

(Coffin, 1950, pp. 5–6)

Such variations, which have long been noted by ballad scholars, could be explained as devices by which a singer can cover up 'his lagging memory' or as deviations from the original authentic form of the ballad – the kind of 'distortions' that inevitably occur in a long chain of memorised transmission. But it is now more common to interpret them in the light of the Parry–Lord approach, according to which there is no one 'correct' original; each ballad is created as a unique piece by a process of simultaneous composition/performance. The approach works with the ballads, which clearly have much in common with other oral narratives in their use of stock episodes and phrases (it seems over-precise to call them 'formulae'): the kind of 'commonplaces' which, as Jones says in an illuminating article which brings out this aspect, 'freed [the singer] from the restrictions of memoriz- ation' and enabled him 'to compose rather than merely transmit' (Jones, 1961, p. 103). Through these set pieces, the ballad singer can vary and adapt the basic story, can in a sense compose, if he wishes, as well as transmitting. Consider, for instance, the many variants of the first two lines of *The unquiet grave* – one of the ballads accepted as 'traditional' in Child's defini- tive collection which it is surely reasonable to attribute to individual re-creation rather than merely 'faulty memory'.

> The wind doth blow today, my love,
>   And a few small drops of rain.

> How cold the wind do blow, dear love,
>   And see the drops of rain.

> Cold blows the wind o'er my true-love,
>   Cold blow the drops of rain.

> Cold blows the wind today, sweetheart,
>   Cold are the drops of rain.

> Cauld, cauld blaws the winter night,
>   Sair beats the heavy rain.

> How cold the winds do blow, dear love!
>   And a few small drops of rain.

> Cold blows the winter's wind, true love,
>   Cold blow the drops of rain.

> (quoted in Gerould, 1932, pp. 171–2)

Again, a common episode in ballads has someone looking over a castle wall and seeing a variety of happenings (according to the needs of the story).

> The queen lukit owre the castle-wa,
>   Beheld baith dale and down,
> And ther she saw Young Waters
>   Cum riding to the town.

The same commonplace is varied to beautiful effect in *The bonny earl of Murray*:

> Lang will his lady
>   Look ower the castle down,
> Ere she see the Earl of Murray
>   Come soundin through the town.

> (quoted in Jones, 1961, p. 104)

Stock phrases, lines and topics of this kind abound in British and American ballads. *Johnie Scot* is recorded in at least twenty versions. Though the basic story (essentially that of a rescue) remains the same, there are many differences – not just of verbal details. In some, only one message is sent for Johnie telling of his sweetheart's imprisonment, while in other versions there are two messages (one from Johnie calling his love, the other from her explaining why she cannot come). The message incident itself can be extended to as many as ten stanzas in one version, whereas in other versions it takes eight, seven, five or four or even less. Versions having the same number of stanzas do not necessarily treat the incident in the same way. Here are three variants:

> O Johnie's called his waiting man,
>   His name was Germanie:
> 'O thou must to fair England go,
>   Bring me that fair ladie.'
>
> He rode till he came to Earl Percy's gate,
>   He tirled at the pin;
> 'O who is there?' said the proud porter,
>   'But I daurna let thee in.'
>
> So he rode up and he rode down,
>   Till he rode it round about,
> Then he saw her at a wee window,
>   Where she was looking out.
>
> 'O thou must go to Johnnie Scot,
>   Unto the woods so green,
> In token of thy silken shirt,
>   Thine own hand sewed the seam.'

Version E used only two stanzas:

> 'O do you see yon castle, boy,
>   It's walled round about;
> There you will spye a fair ladye,
>   In the window looking out.'
>
> 'Here is a silken sark, lady,
>   Thine own hand sewed the sleeve,
> And thou must go to yon green wood
>   To Johnie, thy true-love.'

Finally, and perhaps not least effectively, Version J used only a stanza and a half:

> (The lady was laid in cold prison,
>   By the king, a grievous man;)
> And up and starts a little boy,
>   Upon her window stane.

Says, 'Here's a silken shift, ladye,
 Your own hand sewed the sleeve,
And ye maun gang to yon green-wood,
 And of your friends speir na leave.'

(Jones, 1961, pp. 109–10)

Variation in ballads can extend beyond this kind of verbal change and affect the characters and scene of the story. Local heroes or settings are often introduced in ballads. Thus the ballad better known as *Lord Randal* becomes one about Johnnie Randolph in Virginia where the illustrious Randolph family lived; in a cowboy version of *Barbara Allen* the scene shifts to the prairie, while the same ballad in a New York village makes Barbara a poor blacksmith's daughter and her lover the richest man in the world (Coffin, 1950, p. 3). The changes sometimes affect the basic plot. One version of *Barbara Allen* was circulating in the Smoky Mountains earlier this century in which the lover recovers instead of dying, and curses Barbara Allen; she dies, and he dances on her grave. This version was composed by a local singer, fiddler and ballad-maker, John Snead. He reworked the ballad and gave it a different ending because, as he said, 'that dratted girl was so mean'. His version caught on locally, and started circulating as a ballad in its own right, and preferred to versions based on the more common story (Leach, 1957, p. 206). Again the 'traditional' framework of the well-known story in *Gypsie Laddie* in which a noble lady leaves her comfortable life to flee with her gypsy lover, became in a West Virginia version a tale set in a local context and with local names, about 'Billy Harman whose wife had gone off with Tim Wallace, Harman's brother-in-law. Wallace was very ugly and the wife very pretty. She never came back; he did' (Coffin, 1950, p. 12). The result is a ballad in which some episodes included in other versions are left out – the meeting with the elopers, and the scorning of the husband – but one which presents its own self-sufficient story.

The older models of transmission in terms of exact reproduction or (fallible) memorisation cannot easily account for this extent of variation – and certainly not for deliberate changes like John Snead's reworking of *Barbara Allen*. The most recent trend in ballad scholarship is to interpret this variability as one instance of the potentialities of any oral poetry – the possibility that it will be changed in the course of performance (see e.g. Jones, 1961; Buchan, 1972; Hodgart, 1971).

This new view of variation in ballads is explicitly based on the findings of Lord and Parry and the 'oral-formulaic school', so the emphasis is very much on the concept of 'composition' rather than on 'transmission'. As was argued in chapter 3, the extreme and exclusive version of the Parry–Lord theory is questionable and we cannot accept entirely Hodgart's comprehensive claim that 'no two versions of a ballad are ever exactly alike; and

every singer is both a transmitter of tradition and an original composer'
(Hodgart, 1971, p. 14). But the oral-formulaic theory brings some insights.
It does now seem clear that ballads must be understood as sometimes subject to the same range of influences towards change due to the individual
personalities of singers, local events, the creative impulse stirred by the
performance itself and the nature and circumstances of the audience.
Bringing the analysis of ballads into touch with comparative work on oral
poetry elsewhere suggests that, as far as transmission goes, ballads are not
a special category but are subject to the same blend of memorisation and
(possibly more frequently) of variability in performance that one would
expect from studies of the composition and transmission of oral poems
generally.

Most of this discussion has concentrated on the British and American
ballad, where the best case for long oral transmission based on memorisation and/or the force of inert tradition has often seemed to be found (apart
from the *Rgveda*). But similar analyses can be made of other cases that might
seem to lend support to the romantic view. The Gésar epic, for instance,
circulating so widely in Tibet, China and Mongolia, is not confined to a
static and exact text, for

> la création poétique est continue du seul fait du caractère médiu-
> mique du barde. Elle respecte toujours le cadre donné, mais peut,
> en improvisant, le déborder ou le crever à l'occasion. L'épopeé est
> une oeuvre vivante qui s'enrichit encore, ou s'est encore enrichi tout
> récemment, de nouveaux chapitres, sans parler des variations dues
> à l'omission ou à l'addition de thèmes et récits par des conteurs plus
> ou moins informés.
>
> (Stein, 1959, p. 586)

Here, as with similar cases, the overall structure of incidents as well as
certain conventions of phrasing recur again and again; but transmission
of the poems in the form of finished oral art – as *literature* – has to take into
account other factors besides the passive handing on of some 'oral tradition'. The creative role of whole series of individual poets and performers
has also to be remembered.

This applies even in an instance where one would expect little creative
adaptation and which is sometimes cited as a good example of long-lasting
'oral tradition' – nursery rhymes and children's verse. Of course, memorisation and more or less exact transmission *are* sometimes involved, and some
basic forms and motifs are known to have a long history. But this does not
rule out variability; this is clear from a large number of examples which
are difficult to explain in terms of 'faulty memorisation'. Here for instance
are a few of the Irish versions of what many of us know as 'How many
miles to Babylon?'

County Louth version

How many miles to Babylon?
  Three score and ten.
Can I get there by candle-light?
  There and back again.
Here's my black (*raising one foot*),
And here's my blue (*raising the other*),
Open the gates and let me through.

Belfast version

How many miles to Barney Bridge?
  Threescore and ten.
Will I be there by candle-light?
  Yes, if your legs are long.
If you please will you let the king's horses through
  Yes, but take care of the hindmost one.

Dublin version

How many miles to Barney Bridge?
  Threescore and ten.
Will I be there by Candlemas?
  Yes, and back again.
A courtesy to you, another to you,
And pray fair maids, will you let us through?
Thro' and thro' you shall go for the king's sake,
But take care the last man does not meet a mistake.

(Marshall, 1931, p. 10)

Besides Babylon and Barney Bridge, other places that appear are Bethlehem, Aberdeagie, Burslem, Curriglass, Gandigo, Hebron and Wimbledon (Opie 1955, p. 64). A large number of variants on other well-known rhymes can be found in the Opies' well-documented *Oxford Dictionary of Nursery Rhymes*.

So even in the apparently tradition-bound sphere of children's verse, creation and re-creation is to be found. Add to this all the other examples of re-creation and re-composition in performance pointed out by scholars all over the world, above all by those inspired by the researches of Milman Parry and Albert Lord: the overall picture that emerges is that though themes and forms persist, and though transmission by exact memorisation *does* sometimes occur, to describe the transmission of oral poetry in terms only of exact and inert oral tradition is incorrect.

There remains the difficult case of the *Rgveda*. It has been claimed by generations of Indian scholars that its transmission over centuries and millennia has been essentially due to exact memorisation. This is a strong claim and, if justified, would provide an unparalleled instance of the exact oral transmission of an extremely long text – around 40,000 lines in all –

over an enormous expanse of time. The religious and liturgical context of the text lends some support to this interpretation, for this is the kind of circumstance that puts a premium on exact rendition. In addition, it seems that in Indian tradition, in contrast to that of the west, writing was held in low regard – even regarded in some respects as impure – and 'extraordinary importance accorded to memory' (Staal, 1961, p. 15). Staal explains the process of Vedic transmission and its underlying idea that

> the words, which are one with the meaning and themselves sacred, should be preserved for the world and for posterity. In this sense the *śrotriya* who recites without understanding should not be compared with a clergyman preaching from the pulpit, but rather with a medieval monk copying and illuminating manuscripts, and to some extent with all those who are connected with book production in modern society. To the copyists we owe nearly all our knowledge of Antiquity, to the reciters all our knowledge of the Vedas.
>
> (Staal, 1961, p. 17)

Accuracy was not just ensured by the strict training and supervision of reciters, but enjoined as a religious duty: by reciting the sacred Vedic literature correctly, man contributed to the divine plan. The whole background of religious belief and training, therefore, served to uphold the accuracy of memorised oral tradition.

Certain doubts occur, however. First, can we in any case be *certain* about this exact transmission over many centuries of time? There is no external written evidence about the exact form and content of the *Rgveda* in, say, 1000 or even 500 B.C. (and, if there *were* written versions within the tradition, how could one be sure that writing did not play some part in the process of transmission?); and the 'archaic' nature of the language, sometimes cited, cannot be regarded as definitive evidence of the original date of final composition or of the text's having remained unchanged in all respects over the centuries (on this see also chapter 4, section 4). The essential contention about the *Rgveda* is that it was directly inspired: with some later works it is collectively known as *śrti* or 'heard', because it is deemed to have been divinely dictated. For someone working within this culture, this must seem as solid a piece of evidence for the lengthy and exact transmission of Vedic literature as belief in the Bible as 'The Word of God' did to Biblical scholars suspicious of the higher criticism of Biblical texts. Statements by priests or poets (or even by their foreign admirers) about the long tradition which lies behind their words cannot – as sociologists know only too well – always be taken at their face value, and further evidence always needs to be sought. Long and unchanging oral transmission over the centuries used to be claimed for all traditional Indian literature, but it is now apparently accepted that this does not necessarily apply to some of the 'later' less sacred pieces. It is possible that a similar re-thinking of the evidence may take place in the case of the *Rgveda* also. There is also the possibility (discussed later) that writing may have played a larger part than is sometimes recognised in the process of Vedic transmission. The overall conclusion must be that, while the evidence seems to point to a remarkable degree of exact oral transmission of a very lengthy text over a long period of time, the argument is not closed and further detailed examination of this case might prove illuminating.

One is forced to the conclusion that there is, after all, no single process of 'oral transmission' – no universal 'laws' – applicable to all oral poetry (or all oral literature). Rather, a number of different elements may be in play: exact verbal transmission (as, apparently, with the *Rgveda* and perhaps with other religiously sanctioned texts like the cosmological poetry of Hawaii); memorisation (often fallible) as with a number of versions of Anglo-American ballads, popular hymns, some Zulu and Ruanda panegyrics and so on; and several variants on the themes of re-creation, re-composition, or original composition-in-performance on the oral-formulaic model. In any one case, different elements among these, or different combinations of them, may be in play in a way that cannot be predicted simply from the nature of the piece concerned.

It is impossible, therefore, to predict in a given instance what the detailed form of oral transmission is likely to be. The earlier hope that, by further study of oral transmission and careful checking of results we may 'eventually arrive at a generally acceptable theory' (McMillan, 1964, p. 309) must be abandoned. There are too many variables involved – not only the different elements so far as memorisation is concerned, but also the variations attaching to differing cultural traditions, different poetic genres, changing historical circumstances, the specific occasions of delivery and the differing personalities of poets and 'transmitters' themselves. We can no longer assume that generalised theories about oral transmission *universally* apply: that it is always through inert tradition; or always through memorisation, faulty or otherwise; or, as in some recent claims, always composition-in-performance. The truth is more unromantic. This is that despite the clear evidence of the widespread distribution of certain themes, plots and forms, the means by which they are actually worked out as literature and distributed orally to their audiences has to be discovered by detailed and painstaking research rather than assumed in advance on the basis of generalised models based on earlier theories.

I have spent so much space on this question whether exact oral tradition over long periods is *the* normal process for the transmission of oral poetry because romantic views about 'oral tradition' are still so prevalent, both in popular understanding and even in many assumptions by scholarly researchers working in related areas; and the idea that there is one proven mode of 'oral transmission' is at first sight so attractive and plausible. Until these ideas are challenged, it is difficult to make a dispassionate appraisal of what is known of the differing ways in which oral poems are transmitted and distributed to their audiences.

The purpose of this discussion has thus been largely negative: to raise questions about assumptions sometimes taken for granted. But it has also emphasised certain more positive points. First, so far from there being one 'normal' means for the transmission of oral poems, there are in fact a number of different ways in which this can take place, depending among other things on historical circumstance, the poet, the performer, the audience and the type of poem. Secondly, even when themes and basic forms are very stable, verbal variability and originality in oral performance are extremely common, and almost certainly more typical than unchanging transmission, even though the extent of memorisation as against originality cannot be predicted in advance from some universal theory. And third, questions of transmission very quickly lead into the discussion of composition and creativity – the two aspects are so closely linked that in this discussion of transmission it has proved impossible not to recur constantly to points previously considered under the head of 'composition'.

These points are reinforced if we turn to a more detailed discussion of some ways in which oral poems can be distributed and thus reach their audiences.

3 How do oral poems reach their audiences?

Some of the means of diffusion have already been touched on in the discussion of ballads. Emigrants sometimes take their songs with them when they travel and sing them with varying degrees of adaptation and new composition in the countries to which they go – as happened with British ballads in America or Australia, or perhaps with African songs brought by slaves to the American South and to the West Indies. Or they are transmitted along trade-routes, like those between Scotland and Scandinavia in the sixteenth and seventeenth centuries, areas whose ballads show close resemblance. Detailed studies of this type of historical diffusion have been carried out by theorists of the historical-geographical school, like Archie Taylor's tracing of the ballad *Edward* from its British source to its widespread occurrence in Scandinavia (Taylor, 1931). In other cases, the transmission is within a single culture; when this is over a protracted period it is often backed by religious authority, as with the transmission of liturgical forms (like the *Credo* or *Magnificat*) within Western Christianity or the *Rgveda* in India. When there are strong religious sanctions on continuity there is less likelihood of variation (though it is not impossible) and diffusion is often relatively straightforward, largely through memorisation reinforced by frequent reiteration in formalised situations (and not infrequently by writing). In other cases, there is not the same sanction on continuity, and how far transmission becomes an aspect of composition is not predictable in advance: it depends on a range of factors like the occasions on which the pieces are delivered, the personality of the performer/poet, the function(s) of the oral poem in question, and the range of variation accepted within a given community.

It is more illuminating to turn from the often speculative studies of lengthy transmission so beloved by romantic theorists and scholars of the historical-geographical school, to consider the more detailed ways in which oral poems are distributed through space, as it were, and on a much shorter time-scale. Basically this comes down to a consideration of the occasions on which poems are delivered to audiences and thus realised as oral literature.

The simplest case is presented by poetry performed communally – by a group singing for themselves rather than for an audience. Work songs are typical. In so far as these songs are relatively unchanging, within short periods at least, the singers learn them through being members of the group, and reinforce their knowledge by singing them. This applies to other songs mainly performed through choral singing – songs like *The people's flag, God save the Queen* or well-known hymns in own culture, the secret society songs ritually sung by initiates in West African groups like the Limba, jointly sung children's songs, Irish pub songs, or Aranda dance songs in Central Australia. In these cases the emphasis tends to be on memorisation, and transmission is at the face-to-face level within the group. Changes in group membership, with individuals taking knowledge of particular songs with them and, if accepted, teaching them in new groups can lead to such songs having quite a wide distribution at times. Though the tendency in these cases of group singing is towards memorisation rather than individual originality, this is not always rigidly the case, and new compositions do arise – it is obvious they must do, since the songs have to have a beginning somewhere.

It is probably more common, however, with work songs (and many other group songs) for the whole group not to sing all the song but for there to be solo lines or stanzas for a leader. Here the opportunities for individual composition can be extensive – depending on the context and form. The kind of creativity illustrated in Jackson's account of originality in work songs among Negro prisoners in Texas has been widely documented elsewhere. He shows how the lead-singer uses many phrases and partial lines from traditional prison songs, but by this means can compose his own personal verses. Sometimes this involves little more than 'slotting-in' appropriate names into formulaic lines or re-assembling new songs from accepted phrases, but others can use even the prison work song context to produce highly creative work: 'They sing not only well-known lines and stanzas, but they add many of their own or vary the existing ones. J. B. Smith is such a song leader...Working within a traditional framework and using some traditional elements, he has woven an elaborate construct of images' (Jackson, 1972, pp. 34, 144). Thus even in the largely choral songs – and so at the simplest level of the work song – it is hard to keep questions about transmission and distribution wholly separate from composition.

This is even more clear when we move to the other extreme: the distribution of oral poems by a highly specialised poet delivering his compositions as a special performance to a gathering of admirers. This type of occasion is widely documented throughout the world from the Kirghiz and Kazakh epic minstrels of the Soviet Union or the Yugoslav *guslari* to the Zulu praise poets, Irish ballad singers or Fijian heroic poets. The picture we are given in *The Odyssey* of the rhapsodist's performance is very similar, and many have speculated that Homer himself – whoever he was – used to perform to groups of listeners in much the same way. A common pattern here is for the poet to engage in the kind of simultaneous performance and composition analysed by Radlov, Parry and Lord. So, although in a sense transmission is involved, in that the poet may be working with known themes and plots and composing within a traditionally accepted system of conventional patterns of various kinds, the composition and performance of a uniquely shaped piece meeting the requirements of a specific occasion, audience and performer's personality are really more in question than 'transmission' of an already existing piece. Insofar as performance of this kind involves the unique realisation of a particular oral poem, the term 'publication' is here better than 'transmission' or even 'distribution'.

Not all public recitations by specialist poets follow this model of blended composition and performance. There is also the opposite case – with shades of difference in between – when the composition takes place separately from the performance, and may even be by a different person from the reciter who merely learns and delivers it. Examples of this type of transmission were described briefly in chapter 3. Here it *does* make sense to speak of 'transmission'. Not much detailed research documents the process by which poetry is transmitted in this way. But at times, this method of transmission can result in remarkably widespread and rapid distribution of poems once composed. In Somalia, for instance, partly owing to traditional nomadic patterns of movement, poems 'spread very quickly over wide areas' (Andrzejewski and Lewis, 1964, p. 45), and this is nowadays accelerated by modern means like trains or lorries, for the singers and teachers of such songs still sometimes travel throughout the country, as wandering minstrels did at a slower pace in the past. The radio is also becoming an increasingly frequent medium for this type of distribution.

Electronic transmission is no abnormal or odd context for oral poetry; indeed radio is becoming extremely important both in industrial and (perhaps even more) in developing countries as a vehicle for oral poetry. We hear of classical and contemporary oral poetry being broadcast over Somali radio, of the Mandinka 'Sunjata epic' being transmitted over both Radio Dakar and Radio Gambia, religious lyrics being broadcast by Radio Ghana, or *mvet* songs by Yaoundé radio; and of course 'folk ballads' and 'folk poetry' as well as pop songs are now widely propagated in western industrial society by radio and television. Thus by means of face-to-face recitations by travelling minstrels and poets, and by mass broadcasts to wider audiences, poems that have been – more or less – formed by prior composition can be transmitted widely to various audiences by the poet himself or by reciters who have learnt the text from the composer or other performers.

Sometimes the performance of a poem following prior composition by the poet takes the form of a carefully-rehearsed set-piece concert, rather than frequent recitations by performers throughout a wide area on what could be dubbed the Somali model. One example of this is the performance that sometimes follows after the long process of careful composition by the Gilbertese poet described in chapter 3. After the song has been composed the poet, Grimble tells us, then teaches it to those who will perform it, a group as much as two hundred strong. They learn the words 'phrase by phrase' and develop the dance to go with it. The rehearsals are elaborate and protracted affairs:

> As each passage becomes known, the experts sketch out the appro-priate attitudes, which are tried and retried until satisfaction is reached. There are interminable repetitions, recapitulations, re-visions, until the flesh is weary and the chant is sickeningly familiar. But from a ragged performance of ill-timed voices and uncertain attitudes, the song-dance becomes a magnificent harmony of bodies, eyes and arms swinging and undulating in perfect attunement through a thousand poises, to the organ tone of ten score voices chanting in perfect rhythm. Then dawns the poet's day of glory.
>
> (Grimble, 1957, p. 206).

Clearly the music and dance play a significant part in such performances, and so long rehearsals are necessary for their effective rendering – but this does not make the performance any less significant as the occasion when the poet's verbal composition is delivered, in the setting locally accepted as suitable, to the local audience: it is indeed 'the poet's day of glory'. Grimble does not record how frequently performances like this took place or how often the same poem was delivered in this way – but it seems reasonable to guess that such a large scale event was not repeated with great frequency, even if the poem was also sung informally in more personal contexts.

This type of carefully-rehearsed performance is not unique to the Gilbert Islands. The Chopi of southern Africa spend long periods working at the joint music and words which make up the nine- to eleven-movement orchestral *ŋgodo* dance which certain skilled and known musicians compose anew about once every two years (Tracey, 1948, pp. 2ff), and a number of other deliberately rehearsed occasions are recorded for the performance of oral literature in Africa (Finnegan, 1970, pp. 103–4, 269f). And of course rehearsals of 'jazz poetry' in Western Europe, or of dramatic performances in many parts of the world rest on similar long preparation and the co-operation of numbers of people, and result not in multiple distribution of the poetry involved but, more often, in just a few performances (for with *oral* as distinct from written literature, later revivals after a protracted period are unlikely). The exceptions are when there are groups of professional or semi-professional players who either command a sufficiently large and varied public to give a series of repeated performances or (more likely except in highly populated urban areas) travel the country in a troupe performing known pieces from their repertoire – like the travelling Malay story-tellers, and perhaps the strolling players of mediaeval Europe. Thus repeated distribution to changing audiences can take place. Cases such as these, as well as the long-rehearsed Gilbertese performances, show how wide of the mark are older assumptions about some uniform and 'natural' form of distribution of oral literature.

Enough has been said to illustrate the basic contention of much of this chapter – that oral poetry is not distributed and transmitted by a single means that can be automatically assumed in advance of the evidence, but takes place in different ways. Some other processes of distribution should be mentioned briefly before I move on to oral/written interaction and how this enters into the distribution process.

In one common situation topical and ephemeral poems, usually short, 'catch on' in a community and pass from mouth to mouth, often in an incredibly short time, to become widely popular (or popular within a particular group of people) and then, often, to be forgotten again. This phenomenon is well known with 'pop' songs in the west (where word-of-mouth transmission is supplemented though not replaced by broadcast media, records and tape) but it also occurs widely in less industrialised contexts – among the Ibo and Tiv of Nigeria for instance (Finnegan, 1970, pp. 266, 279–80). This sort of transmission is often informal and perhaps ultimately depends on face-to-face and unorganised contact (despite the commercial backing given to it in some western contexts).

There is also the not uncommon situation where oral poems are delivered in the context of a public duel or competition. Eskimo taunting songs are famous examples of this, when two hostile singers work off grudges and disputes through both traditional and specially composed songs which ridicule their opponents. The winner is the singer most loudly applauded

(Hoebel, 1972, pp. 93ff). In this case the distribution to listeners depends on formally organised occasions when these songs – whether previously prepared or not – are delivered.

The same goes for the widely held poetic competitions where the emphasis is (in varying degrees) on display and poetic accomplishment rather than on resolving or maintaining hostilities. Organised competitions by poets used to be held in several areas of East Africa. In Tanzania, for instance, two singers, each with his own supporting group, sometimes decided to compete on an agreed day. They taught their followers new songs of their own composition and on the day the competition was won by the group which drew the greatest number of spectators. On other occasions the local Sultan arranged the competition and acted as umpire between the two sides, each of whom tried to find out their opponents' songs in advance so as to prepare suitably insulting and sarcastic replies (Finnegan, 1970, p. 103). Similar song competitions were widespread among Polynesian poets (Chadwicks, III, 1940, pp. 415, 462) and Russian poets like the Kazakh and Kirghiz (Chadwick and Zhirmunsky, 1969, p. 329). Japanese court poetry too was often 'published' at poetry matches (*utaawase*). These were at first informal and purely for entertainment, but were later conducted according to very formalised rules and even developed into the special form of a 'poetry match with oneself' (*jikaawase*) in which 'the poet took two roles and played a kind of poetic chess with himself, sending the results to a distinguished judge for comment' (Miner, 1968, p. 31). Poetry competitions and duels thus provide yet another organised mode through which the process of publication and distribution of oral poetry can take place.

Another pattern worth notice is that which can result from the exertion of political authority. It may seem odd to single out political and propaganda songs for special mention here since *any* poem can have a political flavour and the most propaganda-oriented song can, in turn, give enjoyable or humorous effects far beyond the originators' intentions. But any consideration of how poems are distributed must involve specific mention of situations where the main role in such distribution is not, as it were, played by commercial motives or the attraction of aesthetic and recreational appeal but is deliberately organised by political authorities for their own purposes.

The radio is a much used vehicle by governments with largely illiterate populations, and one medium is oral poetry – such as the songs used in the Indian government's birth control campaign, or the patriotic songs broadcast by Arab radio stations during the 1973 Middle East War. On a less public but equally effective level are the poets and reciters encouraged by government or political parties to give performances of poetry designed to put their own case – the various singers, for instance, hired by opposing political parties in the Western Nigerian elections in the 1960s, or the Tanzanian government's appeal to musicians in 1967 to help propagate its new policies of socialism in their songs (Finnegan, 1970, chapter 10), or the *aqyn* bard in Kazakhistan who travels the country to laud the new Soviet leaders and their policies (Winner, 1958, pp. 157ff). Enthusiastic supporters of particular groups or policies may make it their business to see that their view is well represented in song. One instance was the campaign of the local R.D.A. (Rassemblement Démocratique Africain) against the French government in Guinea in 1954–5. The campaign was greatly assisted by songs in praise of the R.D.A.'s symbol (the elephant) and its leader Sékou Touré. The final success of the R.D.A. was partly due to this effective propaganda, unwittingly aided by the French administration who tried to disperse the apparent agitators ('the vagrants') and send them home.

> They were piled into trucks, and sent back to the villages. R.D.A. militants tell of their delight at these free rides. The overloaded open trucks carried many R.D.A. supporters on impromptu propaganda tours. This is what they chanted on their trip:

> They say that the elephant does not exist.
> But here is the elephant,
> The elephant no one can beat.

> (Schachter, 1958, p. 675)

Many parallels can be found in the industrialised west, such as Irish 'rebel' and IRA songs, or left wing 'protest' songs. The various types of praise poems of local rulers may not be subject to quite such deliberate distribution among the people, but in highly organised states like, say, the Muslim states of West Africa or Polynesian kingdoms of the Pacific, it is hard not to believe that the performance and reception of these panegyrics were not actively encouraged by those in authority.

The various means of distribution mentioned here have been put forward in the most schematic way. Obviously each of the contexts mentioned has possible variations which shade into each other. And there are specific forms of distribution that could not be covered in a quick survey like this, though they share aspects with the types mentioned – forms of performance like the Ibo taunting songs sung outside a victim's hut, cowboy songs around a camp fire, or a lover's solitary serenade to his beloved. There are also cases where 'transmission' and 'distribution' are not involved, but rather there is a unique performance of a particular oral poem by an individual poet. But enough has been said to show the wide variety of ways in which oral poems reach their audiences and are (on occasion) transmitted over space or time.

Awareness of these many possibilities makes one realise how many questions are opened up by considering not only the traditional problem about 'transmission' over long periods of time, but also the more general topic of the manifold ways in which oral poems are distributed and 'published'. The romantic theory turns out to be not only mistaken in its assumptions that there is a single mode of transmission for oral poetry, but also to be unfruitful in that concentrating primarily on *one* mode of transmission draws attention away from other equally interesting possibilities.

4 'Oral transmission' and writing

One difficulty about the romantic view was mentioned earlier, and must be considered further. This is the assumption that lengthy transmission of oral poetry such as the Gésar or Gilgamesh epics, the *Rgveda* or – the case *par excellence* – Anglo-American ballads is likely to have taken place by some pure 'oral tradition' untouched by influence from written and printed sources. Allied to this, one sometimes finds the view that writing is incompatible with, or even destructive of, oral literature. Carpenter in his study of the Homeric epics is categorical that writing kills oral literature, for 'the spread of literacy has remorselessly been destroying the oral literary forms and only the lowest cultural levels preserve their preliterate traditions' (Carpenter, 1958, p. 3). Evidence for this is suggested in statements like that of the old woman who was the source for several of the ballads in Sir Walter Scott's *Minstrelsy of the Scottish Border*: 'There war never ane o' ma sangs prentit till ye prentit them yoursel', an' ye hae spoilt them awthegither. They were made for singing an' no for reading; but ye hae broken the charm now, an' they'll never be sung mair' (Hogg, 1834, p. 61).

Even Lord sees the 'oral' and the 'literary' techniques as 'contradictory and mutually exclusive' and holds that once the idea of a set 'correct' text arrived 'the death knell of the oral process had been sounded' (Lord, 1968a, pp. 129, 137).

Detailed evidence tells strongly against both facets of this general view. In practice, interaction between oral and written forms is extremely common, and the idea that the use of writing *automatically* deals a death blow to oral literary forms has nothing to support it.

The following section gives brief instances of this claim. These instances also fill out the sketch already given of the distribution and publication of oral poetry – for, the reader will already have gathered, writing sometimes plays a part in this process even in largely *oral* literature.

The essential point in this context is that writing has been in existence for a longer period and over a wider area of the world than is often realised. The image of the non-literate, untouched and remote 'primitive society' goes so deep in western thinking over the last few centuries that it is easy to think that it was only in certain favoured areas of, say, western civilisation that writing has for long played a significant part in society; and that elsewhere (with perhaps some slight recognition of certain achievements in the Far East) writing has been introduced recently as a foreign innovation brought by western penetration. This is seriously misleading. It is true that many groups in Africa, Australia or the Pacific were almost entirely illiterate for many years (and the overall adult illiteracy rate for the world as a whole is reckoned by UNESCO as *still* around thirty per cent) and that for some cultures their first serious contact with reading and writing was first through Christian missionaries and later through colonial administrators. But it is not true that most of the 'developing' world had no contact with writing until two or three generations ago. As Jack Goody sums it up:

> At least during the past 2,000 years, the vast majority of the peoples of the world (most of Eurasia and much of Africa) have lived...in cultures which were influenced in some degree by the circulation of the written word, by the presence of groups or individuals who could read or write...It is clear that even if one's attention is centered only upon village life, there are large areas of the world where the fact of writing and existence of the book has to be taken into account, even in discussing 'traditional' societies.

(Goody, 1968, pp. 4–5)

Writing is not an abnormal or oddly 'extraneous' phenomenon even in a society whose main channels of communication may be oral, and which is characterised by the development of oral rather than written literature. One would *expect*, in fact, that in many such societies written forms would, from time to time, be used in the process of transmitting, composing or memorising forms of oral literature. This indeed is precisely what one finds.

Take, first, the British and American ballads. It is clear that there was and is constant interaction between written and oral forms. A distinction used to be made between 'traditional' ballads (like *Lord Randal* or *The elfin knight*) which were taken to have originated and been transmitted orally as far back as mediaeval times, and the later 'broadside' or 'street' ballads which specifically began in printed form, but then sometimes became accepted into the 'oral tradition'. Though there is some truth in this distinction, a clear differentiation in terms of *mode of transmission* does not hold up. Many 'traditional' ballads have much in common with earlier literary romances and lais (e.g. *Hind Horn* from the Horn cycle of romances, *Thomas Rymer* directly from a fifteenth-century poem about Thomas of Erceldoune, *King Orfeo* a reworking of the Middle English lai *Sir Orfeo*) and have themselves inspired later literary poems, particularly by romantic poets. Similarly many street ballads have connections with 'traditional songs', for one way in which ballad printers acquired material for their texts was to send their agents into the country to collect the words of songs being sung there. In turn, some literary poems are based on earlier street ballads – Campbell's *Ye mariners of England,* for instance, is clearly inspired by Martin Parker's seventeenth-century street ballad *Saylors for my money* (see Pinto and Rodway, 1965, pp. 19 and 221ff).

Another apparent distinction – between street ballads and 'proper' literature – cannot be pressed very far either, for there was continual interchange between the two from the sixteenth century. A number of well-known English poets are known to have written 'street ballads'. Marlowe's *Come live with me* and Raleigh's reply, for instance, were printed together anonymously on a single broadsheet. Again, in the corpus of poetry attributed to or deriving from Burns, it is almost impossible to draw a clear line between what is oral and what written: some poems perhaps originated from popular poetry crystallised and written down by Burns, others were perhaps originally conceived by him but now circulate orally in various renderings. Here and elsewhere clear-cut distinctions in terms of transmission cannot be applied.

The 'broadside' ballads are a particularly instructive instance of the interaction in distribution between written and oral modes. In England around the early sixteenth century, ballads were distributed in broadside form: at first on single large unfolded sheets of paper in 'black letter' (or gothic) type, later in various formats, including the 'chapbooks' (or pamphlets of 8–16 pages) and the small collections of songs or ballads known as 'garlands'. They were designed for wide distribution and cheap sale, and printed in very large numbers. A nineteenth-century ballad about a particularly sensational murder ran to 250,000 copies (Laws, 1957, p. 39). Several hundred ballad printers are known to have practised throughout the British Isles (in the first ten years of Elizabeth's reign alone, at least forty publishers of ballads are mentioned in the incomplete records of the Stationers' Company) and all in all 'ballads were printed and circulated in enormous numbers' (Rollins, 1919, pp. 258–9).

The main way in which these broadside ballads reached their public was by ballad singers going around the towns or countryside singing samples of their wares, and trying to sell broadside sheets. They were a familiar sight at fairs and markets, and broadsides were among the common stock carried by pedlars throughout the country. In the cities, ballads were sold both by street singers and in small shops and stalls. The initial distribution and publication was thus a mixture of print and performance, with the ballad singer actually performing samples of his ballads to entice people to purchase them. After that, it seems clear that the ballads often circulated orally, with people singing the currently popular ones, or adopting and adapting their own favourites – so that many ballads which started as printed broadside texts then circulated largely through oral means, subject to the variability and re-composition so common in oral literature. This oral transmission in turn sometimes mingled with written distribution, for there is no reason to suppose that popular singers eschewed all contact with the printed versions of their songs, and it is known that singers sometimes wrote down words in manuscript ballad books to assist them (Laws, 1957, p. 44).

The apparently clear-cut 'start' from the printed form may itself give an over-simplified picture; for the origins of broadside ballads too sometimes involve a similarly complex mix of oral and written forms. In some cases, the printers employed ballad writers who produced not only 'timeless' ballads on various romantic and legendary themes, but also wrote up topical incidents: they were sent to 'cover' events of interest and produced many ballads about recent deaths, battles, storms, shipwrecks, murders, executions and the criminal's 'confession', incidents at court and so on. Agents also went into the country to search out 'traditional' songs, and used them as a basis for printed ballads. It is often impossible to say which came first, printed broadsheet or popular song, and the detailed origins of particular broadside ballads are usually not known. It is certain, however, that some broadside ballads are 'indistinguishable in style and content from various Child Ballads' (Laws, 1957, p. 78) and that far from pure 'oral tradition' being unquestionably the norm for ballad transmission, the practice over the last few centuries in Britain, Ireland and (later) America has been for ballad distribution to proceed through a complex interplay of written, printed and oral media. There is no indication that these are incompatible or mutually destructive. On the contrary, as Laws claims, 'One of the strongest arguments against the harmful effects of print is the remarkable vitality of the broadside ballad tradition '(Laws, 1957, p. 59; see also Holloway, 1970).

One could quote many examples of ballads which began in broadside form, and then started to circulate in part orally, in part in print. Greene, for instance, discusses the detailed history of *The lady and the dragoon*, normally accepted as a 'traditional ballad'. He shows that it does not just start off from a seventeenth-century origin, from which it was transmitted by 'oral tradition' (the conventional view). Rather, it can be closely related to a nineteenth-century broadsheet published by Nathaniel Coverly of Boston, itself based partly on earlier broadsides as well as on oral tradition. In the twentieth century 'at least forty versions of it have been collected from the American folk...the most noteworthy fact about all of these American traditional variants is that they resemble the Coverly broadside very closely – far more closely than it resembles its British ancestors of the seventeenth century' (Greene, 1957, p. 223). Other ballads begin in yet other ways. *O, bury me not on the lone prairie*, for example, apparently originated with a commercial parlour ballad, then started to circulate orally as part of the folksong repertoire of cowboys, and finally surfaced again among collectors (Lathrop, 1957). It seems probable that detailed research on other 'traditional folksongs' and ballads would reveal the same interaction between written and oral modes of transmission and distribution as in these examples, rather than the exclusively oral tradition sometimes automatically assumed.

Even the classic 'traditional' ballads brought to the secluded Appalachian region by the 'British forefathers' and since – in Sharp's account – surviving by 'oral tradition' may have been affected by the same kind of oral/written interaction. Though Sharp himself found no printed song-sheets, he does admit that some of his singers 'produced written copies, usually made by children, which they called "ballets"' (1932, I, p. xxviii). Perhaps more important, it is likely that the isolation of the American South, so much emphasised by Sharp and his followers, has been exaggerated. One of the leading American folklorists of today, D. K. Wilgus, is quite clear on this point:

> The 'isolation' of the Southern Highlander is a myth celebrated as much in the in-group folk jests as in the ethnographic accounts. By steam packet, by railroad, by returning loggers who had rafted timber, by returning westward migrants, by those who drove the jolt wagons to the settlements – selected musical materials reached our 'contemporary ancestors'. The South has been 'backward', but it has not been totally isolated. Throughout the later nineteenth century the entire rural South was accepting, rejecting, absorbing, reshaping the cultural influences and artifacts of the encroaching urban civilisation.
>
> (Wilgus, 1965, pp. 196–7)

Similarly Cray has demonstrated in a detailed study that *Barbara Allen's* popularity in America is at least partly due to its frequent inclusion in cheap print versions. He lists 43 appearances in print in the United States between about 1830 and 1910, many of them with wide circulation, such as the *Forget-Me-Not-Songster* of the 1840s or the version in *Harper's Magazine* in 1888, and considers that 'without a doubt, this bibliography could be doubled or trebled by working through further collections of ephemera since the ballad was as popular with the printing houses as it was with folk singers' (1967, p. 45). It is difficult to continue to assume that given instances recorded from local performance, whether in the Appalachians or elsewhere in America, must necessarily have come down through pure and non-literate 'oral transmission'.

That this sort of interaction between oral and written modes of distribution should need explicit documentation is a tribute to the strength of romantic theories about oral tradition. For it is, in the end, just what one would expect to find, wherever both literacy and illiteracy were significant.

There are many parallels to this kind of interaction. Popular Irish songs provide a familiar example of circulation in both written and sung forms, with constant fruitful interaction between the two, or the Turkic oral epics which now appear in popular editions and 'still retain their appeal as modern "chap books"' (Chadwick and Zhirmunsky, 1969, p. 290). Again, the American cowboy songs made so famous in John Lomax's collections and at one time supposed to have originated in oral circulation alone, now turn out (according to a recent study by John West, 1967) to have early sources in print as well as in performance around the camp fire. There are also the many forms in developing countries today which circulate both in written forms and by oral means (often radio, tape and records as well as word of mouth): the political songs, for instance, in Zambian elections in the 1960s which were performed at mass rallies to inspire and attract potential supporters, and *also* appeared in written form; or the Zulu hymns of the separatist church of Shembe in South Africa which were disseminated and performed orally among Zulu congregations but were also published. Similarly Malay oral poetry takes some of its inspiration from traditional Hindu and Muslim written forms (the *Ramayana* for instance appears in a local 'folk version') as well as from recent topical events; and, in their turn, oral poems become accepted into the written texts. There is no basic incompatibility between written and oral forms, so there is no reason why a poet should try to keep his art free from the influence of oral modes nor why a local singer should refuse inspiration from a poem just because it happens to have been printed.

Ortutay gives a nice case of a printed poem becoming what he terms 'folksong'. This is Petöfi's song 'I am sitting on a hill', where the last verse of the original poem is

> Szeretném, ha vadfa lennék erdöben.
> Még inkább: ha tüzvész lenne belőlem;
> Elégetném ezt az egész világot,
> Mely engem mindörökké esak bántott.

> (Wish I were a wild tree in a great forest.
> Still more if a great fire became of me,
> Burn would I all the world around me,
> Which did nothing but torment me without rest.)

Its folk song version is this:

> De szeretnék –
> De szeretnék fa lenni az erdöben,
> Ha valaki tüzet rakna belőlem;
> Felgyujtanám ezt a cudar világot,
> Közepéből –
> Két széléből szakajtanék virágot.

(How I would like –
How I would like be a great tree in forest
Oh, if someone made a fire out of me,
I would set then all the world well aflame
From its middle –
From its edges would I pluck a nice flower...)

(Ortutay, 1959, pp. 211–12)

This combination of written and oral media for the distribution and publication of literature goes back a long way. In classical Greece and Rome, public or semi-public readings and dramatic performances sometimes took place and formed one means by which a work that was initially written found its publication through an oral medium (Hadas, 1954, pp. 50ff; Crosby, 1936, pp. 88–9). Similarly in Europe in the Middle Ages it was common for literature to be recited or read aloud for the pleasure or edification of largely illiterate audiences. The original composition of the pieces may have been in writing but their transmission and main distribution was, in practice, oral.

> The romances are full of passages showing that minstrelsy, not music alone, but chanting or reciting of stories as well, was the almost inevitable accompaniment of feasting, particularly in celebration of such a great event as a wedding or a coronation. The professional minstrel was often employed also merely to help some king or nobleman while away his leisure hours. Often, too, on journeys, whether on horse-back or shipboard, the song or recitation of the minstrel was heard. Not only before the nobility but for the benefit of the common people in the streets the professional story-teller recited his tales and paused at interesting points to pass his hat for contributions. Finally, though the church frowned upon the jongleur, especially in the days of his decline, she allowed him within her precincts when he confined himself to such literary pieces as chansons de geste, lives of the saints, and miracles of the Virgin. From all the evidence that has been many times discussed, the popularity of the minstrel in the days when books and readers were few and when theaters offered no rival attractions, cannot be overestimated.

(Crosby, 1936, pp. 92–3)

This point about the importance of oral communication in the Middle Ages is worth emphasising, for since written texts are among our main continuing sources for the period it is tempting to overestimate their importance as a medium – and this tendency is supplemented by the common model of mediaeval European society which sees it as dominated by the formal learning of the Church. But at the time, everyday communication was largely oral; as one analyst puts it, 'medieval history is marked by large-scale popular movements: people's crusades, heresy, preaching, pilgrimage, cults of relics, songs, and stories are among them' (Morris, 1972,

p. 5). In many of these orally communicated songs and poems, written and orally-composed forms interacted and mutually influenced each other. Take, for instance, the *Song of the ass*, a song belonging to a ceremony when a donkey was brought to the church during Epiphany. The song is, as Morris points out, 'a rich cultural mixture'

> combining as it does liturgical and popular music; a clerk's knowledge of the Bible, the touch of a satirist, and a French response for the people.

Orientis partibus	In the eastern regions, there
Adventavit Asinus	Once arrived a donkey fair.
Pulcher et fortissimus	Brave as any ass may be,
Sarcinis aptissimus.	Good at carrying loads was he.
Hez hez sire asnes hez.	*Hey, Sir Donkey, hee-haw.*
Aurum de Arabia	Gold, which came from Arab lands,
Thus et myrram de Saba.	Myrrh and scent, from distant strands,
Tulit in ecclesia	Carried down the church's length
Virtus asinaria.	With a donkey-given strength.
Hez hez sire asnes hez.	*Hey, Sir Donkey, hee-haw.*
Dum trahit vehicula	He can pull a wagon-train,
Multa cum sarcinnula	And a bundle well sustain,
Illius mandibula	While he vigorously gnaws
Dura terit pabula.	His rough fodder with his jaws.
Hez hez sire asnes hez.	*Hey, Sir Donkey, hee-haw.*
Cum artistis ordeum	So he eats the ears and bristles
Comedit et carduum	Of his favourite corn and thistles,
Triticum a palea	All around the threshing-floor,
Segregat in area.	Segregating wheat from straw.
Hez hez sire asnes hez.	*Hey, Sir Donkey, hee-haw.*
Amen dicas, asine	So proclaim 'amen', you ass,
Iam satur ex gramine	Now that you are full of grass,
Amen Amen itera	Then repeat 'amen' again,
Aspernare vetera.	And all former things disdain.
Hez hez sire asnes hez.	*Hey, Sir Donkey, hee-haw.*

(Morris, 1972, p. 8)

This mixed mode of literary distribution – popular song arising in part from a knowledge of written forms and written literature often transmitted by oral means: recitation, chant or reading aloud – was characteristic of mediaeval Europe. Similar situations are found throughout the world, particularly where there is a smallish educated literate group and an illiterate majority. In East Africa the long written *tenzi* – didactic or narrative poems composed in the framework of earlier Arabic models – often originate in writing but are designed for public performance. They are sung or intoned aloud, sometimes by the composer himself, with a musical accompaniment, and this public recital ensures that these poems are widely transmitted and 'would reach the ears of the ordinary man' (Harries, 1962, p. 24). Similar public performances of written Hausa poems are given to illiterate audiences in Northern Nigeria (and the radio is used in this way too), as well as being transmitted in oral form, chanted by beggars for instance, or snug on the streets at night (Last, 1972, pp. 8–9; Hiskett, 1964, p. 540; Paden, 1965, pp. 33, 36). Other parallels are manifold: the mediaeval Chinese ballads where the singers performed sometimes from a written text, sometimes from notes 'to jog their memory before or during the performance' (Doleželová-Velingerová and Crump, 1971, p. 2); eighteenth-century Malay romances (*hikayat*) 'read, sung, or recited from a book by an educated reader to an audience of paying listeners' (Wilkinson, 1924, p. 29); or the way some traditional ballad singers or modern performers use written versions as an occasional aid to oral delivery.

It is no surprise that what at first sight seems like pure 'oral transmission' of a particular series of oral poems proves to include interaction with *written* forms. This is so with the Gésar epic cycle mentioned at the outset of this discussion as one apparent instance of long and widespread oral transmission. It turns out that the many oral and written versions have almost certainly been interdependent over at least three centuries (Stein, 1959, chapter 3). The same goes for the famous heroic epic songs of Yugoslavia, where over many years oral and written forms have 'flowed into each other: the heroic songs chanted by the *guslari* found their way into literature while written stories reached the *guslari* who turned them into decasyllabic lines' (Subotić, 1923, p. 90). Even that case of oral transmission *par excellence*, the *Rgveda*, turns out to have contacts with written versions. As Emeneau concludes: 'oral transmission down to the present day by memorization is undoubted – but at the same time suspect, since it is clear that there has at times been recourse to good old manuscripts to correct corrupt oral tradition' (Emeneau in Hymes, 1964, p. 331). In all cases of claimed 'oral transmission', in short, we need to ask whether writing might not also have played a part in the transmission.

5 *Conclusion*

The modes of transmission, distribution and publication of oral poetry turn out to be complicated, and not, as used to be commonly supposed, confined neatly to two distinct traditions, one oral, the other written. In practice one always has to envisage the possibility of more complex interactions between many different modes of transmission and distribution. Classifying a poem as, say, 'folk' or 'oral' or 'popular' on the basis of its style, expected audience or origin, gives no *automatic* information about its likely mode of distribution and transmission.

In the twentieth century too, besides the overlap of written and oral face-to-face media, there is also the contribution of new media like radio and television, gramophone and tape-recorder. These are clearly 'oral' media, but not in the sense used in traditional ballad scholarship. The purist is tempted to try to exclude them from his study of transmission, but this is unrealistic. In this century they form one of the main means of distribution of oral poetry – and not just in industrial countries.

The many contributory means of distribution are thus now even more complex than in earlier centuries; one must look not only at interaction between written text and word-of-mouth forms, but also at the involvement of mechanically reproduced oral means by which large audiences can (on occasion) be reached, and multiple identical versions of the same poem produced and distributed.

This chapter shows that it has increasingly become necessary to treat 'transmission', 'distribution' and 'publication' together. It *is* possible to make analytic distinctions between them and even (though this is more difficult with oral than written literature) to apply the distinctions in practice. But with oral poetry they shade into each other and discussion of one inevitably involves others. The aspect of composition, too, quickly enters in. (This chapter is thus in some respects a continuation of the discussions of composition in chapters 3 and 4).

One final point. A main theme of this chapter has been the rejection of a cluster of romantic theories about the nature and purity of 'oral transmission'. I have stressed the frequent significance of written and printed forms, and tried to remove 'oral transmission' from the unique position in which it has often been placed in such theories. But it would be wrong to imply that transmission by word of mouth has little importance – or has lost its importance in the modern world. On the contrary, it is, even now, one of the most important means of communication (perhaps *the* most important) for literary as well as other forms; and the communication of both print and modern mechanical means of communication is still often through word of mouth. The characteristics of 'oral transmission' and 'oral distribution' are important in the initial assessment of any piece of literature as 'oral', even if the mode of transmission is more complex and unpredictable than used to be believed. It is good to remember the sensible emphasis of folklorists and others on the significance of oral transmission, even if we reject the more extreme and unsubstantiated assumptions of romantic theorists and those who postulate a single and universal set of laws of 'oral transmission'.

6

Poets and their positions

In any consideration of oral poetry, one obvious question is: *who* are the poets? Who composes and performs oral poetry? The quick answer is that it can be almost anyone. An immense variety of people are, and are expected to be, poets in different groups and societies. Despite some confident pronouncements on the subject, there seems no one predictable pattern in type of personality, relationship of the poet to his society, or the economic and social rewards of poetry. The role of poet is occupied and envisaged in a variety of ways – from the official court poets of kingdoms in mediaeval Europe or Asia or recent West Africa, to a Malay or Eskimo shaman, or an American preacher claiming poetic inspiration from the spirit, or the unpaid lead singer in a working group of canoeists or agricultural workers or prisoners. And yet the position of the makers of oral poetry is neither random nor totally unpredictable. There are recurring patterns found in widely separated parts of the world; and the opportunities and duties of the oral, as of the literate, poet are regulated by social conventions and co-ordinated with the social and economic institutions of his society.

It may be helpful to start with portraits of individual poets. Case studies can usefully give a preliminary illustration of the variety of oral poets, as well as an initial basis for exploring the still prevalent theory that oral poetry is composed anonymously, perhaps even 'communally', rather than by individual named poets. We also gain some idea of how poets themselves see their work, and of their interpretation of their role.

1 The poet: five case studies

The first example is Velema Daubitu the poet and seer, at the village called The-Place-of-Pandanus (Namuavoivoi) in the island of Vanua Levu, Fiji. He was an old man in the 1930s, when Quain recorded and translated a number of his songs (published in 1942). Velema was the composer and performer of several kinds of poetry, but chief among them were heroic poems about the deeds of far-off ancestors who belonged to the legendary kingdom of Flight-of-the-Chiefs, from whom the present chiefs and their subjects believed they were descended. This was the most valued form of oral literature among the Fijians, and it was held that the appropriate person to compose them was a man who – like Velema – was seer as well as poet.

When Velema was still a child, people began to notice in him the kind of personality and behaviour which made them feel he was destined to be a seer. They noted in particular his diffidence and his excitability, as well as his curiosity about serious things. Because of this Velema was chosen by his mother's brother to succeed him as priest and guardian of the sacred objects of the village. Over many years Velema learnt from his uncle how to perform the rituals of his landgroup, and inherited the sacred war club and axe as well as the dancing spear – all of which played a part in his composition of songs. At the same time he was trained in the arts of singing and composition, and learnt the secret mysteries of communing with the ancestors, the inspirers of poems. He 'learned how it felt to speak with them and even let them use his tongue to speak.' (Quain, 1942, p. 14.)

In Fijian poetic theory, the ancestors teach and form the songs. This is believed to go further than mere inspiration: with the 'true-songs' or epic songs the ancestors themselves chant the songs as they teach them to the poet, and it is in their name that they are delivered.

> During one of my sojourns at Flight-of-the-Chiefs
> The-Eldest is calling

is the opening of one of Velema's 'true-songs' (p. 21) in which the ancestor is speaking through Velema's mouth, and describing how he himself was there in the ancestral home and observed the incidents of the poem which follows. These poems are given to Velema in trance or sleep. He acts only as the mouthpiece of his mentors: 'he takes no personal credit for his composition, does not even distinguish between those which he has composed himself and those old ones which his mother's brother must surely have taught him. All contribute to the glory of his ancestors' (Quain, 1942, p. 14). Even the special liberties that Velema took with language so as to fit the musical and rhythmic requirements of the verse are attributed to the ancestors' chanting. When Velema chose 'archaic words from his own background, words which he alone understands' (ibid. p. 16) so as to fit the rhythm, this too has the implied sanction of ancestral approval.

This insistence on the personal involvement of the ancestors in the poems is made more effective by the stylistic device of first-person interpolations into the epic narrative. From time to time the poet's recounting of historic events is replaced, as it were, by the direct speech of one of the ancestral actors. This comes out well in the opening sections of one of Velema's 'true' poems, where he describes how the gods of the mythical village of Flying-Sand plot to attack Flight-of-the-Chiefs, the ancestral home of Velema and his compatriots. Their ancestor Watcher-of-the-Land discovers the plan, and after vainly trying to find a safe refuge for his friends, comes to Flight-of-the-Chiefs to warn their leader (The-Eldest) of the threatened

attack. From time to time Watcher-of-the-Land speaks in his own person
(printed in italics).

> Those at Flying-Sand hold council;
> They hold council there, those Gods of the Beginning.
> They decide that Flight-of-the-Chiefs be eaten.
> It stings, the foot of Watcher-of-the-Land;
> And Sir Watcher-of-the-Land wails forth
> So that Flight-of-the-Chief resounds.
> *And quickly I came outside.*
> *I took up my staff.*
> *I descended to the shore at Bua*
> *I dived down to the Cave of Sharks.*
> *Creeping, I explored the grotto*
> *That those of Flight-of-the-Chiefs might be hidden there.*
> *I crawled outward to the open sea.*
> *I climbed to the village at Levuka.*
> There are shallows in the open sea,
> And Watcher-of-the-Land dives again.
> *I dived among the white coral rock.*
> *I climbed to the village at Peninsula.*
> *I climbed upward again to Flight-of-the Chiefs.*
> *I entered into The-Land's-Beginning.*
> And there is the wailing of Watcher-of-the-Land
> And it re-echoes through Flight-of-the-Chiefs,
> And Watcher-of-the-Land stands up
> And takes again his staff.
> *And quickly I came outside.*
> *I climbed upward to The-First-Appearance.* [a high cliff]
> And Watcher-of-the-Land digs a hole
> And he disappears down into the second depth in the earth.
> And then Watcher-of-the-Land says:
>> 'The people of Flight-of-the-Chiefs be hidden here,
>> Then the Gods of the Beginning will find them.'
> And Watcher-of-the-Land returns again.
> *I entered into It-Repels-Like-Fire.* [his own village]
> And Watcher-of-the-Land is weeping there.
> And he takes up his staff.
> *And quickly I came outside.*
> *And I hurtled downward to Flight-of-the-Chiefs*
> *I hastened to The-Eldest.*
> Watcher-of-the-Land is weeping there
> And now-The-Eldest asks:
>> 'What report from The-Land's-Beginning?'
> And now Watcher-of-the-Land answers:
>> 'Listen, then, the-Eldest:
>> Those at Flying-Sand hold council.
>> They decide that Flight-of-the-Chiefs be eaten.'

(Quain, 1942, pp. 45-7)

The most important and serious inspirers of poetry are the 'true ancestors' from whom Velema learns the heroic 'true' songs by virtue of his control of the ancient war club and axe. But there are also other spirits – like the Children of Medicine – who teach him the less serious songs. Velema is a participant in the special Children of Medicine cult, and through this and his possession of his ancestral dancing spear he is able to compose dances and dance-songs as well as serenades. These songs are comparatively short and less complex stylistically than the 'epic' poems. They raise fewer problems of composition, and are believed to be inspired by less revered spirits.

Velema not only practised his art in solemn religious surroundings, but took part in dance festivities and sometimes entertained an evening gathering with his songs. On these occasions he chanted the epic songs himself, accompanied by another old man who accompanied him as a kind of chorus.

His long training and religious responsibilities made use of, rather than changed, his unusual and excitable personality. As he grew up, people came to recognise his strange talents, and to accept from him actions unacceptable in others, like brooding all day in the house or wandering too often alone in the forest. From a poet and seer, such behaviour was even expected. As Quain sums it up, 'Though there are sceptics among modern citizens who suspect that the poet exaggerates the virtues of the heroes at Flight-of-the-Chiefs, yet no one doubts the validity of his talent for literary rapport with the supernatural. His ancestral communications are the only bonds with the distant past' (ibid. pp. 8–9).

The second poet is the Yugoslav epic minstrel, Avdo Mededović. He has become famous through the researches of Parry and Lord, but throughout most of his life he directed his compositions to local audiences in rural Yugoslavia.

Avdo Mededović was born, lived and died in eastern Montenegro, in what is now Yugoslavia. His father and grandfather were butchers, and in his mid-teens Avdo began to learn their trade and, despite spending some years away from his home in the army, he ultimately married and settled down to follow them as village butcher. As a Muslim, he and his family were in great danger in the months just after the defeat of Turkey in the First World War, but he managed to survive and keep his butcher's shop, and to spend the greater part of his life as 'a quiet family man in a disturbed and brutal world' (Lord, 1956, p. 123).

Avdo was born into a culture in which epic singers flourished, and grew up hearing the traditional themes sung in epic poems to the *gusle* (the one-stringed bowed instrument used to accompany singing). This rich tradition behind him provided him with much of the material for his poetry. But he also learnt his art from skilled singers, above all from his father.

He in his turn had been deeply influenced by a famous singer of his own generation, Cor Huso Husein, who still had a prodigious reputation in the area. Cor Huso's main characteristic was apparently the ability to 'ornament' a song, characteristic also of Avdo's work.

Avdo's capacity to compose and perform epic was enormous. Though it makes no sense in the type of combined performance-composition typical of Avdo's art to try to calculate absolute figures of how many poems he 'knew', it is noteworthy that he claimed to have a repertoire of fifty-eight epics. Parry and his assistant recorded thirteen of these in 1935 (to which must be added the recording of additional versions by Lord in 1950 and 1951). The result is 96,723 lines of recorded epic from Avdo's singing alone. His longest single song contains 13,331 lines and represents over sixteen hours of singing time. From the mere point of view of quantity it is hardly surprising that Parry was so impressed by Avdo as a singer. As Lord puts it, 'Avdo could sing songs of about the length of Homer's *Odyssey*. An illiterate butcher in a small town of the central Balkans was equalling Homer's feat, at least in regard to length of song. Parry had actually seen and heard two long epics produced in a tradition of oral epic' (Lord, 1956, p. 125).

Avdo's epic versions of stories tended to be longer than anyone else's because of his 'ornamentation'. He amplified the details, and elaborated what he had heard from others. He did not merely borrow 'ornaments' from other singers, for many came from his visualising the scene himself. As he once told Lord, he 'saw in his mind every piece of trapping which he put on a horse' (Lord, 1956, p. 125).

His ability to extend and ornament a song was well demonstrated in 1935, when he heard another poet, Mumin Vlahovljak sing the tale of *Bećiragić Meho*, previously unknown to Avdo. Mumin was a skilled singer and his song, a fine one, ran to 2,294 lines. As soon as it finished, Parry asked Avdo if he could now sing the 'same' song himself. At first he asked to be excused, because he did not wish to offend Mumin or take the honour away from him. When he was finally persuaded to sing, his version reached 6,313 lines, nearly three times the length of the 'original epic'. 'As [Avdo] sang, the song lengthened, the ornamentation and richness accumulated, and the human touches of character, touches that distinguished Avdo from other singers, imparted a depth of feeling that had been missing in Mumin's version' (Lord, 1968a, p. 78).

A similar example is his great epic *The wedding of Smailagić Meho*. Avdo first heard a song on this theme read aloud from a written version. It had been published in a small songbook that Hivzo, the butcher in a shop next to his, had bought in Sarajevo. Hivzo had taught himself to read, and gradually read out the version to Avdo, making out the words slowly and painfully. The printed version had 2,160 lines – but when Avdo performed the song as one of his epic poems in 1935, it stretched to 12,323 lines.

This capacity to ornament and to introduce his own personal touches, sometimes reflecting insights obviously drawn from his own experiences, runs through all Avdo's poems. It was this, rather than a superlative performance, that gave his poems such force, for his voice was not especially good (it was rather hoarse), and his accompaniment on the *gusle* was only mediocre. But in his poems he could convey the conventional themes of Slavic epic and his own personal commentary on them. He was dedicated to the themes and atmosphere of the epics he performed:

> The high moral tone of his songs is genuine. His pride in tales of the glories of the Turkish Empire in the days of Sulejman, when it was at its height and when 'Bosnia was its lock and its golden key', was poignantly sincere without ever being militant or chauvinistic. That empire was dead, and Avdo knew it, because he had been there to hear its death rattle. But it had once been great in spite of the corruption of the imperial nobility surrounding the sultan. To Avdo its greatness was in the moral fibre and loyal dedication of the Bosnian heroes of the past even more than in the strength of their arms. These characteristics of Avdo's poems, as well as a truly amazing sensitivity for the feelings of other human beings, 'spring from within the singer himself. He was not 'preserving the traditional'; Avdo believed with conviction in the tradition which he exemplified.
>
> (Lord, 1956, p. 123–4)

A very different example is the American Negro prisoner Johnnie B. Smith. He had spent much of his life in Texas prisons and it was in prison that he had developed the songs through which, Bruce Jackson says, 'he has woven an elaborate construct of images that brilliantly details the parameters of his world' (Jackson, 1972, p. 144).

When Jackson, researching on prison songs, met Smith in a Texas prison in the mid-1960s, Smith was in the eleventh year of a forty-five-year sentence for murder. It was not his first sentence, for he had three previous convictions for burglary and robbery by assault. Here he describes the murder:

> I got out of here on those ten-year sentences, that robbery by assault. I lost my people while I was in here and I just felt like I was kind of in the world alone. I wanted to find me a pretty girl to settle down with and marry. I was thirty-five years old then. And I just wanted to marry and settle down. I left my home down at Hearn, Texas, other side of Bryant, and went to west Texas, out in the Panhandle country, to Amarillo. And I married a beautiful girl. She was about three-quarters Indian, I guess. A lot of mixed-breed girls out there, 'specially around Mexico and Oklahoma and Amarillo. I found me that pretty girl, the girl of my dreams I thought, and I had good intentions. But now, I fell in love with her, was what I did, and I got insane jealousy mixed up with love. So many of us do that. Lot of

fellas in here today on those same terms. I was really insane crazy about the girl and I had just got out of the penitentiary and I was working, just trying to make an honest living and to keep from coming back. But I couldn't give her all she wanted and she'd sneak out a little. That went to causing trouble. I was intending to get in good shape, but I hadn't been out there long enough, not to make it on the square, you know. She wanted a fine automobile, she like a good time, a party girl, she liked to drink, she liked to dress nice. So did I, and so I was living a bit above my income. And she would sneak out to enjoy these little old pleasures and that caused us some family trouble. On a spur of the moment I came in one day, we had a fight and I cut her to death. And regret it! Because I loved her still and still do and can't get her back.

(Jackson, 1972, pp. 143-4)

Forty-five years is to all intents a life sentence. In prison on this long sentence Smith composed the poetry under his name in Jackson's collection of Texas prison work songs.

This poetry takes the form of the solo part in songs designed to accompany the work prisoners have to do throughout the day. Some of these songs give small scope for originality. These accompany strictly metered work, in which the timing is critical for effective working and to avoid injury to co-workers – where several men are simultaneously chopping down a tree, for instance. In songs for work like this, the verbal element is relatively simple, with short lines and automatic repetition giving the lead singer time to prepare his next line. But for songs to accompany less strictly timed work – cane cutting or cotton picking for instance – there is more opportunity for the soloist. They tend to be more complex in text as well as in melody and ornament, and offer the soloist scope for experiment.

Smith was an effective leader in the strictly timed songs, and even there he set his own stamp on the words. But in the solo verses of songs for less rigidly metered tasks Smith had the fullest scope for originality. Jackson's collection of non-metered work songs by Smith runs to 132 separate stanzas. Though the sections were often sung separately (and even sometimes given separate titles) Smith usually thought of them as really *one* song, and sometimes talked of them in that way.

His songs are very much a function of his surroundings and reflect his and his co-prisoners' concerns. As Smith once said, 'Guy down here, if he's thinkin' about anything at all, he's thinking about his freedom and his woman' (ibid. p. 37). Eighteen stanzas are indeed about 'his woman', and there are frequent mentions of places outside prison, in the world of freedom. But it is the negatives of his basic concerns that Smith is thinking more of – the constraints and bonds that keep him *from* his woman, and restrict his freedom. Thus many of the stanzas refer to the length of his sentence, or the possibility of escape, and there are constant references to the guards and the prison officials, to firearms and to sickness and death. As Jackson puts it,

> The reason Smith (he is the most creative song leader I met; the statements here apply even more to the others) cannot dwell at any length on his woman or his freedom is that he does not really think of *them* so much as of their *absence*; he perceives the negative, and in his imagistic song-world there are no terms to present these feelings (for they are not *things*) directly. All he can do is deal with the *devices* of control: the number of years he has to do, the weapons of the guards, the presence of the guards, the existence of other places to which he has no access. To express both hope and longing, both his sense of self and his lack of control over that self's movements, the singer is forced to document the concreteness of the enemy, the prison itself, because that is all that *is* concrete, and depend on rhetoric to return to his real themes.
>
> (Jackson, 1972, p. 39)

This is evident in the opening of his song 'No More Good Time in the World for Me'

> No more good time, buddy, oh man, in the wide, wide world for
>   me,
> 'Cause I'm a lifetime skinner, never will go free.
> Well a lifetime skinner, buddy, I never will go free,
> No more good time, buddy, in the wide, wide world for me.
>
> Lifetime skinner, skinner, hold up your head,
> Well you may get a pardon if you don't drop dead.
> Well you may get a pardon, oh man, if you don't drop dead,
> Oh well lifetime skinner, partner, you hold up your head.
>
> I been on this old Brazos, partner, so jumpin' long,
> That I don't know what side a the river, oh boy, my home is on,
> Don't know what side a the river, oh man, oh boy, my home is on,
> 'Cause I been down on this old river, man, so jumpin' long.
>
> Well I lose all my good time, 'bout to lose my mind,
> I can see my back door slammin', partner, I hear my baby cryin'.
> Yeah, I'm a hear my back door slammin', man, I hear my baby
>   cryin',
> I done lose all my good time, partner, I'm 'bout to lose my
>   mind...
>
> (Jackson, 1972, p. 148)

There is a full account of Smith's style and the way he built up his own individual insights and imagery in a traditional framework in Jackson's book (1972, esp. pp. 143ff). Despite his obvious talent and creativity, Smith felt that it was his circumstances rather than his own application that generated his poetry.

7

Now these songs, we can, you know, you stay here so long, a man can compose them if he want to. They just come to you. Your surroundings, the place, you're so familiar with them, you can always make a song out of your surroundings. I read about some great poetry, like King David in the Bible, he used to make his psalms from the stars and he wrote so many psalms. A little talent and surroundings and I think it's kind of easy to do it.

(Jackson, 1972, p. 144)

The fourth example is the Eskimo poet, Orpingalik. Although we do not know much about his life or his economic position *qua* poet, his articulateness about his poetry and his greatness as a poet in the eyes of Eskimos and foreigners make him an interesting member of this group of brief case studies.

Orpingalik was a member of the Netsilik group of Eskimos in the interior of the Rae Isthmus area of northern Canada, which was visited by Rasmussen in his great expedition through Eskimo country in the early 1920s. Our knowledge of Orpingalik's personality and poetry derive from the publications in which Rasmussen reported his findings from that expedition.

Orpingalik – 'He-with-the-willow-twig' – was a man of mature years when Rasmussen met him, with several full-grown sons, a daughter, at least one grand-child, and a wife, Uvlunuaq ('The-little-day'), who was herself a notable poet. Orpingalik himself was accepted by local people as outstanding in many ways: 'a big man'. He was a great hunter – important to an Eskimo group living under the constant threat of starvation if the game on which they depended eluded them. He was also a strong and deadly archer, and 'the quickest kayakman of them all when the caribou herds were being pursued at the places where they crossed the lakes and rivers' (Rasmussen, 1931, p. 13).

Orpingalik was revered as a shaman as well as for his physical skills. He was an *angakok* who could communicate with the spirits in séance, and he had his own guiding spirits who had chosen him of their own volition and whom he could summon through their spirit songs and commune with in the special metaphorical shaman's language. As shaman he was versed in the intellectual and poetic traditions of his people – he recounted many tales as well as poems to Rasmussen during his visit – and was also the personal possessor of many magic songs and spells. These belong to him alone, and no one else had the right to use them. Even Rasmussen could not record them free, but paid Orpingalik in kind 'giving him in return some of those I had obtained from Aua [another shaman].' (Rasmussen, 1927, p. 161). Control of these spells added to Orpingalik's prestige and power: they enabled him to catch seals, to hunt in a strange country, to injure his enemies and, as in this one, to kill caribou unscathed

1 Velema

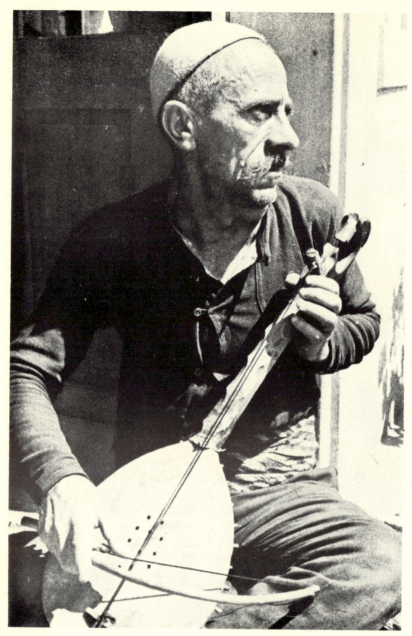

2 Avdo Međedović, Guslar

3 Johnnie B. Smith

4 Granny Riddle singing with her band

Wild caribou, land louse, long-legs,
With the great ears,
And the rough hairs on your neck,
Flee not from me.
Here I bring skins for soles,
Here I bring moss for wicks,
Just come gladly
Hither to me, hither to me.

(Rasmussen, 1931, p. 15)

But the power of a shaman could rebound too – or so it seemed in Eskimo eyes – and Orpingalik's life held suffering as well as leadership and prestige. Only a year before his meeting with Rasmussen, Orpingalik and his youngest son Inugjag had met disaster, and all his power and skill as shaman had not availed to save his son's life. He and Inugjag had been ferrying their possessions over a wide river on an icefloe when the swift current suddenly caught the floe and overturned it. Orpingalik and his son were immediately sucked under.

> When Orpingalik at length came to himself he was lying on the bank, half in the water, with his head knocking against a stone. The pain brought him to his senses, and a glance at the sun told him that he must have lain unconscious a long time. All at once the catastrophe became vividly clear to him and he began to look for his son, whom he found a little way further down the river. He carried him up to the bank and tried to call him to life with a magic song. It was not long before a caterpillar crawled up on the face of the corpse and began to go round its mouth, round and round. Not long afterwards the son began to breathe very faintly, and then other small creatures of the earth crawled on to his face, and this was a sign that he would come to life again. But in his joy Orpingalik went home to his tent and brought his wife to help him, taking with him a sleeping skin to lay their son on while working to revive him. But hardly had the skin touched the son when he ceased breathing, and it was impossible to put life into him again. Later on it turned out that the reason why the magic words had lost their power was, that in the sleeping skin there was a patch that had once been touched by a menstruating woman, and her uncleanness had made the magic words powerless and killed the son.
>
> (Rasmussen, 1931, pp. 11–12)

Other Eskimos explained the incident differently. They pointed out that the icefloe would not normally have capsized – 'it was as if the floe suddenly met with some resistance that forced it down under the waters of the river' – and that the cause of the disaster was magic words that had rebounded on their master after Orpingalik had tried to kill another shaman. He turned out to be more powerful than Orpingalik and the evil spell turned back against its maker: since it could not kill Orpingalik himself – for he too was a great shaman – it took his son's life instead. 'For a formula of wicked words like that *must* kill if there is any power in it; and if it does not kill the one it is made for, it turns against its creator, and if it cannot kill him either, one of his nearest must pay with his life' (Rasmussen, 1931, p. 201).

So the position and insights of a shaman among the Eskimo involved hazards and suffering as well as prestige. They could not help, either, to save Orpingalik's other son, Igsivalitaq, from the bitterness of long exile from his family after he had murdered a hunting companion in a fit of temper. He had to live as an outlaw in the mountains, cut off from his people. His mother Uvlunuaq described the pain of his deed and his exile in a long poem

> When message came
> Of the killing and the flight,
> Earth became like a mountain with pointed peak,
> And I stood on the awl-like pinnacle
> And faltered,
> And fell!
> (Freuchen, 1962, p. 283)

We must set Orpingalik the poet against this background of experience and suffering. For him his songs were his 'comrades in solitude', and 'all my being is song' (Rasmussen, 1931, pp. 16, 15). Rasmussen thought him the most poetically gifted man he had met among the Netsilik Eskimo, with a luxuriant imagination and most sensitive intelligence (ibid. p. 15). Orpingalik was always singing when he had nothing else to do, and felt that his songs were a necessity to him, as much so as his breath: part and parcel of himself.

> How many songs I have I cannot tell you. I keep no count of such things. There are so many occasions in one's life when a joy or a sorrow is felt in such a way that the desire comes to sing; and so I only know that I have many songs. All my being is song, and I sing as I draw breath.
>
> (ibid. p. 16)

One of his most famous songs he called *My breath*, for, as he explains 'it is just as necessary for me to sing it as it is to breathe' (p. 321). He composed the poem when he was slowly recovering from a severe illness. He reflects on his present helplessness and reminisces about the past when he was strong and a hunter who could save the village from famine while his companions still slept. Into his poem he pours his despondency and self-questioning as he struggles to regain his strength and vigour.

MY BREATH

This is what I call this song, for it is just as
necessary to me to sing it as it is to breathe.

I will sing a song,
A song that is strong,
   Unaya – unaya.
Sick I have lain since autumn,
Helpless I lay, as were I
My own child.

Sad, I would that my woman
Were away to another house
To a husband
Who can be her refuge,
Safe and secure as winter ice.
   Unaya – unaya.

Sad, I would that my woman
Were gone to a better protector
Now that I lack strength
To rise from my couch.
   Unaya – unaya.

Dost thou know thyself?
So little thou knowest of thyself.
Feeble I lie here on my bench
And only my memories are strong!
   Unaya – unaya.

Beasts of the hunt! Big game!
Oft the fleeing quarry I chased!
Let me live it again and remember,
Forgetting my weakness.
   Unaya – unaya.

Let me recall the great white
Polar bear,
High up its back body,
Snout in the snow, it came!
He really believed
He alone was a male
And ran towards me.
   Unaya – unaya.

It threw me down
Again and again,
Then breathless departed
And lay down to rest,
Hid by a mound on a floe.
Heedless it was, and unknowing
That I was to be its fate.

Deluding itself
That he alone was a male,
And unthinking
That I too was a man!
    Unaya – unaya.

I shall ne'er forget that great blubber-beast,
A fjord seal,
I killed from the sea ice
Early, long before dawn,
While my companions at home
Still lay like the dead,
Faint from failure and hunger,
Sleeping.
With meal and with swelling blubber
I returned so quickly
As if merely running over ice
To view a breathing hole there.
And yet it was
An old and cunning male seal.
But before he had even breathed
My harpoon head was fast
Mortally deep in his neck.

That was the manner of me then.
Now I lie feeble on my bench
Unable even a little blubber to get
For my wife's stone lamp.
The time, the time will not pass,
While dawn gives place to dawn
And spring is upon the village.
    Unaya – unaya.

But how long shall I lie here?
How long?
And how long must she go a-begging
For fat for her lamp.
For skins for clothing
And meal for a meal?
A helpless thing – a defenceless woman.
    Unaya – unaya.

Knowest thou thyself?
So little thou knowest of thyself!
While dawn gives place to dawn,
And spring is upon the village.
    Unaya – unaya.

(ibid. pp. 321–3)

Besides his powers as poet and shaman, Orpingalik also had the ability
to reflect self-consciously on the process of poetic composition and the

functions of poetry. He had many discussions with Rasmussen about the significance of song both as an outlet for sorrow and anxiety and as a herald of festivity. He also explained how he conceived of a poem being born in the human mind, a passage interesting enough to quote once more

> 'Songs are thoughts, sung out with the breath when people are moved by great forces and ordinary speech no longer suffices.
> Man is moved just like the ice floe sailing here and there out in the current. His thoughts are driven by a flowing force when he feels joy, when he feels fear, when he feels sorrow. Thoughts can wash over him like a flood, making his breath come in gasps and his heart throb. Something, like an abatement in the weather, will keep him thawed up. And then it will happen that we, who always think we are small, will feel still smaller. And we will fear to use words. But it will happen that the words we need will come of themselves. When the words we want to use shoot up of themselves – we get a new song.'
>
> (ibid. p. 321)

Most detailed descriptions of individual oral poets are of men. There *are* references to women poets too, but these tend to be more generalised, and it seems that it is less common for specialist poets to be women. But one expert woman poet about whom we know a good deal is the American singer, 'Granny Riddle', acclaimed by folklorists and public alike as a 'folksinger'. Her memories and songs were recorded on tape by Roger Abrahams and published in 1970 as *A Singer and her Songs*.

Almeda Riddle was born in 1898 in the Ozarks, Arkansas, and spent most of her life in the region. Her father was part-Irish (his mother's people had come to America from Ireland) and he lived first from timber-working, then farming. He was also a singing master and enthusiastic singer: 'He sang all the time. He'd go into any community that we went into, and if they didn't have a singing class, he immediately taught a ten-day school. Those that could pay him, paid him, and those that couldn't, couldn't' (Abrahams, 1970b, p. 6). He himself was accustomed to using written versions – 'he sang most of his songs from the books' (ibid. p. 6) – and in this way helped to form his daughter's musical experience. She says 'Every morning before breakfast...I don't ever remember a time that he didn't sit down with his book and sing a song or two. And after supper each night, he'd always sit down and sing awhile. And from the time I can remember, I got 'round and sang, too. I knew my notes before I knew my letters' (ibid. p. 6).

Her mother, by contrast, relied more on oral transmission, and passed on to Almeda Riddle a number of songs she had learnt from her own mother. Of one song, 'My mother [said] she had learned that from her mother and her mother said she could remember her own mother singing it to her. And I am now singing it to *my* great-grandsons. And as her own mother came from Ireland, she supposed she learned it in Ireland' (ibid. p. 42). Other songs she learned from members of her mother's family, or from a wide circle of friends and acquaintances – for, as she describes it herself, Almeda Riddle had a 'passion' for collecting songs.

Not surprisingly, Almeda's method of learning and performing songs used both written and oral sources from the start. She clearly had a remarkable verbal memory and very quickly picked up songs she heard. But at the same time she liked to keep a written record – what she termed 'ballets' – and from an early age had a large collection of written texts.

In her recollections, Almeda Riddle speaks vividly of the effect her early upbringing had on her development as singer. Her father's influence, in her account, was the strongest of all, but it is clear that singing also formed part of her family life generally, and of much contemporary life around her. She used to sing with her sister and school friends, or creep in to listen to older girls singing ballads. When she and her future husband were courting, they used to sing and discuss singing together: 'We'd sit on the back porch and talk of books we'd read or things we'd seen or of songs we knew. Sometimes we'd just sing' (ibid. p. 67).

Singing often accompanied work – it went with sewing or spinning or making soap – and Almeda Riddle says that one reason she can remember so many songs was that she used to sing them to her cow as she milked. Song was also associated with the Primitive Baptist church of which she was a member, and a number of her songs were learnt there.

Her life was interspersed with tragedy. After only nine years of marriage, her husband and baby were killed in a cyclone in 1926, and she returned home to her father's farm with her three small children. An experience that in some ways affected her even more deeply was the death of her elder sister Claudia, with whom she used to sing.

> One of the earliest remembrances I have in life was playing with my sister, Claudia, who was four years older than I. We were rocking our dolls to sleep and singing to them. My father, who was a singing teacher, always sang with us a while almost every night before bedtime. I don't remember the songs we sang while Claudia was with us, but I do remember she sang very well and had a beautiful face, long golden hair, and a very sweet voice. She died after only three days' illness in August before I was six years old. I do remember the day she was taken sick quite well. We sat out in a peach tree in the backyard and sang and ate half-ripe peaches. She said she was getting cold, so we went inside. She was put to bed with a chill, what at that time, 1904, was no unusual thing in Arkansas. There was so much of what people called chills and fever – malaria. And she died the third day of her illness, after two more chills. I had what I guess you would call today a 'mental breakdown', and my father had to take me out in the woods with him each day. And for many months I remember I would only cry and say No when I was asked to sing.
>
> (ibid. p. 5)

Despite this, her passion for singing and song collecting continued, and in later life this was recognised by folksong collectors throughout the United States, who dubbed her 'Granny', for by her 60s she was already a great-grandmother. She sang for commercial recording companies[1] and with well-known bands as well as for local and family audiences, 'folk festivals' and university concerts.

Her repertoire covered both her favourite 'classic' ballads, as she called them – mostly those included in the Child canon, like *Barbara Allen*, *The four Marys*, *Lady Margaret* – but also some popular songs of the day, and even songs she had based on printed texts in newspapers or developed from recitations. Though she apparently laid great store on her songs being old and belonging to authentic tradition in some sense, she was by no means a passive traditor only. She explains herself how she changes a song in certain ways while singing, even though she dislikes the idea of over-dramatising her performances: 'Now, it's scarcely ever, if you sing a song from memory, that you'll sing it exactly word for word each time. You'll probably change a word here and there, which keeps it changing. This is true of all songs, the classic songs and other kinds' (ibid. p. 117). Her musical interpretations are noted for their richness and individuality. She uses variations to enhance the meaning of her story, so that almost every verse has its own nuances in actual performance. As one observer explains, 'She not only cultivates meaningful texts but creates a rich flexibility within the tune to accommodate the changing speech from stanza to stanza' (Foss in Abrahams, 1970b, p. 162).

In what she calls the 'classic songs' she emphasises that she is less prepared to make changes than in what she regards as newer songs. In the classics, she insists on keeping the 'meaning' as it has come to her even when she makes verbal changes

> The words, you know, are fluid...they might change this way or that, but never the meaning. I wouldn't consciously change the words of a song, and I'd be *very* careful not to change the meaning. But now I might sing you 'Barbara Allen' today one way, and I have at least six or eight versions of that, so tomorrow some of this version or that might creep in.
>
> (ibid. p. 120)

With other songs she is more prepared to claim a piece as her own. Her account of the way she worked out her own interpretation of *Go tell Aunt Nancy* is worth quoting at some length.

> Well, 'Go tell Aunt Nancy' is not a classic; it's my own version. Most of it I wrote...for the kids, and just to sing it to them...This arrangement of mine, I never heard of it except we kids just made it up, and sang it along as a child. Probably it's not any more authentic than I am...

---

[1] Among her records is Vanguard VRS 9158, *Almeda Riddle: Songs and ballads of the Ozarks*.

The first of that I heard was as a child. A little girl, Merty Cowan, sang that. I was very small, first school. And then my mother sang some verses of this. I guess the original is really the old goose who was always in the millpond. But I've always sung where she was killed by a walnut, definitely – the walnut hit her on the top of the head and killed her. Aunt *Nancy's* goose, and I remember as a child having some fierce arguments with school children over this song. Now, Merty Cowan sang it, the first time I heard it. She sang it as Aunt Nancy, and a walnut killed it. This was an older girl. I was about six, and I got it into my mind like that. Now these other verses have been picked up along the way from other children's versions of 'Aunt Nancy' and from my mother's. I remember one fight I had about the way she was buried and the way that the old goose 'died in the millpond, standing on her head'. And I said it definitely was Aunt *Rhody's* goose and not Aunt Nancy's. And so, I still say Aunt Nancy's goose was definitely killed by a walnut. She didn't die in the millpond.

And children like the way it's done now, and it's recorded like that. That's just Granny's version of 'Aunt Nancy' and I think it's nobody else's. I've sung that thing so long that I don't remember where it all comes from...

Go tell Aunt Nancy, go tell Aunt Nancy,
Go tell Aunt Nancy, her old grey goose is dead.
The one that she's been saving, one that she's been saving,
The one that she's been saving, to make a feather bed.
Down come a walnut, down come a walnut,
Down come a walnut and hit her on the head.
Go tell Aunt Nancy, poor old Aunt Nancy,
Go tell Aunt Nancy the old grey goose is dead.

The gander is weeping, gander is weeping,
The gander is weeping, because his wife is dead.
Her goslings all crying, and weeping and peeping,
Her goslings all crying, their mammy they can't find.
Down come a walnut, down come a walnut,
Down come a walnut and hit her on the head.
Go tell Aunt Nancy, poor old Aunt Nancy,
Go tell Aunt Nancy her old grey goose is dead.

Go tell Aunt Nancy, go tell Aunt Nancy,
We took her in the kitchen and cooked her all day long.
And she broke all the forkteeth, broke all the forkteeth,
Broke all the forkteeth, they weren't strong enough.
Broke out Grandad's teeth, broke all Granddad's [sic] teeth,
Poor old Granddad's teeth, the old grey goose was tough.
Go tell Aunt Nancy, go tell Aunt Nancy,
Go tell Aunt Nancy that the old grey goose is tough.

> Go tell Aunt Nancy, go tell Aunt Nancy,
> Go tell Aunt Nancy, we hauled her to the mill.
> We'll grind her into sausages or make her into mincemeat,
> Grind her into sausages, if the miller only will.
> She broke all the sawteeth, broke all the sawteeth,
> Broke all the sawteeth, it was not strong enough.
> Broke all the sawteeth, tore down the saw mill,
> Broke up the circle saw, that old grey goose is tough.
>
> Go tell Aunt Nancy, go tell Aunt Nancy,
> Go tell Aunt Nancy, we know this is a shock.
> But go tell Aunt Nancy, poor old Aunt Nancy,
> Go tell Aunt Nancy we buried her under a rock.
> Go tell Aunt Nancy, go tell Aunt Nancy,
> Go tell Aunt Nancy the old grey goose is dead.
> Down come a walnut, down come a walnut,
> Down come a walnut and hit her on the head.

(ibid. pp. 117–20)

Granny Riddle's success as a 'folksinger' seems to be due to her abilities as a *performer* and interpreter as much as to her powers of original composition – insofar as these can be distinguished. But to her what is of explicit and first importance is not her performing skill but the songs themselves, 'classic' or otherwise: these she regards as of enduring value. Typically she ends the tape-recorded account of her life with the words

> So that's all there is about my songs and myself. And as far as I'm concerned, that's a good deal too much about me – and maybe not enough about the songs. But I'll tell you one thing: I've sung ever since I remember. I intend to sing as long as God gives me a cracked-up voice to do it with. And I intend to sing these songs. But my own greatest, pushing ambition is to get all of the songs I know either on tape or in book form and leave it. Free for anybody that wants to use it. And you can sign that: Granny Riddle.

(ibid. p. 146)

Collectors of oral literature have not always taken much interest in individual poets, so there is a relative dearth of material on the personalities and careers of individual poets. Even so, there are others who could have been described here if space permitted. There was the famous nineteenth-century Somali poet Sheikh Mahammed 'Abdille Ḥasan for instance, better known to European historians as the 'Mad Mullah' and leader of the fighting Dervishes (Andrzejewski and Lewis, 1964, pp. 53ff). Among women poets one could mention the opulent Moorish poet in Mauretania, Yāqūta mint 'Alī Warakān, who can support a comfortable well-furnished house from her art, and is efficient at guarding her own songs from piracy by others and ready to sing her own praises

From what ruby, O Lord of the throne, is Yāqūta?
From the source of pearl and ruby she is fashioned...
She is the full moon, but without a blemish in it...

(Norris, 1968, p. 53)

There is the flirtatious Maori poet Puhiwahine who died in 1906, the daughter of the poetess Hinekiore, who was both skilled in traditional poetic forms and prepared to innovate in poetry from new experiences and contacts – famous not only for her poetry but also for her personality and many love affairs (Jones, 1959–60). Again, there are studies of recent oral poets, like Larry Gorman, Leadbelly, the Beatles, or Bob Dylan. It is probably clear from the portraits given here that something is known about individual oral poets, and that further knowledge would be useful for what it tells us about modes of oral transmission and composition, local theories about poetry and the role of poets, as well for the help it provides in testing older theories about the anonymity of oral poetry or the communal and basically un-individualised nature of oral composition.

Something of the variety of the poet's personality, training and circumstances emerges from this glance at a few creators of oral poetry. This variety is the main point to emerge when one tries to compare the positions and activities of oral poets throughout the world. But there are also common ways in which societies have come to arrange their literary institutions, and the activities of poets can thus be seen to fit, quite often, into recurrent patterns. Though these are not comprehensive or exclusive, it is illuminating to glance at some of them.

2 Some types of poets: specialists, experts and occasional poets

In some societies the role of poet is a specialised one – at any rate for the poet of certain approved kinds of poetry. There are the priest-poets once found widely throughout Polynesia, the highly trained and honorific poets of Ruanda or Ethiopia and the recognised high-status grade of fili in early Ireland. In these cases the practice of poetry (of a particular kind) fits with other honoured institutions in the society – most often religious or political. Like the Fijian Velema, the practitioners of this poetry have an approved position consonant with the recognised values and power-structure of the society.

This is particularly obvious with the praise poets often attached to the courts of rulers. In the Zulu kingdoms of South Africa, every king or chief with pretensions to political power had his own praiser or imbongi among his entourage. At the more elaborate courts of West African kingdoms, there were often whole bands of poets, minstrels and musicians, each with his specialised task, and all charged with the duty of supporting the present king with ceremonial praise of his glory and the great deeds of his ancestors. The old and powerful kingdom of Dahomey had a whole series of royal orchestras, while in Hausa states teams of praisers included musicians and singers with their own royal titles permanently recognised at court. In Hawaii a poet termed the 'master-of-song' (*haku-mele*) was attached to a chief's court, with the duty of composing 'name chants' to glorify the exploits of the chiefly families as well as transmitting and performing older praise poems and genealogies handed down from previous poets (Beckwith, 1951, p. 35). Court poets are common in aristocratic or hierarchical societies, from the poets of mediaeval Wales, Ireland and Scotland to the early Tamil bards or the minstrels of nineteenth-century Kirghiz sultans.[1]

In these contexts, the role of poet is often highly skilled and involves specific training. This may involve personal apprenticeship to a qualified practitioner. The Fijian Velema was taught his craft by his maternal uncle, who at the same time passed on to him the authority and mystique of a seer and priest. Or the apprenticeship may – as with the Ifa oracle priest-poets in Southern Nigeria – involve a course of learning in which the novice goes to a number of qualified experts, often over several years, before he is considered to have mastered his craft. Training of poets is a fairly common pattern, found in places as far apart as mediaeval Ireland and Scotland, Polynesia and Central Africa, and shows the seriousness with which the acquisition of poetic skill and knowledge is locally regarded.

This is taken even further, with the institution of a fully organised 'school' or official system of training. This is not uncommon even in largely non-literate societies. The Maori 'school of learning' is an example. This was a house, often specially built, in which selected youths of well-born parents were formally taught the traditional poetry and sacred knowledge of the priest-poets. There were grades of proficiency through which the candidates could pass, and moving upward depended on passing examinations conducted by expert teachers (Best, 1923). Similar formal training for poets in schools for the well-born was common in the major islands of Eastern Polynesia (Luomala, 1955, p. 45). Again, there is the training in poetry received by the high-status poets in Ruanda under the overall supervision of the president of the poets' association. There were Druidic schools in Caesar's Gaul, mediaeval Irish bardic schools and schools of rhetoric designed to train the Ethiopian *dabteras* poets in the art of *qene* composition.

With a publicly recognised and specialised role, poets have often become a power in their own right. They help to uphold the authority of state or religion – which gives them their own position – and also sometimes keep

---

[1] However they are not, contrary to some suggestions (e.g. Dillon, 1947, p. 15; Williams, 1971, p. 17), peculiar to 'Indo-European Society'.

a firm hold on their monopoly by conducting their own examinations or other controls over the entrance of new recruits. This is the case with Maori and Ruanda poets. Succession to the powerful positions which poets may hold is not infrequently hereditary, so that powerful dynasties of poets can establish themselves, sometimes forming a recognised and dominant grade within society as with the Marquesan and Mangarevan master bards in Polynesia, the privileged early Tamil minstrels, the early Irish or Scottish poets and perhaps the Brahmanic reciters of the sacred Vedic literature.

Among these more specialised types of poet, there is often a split between reciters and composers. This is especially so when the delivery of the poem involves a group of specialists working together – the West African orchestra, for instance, or Mangarevan song groups, who must to some extent rehearse their performances. It is particularly common with specialist religious poets preserving a conservative tradition where, in theory and often in practice, they are delivering or interpreting traditional material. This is so, presumably, with many transmitters of Vedic literature in India, just as it can also be said of the priests and ministers who carry on and disseminate the literary heritage of the Christian Church, some of which must be classed as a kind of oral poetry. Some praise poets learn the praises of older rulers from previous poets, and may do little more than preserve these in their public recitations, reserving their newer compositions for more recent events. But there are also cases of a joint performer/composer role, and even with the more powerful and specialised type of poet, there seems to be no absolute need for this further specialisation into reciter as distinct from composer.

One corollary of the special status of such poets is the return they get from practising their craft. Sometimes they are mainly (even perhaps fully?) supported by it and so can be regarded as professionals. A king's *maroka* praise teams in Northern Nigeria rely heavily on their position for their livelihood: 'they are allocated compounds, farm-lands, and titles by the king, who may also give them horses and frequently provides them with clothes, money, or assistance at weddings, as well as with food' (Smith, 1957, p. 31). Mediaeval Scottish bards built up powerful hereditary families with extensive lands (Thomson, 1974, pp. 12ff) and the Irish court poet expected lavish generosity and 'an estate of land of the best kind and an abode near his chief's court' (Williams, 1971, p. 3). Their earlier counterparts, the *fili* or *ollam*, could expect the reward for a poem to be reckoned in cattle or horses. When poets formed a special hereditary class or caste (as sometimes, for example, in Polynesian, Indian and Gaelic society) their economic as well as their socio-political status were related to the practice of their art, and their right to land and other capital possessions followed from this.

Considering the authoritative position often held by such poets, it is not surprising that the view of the poets' role held by them and by members of their culture often involves reference to a higher sanction underlying their words and position. This is particularly so for poets with religious authority. It is common for the poet's words to be attributed to some power beyond him. Velema's poems were composed by some 'true ancestor'; the Vedic scriptures were divinely revealed rather than composed by human poets, and the hymns of the great Zulu prophet and founder of the Church of Nazareth, Isaiah Shembe, were felt to have been directly imparted to him by God. Many other instances of this emphasis on inspiration in early Europe as well as recent oral literature elsewhere are recorded in Nora Chadwick's analysis, *Poetry and Prophecy* (1942). The claim to divine inspiration in the production of poetry is likely to assist such poets to retain their positions of power or prestige.

A second common type of poet could be called the free-lance and unattached practitioner. Admittedly the distinction can never be clear-cut; for even the most aggressively individualistic poet may form part of the power structure of a society, and what counts as an official role from the point of view of one group (say, a group of Ifa worshippers) may seem more like commercial self-interest from another (say, by certain Christian sects among the Yoruba). Nevertheless the rough distinction is useful: between poets who can rely on relatively permanent and accepted patronage as part of the political and religious establishment, and those who make a living by the effectiveness of their appeal to a succession of potential patrons.

Wandering poets and minstrels who live on their art and their wits are common in many societies. The mediaeval European poet-musicians are one well-known example, or the Moorish troubadours of modern Mauretania, and professional Tatar minstrels on the Central Asian steppes. It is also common in West African kingdoms: itinerant Hausa praise singers, unattached to an official court, can make a living by moving round the villages, picking on wealthy and powerful men to 'praise' in return for gifts in cash or kind. The attempt by the object of the songs to avoid paying the required largesse is likely to result in hurtful and derogatory 'praise songs', so the victim pays up. Similar power was held by the special 'caste' of poets in the Senegambia region known as *griots*. As holders of the hereditary rank of poet, these *griots* had special impunity: they had the right to insult anyone and – like the Moorish troubadours – to switch to outspoken abuse if they failed to get a reward of the expected size. Poets with this power are naturally feared (even despised) as well as admired and patronised, and hold an ambiguous position in society.

Not all free-lance poets take this aggressive route to their commercial objective. The Kirghiz minstrels work more subtly on a wealthy patron's susceptibilities. Though they make a living by going from feast to feast,

singing in honour of the host and for the delight of the guests, they take
care to gauge the interest of the audience and compose effective and
elaborate panegyrics to their patrons without appealing directly for largesse. It is worth quoting Radlov's vivid description of these performances
once more

> One sees from a Kirghiz reciter that he loves to speak, and essays
> to make an impression on the circle of his hearers by elaborate
> strophes and well-turned expressions. It is obvious, too, on all sides
> that the listeners derive pleasure from well-ordered expressions, and
> can judge if a turn of phrase is well rounded off. Deep silence greets
> the reciter who knows how to arrest his audience. They sit with their
> head and shoulders bent forward and with eyes shining, and they
> drink in the words of the speaker; and every adroit expression, every
> witty play on words calls forth lively demonstrations of applause.
>   Since the minstrel wants to obtain the sympathy of the crowd, by
> which he is to gain not only fame, but also other advantages, he tries
> to colour his song according to the listeners who are surrounding
> him...The sympathy of the hearers always spurs the minstrel to new
> efforts of strength, and it is by this sympathy that he knows how to
> adapt the song exactly to the temper of his circle of listeners. If rich
> and distinguished Kirghiz are present, he knows how to introduce
> panegyrics very skilfully on their families, and to sing of such episodes
> as he thinks will arouse the sympathy of distinguished people...It
> is marvellous how the minstrel knows his public. I have myself
> witnessed how one of the sultans, during a song, sprang up suddenly
> and tore his silk overcoat from his shoulders, and flung it, cheering
> as he did so, as a present to the minstrel.

> (Radlov, *Proben* v, pp. iii, xviiif, translated in Chadwick, iii, 1940,
> pp. 179 and 184–5)

The Yugoslav poets such as Avdo Mededović do not make a direct appeal
for reward in their singing. But such a singer can make, if not his full
livelihood, at least some profit from his songs. In Avdo's Yugoslavia, the
singing of epic poetry formed the main entertainment of the adult male
population in villages and small towns, and people were prepared to give
the poet a reward in return for pleasure. The coffee houses in the towns
were·places where a singer could make money (as well as getting his
audience to buy him drinks). During the period of Ramadan most Muslim
coffee houses engaged a singer several months in advance, paying him a
basic fee and organising a collection from the guests at the time of the
performance (Lord, 1968a, pp. 14ff). So popular Yugoslav epic singers could
attain semi-professional status and make some profit from time to time even
though (except for those who were beggars) they were not professional
singers in the sense of depending on their art for their livelihood.

The views such poets hold of their role vary a great deal. One would
expect less stress to be laid on inspiration than in the case of poets with

religious authority. This is so, in that the direct sanction of a poet acting as mouthpiece for the spirits in the authoritative religious system of the society is not here in question. But stress on the personal inspiration of the poet, even sometimes on his prophetic insight, is often found among free-lance poets, and is an aspect of the role which naturally adds to acceptability (and thus the likelihood of profit). This view may go alongside deliberate and professional training – which in some senses it might seem to contradict. Among the peoples of Central Asia, where the free-lance poet receives the most specialised training, it is believed that

> the art of poetry is a kind of mysterious gift bestowed on the person of the singer by a prophetic call from on high. The biographical legend of the singer's call is much like that of Caedmon, the first Anglo-Saxon poet, and has been taken for fact by the majority of the epic singers in Central Asia and South Siberia, both Turkic and Mongolian. The future manaschi, for example, is visited in a dream by the hero Manas and his forty followers, or by his son Semetei, or by another of his famous warriors, and is handed a musical instrument (the dombra) and commanded to sing of their deeds. If the chosen singer disregards this call, he is visited by illness or severe misfortune, until he submits himself obediently to their will.

(Chadwick and Zhirmunsky, 1969, pp. 332–3)

Similarly the long practice and the knowledge of conventional runs and motifs that lie behind the art of an accomplished Kirghiz minstrel, is played down in his own account of his role where he stresses inspiration rather than deliberate art: 'I can sing any song whatever; for God has implanted this gift of song in my heart. He gives me the word on my tongue, without my having to seek it. I have learnt none of my songs. All springs from my inner self' (Radlov, *Proben* v, pp. xviff, translated in Chadwick, III, 1940, p. 182).

The training of these free-lance poets is seldom as formal as that sometimes arranged for official poets. It is common for singers to work at learning their craft in a personal and informal way. Potential Yugoslav singers like Avdo Mededović, for instance, begin by picking up the themes and stylistic conventions of the epic poems unconsciously by listening to others, then later start to try to sing for themselves. One singer explained how he learnt his art.

> 'When I was a shepherd boy, they used to come for an evening to my house, or sometimes we would go to someone else's for the evening, somewhere in the village. Then a singer would pick up the gusle, and I would listen to the song. The next day when I was with the flock, I would put the song together, word for word, without the gusle, but I would sing it from memory, word for word, just as the singer had sung it... Then I learned gradually to finger the instru-

ment, and to fit the fingering to the words, and my fingers obeyed
better and better... I didn't sing among the men until I had perfected
the song, but only among the young fellows in my circle (*družina*) not
in front of my elders and betters.'

(Lord, 1968a, p. 21)

Quite often the Yugoslav neophyte chooses some particular singer, often
his father or uncle or a well-known local singer, to follow most closely (Lord,
1968a, p. 22). This style of training tends to be informal and personal, but
involves the deliberate 'learning of a craft'.

Occasionally even free-lance poets had access to more formalised
training, either through specific apprenticeships or in organised schools.
Professional training was usual for instance, with Central Asian tale-singers.
Zhirmunsky describes the system of training for Uzbek singers.

> The most prominent singer-teachers had several pupils at a time.
> Training lasted for two or three years and was free of charge; the
> teacher provided his pupils with food and clothing, the pupils helped
> the teacher about the house.
>
> The young singers listened to the tales of their teacher and accom-
> panied him on his trips to villages. At first, under the teacher's
> guidance, the pupils memorized the traditional passages of dastans
> and epic clichés, and at the same time learned how to recount the
> rest of the poem through their own improvisation. The end of the
> training was marked by a public examination: the pupil had to
> recite a whole dastan before a selected audience of tale-singers,
> after which he received the title of *bakshy* with the right to perform
> independently.
>
> In the nineteenth and the beginning of the twentieth centuries, in
> the Samarkand district of the Uzbek Republic, especially famous for
> its tale-singers, there were two famous schools which were by far the
> most important centres of epic art: the schools of Bulungur and of
> Nuratin. Two outstanding folk-singers of our times belonged to these
> schools: Fazil Yuldashev (1873–1953) and Ergash Jumanbulbul-ogly
> (1870–1938). The Bulungur school was especially known for its heroic
> repertoire (*Alpamysh*), the Nuratin school for its performance of folk
> romances. Their styles of performance differed correspondingly: the
> style of the former was more severe and traditional, that of the latter
> more lyrical and ornamental in accordance with the nature of its
> romantic subjects. The relative artistic 'modernism' of the Nuratin
> school must probably be explained by the stronger influence written
> literature had over it, which can be traced back to Persian romantic
> epos through Tajik or Uzbek chap-books (*kissa*). Ergash and the
> majority of his teachers were literate people (as indicated by the word
> *molla*, usually added to their names), who had received fundamental
> Moslem elementary education.
>
> The centre of the Nuratin school was Kurgan, a small village, the
> birthplace of Ergash. Despite the fact that only seven patriarchal

'large families' lived in the village, well over twenty folk-singers could be found there by the middle of the twentieth century, whose names have been recorded by the Uzbek folklorists on the information given by Ergash and the village elders. Ergash's father and two uncles were outstanding tale-singers, as well as his two younger brothers and his great-grandmother, the woman tale-singer Tella-kampir. Such 'dynasties of singers' in which poetic talent was passed on from one generation to another, were well known among other Central Asiatic peoples.

(Chadwick and Zhirmunsky, 1969, pp. 330–1)

Free-lance poets are clearly of many different kinds, some hereditary, others not. Some depend on the direct approach in order to gain their main livelihood from poetry, others merely supplement their income by their art. Some rely on face-to-face performance; either drawing their public to hear them *in situ* or themselves travelling to their audience. Others, nowadays, use the radio as an alternative source of income and dissemination, like contemporary Somali poets and Mandinka *griots* in Africa, performing in both traditional and modern vein. Or, like Bob Dylan or the Beatles, they make use of the whole range of modern telecommunications: tapes, gramophone records, radio and television. What they all share is the recognition by their society – or of sufficient groups within it – that their craft is a specialist one, worthy of an individual's spending many years to acquire and practise it, and deserving reward in whatever currency is locally offered. The value thus attached to the learning and practice of poetic art, and the consequent specialisation of the poet's role, is not at all the picture of the organisation of oral literature sometimes held: of a communal, undifferentiated and anonymous activity with no opportunity for the development of the specialist individual poet, still less economic profit.

There are also poets – and perhaps this is the largest category – who are less specialised than those already discussed, and cannot be said to depend largely (and certainly not primarily) on their art, but who are nevertheless in some degree recognised as expert. Such poets often co-exist with more professional poets – the Hausa local and occasional singer for instance, practising in the same society as the official court poets and professional free-lance minstrels – while in societies or groups which do not have the poetic interest or the economic resources to support a distinct group of professional or semi-professional poets, these more occasional poets are the main exponents of the art.

Such poets often appear on ceremonial occasions when convention demands poetry and song, rather than on occasions specifically devoted to entertainment as such. These occasions are often crucial points in the social life cycle. Funerals often need music and poetry, and it is common for certain individuals recognised as particularly skilled – often but not always relatives – to be asked to assist in the mourning. Women dirge singers among the Akan of Ghana take on the responsibility for singing or intoning laments during public mourning. Though all Akan girls were expected to show some skill in composing and performing dirges to sing at relatives' funerals, some women were recognised as particularly expert and had a larger repertoire than usual (Nketia, 1955, pp. 2ff). Again, the rituals of initiation or marriage often demand the assistance of an expert singer. Among the Limba of Sierra Leone there are no professional or near-professional poets, but there are recognised experts specialising in different genres of song: songs for the stages of initiation (separately for male and female initiation); different types of funeral songs, each with their own names and styles; songs and declamations for memorial ceremonies; and songs to go with phases of the farming cycle throughout the year. For attending and performing at such ceremonies the expert poet/singer often receives some small fee or, at the least, generous hospitality from those organising the ceremony. With the more specialised poets (for in Limba culture some occasions, especially memorial ceremonies, demand greater expertise in their singers than others), large gifts may be forthcoming from the hosts.

Though poets like these are less highly specialised in terms of economic position or formally organised training, this does not mean that their art is less carefully structured or their poetic insight and detachment necessarily less. Take, for instance, the Luo *nyatiti* singer in East Africa. His speciality is the lament song, and he appears at funerals, which the Luo celebrate on a grand scale. He makes an appearance partly for social and personal reasons – relationship to the deceased or to help out a neighbour – and partly to make a collection from the large and admiring audience he is likely to find there. He composes and performs his songs for the occasion, drawing on accepted themes of honour and mourning for the deceased. Such songs are relatively conventional and soon forgotten; but sometimes a gifted singer, especially moved by sorrow, composes a song in advance with special care and intensity, devoting much time and concentration to it. The song may be so admired that he is asked to sing it again, after the funeral. When he does so, the poem often gains in detachment and depth – 'being freed from the solemnity of a funeral [it] may rove from the fate of a particular individual to that of other people, and finally to the mystery of death itself' (Anyumba, 1964, p. 190).

Again, Eskimo poetry is famed for its insight and careful composition. And yet, among some groups of Eskimos a measure of skill in composition was expected of everyone, and while expert poets were admired they did not hold official or professional status.

Every Eskimo, therefore, whether man or woman, can not only sing and dance, but can even in some measure compose dance-songs. Distinction in this field ranks almost as high as distinction in hunting, for the man who can improvise an appropriate song for any special occasion, or at least adapt new words to an old song, is a very valuable adjunct to the community. Certain individuals naturally possess greater ability than others; their songs become the most popular and spread far and wide. But there are no professional song-makers, no men who make the composition of songs their main business in life.

(Roberts and Jenness, 1925, p. 12)

One has to set against this background the art of an outstanding poet like Orpingalik: a recognised and admired expert, but not economically or socially set apart by virtue of his skill.

Besides performing at recurrent ceremonies or creating songs for their own or others' enjoyment, poets sometimes compose or perform in virtue of their membership of particular associations or interest groups in a society. Societies like the Yoruba hunters' society, the Ghanaian military association of the Akan, or the Hopi flute societies have special music or poetry associated with them and one or more members who are skilled exponents of it. Here the poet performs largely in fulfilment of his social obligation as a member, though he may also derive some small material profit from his performance.

One of the roles often taken by the kind of occasional poets considered here is that of lead singer with a choral group, the position filled by the American Negro poet Johnnie Smith. The soloist who takes the lead in antiphonal or responsorial patterns with a chorus can create poetry of real originality and depth, as we have seen. It may not be so clear that this context for the practice of poetry is extremely common. From work songs by prisoners in Texas, Indian road-makers, or Limba peasants in their rice fields, to wedding songs and dance songs and public entertainment throughout the world, lead singers perform and compose their poems, usually with little or no material recompense.

As amateurs, such poets often have no formal training. Their method of learning is likely to be through the informal process of watching and listening, and gradually absorbing the conventions appropriate to different genres of song in their differing contexts. A child growing up in Ireland is likely to hear the typical eight-line stanza and traditional tunes from his earliest years, and when he comes to sing himself to find it natural to compose and perform within these conventions. Similarly Yoruba children grow up with an increasing awareness of the potentialities of 'their tonal, metaphor-saturated language which in its ordinary prose form is never far from music in the aural impression it gives' (Babalọla, 1966, p. v). A member of traditional Hawaiian culture is likely to be socialised from an early age into the kind of playing on words and complex figurative expression so important in his oral poetry.

These poets are not highly specialised professionals, and might not be noticed in an account of the economic and social division of labour. They tend to make the same kind of living as people around them – farmers, industrial workers, fishermen, building labourers, prisoners, house-wives – and have no recognised status or high reward. But they perform an important role in publicising and realising the art of poetry. This is so in whatever society they practise, but most noticeably in cultures where professional and specialised poets are lacking.

It is interesting that women poets and singers are mentioned more frequently in this relatively amateur group than among the more profes-sional. Men may still predominate, but women frequently take the lead in songs designed for ceremonial occasions associated with crucial points in the life cycle, above all in laments and wedding songs.

As might be expected, these amateur poets are less articulate about their roles and sources of inspiration – if only because they have less of a position to keep up and less pressure to theorise about it (or have researchers just taken less interest in the views of these less conspicuous poets?). But some have produced interesting comments on the aims and processes of poetic composition or performance. An aspect often mentioned is the poet's interest and pleasure in his own songs. There was J. B. Smith's comment on the way 'you can always make a song out of your surround-ings'. The earlier American Indian Hopi poet Lahpu describes how he composed his song about 'butterfly maidens' in the fields: 'I had been a long time away, and so my heart was happy as I came through the fields. I saw the Hopi girls playing among the corn-plants, chasing one another and laughing and singing, and – I liked it; it was pretty, and I was happy, so I made this song about it' (Curtis, 1907, p. 483).

A different situation is found in cultures (or poetic genres within them) where everyone is expected to master the specific craft involved. This contrasts with the amateur poets just discussed, where it was important for *one* person to take the lead or have enough recognised and specialist skill to play a role in a specific ceremony. But certain poetic skills are often very widely demanded.

This is sometimes a matter of merely being able to take part in kinds of choral singing where there is practically no specialisation at all: poems for children's action games, work songs, the chorus parts of antiphonal songs led by more skilled soloists. In such cases, the main skill involved is that of performance rather than composition, but even here some aware-ness of poetic art is needed, and a practised readiness to pick up and transmit newly composed poetry – so that those who take this part in the realisation of oral poetry within a culture are not irrelevant to discussion of the position of poets within it.

Sometimes the poetic skill widely expected of 'ordinary' people is more demanding. In Southern Africa, all Sotho boys had to become proficient in the composition and performance of praise poetry as part of their initiation, and had to declaim their own praise composition in public when they emerged from their exclusion as initiates (Laydevant, 1930, p. 524). Similarly among some Zambian peoples a young man had to sing a song of his own composition at his marriage, while each woman must have her own personal repertoire of *impango* songs to sing publicly as solos (Jones, 1943, pp. 11–12). Among the Ibo of Eastern Nigeria self-praises are widely composed. They can be illustrated by two, one that of a wine-tapper, celebrating his ability to make good money from his perilous ascent of tall palm-trees for their wine, and one by a powerful man expressing his sense of achievement

I am:	I am:
Height that is fruitful	Tiger that defends neighbours
Climbing rope that makes king	King that is liked by public
Knife that harvests money	Fame that never wanes
Wealth from height.	Flood that can't be impeded
	Ocean that can't be exhausted
	Wealth that gives wisdom...

(Egudu and Nwoga, 1973, pp. 21, 22)

Even when the requirements for personal composition and performance are not formally prescribed as for these set-piece occasions, the convention that individuals either have their own personal poems (as among the Eskimo or the Pacific Dobuan islanders) or are just able and ready to take part in the poetic practice of the society, is widely-spread. Mothers in countless societies sing lullabies to their babies – and these are not necessarily derivative or simplified – lovers among the Gond, Pueblo, Dobuans and many many others evoke love or deplore faithlessness or plan elopement. Herdsmen like the contemporary Dinka guardians of cattle or earlier Scottish or Hebrew shepherds in the hills, sing and chant their poems in lonely pastures. Irish travellers celebrate in the traditional 'rebel' song style in the bars of cross-channel ferries, just as Somali lorry drivers sing *balwo* lyrics to liven the tedium of their long journeys, and countless western teenagers transmit and mould popular songs from every kind of origin.

Examples like these may seem trivial, but it must be remembered that it is largely by these practitioners, as well as by the more skilled and spectacular craftsmen, that the poetic heritage of a society is realised. Such practitioners may be performers only, and 'merely' pass on the compositions of others. But one must not forget that *oral* poetry, being oral, depends fundamentally on its expression and realisation in words – the performer is not a 'mere' performer but an essential part of the whole process of poetic creation. In considering the position of the oral poet one has inevitably to take account of performers as well as composers, wherever the two roles are split. Further, it is by no means clear that these unspecialised practitioners *are* always mere reflections of the originality of others. It was an ordinary Somali lorry driver who made the first *balwo* lyric – the new genre that then swept through the Somali younger generation – and the whole sense of variability in oral transmission that inevitably emerges from research pays tribute to the originality and ingenuity of ordinary singers and reciters without specialist status. To understand the way in which poetry is created and practised in any society one has to take account of non-specialist practitioners like these, as well as the more professional poets, when they exist.

The categories of poet discussed here are not absolute nor clearly differentiated. They cannot be set up as definitive typologies, if only because their differential characteristics do not include clear-cut single criteria, and there is in practice much overlap between them. Thus the Eskimo poet Orpingalik comes nearest to my third pattern – the expert among equals – but in his role of shaman he has an element of the religious position held by the seer Velema; while Almeda Riddle, again close to the third type, also shares the economic reward (not necessarily monetary) and relatively formal training more usually associated with the second 'free-lance' type. But, accepted as a rough and ready distinction, the categories distinguished above *are* frequently found, and the arrangements by which poets practise their craft often roughly coincide with one or more of the common patterns discussed here. The categories serve their purpose well enough.

Which types of poets practise in a given society is of some social importance. For it makes a difference whether poetry is composed and performed by professional poets with official and permanent positions (perhaps organised into a self-perpetuating and powerful group), by free-lance and unattached poets who are nevertheless often highly specialised and effective, by less specialised experts who practise mainly in particular genres and contexts, or by the kinds of unspecialised poets who emerge when poetry is diffused widely throughout society and poetic craft expected in a measure from everyone. In some societies – especially those with a marked division of labour and enough economic resources to support specialists in what is not an economically productive role – all or several of these categories often co-exist: in the wealthy and powerful kingdoms of West Africa or Asia, in mediaeval Europe or in some Polynesian islands. In other cultures or groups with less interest or opportunity for this kind of division of labour, only the last two categories are, broadly, likely to be found (perhaps sometimes only the last) – in Texas prisoner groups, for instance, or possibly some of the poorer peasant economies.[1]

This general account of the status and role of oral poets is inevitably sketchy. But the picture that emerges throws light on some of the controversies in the general area, especially when considered in conjunction with the brief case studies presented earlier.

3 Are oral poets anonymous?

It is often suggested that oral poetry is produced anonymously and 'communally'. This idea is particularly applied to oral poetry in non-literate (or mainly non-literate) societies – though the concept is sometimes extended more widely, especially to poetry regarded as subject to 'oral transmission'. It is already obvious that my immediate answer to the basic question posed above is 'no', and that I reject the older ideas about oral poetry as necessarily anonymous and somehow communal. But a summary dismissal is not enough; there are some points here that require discussion.

In one sense it is an attractive possibility that there are elements of anonymity and communal participation in oral poetry. For instance, it is true that audiences play a more directly influential part in the creation of oral literature than is common with written literature; and the process of variability in oral poetry and the influence of the traditional conventions from which a poet selects means that in one sense *many* poets play a part in the composition of a piece of poetry, and not just one original composer on the model of written literature.

It is easy to exaggerate this, and easy to misrepresent both oral and *written* literary composition by pressing it too hard (do not literate poets make use of traditional conventions, which others have had a hand in shaping?). And when one comes to the more extreme formulations of these concepts (those emphasised by romanticist writers) the contrary evidence seems overwhelming. Where oral poetry involves simultaneous performance and composition – as it often does – it is clearly *not* all produced anonymously and 'communally'. The poet, the author of the poem at that particular performance, is, by definition, a known individual, enunciating his poem in his own person before an audience. Among the cases cited here it is clear that Velema or Avdo Mededović or Johnnie B. Smith are neither anonymous nor communal: they are named and known individuals.

When there is a split between performance and composition, with the element of memorisation entering in, the name of the original poet *is*

---

[1] Once again, what is being commented on here is not the quality of the poetry in any aesthetic and evaluative sense; only the *social arrangements* concerning the production of poetry and the position of the poet.

sometimes unknown. Equally, it is often carefully preserved, as with the
Somali poets Mahammed 'Abdille Ḥasan, or Faarah Nuur, or Salaan
'Arrabey. In cases when the author *is* apparently unknown, this is sometimes a mere function of *our* ignorance (rather than that of the people
themselves) or of the theoretical assumptions of researchers who felt it
inappropriate with oral art to enquire about the names of the poets. In the
light of the available evidence it seems that anonymity of the poet may
sometimes be the case – but often it is not.

The idea that the communal creation of oral poetry is the normal
process is also, in its literal sense at least, decisively negated by the existence
in many societies of specialist poets. Poems composed by the Ruanda poetic
élite, Hausa or Zulu court poets, trained Uzbek epic-singers, or Polynesian
nobles cannot be regarded as 'communal' – they are in no way the product
of 'the people' (far less 'the tribe'), but the compositions of members of
a specialised and to some extent separate group within the society. This
type of social arrangement for the production of poetry is *not*, furthermore, an unusual and aberrant phenomenon with oral poetry: on the
contrary, it is extremely common in societies with the economic resources
to support an extended division of labour.

The question of the ownership and control of poetry is also relevant here.
It is true that 'copyright' is a concept that goes with the printed word and
is not characteristic of oral, but of written poetry. This is particularly so
in contexts where the primary realisation of a poem is by its performer,
and the performer's responsibility for the poem is in any case there for
all to see. Thus the attitude to what we would call 'copyright' in oral poetry
is very widely of the kind well summed up by Wilkinson writing of Malay
poets:

> The horror of literary piracy which characterises European work has
> no place among primitive peoples. A jester whose jokes are repeated
> is only flattered by the repetition; a Malay song-writer who objected
> to other people using his songs would be regarded by his fellow-
> countrymen much as we should regard a man who went to Stationers'
> Hall and applied for permission to copyright his own conversation.
> A native author likes to claim the monopoly of a recognised classic
> such as 'Esop's Fables' or the 'Arabian Nights' or the local 'Si-Miskin'
> romance which is at least two centuries old; he does not care so much
> about securing rights over his own original work. A native dramatist
> picks up his plots anywhere; he stages 'Aladdin' or 'Ali Baba' one
> night, and tries 'Hamlet' for the night after. He would be horrified
> at the charge of lack of originality; indeed, he glories in the fact that
> he has treated 'Hamlet' in a novel manner – quite unlike the way in
> which his predecessors treated that very hackneyed theme. he would
> compare himself rather to the great Greek tragedians who dealt in
> 'slices from the great banquet of Homer' and who related the same
> Orestes legend from characteristically different points of view. He
> would curse as a 'plagiarist' any man who crimped his clown or

enticed away his poet, but he would not stoop to quarrel about mere words, which, once uttered, are to him as stale as the jokes of yester-year.

(Wilkinson, 1924, p. 41)

This is not the only possible attitude to ownership of oral poetry. There are also societies in which the practice of having 'personal poems' is both recognised and encouraged, and in such cases the individuals presumably 'own' their own songs in the sense either that they alone know and are able to sing them, or that they alone have the *right* to sing them. (This is another topic on which further research is needed). Among the Dinka of the Southern Sudan, songs are owned in the sense that all individuals and groups have their own songs, composed either personally or by an expert on their behalf. 'Only the owner of a song may present it formally, but informally any person may sing any song almost anytime and anywhere' (Deng, 1973, p. 78).

There are also societies in which legal ownership is quite explicitly recognised for at least some categories of poem. The Dobuan islanders in the Pacific lay great stress on originality of content and words and recognise the ownership of poems: 'The song-maker is proud of his creation, proud of its originality, and he has rights to prevent others from using his song, at least for a while. The song-maker must give his permission before his song is used for the dance' (Fortune, 1963, p. 251). Again, the Rwala Bedouin recognise the concept of authorship and copyright in poems, even if proving this in practice is difficult.

> The begging poets are not held in much esteem, being reproached for their insatiability, for their disregard of honesty in praising even scamps for a reward, and also because they lie and steal. They steal the ideas, sentences, and even whole verses of others. It often happens that the hearers assail such a poet with the words: 'Thou liest. Thou stolest it from So-and-So!' The poet defends himself, calling on others to be his witnesses, but the confidence of his hearers is gone, and they say: 'A poet is a liar, ḳaṣṣâd ḳaḍḍâb.' When the poet learns that his composition or some of his verses are claimed by somebody else, he complains to the chiefs or even in the courts, but they refuse to listen on the ground that a poet cannot be trusted.
>
> (Musil, 1928, p. 283 (quoted in Greenway, 1964, p. 165))

The 'ownership' of a poem is not necessarily wholly vested in the person who – in our terms – was the composer. In Hawaii, writes Pukui, 'chants "belonged" to the person, or the family of the person to whom they were dedicated and for whom they had been composed. Others were not allowed to use them, except to repeat them in honour of the owner' (Pukui, 1949, p. 255). In Polynesia generally poems are not only owned but often given and received as precious gifts. The poem

If I give a mat it will rot,
If I give cloth it will be torn,
The poem is bad, yet take it,
That it be to thee boat and house,
For thou art skilled in its taking,
And ever have I joyed
When the ignorant of heart have conned a poem
In companionship with the wise

was from a one-hundred-and-one-line poem that a Tongan sailor and poet chanted as a gift to a friend who was also a poet. The poem was highly appreciated, as being of greater value than a material gift, and the friend showed his delight in it by responding '"Thanks for the..." and reciting the entire poem back to its composer' (Luomala, 1955, p. 43).

Poems which – like charms or incantations – are regarded as in themselves powerful are often the subject of ownership by an individual or social group, and sometimes sold to another or inherited along with other property. Thus one Apache priest described how his family had owned a powerful 'medicine song'

> The song that I will sing is an old song, so old that none knows who made it. It has been handed down through generations and was taught to me when I was but a little lad. It is now my own song. It belongs to me.
>
> This is a holy song (medicine song) and great is its power. The song tells how, as I sing, I go through the air to a holy place where Yusun[1] will give me power to do wonderful things. I am surrounded by little clouds, and as I go through the air I change, becoming spirit only.
>> O ha le
>> O ha le!
>> Through the air
>> I fly upon a cloud
>> Towards the sky, far, far, far,
>> O ha le
>> O ha le!
>> There to find the holy place,
>> Ah, now the change comes o'er me!
>> O ha le
>> O ha le!
>
> (Curtis, 1907, p. 324)

Among the Eskimo too, magic songs are sometimes owned and handed down from father to son, while for the Australian Aborigines of Arnhem Land, the 'ownership' of a song cycle by a particular 'songman' entails not so much exclusive knowledge of the story involved – many people in practice know this – but 'the right of access to the dream-spirits manifested

[1] The Supreme Being.

in the stories...the songman is in direct contact with these live spirits' (Berndt, 1970, p. 588).

'Ownership' of poetry thus turns out to be a remarkably complex phenomenon. The overall picture that emerges is not of the type of 'communal' poetry envisaged by early theorists. Oral poetry is composed, performed and even sometimes owned by individuals, and its production and publication is not infrequently under the control of specific and differentiated groups within the society, rather than of 'the tribe' or 'the society' in general.

This leads to a final point concerning the communally shared aspect of poetry. It is sometimes tacitly assumed that the productions of poets in some sense stand for the whole society; reflecting the views and aspirations of the people at large and being essentially 'their' culture; so that even if one individual poet can be recognised as the composer or performer, he is really speaking not as himself, an individual, but as the 'voice' of the community. This is a readily-held idea, applied as often to the productions of literate societies as to those of more 'primitive' cultures. There is a sense in which it is true, but too facile an acceptance of this stance can lead to misassessment of the role of poets and poetry. This has been forcefully pointed out by Cesar Graña:

> The normal ways of sociology require that statements about the 'values' of a culture should rest on whatever one can find out about behavior and belief among a *number of people* which, with one or another justification, might be regarded as representative. Some sociologists of culture, however, embracing what is in fact a traditionally romantic view of the relationship between social life and aesthetic expression, fall to writing as though the work of artists, the work, that is, of a minority of the uncommon, should be taken as the final testimony of a culture's true character, or as the act or gesture *defining* the quality of a social period.
>
> It seems clear, at least to me, that a sociology of art moving at such a glamorous level of abstraction would be constantly faced with the temptation of taking the unique eloquence of art as *proof* of its social representativeness, thus circumventing the very thing that sociologists should be required to demonstrate: the connection between ordinary, unselfconscious experience and the memorable creations of the few.
>
> (Graña, 1971, p. 66)

Graña's comment applies equally to oral literature. The traditional emphasis on the communal and homogeneous nature of non-literate society or the democratic connotations of the term 'folklore' might lead one to suppose that oral poetry is always equally shared and approved throughout the society and the poet merely the spokesman of that society (of 'the folk'). But so far as its *production* goes this is not always the case. In non-literate as in literate societies, powerful groups of poets can retain their positions in conjunction with religious and political interests, can maintain a monopoly over the production of certain types of poems (usually those which express certain points of view) and in addition receive good reward and control the entrance of new recruits to their profession. The *reception* of their openly performed poetry may be in principle more widespread than when the appearance of such poetry can be confined to small numbers of inaccessible or expensive books. But even this contrast can be exaggerated, for official poets sometimes address themselves to restricted audiences (wealthy and powerful patrons at court, or members of particular esoteric groups) and in some cases such poets may not travel far beyond the main political and economic centres of the culture of which they are sometimes taken to be the 'representatives'.

The point is obvious, but worth stressing, for it is tempting in any study of poetry, especially of a non-literate society, to be so impressed by the insight or art of certain poetry that one forgets the touch of cynicism which any sociologist needs in order to study any social phenomenon with detachment. So it has to be said explicitly that in societies where there is a marked division of labour affecting the production or circulation of poetry, it cannot be assumed without evidence that the official and established poets in every sense represent the people at large in the sentiments they express or the means of expression. Marx's comments in *German Ideology* on the vested interests of groups of intellectuals might apply equally to certain oral poets:

> The class which has the means of material production at its disposal, has control at the same time over the means of mental production, so that in consequence the ideas of those who lack the means of mental production are, in general, subject to it. The dominant ideas are nothing more than the ideal expression of the dominant material relationships, the dominant material relationships grasped as ideas, and thus of the relationships which make one class the ruling one; they are consequently the ideas of its dominance. The individuals composing the ruling class possess, among other things, consciousness, and therefore think. In so far, therefore, as they rule as a class and determine the whole extent of an epoch, it is self-evident that they do this in their whole range and thus, among other things, rule also as thinkers, as producers of ideas, and regulate the production and distribution of the ideas of their age...
>
> (Marx in Bottomore and Rubel, 1963, pp. 93–4)

The representativeness or otherwise of specialist oral poets always needs empirical investigation, for it cannot be predicted in general terms. To assume any one interpretation – whether 'Marxist', 'folklorist' or other – in advance of detailed enquiry is likely to be misleading.

4 The poet as seer

Another interpretation of the role of oral poets has been put forward by some scholars: namely that the poet is essentially and always a seer or prophet, who reveals what is hidden through divine inspiration and communication with spirits. He speaks in an exalted and trance-like manner and through his poetry links his fellow men with the spirit world. Nora Chadwick was a leading exponent of this view. In *Poetry and Prophecy* she wrote:

> The fundamental elements of the prophetic function seem to have been everywhere the same. Everywhere the gift of poetry is inseparable from divine inspiration. Everywhere this inspiration carries with it knowledge – whether of the past, in the form of history and genealogy; of the hidden present, in the form commonly of scientific information; and of the future, in the form of prophetic utterance in the narrower sense. Always this knowledge is uttered in poetry which is accompanied by music, whether of song or instrument. Music is everywhere the medium of communication with spirits. Invariably we find that the poet and seer attributes his inspiration to contact with supernatural powers, and his mood during prophetic utterance is exalted and remote from that of his normal existence. Generally we find that a recognised process is in vogue by which the prophetic mood can be induced at will. The lofty claims of the poet and seer are universally admitted, and he himself holds a high status wherever he is found.

(Chadwick, 1942, p. 14, cf. also pp. 27–8, 41, 57, 72)

On this general view, it has been observed that the so-called 'shaman' in Eskimo and North Asian cultures often has close associations with poetry as well as having the prophetic and visionary personality that can, according to accounts like Chadwick's, be widely expected of the poet. Some scholars have extended this observation into a theory that one of the main historical origins of epic poetry in these areas is in 'shamanism': a complex of characteristics which cover the personality and function of the poet and typical elements of content and style in the poems – for instance a hero's journey to the other world, or narration in first person dream-like style (Hatto, 1970). Shamanism, in Hatto's view, has

> left its traces in the epic traditions of Northern Asia in these ways: in the excitement bordering on ecstasy of improvisation; in a dream- or trance-like style of first-personal narration; in narrative content in the form of initiatory tests and heroic journeys to the Otherworld, marked by battles with spirits and monsters or by other encounters by land, air or water.

(Hatto, 1970, p. 3)

He extends this by finding a link between Northern Asian epic and others further afield, including the old Sumerian epic of Gilgamesh: 'the link', he asserts, 'is through shamanist tradition' (1970, p. 19).

A similar – but even more generalised – approach is taken by Caerwyn Williams who, reflecting the views of a number of other writers, asserts categorically that 'Every primitive poet was to some extent a shaman or magician, in other words he claimed the ability to exercise power over things, and his poetry was the means to that end' (Williams, 1971, p. 25). This general approach has influenced interpretations of the role of poets in a number of societies (e.g. Kailasapathy, 1968, pp. 61ff).

Sweeping generalisations like these (even Hatto's, though confined to the one genre of epic, is extensive geographically) can at times be illuminating. Certainly poetry is often associated with religion and with a highly-wrought and nervous personality in the poet; it is, furthermore, useful to be reminded of the prophetic calling of the poet which is a part of poetic theory widely held in northern Asia and the Pacific.

But there is no *necessary* connection between these characteristics; nor do they apply more widely as a general characterisation of all poets (or all oral poets in non-industrial contexts). It may be helpful to separate these traits, and consider them separately.

First, poets indeed often have religious roles. There are the established poets of official religion and the carriers of authoritative religious tradition – like the Vedic poet/priests of India, the practitioners of the Christian literary heritage or, at a more specialised and local level, poets and priests expressing the poetry of one particular cult in society (like the Yoruba Ifa cult) or, like Velema, representing religious authority in one particular village. Such poets may add to their position the extra sanction of claiming to be directly and supernaturally inspired. But the manic personality sometimes associated with shamanism and possession is not necessarily a feature of this kind of poetic practice. In some cases, religious poets prefer to present a dignified and austere mien. On the other hand there *are* many poets who resemble mediums in that, like the Malay magician or, in some cases, the Eskimo shaman, they receive and deliver their poems in the context of a kind of spiritualist séance where trance and dream are elements and the poet claims direct access to a possessing spirit. Such poets may be associated with the main established religion of the area – but often they are not. Their poetry is a means for gifted or unusual individuals to make a mark outside the official ranking system in the society and practise on a free-lance and individualistic basis.

But though poets with religious functions do exist widely, they do *not* comprise the whole body of oral poets. There is also a great number of secular poets, from official court poets lauding the military achievements of their patrons to entertainers like Avdo Međedović and countless others,

who seek primarily to tell a good and gripping story and for whom passing
religious allusions are of secondary importance; or there are local poets
interested mainly in love or recent political events or, like Johnnie Smith,
in interpreting and enduring prison life. Such poets have little in common
with prophets and shamans.

The same argument applies to the question of personality. In other
words, many poets *are* characterised by a manic and highly charged personality – either because such individuals are more likely to turn to poetry
or (perhaps) because social pressures can encourage individuals of this type
to become poets. But not all poets are like this. And as Nora Chadwick
herself points out on the basis of a wide study of the subject, while it is
true that 'nervous and highly strung people make likely subjects for
ecstasy and other forms of manticism...that people who...are actually
mentally abnormal or diseased, make good shamans has yet to be shown.
Nor have I found satisfactory evidence elsewhere that people who are
obviously mentally diseased are held in high esteem for mantic gifts in their
own community' (Chadwick, 1942, p. 65).

One *could* so define the poetic art that insight akin to prophecy and a
'sensitive' and 'highly strung' personality in the poet are defining characteristics. Up to a point, this would fit well with some of the cases discussed
here: Velema's strange personality, Almeda Riddle's 'mental breakdown'
after her sister's death, Johnnie Smith's uncontrollable jealousy and murder
of his wife. But one must not be tempted to turn an empirical matter into
a value judgement, or a tautology, and include under the term 'poet' only
those whom the analyst regards as 'good' or 'true' poets. This is to ignore
the commonsense point that local classifications of poet widely include the
second-rate practitioner as well as the truly original and insightful creative
artist: and many recognised poets do not have neurotic and manic personalities, even if some of the most gifted do.

It sometimes causes ambiguity that poets claim that their words are
inspired – that they arise not from conscious deliberation but from some
deep unconscious impulse within, for which the poet is not fully responsible,
or from some outside supernatural source. Such claims are at least evidence
of local poetic theories and of how poets envisage their role; and it is clear
that in some cultures – early Ireland for instance – poets *were* seen as
essentially seers. But it can be a mistake to treat such claims literally as a
complete account of poetic creation. This is partly because poets do not
necessarily speak equally strongly about all aspects of their craft, or necessarily analyse accurately what contribution is made by different activities.
The Eskimo poet Orpingalik stresses the element of improvisation and
spontaneity in his statement that 'the words we need will come of themselves...shoot up of themselves' (Rasmussen, 1931, p. 321), yet he also
gives his poetry all the deliberate and time-consuming attention typical of

Eskimo poets. One has, too, to preserve some detachment about such apologias, remembering the practical purposes that can be served by powerful poets claiming, sincerely or not, to be inspired by divine sources beyond themselves. In some cases, references to inspiration are merely conventional: for instance, Virgil's or Milton's invocation to the muse are not evidence that they composed the rest of the poem in an inspired shamanistic trance. So claims to inspiration from supernatural or mystical sources cannot be taken at face value, and do not *necessarily* mean that the poet speaks in inspired ecstasy or that all the characteristics which Hatto claims as typical of 'shamanism' are simultaneously present.

Many of the characteristics variously associated with prophets or mediums are found among oral poets. But none of them applies *universally* or to *all* oral poets, and the varying characteristics do not necessarily always go together. To produce wide generalisations from scattered evidence or to draw together different characteristics into some over-all term like 'divine inspiration' or 'shamanism' is to over-generalise.

5 The poet as individual genius

The final assumption on which this sketch of poets' positions can throw some light is that of the poet as individual genius, above and untrammelled by society: the poet as defined by the romantic theorists. On this view the artist represents the extreme individual guided by his own canons of sincerity and emotional integrity, independent of the accepted conventions of society. Emphasis is placed on the individual emotional genesis of poetry, embodying the poet's personal and deeply experienced vision.

Again, in one sense this is true. The 'best' poets are extraordinarily gifted, and many must have been drawn to poetry by their creative ability. In non-literate as in literate society, poetry is one medium through which an individual can, in a sense, free himself from the here and now and, through his creative genius, both re-interpret and rise above his environment.

But taken to extremes the approach can be misleading. It is easy to be moved by Whitman's famous panegyric: 'The greatest poet hardly knows pettiness or triviality. If he breathes into anything that was before thought small, it dilates with the grandeur and life of the universe. He is a seer; he is individual; he is complete in himself' (Whitman, Preface to *Leaves of grass* in Anderson and Warnock, 1967, p. 343). But the statement, illuminating in one sense, is no full or safe guide to the position and activities of all poets in all contexts. For one thing this approach too assumes a circular and limiting definition of the poet as 'the good poet' (or some particular ideal of the good poet). It ignores the part played by *social* conventions and opportunities, and concentrates on the genesis of poetry from the individual and spontaneous genius of the poet. This theory of creation may be acceptable and helpful to poets, but does not for that reason necessarily coincide with the facts.

This is particularly so in the extreme version implied in statements that the poet is free from external constraints or stimuli, uninfluenced by the background or opportunities of society around him. That this cannot be so is already clear: the poet's language, style, mode of composition, local poetic theory, role, type of training and mode of reception are surely socially and not individually generated. They are moulded and developed (sometimes changed) by individual poets, without whom the conventions would not persist. But no poet creates in a vacuum, looking only to himself and never to the social and economic world within which he must practise, the audience to which he must direct himself or the acceptable artistic conventions on which he can draw.

The position of poets in society is incorporated in the wider social, political and economic institutions in which they practice. Take as example Emerson's vivid description of the way Hawaiian hula singers used to make their way. He writes:

> The king overhears remark on the doings of a new company of hula dancers who have come into the neighborhood. He summons his chief steward.
>
> 'What is this new thing of which they babble?' he demands.
>
> 'It is nothing, son of heaven,' answers the kneeling steward.
>
> 'They spoke of a hula. Tell me, what is it?'
>
> 'Ah, thou heaven-born (lani), it was but a trifle – a new company, young graduates of the halau, have set themselves up as great ones; mere rustics; they have no proper acquaintance with the tradition of the art as taught by the bards of * * * your majesty's father. They mouth and twist the old songs all awry, thou son of heaven.'
>
> 'Enough. I will hear them to-morrow. Send a messenger for this new kumu. Fill again my bowl with awa.'
>
> Thus it comes about that the new hula company gains audience at court and walks the road that, perchance, leads to fortune. Success to the men and women of the hula means not merely applause, in return for the incense of flattery; it means also a shower of substantial favors – food, garments, the smile of royalty, perhaps land – things that make life a festival. If welcome grows cold and it becomes evident that the harvest has been reaped, they move on to fresh woods and pastures new.
>
> (Emerson, 1909, p. 27)

This is far from the romantic view of the detached and self-sufficient poet. And yet their involvement in the political and economic realities of their society has not prevented the Hawaiian singers from producing the highly metaphorical and beautiful poems translated in Emerson's great collection *Unwritten Literature of Hawaii. The sacred songs of the hula* (1909).

Inevitably, the way in which poets and poetic activity fit into the social, economic and political institutions of their society varies in detail. The relationship may be functional and official – as with those poets discussed above who are a part of the current power structure of society. Other poets occupy an ambivalent or even marginal role in society, where they are both admired and feared, or where they can act as unaligned and above partisan interest. Thus early Irish poets were a national and not a local group, and travelled widely even through warring and hostile groups (Knott, 1922, p. xli), while Manding *griots* 'could pass freely through enemy territory, for the person of a *griot* was inviolable' (Innes, 1974, p. 8). Poets are also sometimes regarded as outcasts or lower caste: the Senegambian *griots* belonged to the special low caste of poets and musicians, the mediaeval Chinese ballad singers sometimes belonged to the ambiguous category of prostitute, the Moorish troubadours are both feared and despised, and the famous travelling minstrels of mediaeval Europe were often subject to legal disabilities and positive discrimination. But even these ways of signalling the special status of certain poets result in a role that is socially recognised, pertaining to an accepted social category; so that the individual poet is not 'outside' society nor free from its claims.

The involvement of the poet in society can also be seen in a whole range of factors affecting his life and livelihood *qua* poet. The mode by which a poet receives his initial training in his craft is socially organised and in a sense comes to him from outside, whether in the form of official and continuous instruction and schooling or through the informal socialisation into poetic conventions common in relatively non-specialised contexts. Again, the occasions on which he can practise his art do not depend only on the poet, but on the ways in which special ceremonies, entertainments or specialist associations are organised in his society. The patronage available is likely to affect his art considerably, for though solitary poems and songs do occur, by and large an oral poet with no patrons is scarcely likely to regard it as worth persisting – unlike literary poets, he cannot console himself by 'writing for posterity'. This need for patronage refers both to the wealthy and powerful patrons who often support the more specialised poets, and to the ordinary audiences to which a poet is likely to address himself. This is a particularly pressing problem for poets in a period of changing fashions and economic circumstances, when genres once in demand have lost their appeal. Some Hausa singers still want to perform certain types of traditional poetry, but their old audiences have turned to other interests – just as the street ballad singers had to give way to music hall artists, and face-to-face performers turn to television and radio. The more committed a poet is to his craft – the nearer he is to the model of the individual committed Artist – the more likely he is to have to take account of economic pressures, for he is more dependent on the practice of his art for his own livelihood than part-time experts.

Not every poet makes careful material calculations – after the manner of the classical economic man – before making a conscious decision about whether and how to ply his craft. But it is clear that these are factors which, consciously or not, help to mould his expectations for himself as poet, the practical exercise of his art, and the way he composes and performs poetry. They are the parameters within which he works, and present him both with constraints and with the opportunities and incentives which help to feed his poetry.

In poetry – as in any other part of life – there is a constant interplay between individual insight and originality and the constraints and opportunities afforded by society. The oral poet is not merely the voice of communal pressures, neither is every poet an individual and untrammelled genuis: poetry is the creation *both* of a particular community *and* of a particular individual. This dual genesis applies as much to oral as to written poetry, and for a satisfactory study both aspects need to be remembered.

7
Audience, context and function

Oral poetry is subject to the same disputes as written literature about its role in society. The same questions arise that have been battled over so long in the analysis (sociological and other) of literature. What is the relationship between poetry and society? Does oral poetry 'reflect' the society in which it exists? Does it form a kind of mythical charter, supporting tradition and the *status quo*? Or is it a force for social change, even a democratic weapon in the hands of the people?

Large questions of this sort – the typical concerns of the sociology of literature – are abstract and elusive. They cannot be avoided in any socio-logical approach to poetry, but to move only on the level of such abstract and vague questions can lead to frustration – or to tautology. Instead of trying to tackle them directly and in general terms it seems more illuminating to turn first to a consideration of the occasions on which oral poetry is performed and to some of the more obvious purposes and effects involved, and then to return to the general theoretical problems. Otherwise, it is easy to fall into the trap of trying to start from first principles and deduce theoretical and would-be general propositions which sound elegant in the abstract, but operate at several removes from the actual practice of oral literature.

1 *Some types of audience*

It is as well to begin with some consideration of the audience to which a piece of literature is directed and delivered. This is a factor sometimes neglected or taken to be merely secondary, particularly in the kind of study which concentrates on the structure and effect of the text or on the model of poet/writer as individual genius. But the nature of the audience is surely an important factor in the creation and transmission of literature. This is noticeably so in *oral* literature, for here the typical context is delivery direct to an audience. The audience, even as listeners and spectators – but some-times in a more active role – are directly involved in the realisation of the poem as literature in the moment of its performance. It is never a mere after-thought which can be ignored throughout the major part of a theoretical analysis of the functions and contexts of oral poetry.

If delivery to an audience is indeed the characteristic setting for oral poetry, it has to be conceded that there *are* also occasions where there is no audience, and the performance is a solitary one. This is less typical (and seldom or never happens in the better known case of oral prose narrative) but it does occur. The Nuer and Dinka pastoralists of the Southern Sudan sing solitary songs as they watch their cattle. The cattle are perhaps a kind of audience – to the Nuer and Dinka they are indeed closely approximated to human beings – and some of the songs of praise to particular oxen might be regarded in this way. But these are *also* songs in which an individual can represent to *himself* his view of his own role and of 'the whole world of beauty around him' (Lienhardt, 1963, p. 828). Among the Dinka

> a person may find entertainment in singing to himself while walking along the road, herding in the forest, or tethering the herds at home. During the season of cultivation, many people can be heard, each singing loudly in his own field. In the stillness of the night, a mother may be heard singing any song as a lullaby at the top of her voice
>
> (Deng, 1973, p. 78)

Again, the Eskimo and Somali and Gilbertese and many others compose and practice songs in solitude as well as performing them in public. Solitary work songs are not at all uncommon (some lullabies may be a marginal case in the same category). There are songs for grinding corn, milking cows, working in the fields, paddling a boat – activities often carried out on one's own. Again, there is the famous song which started Sharp off on his protracted collecting of English and American folk songs – when by chance he overheard the gardener John England quietly singing 'The Seeds of Love' to himself as he mowed the vicarage lawn:

I sowed the seeds of love, And I sow'd them in the spring; _____ I ga-ther'd them up ___ in the morn – ing so soon, While the small birds so sweet – ly sing, While the small birds so sweet-ly sing.

My garden was planted well
With flowers ev'rywhere;
And I had not the liberty to choose for myself
Of the flowers that I love dear. (*bis*)

The gard'ner was standing by;
And I asked him to choose for me.
He chose for me the violet, the lily and the pink,
But those I refused all three. (*bis*)

The violet I did not like,
Because it blooms so soon.
The lily and the pink I really overthink,
So I vow'd that I would wait till June. (*bis*)

In June there was a red rosebud,
And that is the flow'r for me.
I oftentimes have pluck'd that red rosebud
Till I gained the willow tree. (*bis*)

The willow tree will twist
And the willow tree will twine.
I oftentimes have wish'd I were in that young man's arms
That once had the heart of mine. (*bis*)

Come all you false young men,
Do not leave me here to complain;
For the grass that has oftentimes been trampled under foot,
Give it time, it will rise up again,
Give it time, it will rise up again.

(quoted from Karpeles, 1973, pp. 93–4)

It is worth remembering these solitary settings, as a counter to the frequent emphasis on the public and community functions of oral literature. Sociologists of literature, in their reaction against the romantic models of the individual and, as it were, a-social poet, sometimes imply not only that the conventions and forms of literature are socially created but – an illegitimate but tempting next step – that all (oral) literature is attached to the public occasions of our lives. This is to forget the personal and contemplative side of literature – particularly characteristics of a number of these solitary songs. They remind us forcefully of the need to leave a place in our sociologies of literature for the human desire to formulate experience in pleasing words and to articulate 'the secrets of the heart' in aesthetic verbal form – and even if it is partly a matter of just warding off boredom in a long and tedious task, to do this with beauty and imagination.

In most performances of oral literature, however, an audience is involved. Sometimes the audience is really part of the performance itself, as in songs for choral singing, or is so at times, as when a lead singer performs partly as soloist, partly as leader in a joint singing with the audience. In such cases the audience participates directly in the performance. In other cases, which need to be distinguished, the occasion is a specialist one in that the demarcation between performer(s) and audience is clear, and the audience is functionally separate.

In discussing the functions and purposes of particular performances of oral poetry it can be useful to distinguish between these different kinds of audience. Even if they shade into each other, there is a difference in purpose and function between poetry delivered to and by a participatory audience and to an audience that is separate. Unfortunately this is just the kind of information often lacking in accounts of oral literature, so that the grander theories are often based on little detailed evidence.

But enough is known to delineate tentatively some common situations, as far as the audience is concerned. First, there is the situation where almost all those present are involved in the performance. This can be a *total* involvement, as when the oral poetry takes the form of joint choral singing or praying, but more often it is a matter of one (or perhaps two) people taking the lead and the rest of the group joining in responses or refrain. In this situation, as with oral art generally, there is no set list of aims and functions, and there seems to be almost infinite variability in the purposes such oral poetry can achieve for its joint performers and audience. There are, however, certain commonly recurring patterns.

In one of these, the joint performance of oral poetry expresses and consolidates the cohesiveness of the group of performers. This is obvious, for instance, with political 'protest' songs in contemporary America and Western Europe. Jointly sung verses like

> We shall overcome
> We shall overcome
> Just like the tree that stands beside the water
> We shall overcome

or the Swahili trade union song in East Africa

> We do their work, bring them in their money
> Clothes sprout on them through the efforts of the workers
> ...So let us unite and crush the employers
>
> (Whiteley, 1964b, p. 221)

help to draw the participants together and make them aware of forming a 'movement' as well as articulating a particular view. Or it may be a matter of accepting membership in a jointly-working group, not necessarily opposed to outside bodies, like the daily hymn still chanted by Japanese workmen at the Matsushita Electric.

> Let's put our strength and mind together,
> Doing our best to promote production,
> Sending our goods to the people of the world,
> Endlessly and continuously,
> Like water gushing from a fountain.
> Grow, industry, grow, grow, grow!
> Harmony and sincerity!
> Matsushita Electric!
>
> (Macrae, 1975, p. 16)

Parallels are easy to find in religious as well as political contexts: Methodist hymn-singing, songs at political rallies, the joint performance of special initiation songs by groups of initiates, school songs, liturgical chanting, party political songs, and many others.

Work songs are a particularly clear example of the way in which oral poetry can create excitement and aesthetic pleasure in a participatory audience doing tedious or even painfully laborious work. This comes out in many descriptions of work songs and their functions. It is described particularly vividly in a recent collection of Hebridean 'waulking' songs – songs sung by women engaged in the heavy job of 'waulking' or beating home-made cloth to shrink it and give it an even texture. This was exhausting work, but the women were elated and light-hearted on these occasions. An eye-witness and participant from the end of the nineteenth century describes the scene

> The web, saturated with the soapy water, was laid loosely upon [a makeshift table], and forthwith the work began. All seemed full of light-hearted gladness, and of bustle and latent excitement, and as each laid hold of the cloth, with their sleeves tucked up to the shoulders, one could see the amount of force they represented...These good women, with strong, willing hands, take hold of the web, and the work proceeds, slowly at first, but bye and bye, when the songs commence, the latent excitement bursts into a blaze.
>
> (Mary MacKellar, quoted in MacCormick, 1969, p. 12)

This atmosphere of enjoyment and excitement in the midst of exhausting work must surely be ascribed at least in part to the songs. In this Hebridean case, the songs were often quite long and elaborate – not all work songs are short and crude. They included love songs, panegyric, and narrative poetry, sung sometimes in unison, sometimes with the group following and repeating a soloist's words. One relatively short one is *Far away I see the mist*, translated from the Gaelic in MacCormick's edition

> Far away I see the mist,
> I see Ben Beg, Ben More as well,
> I see the dew on grassy tips.
> Heard ye how my woe befell?
> The traveller broke, the sail was rent,
> Into the sea the mast it went,
> The gallant boatmen further fared.
> O would my father's son were spared –
> My mother's son 'tis makes my woe,
> He breathes not in the wrack below,
> No raiment now his body needs,
> His foot no covering but the weeds.

> Hearty fellows be ye cheerful,
> Let us prove the tavern's hoard,
> Fetch the glass and fill the measure,
> Tossing bonnets round the board,
> Banish sorrow unavailing,
> The dead come not to life with wailing.

(MacCormick, 1969, p. 155)

Other work songs may have words which seem less elaborate, but give scope for originality and for enjoyment in a different way: they give a soloist the opportunity to improvise and adapt to the needs of the moment and the audience the chance to participate, whatever the new words initiated by the leader. Many of the songs designed to go with strictly timed work seem to be of this kind, the emphasis on repetition going well with the needs of a participating and working group. Lloyd quotes a typical 'one-pull shanty' of this kind

> A Yankee ship came down the river.
> *Shallow, Shallow Brown.*
> A Yankee ship came down the river.
> *Shallow, Shallow Brown.*
> And who do you think was master of her?
> *Shallow, Shallow Brown.*
> And who do you think was master of her?
> *Shallow, Shallow Brown.*
> A Yankee mate and a limejuice skipper.
> *Shallow, Shallow Brown.*
> A Yankee mate and a limejuice skipper.
> *Shallow, Shallow Brown.*
> And what do you think they had for dinner?
> *Shallow, Shallow Brown.*
> And what do you think they had for dinner?
> *Shallow, Shallow Brown.*
> A parrot's tail and monkey's liver.
> *Shallow, Shallow Brown.*
> A parrot's tail and monkey's liver.
> *Shallow, Shallow Brown.*

(Lloyd, 1967, p. 302)

In all these cases, the performers themselves are a kind of audience. Thus we must look in the first place at the influence on *them* for the direct effects of the performance of oral poetry – the way that it alleviates or rhythmically encourages and co-ordinates their work – rather than at the level of Society at large.

These poems with participatory audiences can enable the performers somehow to control their environment by capturing it in words. This is not the kind of point that can be proved or measured but it is hard to deny its significance. Jackson finds it in the songs which Texas prisoners sing as they labour:

> The songs have one other function. I am not so sure of it that I can list it with the clear and definite group of functions above [supplying rhythm for work, helping to pass the time and providing an outlet for tensions and frustration], but I am interested enough in it to offer it here as a suggestion: the songs change the nature of the work by putting the work into the worker's framework rather than the guards'. By incorporating the work with their song, by, in effect, co-opting something they are forced to do anyway, they make it *theirs* in a way it otherwise is not.
>
> (Jackson, 1972, p. 30)

People contending with boredom or oppression or grief can control or come to terms with it by expressing it in the literary form of a poem. This must in a measure be true of all oral art (though it may apply somewhat differently to the poet and/or performer than to a merely listening public); with a participatory audience such significance is likely to be shared widely with the whole performing group. Again, therefore, it is worth asking who and of what kind the audience is.

In a number of oral poems, the participating singers are trying to control their environment in a more direct and active way. In a sense this is true of most religious songs for joint singing, particularly those with an emphasis on salvation or on the blessings of this or another world, but it is most noticeable in political songs. Election songs have become very important in modern Africa since the late 1950s. In these songs – which are sometimes written down but basically circulate by oral means – the singers often state their political policies, and in doing so both reinforce their own beliefs and ensure that all members of the movement have a mastery of their political aims and the means needed to achieve them. One infectious calypso in the 1962 elections in (then) Northern Rhodesia made sure that the voters understood the electoral machinery:

> Upper roll voting papers will be green.
> Lower roll voting papers will be pink.
>
> *Chorus* Green paper goes in green box.
>   Pink paper goes in pink box.
>
> (Mulford, 1964, pp. 134–5)

The leader-chorus pattern can be particularly effective in this context, and seems to be commonly used in elections when leaders wish to involve and stir up loyalty from a largely illiterate electorate. This comes out clearly in another election song from Northern Rhodesia, when the African National Congress took up ill-defined popular grievances and articulated them into definite aims in a party programme, carrying the participatory audiences with them. In this song the soloist sings in his own person and involves the audience all directly in the chorus.

> One day, I stood by the road side.
> I saw cars passing by.
> As I looked inside the cars
> I saw only white faces in them.
> These were European settlers.
> Following the cars were cyclists
> With black faces.
> They were poor Africans.
>
> *Refrain*   The Africans say,
>   Give us, give us cars, too,
>   Give us, give us our land
>   That we may rule ourselves.
>
> I stood still but thinking
> How and why it is that white faces
> Travel by car while black faces travel by cycle.
> At last I found out that it was that house,
> The Parliamentary House that is composed of Europeans,
> In other words, because this country is ruled by
> White faces, these white faces do not want
> Anything good for black faces.
>
> (Rhodes, 1962, p. 19)

An extended form of the basically participatory audience occurs when a group is relatively self-sufficient in itself and has no sustained audience outside, but nevertheless throws out occasional comment for the benefit of someone outside the group who is assumed or invited to listen in at that point – a temporary and occasional audience. This is not uncommon. Texas prison work songs are primarily sung by and for the working prisoner group, who constitute the primary audience. But there are also references to guards or prison officials who appear to be listening. Similarly, political songs may be sung mainly as an expression of solidarity or joyful participation by a united group, but are also secondarily directed to occasional bystanders or assumed opponents: think, for instance, of the enthusiasm which Campaign for Nuclear Disarmament marchers in England in the late 1950s gave to the songs they had been singing all along when they found they were marching past potentially interested spectators; or the way Mau Mau supporters in Kenya stood up with extra fervour for the tune of the British National Anthem – their European opponents did not know that new subversive words in Kikuyu had been set to the tune, and merely remarked on the apparently increased loyalty of the Kikuyu to the crown (Leakey, 1954, pp. 72–3). Here again, one can only detect the possible functions of friendly teasing, protest, attempted confrontation, conscious persuasion, deception or aggressive solidarity by identifying the primary and the temporary audiences, and the likely effects on them.

Another situation – overlapping with the first, but distinct enough to be noted as a commonly recurring pattern – occurs where the performance of oral poetry is part of a ceremony associated with one of the recognised turning-points of social and personal life. These are the performances that in many societies accompany weddings, funerals, coronations, initiations, the recognised events of the farming or pastoral year, even military rituals and legal proceedings. In societies with complex forms of specialisation affecting the arts, oral poetry at such ceremonies is sometimes by professionals or experts performing to clearly separate audiences; but in the situation I am distinguishing here songs are primarily performed by members of the social group immediately associated with the ceremony, with a larger public directly or indirectly involved and in some sense acting as audience. These amateur-dominated occasions are common even in our own society where professionalisation of the arts has in other contexts gone a long way.

One characteristic example can be taken from the ceremonies associated with death among the Limba of Sierra Leone. Here both the initial notification and mourning of the death and, later, the actual burial are marked by the lavish performance of oral poetry in the form of song. This is primarily initiated and led by a close woman relation of the dead man, supported by other women closely connected with the family. The songs go on for hours, and can be heard clearly through the rings of thatched huts that, till recently, constituted many Limba villages. The performance is like the participatory audience situation in one respect, for the group are singing for themselves – but differs in that they have an audience in the other inhabitants of the village who see and hear the singing going on in their midst.

This is not a trivial or theoretical difference, for the presence of this relatively permanent outside audience in the village is a significant factor in analysis of the function of the oral poetry which clusters round the fact of death, and plays a part in making it a public and not just a private event.

The prevalence of song on such occasions serves to mark them out as special and significant in social life. Poetry has been said to italicise or put in inverted commas, and this is indeed one of its functions here. Just as special forms of dress or of ritual in other contexts set some act or occasion apart from everyday life, so does the performance of oral poetry here. It helps to give meaning and weight to the event both for the participants and also for the village as a whole – the audience who hear the mourning songs going on among them. Part of this whole process, italicised as it is by poetry, is the public recognition in and through the ceremony of the new social status of both deceased and bereaved.

In this way a whole range of functions can be performed through the

delivery of oral poetry at a Limba death, some mainly affecting the participating singers, others essentially dependent on the wider audience. There
is the sense of consolation and of significance experienced by the performers themselves, as well as the satisfaction of carrying out the due social
obligations at this time of crisis for the group. For the village generally,
the event is marked out with due solemnity and attention largely by virtue
of the performance of oral poetry. It is claimed as a special responsibility
by the close-knit group who take the lead, and also spread abroad as a
significant event for the whole wider audience.

Another variant of this kind of situation occurs when the performance
of poetry and song expresses or resolves hostilities between individuals or
groups. At weddings, for instance, the relatives of bride and groom sometimes sing in turn, 'getting at' each other with both the opposing group
and, presumably, the other attenders at the wedding acting as an audience;
and rivalries between Kirghiz families often used to find expression in the
aitys or public song competitions (Chadwick and Zhirmunsky, 1969, p. 329).
Again, in Eskimo song duels, long and biting poems of derision are
composed and performed: 'Little, sharp words, like the wooden splinters
which I hack off with my axe', as one poem puts it (quoted in Hoebel, 1972,
p. 93). The singer most applauded is the winner – though he is likely to
get little but prestige from his victory. It is customary to identify the effects
of such activities as expressing hostility (which may be latent rather than
explicit) and rendering it more innocuous by ventilating it. But we need
to bear in mind the situation and the likely mood and nature of the
audience. One can surmise that entertainment and amusement are *also*
likely to play a part in such performances.[1] Indeed we know that the East
Greenland Eskimos carry on song duels for years 'just for the fun of it'
(Hoebel, 1972, p. 93). Political songs are sometimes used in a kind of duel
situation too. The 1959 federal elections in Western Nigeria were characterised by this kind of interchange. The supporters of the NCNC party
(symbolised by a cock) and the Action Group (a palm tree) sang against
each other, mocking each others' symbols.

Action Group
The cock is sweet with rice,
If one could get a little oil
With a little salt
And a couple of onions –
O, the cock is so sweet with rice.

NCNC
The Palm tree grows in the far bush.
Nobody allows the leper to build his house in the town.
The palm tree grows in the far bush...

[1] Duels of this kind shade into the more formally organised poetry competitions discussed later.

Action Group
Never mind how many cocks there are.
Even twenty or thirty of them will be contained
In a single chicken basket,
Made from the palm tree.
(Beier, 1960, pp. 66–7)

Sometimes the primary audience consists basically of a single person. This is the third common situation. It can be illustrated by Merriam's account of Bashi singers in the Kivu area of the Congo. Girls working on a plantation were dissatisfied with their conditions, but did not feel able to raise this directly with their employer. But they did seize the opportunity of singing a song about their grievances in his presence, and so the complaints they did not wish to raise formally were expressed indirectly.

> We have finished our work. Before, we used to get oil; now we don't get it. Why has Bwana stopped giving us oil? We don't understand. If he doesn't give us oil, we will leave and go to work for the Catholic Fathers. There we can do little work and have plenty of oil. So we are waiting to see whether Bwana X will give oil. Be careful! If we don't get oil, we won't work here.

(Merriam, 1954, pp. 51–2)

The convention by which things can be said in a poetic medium that could not be uttered in a more 'direct' form, is a widespread and interesting one. It is as if expression in poetry takes the sting out of the communication and removes it from the 'real' social arena. And yet, of course, it does not – for the communication still takes place. It is a curious example of the conventions that surround various forms of communication in society, where, even if the overt 'content' remains the same, the form radically affects the way it is received – whether or not it is regarded as a confrontation, for example.

The way that expression in songs and poems can be conventionally regarded as not offering the same direct challenge as prose communication is very widely documented. In the Texas prison songs, references – even derogatory references – to prison officials are regarded as acceptable in song even when they could never be articulated directly in what, for this purpose, is classified as 'real life'. This is a common pattern throughout the American South, where it is a long-standing convention for Negroes to express in song insult and hostility that could not be spoken (Jackson, 1972, pp. 126, 193). Again, social conventions often make it difficult for complaints by a wife about her husband (or, perhaps less often, the other way round) to be expressed directly, but are not infrequently voiced in song. A Maori woman, for instance, who was accused of being lazy by her husband often retaliated by composing a song about it (Best, 1924, p. 158) while among the Mapuche of Chile, where women normally held a subordinate role, it was accepted that wives blew off steam about marital problems in a song. It was incumbent on the husband whose faults were thus publicised to take it in good part. This comes out in the following Mapuche exchange, when the wife in her song publicly hints that her husband is a thief and wrong-doer.

Wife's song
I dreamed of a fox. It was bad for me, but there is no help for it now, since that is the way it turned out to be.

Man's reply
Things are not as bad as you have said, my little cousin (wife). If I have done anything wrong, it's all over now. Only on you do my eyes gaze. Let everything bad be ended.

Wife's counter-reply
Just now, dear cousin (husband), I have heard what I wanted to hear from your own lips. Now my heart is restored to its proper place. If you do what is right, I shall love you more than ever.

(Titiev, 1949, pp. 8–9)

Sometimes the presence of a secondary audience, as it were, can be important in these cases. The song or poem may be directly against one person as the primary audience and the one the poem is designed to affect, but the presence of a wider audience who overhear the communication can also be significant – as in the Mapuche case just quoted where interested auditors joined the wife in pressing her husband to mend his ways. The secondary audience forms the background of potential support against which the singer or speaker tries to reach the primary target. When two Yoruba women have quarrelled, they vent their enmity by singing aloud at each other in public places like the washing area *where other women will hear them* (Mabogunje, 1958, p. 35). Again, the verse directed against the Chopi youth trying to seduce a young girl was designed to stir up public opinion as well as express a rebuke in the acceptable medium of poetry.

We see you!
We know you are leading that child astray...
We know you!
(Tracey, 1948, p. 29)

It has frequently been pointed out that one way in which subjects can exert sanctions against their rulers is through poetry. This too gives the possibility of saying things which are normally unacceptable (often with additional conventional requirements about the permitted speaker and occasion). Thus the Somali poet could address a poem to a local sultan who was trying to assume dictatorial powers; with the backing of the wider audience of the poem, it finally led to the sultan's deposition.

> The vicissitudes of the world, oh 'Olaad, are like the clouds of the
>   seasons
> Autumn weather and spring weather come after each other in
>   turn...
> When fortune places a man even on the mere hem of her robe,
>   he quickly becomes proud and overbearing
> A small milking vessel, when filled to the brim, soon overflows
>
> (Andrzejewski, 1963, p. 24)

A similar device was used by Yoruba singers to give instructions to the local Mayor of Lagos. Cast in the form of a piece of popular dance music and ostensibly praising the Mayor Olorun Nimbe, it gives firm advice about the way he should act.

> I am greeting you, Mayor of Lagos,
> Mayor of Lagos, Olorun Nimbe,
> Look after Lagos carefully.
> As we pick up a yam pounder with care,
> As we pick up a grinding stone with care,
> As we pick up a child with care,
> So may you handle Lagos with care.
>
> (Beier, 1956, p. 28)

Parallels to this type of communication are very widespread, from the Chopi and Hottentot poetic attacks on chiefs in Africa (see Finnegan, 1970, p. 273ff) to the early Irish poets' satires on rulers, which were thought powerful enough to raise blemishes on the victim's face – and 'a man with a blemish shall not reign' (Knott and Murphy, 1967, p. 79).

Praise of rulers and other patrons can be regarded in the same light. The poem is directed at one known person (occasionally a small group), who forms the primary target, but with a larger audience who are expected to hear and applaud. Here again sentiments can be expressed not normally considered appropriate in straightforward prose or the medium of every-day conversation – the lengthy and hyperbolic praises involved would be too fulsome or too tedious to be readily acceptable in a more 'ordinary' medium – for instance, this extract from the panegyric of the famous Zulu king Shaka:

> ...He who is alone like the sun;
> He who bored an opening through the Chube clan,
> He came with Mvakela son of Dlaba,
> He came with Maqobo son of Dlaba,
> He came with Khwababa son of Dlaba,
> He came with Duluzana from among the Chubes...
>
> (Cope, 1968, p. 104)
> and so on through 450 lines

This is beautiful and elevating in poetry and doubtless did much to commend the poet to the ruler, to fortify his own pride in his actions, and to stir up and consolidate the admiration of the attendant audience for their ruler – but in everyday conversation it is less likely to be appealing or effective. Similar situations are found all over the world where court poets flourish. The primary audience may be the ruler, but the poems are given meaning and effect by the wider audience of those present during his performance.

In all these contexts the poet's communication with his intended primary audience is facilitated by the common convention that sentiments can be communicated through poetry that would be impertinent, boring or embarrassing in more direct form. Lovers exchanging passionate declarations of love or invitations to secret meetings, children mocking a teacher, beggars importuning wealthy passers-by, or wandering singers, like the Hausa, veiling aggressive attacks and abusive demands for payments in the acceptable medium of poetry – all perform in a context made possible by the social convention that communication in poetry is not just abuse, or immodesty, or flagrant begging, but an acceptable and pleasing social activity.

With situations of these kinds, it is easy to see the social function they perform in terms of social pressures and sanctions against rulers and others, or subtle and oblique communication, and these functions have frequently been commented on. But when one takes the contexts and audiences into account, especially the secondary audiences often involved, it becomes obvious that there are also elements of aesthetic pleasure and sheer enjoyment. It is, after all, the aesthetic setting which makes this type of special communication feasible, and clothing the message in appealing or magnificent or witty language gives spice and effect to the whole occasion.

This aesthetic aspect is usually taken for granted, and left for us to guess at from a knowledge of the general context. A few writers have commented on it directly. It comes out clearly, for instance, in Green's description of Ibo singers. Here songs are used as a direct sanction to coerce an offender. One woman had refused to pay a fine levied on her for a false accusation. The other women went in a group to her house to sing and dance against her. The songs were explicitly obscene – another instance of poetry as a medium for the normally unsayable – and had the effect of making the offender pay her fine. So far, the aim and effect of the songs are clear. But this was not all there was to it; sheer enjoyment was also involved, both for the participatory audience and for any by-standers.

> As for the women, I never saw them so spirited. They were having a night out and they were heartily enjoying it and there was a speed and energy about everything they did that gave a distinctive quality to the episode. It was also the only occasion in the village that struck one as obscene in the intention of the people themselves. Mixed with

what seemed genuine amusement there was much uncontrolled, abandoned laughter. There was a suggestion of consciously kicking over the traces about the whole affair.

(Green, 1964, pp. 202–3)[1]

One other situation is worth drawing attention to. Here the audience is clearly and specifically separate from the performer(s) and is present mainly, or largely, to listen to a performance. This kind of situation is worth special attention, for amidst the frequent comments on the functional aspects of oral art and its role in an actual social context, it is easy to forget that the performance is sometimes a specialised activity, explicitly valued as an end, with a special time and place set aside for its enjoyment.

Contrary to the once-prevalent theories about the communal or utilitarian nature of art in non-industrial societies (or elsewhere), such specialized situations are fairly common. It is clear in a number of accounts that enjoyment or entertainment were from the audience's point of view the main purpose of oral performances. Take, for instance, Vambéry's description of Turkoman performances by the heroic poets, *bakhshi*, in the nineteenth century:

> On festal occasions, or during the evening entertainments, some *Bakhshi* used to recite the verses of Makhdumkuli! When I was in Etrek, one of these troubadours had his tent close to our own; and as he paid us a visit of an evening, bringing his instrument with him, there flocked around him the young men of the vicinity, whom he was constrained to treat with some of his heroic lays. His singing consisted of certain forced guttural sounds, which we might rather take for a rattle than a song, and which he accompanied at first with gentle touches of the strings, but afterwards, as he became excited, with wilder strokes upon the instrument. The hotter the battle, the fiercer grew the ardour of the singer and the enthusiasm of his youthful listeners; and really the scene assumed the appearance of a romance, when the young nomads, uttering deep groans, hurled their caps to the ground, and dashed their hands in a passion through the curls of their hair, just as if they were furious to combat with themselves.
>
> (Vambéry, *Travels*, p. 322, quoted in Chadwick, III, 1940, p. 175)

Kara-Kirghiz singers too were valued for their power to stir the enthusiasm and admiration of the audience, who came specially to hear them. The Russian traveller Venyukov heard one of the most famous of these minstrels in 1860

> He every evening attracted round him a crowd of gaping admirers, who greedily listened to his stories and songs. His imagination was remarkably fertile in creating feats for his hero – the son of some

---

[1] For other examples of the element of enjoyment in pressurising poems in Africa, see Finnegan, 1970, pp. 278ff.

Khan – and took most daring flights into the regions of marvel. The greater part of the rapturous recitation was improvised by him as he proceeded, the subject alone being borrowed usually from some tradition. His wonderfully correct intonation, which enabled everyone who even did not understand the words to guess their meaning, and the pathos and fire which he skilfully imparted to his strain, showed that he was justly entitled to the admiration of the Kirghizes as their chief bard!

(quoted in Chadwick, III, 1940, p. 179)

The details of such occasions naturally vary, but the general pattern, in which a poet addresses himself specifically to an audience who are present to enjoy his poetry is a common one. The audience may at the same time be drinking, dancing, or otherwise relaxing – but the poetry being delivered in speech or song is often a central part of the entertainment involved. This sort of occasion occurs all over the world, from the 'singing pubs' or fireside literary circles of Ireland (Delargy, 1945, p. 192) to home gatherings in the Yugoslav countryside where men come from the various families around to hear an epic singer perform, or the coffee houses in Yugoslav towns where the minstrel must please his audience with exciting and well-sung heroic tales so as to reap a reward from listeners who have come into town for the market (Lord, 1968a, pp. 14–15). The same general pattern is found in the fairly common contexts of poetic competitions, where single poets or contending groups of performers compete to gain greater applause than their opponents from the audience and thus be declared the winner. Such competitions are found all over the world, from Central Asia and Japan to Africa and Polynesia.

In the case of a performer like Avdo Mededović or the Kirghiz 'chief bard' it is easy to see such occasions as primarily 'aesthetic', comparable to concerts or poetry recitals in our own culture where the purpose is the appreciation of an artistic performance. But it is not always easy to delimit the specific purpose of a set occasion (even in our own culture people have a variety of reasons for attending such performances!), still less all the possible functions. Certainly, many of the occasions on which there is a specific audience assembled to hear one or more performers are, arguably, describable as specialised and deliberate 'artistic occasions'. But there are also contexts where this aim may not be specifically differentiated from others, or where the aim is overtly of some other kind – religious say, or political. Hearing the chanted sermons in the American South described by Rosenberg, the outsider may wish to analyse the aesthetic and poetic characteristics of the chants, but the audience comes for religious reasons, 'to hear the Word of God'. Or take the Northern Rhodesia party songs again. In the election campaign meetings of 1962, songs formed a recognised and popular part of mass meetings, and were, we assume, one inducement to large numbers to attend. Mulford describes a typical rally by the UNIP party

> Thousands were packed in an enormous semi-circle around the large official platform constructed by the youth brigade on one of the huge ant hills. Other ant hills nearby swarmed with observers seeking a better view of the speakers. Hundreds of small flags in UNIP's colours were strung above the crowd. Youth brigade members, known as 'Zambia policemen' and wearing lion skin hats, acted as stewards and controlled the crowds when party officials arrived or departed. UNIP's jazz band played an occasional calypso or jive tune, and between each speech, small choirs sang political songs praising UNIP and its leaders.

> Kaunda will politically get Africans freed from the English,
> Who treat us unfairly and beat us daily.
> UNIP as an organization does not stay in one place.
> It moves to various kinds of places and peoples,
> Letting them know the difficulties with which we are faced.
> These whites are only paving the way for us,
> So that we come and rule ourselves smoothly.

> (Mulford, 1964, pp. 133–4)

In these situations, obviously, different effects can be accomplished by the poems and their performance: economic transactions (between audience and poet), expressions of hostility and consequent consolidation of contending groups, the transmission of religious forms or political viewpoints, and so on. But from the point of view of the audience, the central aim is surely enjoyment. This need not be categorised in reductive terms as 'mere entertainment'. This enjoyment embraces, for instance, the delight of Yugoslav audiences in the beauty of diction, delineation of character and evocation of high heroic deeds in a glorious and remote world by a minstrel like the great Yugoslav singer Avdo Mededović, or the satisfaction of Tongan islanders in unravelling the skilful metaphors with which contending bards assailed each others' work, poems 'laden with two or three strata of meaning' (Luomala, 1955, p. 33), or the Marquesans' appreciation of the intellectual contests of their own bards (ibid. p. 48) or Kirghiz audiences' delight in the polished diction of their minstrels where 'every adroit expression, every witty play on words calls forth lively demonstrations of applause' (Radlov, *Proben*, v, p. iii translated in Chadwick, III, 1940, p. 179). It is tempting in the search for the more abstruse 'functions of art' to neglect this kind of reaction and to brush aside, as too obvious to mention, the element of enjoyment and aesthetic appreciation. But to play down this aspect is to forget what must often be the primary interest of the audience.

These patterns of audience involvement bring home to us how important it is to ask questions about the nature and wishes of the *audience* to which a performance is directed. As with the recurring patterns of relationship between the role and activities of poets (above chapter 6), it would be a mistake to regard these common situations as separate and distinctive categories, or to erect them into theoretical typologies. There is plenty of overlap between the various situations delineated here, and those discussed are not an exhaustive list. All that is claimed is that it is illuminating to see that these *are* commonly occurring patterns, and that we need to identify the nature and situation of the audience in any analysis of the supposed 'functions' of any particular oral poetry.

2 The effect and the composition of audiences

The audience, it is now clear, affects the nature and purpose of performances of oral poetry in various ways. There are also two further questions worth asking: first, the direct effect which the audience may have on the poem at the actual time of performance; and second, the way the audience is itself selected.

As for the first, it is clear that audiences do often have an effect on the form and delivery of a poem. Of course, the nature of the likely audience influences all literature, but with oral literature there is the additional factor that members of the audience can take a *direct* part in the performance. This is obvious in the case of a participatory audience, or in the fairly frequent situation where a basically specialist solo performance is supplemented by the audience joining in the choruses or responses. There are also the cases where (as described in the chapter on composition) the restiveness or receptiveness of the audience affects the length or brevity of the delivery of a piece, or when the presence of certain individuals or groups leads a poet to gear his presentation of, say, events or genealogies to please them. In mediaeval Chinese ballad singing, audience-reaction was a significant part of the whole performance.

> In the case of a Chinese story-teller ballad, the relationship between the originator and his audience is so essential and so tight that the existence and the shape of the production is directly dependent on the audience's reaction. The interpretation gap between the creator and the reader has, in the case of Chinese story-teller literature, disappeared because the story-teller is forced by his profession to foresee his client's expectations, wishes, and moods and to react to them, though they may be very changeable indeed. Either the story-teller knows and reacts to his audience with skill, is successful, and earns his livelihood, or he misjudges them and fails. So in a certain sense audience reaction is not a passive but an active, creative factor in the Chinese story-telling.
>
> (Doleželová-Velingerová and Crump, 1971, p. 13)

This involvement by the audience – even when the audience is primarily separate rather than participatory – sometimes extends to verbal prompting or objections by individual listeners. In Yoruba hunters' songs (*ijala*), for instance, other expert *ijala* performers are often present. If they think the performer is not singing properly, they will cut in with a correction, beginning with a formula like:

> You have told a lie, you are hawking loaves of lies.
> You have mistaken a seller of *àbàri* for a seller of *ègbo*[1]
> Listen to the correct version now.
> Your version is wrong.
> For the sake of the future, that it may be good.

In self-defence, a criticised *ijala*-chanter would brazenly say:

> It all happened in the presence of people of my age.
> I was an eyewitness of the incident;
> Although I was not an elder then,
> I was past the age of childhood.

Alternatively the chanter may reply by pleading that the others should respect his integrity.

> Let not the civet-cat trespass on the cane rat's track.
> Let the cane rat avoid trespassing on the civet-cat's path.
> Let each animal follow the smooth stretch of its own road.
>
> (Babalọla, 1966, p. 61–2)

Such cases are interesting for what they show about the old theories about the possibly 'communal' nature of oral literature, and the part played by the 'folk' in its creation. There are reasons for abandoning parts of these theories, but there remains the genuine point that, with oral literature, the audience can take a direct part in its realisation. There are participatory audiences, for one thing, and then, over and above the way in which any *face-to-face* audience is likely to affect the manner and content of the poetry, there is the accepted convention in some contexts that members of the audience can intervene directly. In the sense of audience involvement, oral literature is more open than written literature to direct group influence on what might otherwise be considered the individual creative genius of the poet.

But one must not labour the point overmuch. In particular, those who have seen this potential involvement of the audience as a sign of the 'democratic' or 'popular' nature of oral poetry are assuming that they know the precise nature of the audiences involved – and that these are indeed

---

[1] *àbàri*: a sort of pudding made from maize, plantain-flour, and beans. *ègbo*: mashed boiled maize grains.

'popular'. This leads to the second question: the nature and extent of the audiences.

It is sometimes assumed, rather romantically, that the audiences of oral poetry are necessarily 'popular' – the public at large – and that knowledge of a particular oral literature is widely diffused through the society. This is not true (see chapter 6, section 3). For though oral literature cannot have the 'private' and 'silent' aspect found in the circulation of written literature, and is always 'public' and 'hearable' by others in its very essence, this does not mean that in a given case the audiences are unrestricted and attendance open to all in the society. In fact, occasions and performers are conditioned by convention, and audiences too are restricted in constitution and distribution.

This is so even with the simplest participatory songs. The work-songs of one occupational group are not always known by others; initiation songs are often separated into those for men and those for women; and adults usually do not know the words of the latest craze among children's songs. Similarly, praise poetry *may* be heard widely throughout a society, but the rich and powerful to whom it is primarily directed are likely to hear it more frequently. Again, how far specialist poets are prepared to make a living by travelling throughout the country and how far they attach themselves to the main centres of wealth and urbanism obviously decides which audiences are likely to benefit from their performances.

The frequent comment that poetry can act as a social sanction by the people against their rulers looks different if – as is sometimes the case – these poems are delivered primarily by poets, themselves members of the establishment, to audiences largely made up of those permanently associated with the court. We often have little evidence on the question of how wide an audience has access to such poetry. It is easy to repeat, for instance, the common claim that ballads speak for 'the people' (e.g. Hodgart, 1965, p. 11) – but which people? when? and is the meaning and role of the ballads the same for all sections of the potential audience?

Again, to claim that certain songs are 'for the folk' inevitably requires a definition of 'the folk'. For a collector like Greenway 'the folk' of modern industrial life are no longer agricultural labourers but modern industrial workers – but he explicitly excludes college students (Greenway, 1953, p. 9); so the provenance of his 'folk songs' is not so wide as one might at first suppose. Similarly, the emphasis in the United States on 'protest' and 'left-wing' songs do not of themselves demonstrate 'democratic' or 'popular' functions for such poetry: to prove this one would have to consider both the performers and the audiences involved, and show that the circulation was not confined to limited social groups. It is not unfair to quote the cynical verse commenting on the political movement associated with 'protest songs' and *The Peoples' Song Book*

Their motives are pure, their material is corny,
But their spirit will never be broke.
And they go right on in their great noble crusade –
Of teaching folk-songs to the folk.

(Quoted in Wilgus, 1959, p. 229)

Even with the apparently public and open transmission of certain types
of oral poetry by modern mass media, audiences may in practice be
restricted, and different sections will react differently to the same performances. The oral poems classified as 'pop songs' in Britain, for instance,
are listened to primarily by one age group, and ignored or actively repu-
diated by most others. This may be *self*-selection rather than arbitrary
restriction by an outside force, but it imposes as real a limitation on the
likely audience. It is a selective process fostered and maintained by social
expectations – conventions which may be more effective (because volun-
tary) than an official order or government censorship.

Similarly, it is easy to make a contrast between the obscurity (hence
restricted circulation) of certain written literature and the more open
nature of oral literature, whose successful performance depends on the
audience appreciating and understanding. This is true. But even primarily
non-literate audiences can consist of initiates and intellectuals, and the
circulation of oral poetry may sometimes take place within circumscribed
limits. In a general way many initiation songs are of this kind – like the
Makua song-riddles, full of allusions that only initiates can understand –
and so are a number of religious poems whose esoteric content and
language confine them to an audience of devotees. This type of restriction
was taken very seriously in parts of India, where there was 'the rule that
no non-Brahman should recite or hear the Vedas, and this was and is
respected by the other castes' (Staal, 1961, p. 33). Similarly, among the
Australian Aborigines of Central Australia, the sacred songs could be sung
only by men, and in some cases 'the women and children were...not
permitted even to listen to them on pain of death' (Strehlow, 1971, p. 637).
Again, some poets may use esoteric or even foreign language unknown to
their audience – like the use of Latin over many centuries, the minstrel use
of Mandingo for song over wide areas of non-Mandingo West Africa, or
the 'special language' used by early Irish poets. Even when a formally
different language is not used, full understanding of the meaning of
certain types of poetry is sometimes deliberately restricted. This was typical
of the aristocratic poetry of Polynesia, where the riddling and figurative
form of expression was 'to exalt language above the comprehension of the
common people, either by obscurity, through ellipsis and allusion, or by
saying one thing and meaning another' (Beckwith, 1919, p. 41). Strehlow
explains how this was a common feature of Aranda poetry in Central
Australia:

The special *form* of Aranda verse increased its effect. Because of the varying ages of the singers it was an advantage that the words sung should be obscure, so that young untried men, who had only recently been initiated, could not from the singing of licentious verses draw the wrong and unwarranted conclusion that they had the approval of their tribal elders to satisfy their drives in real life as well as in a symbolic ceremony. Most of the particularly 'dangerous' verses of this sort were, as I have pointed out earlier, hidden from the young men; others had harmless meanings attributed to them when they were being explained to the untried and the immature. The full meaning of each verse had to be brought out by the accompanying oral tradition; and its old guardians saw to it that no one was told the full truth until his personal conduct had proved him to be a man amenable to strict discipline. Clearly, 'censorship' to protect the morals of the young was not unknown even in a 'primitive' community!

(Strehlow, 1971, p. 681)

So oral poetry is not necessarily widely and democratically diffused through the people; its distribution and audience may in practice be restricted, and its form such as to strengthen the current power structure of society rather than undermine it.

Oral literature does often circulate more publicly and openly than much written literature. Against this, one must set the mass production of printed books to which it is possible in principle for huge numbers of people to have access; contrast this in turn with the restricted audiences to whom (apart from the recent development of radio and television) oral poetry tends to be delivered. Oral literature is dependent for its realisation on performers and audiences, and these are often more restricted than the more naive views of non-industrial societies as essentially 'communal' and 'open' would have us believe. Here again it is essential to look both at the type of performers and poets involved and at the nature of the audience in each case.

3 The purpose and meaning of poetry: local theories

A further point worth noting is the significance of local interpretations, of a poem or of poetry generally. This too needs to be considered, not just the role of poetry in general terms, abstracted from the particularities of the culture in which it occurs.

People trying to analyse the role of poetry have often been tempted to concentrate on objective-sounding terms like 'function' or 'effects'. The focus has thus been the consequences which, seen from the outside, poetry (or poetic activity) can be seen to have for the society in general, or for particular groups or individuals within it – whether or not these conse-quences are locally perceived as such. Sociologists have been drawn more to this 'external' aspect – particularly functional anthropologists – while exploration of the local interpretations of the meaning of poetry or the local philosophy of art tend to be taken up by those interested in 'the arts'. The dichotomy between these approaches has never been complete, and many sociologists and anthropologists have seen the need to understand local interpretations, whether of poetry or anything else. Recently there has been increasing awareness among sociologists of the importance of the 'meanings' that people attach to their actions and to the world around them, and a renewed sense that to look at the role of any social action only from the outside in so-called 'objective' or 'generalisable' terms is seriously to diminish our appreciation of the complexity of reality and of the resources of the human imagination.

It is thus relevant at this point to say something about local views of the nature and purpose of poetry. This is, by definition, not a subject that can be treated in general terms. The whole point is the uniqueness of many such views, bound in as they are with local religious beliefs, particular social experience and symbolism, local theories of psychology, and so on. All I can do here is to illustrate some of the kinds of views that are held on these topics. But even a few examples will help to convey how significant this can be for the study of a particular oral poetry. It also establishes, contrary to some older assumptions, that non-literate like literate people can reflect self-consciously on the nature and purpose of poetry.

The genesis of poetry is often seen in terms of 'inspiration' – though where this inspiration is believed to come from varies. This is obviously relevant to the understanding of local views about the nature – and hence the purpose – of poetry and of particular forms. Thus the outside analyst may note the 'oral-formulaic' structure of American Negro chanted sermons, or their integrative function for the audience; but for the congregation itself 'when the preacher is giving a sermon the words come directly from God' (Rosenberg, 1970a, pp. 8–9). This conviction obviously affects how these chanted poetic sermons are received by their audience and thus their specific effect. Again, the members of the hunters' society among the Yoruba of Nigeria regard the god Ogun as their special patron, and many of their *ijala* (or hunting) songs are connected with the worship of Ogun as well as with popular entertainment. The views of participants in this society about the nature and genesis of poetry are consonant with this background, as will be clear from the following comments on *ijala* songs by members of the society

> No hunter can validly claim the authorship of an ijala piece which he is the first to chant. The god Ogun is the source and author of all ijala chants; every ijala artist is merely Ogun's mouthpiece.

> Certainly there are new ijala chants created by expert ijala-chanters from time to time. The process of composition is intuitive and

inspirational; it springs from the innate talents of the artist. The spirit,
the genie (*àlùjànnú*) of ijala-chanting teaches a master chanter new
ijala pieces to chant. The god Ogun himself is ever present with a
master chanter to teach him new ijala.

It is often through inspiration that ijala artists compose new ijala
chants. They receive tuition from the god Ogun in dreams or
trances.

(Quoted in Babalọla, 1966, pp. 46–7)

Songs which are believed to derive from a divine source of this kind are
likely to affect their audience otherwise than songs seen as primarily due
to the personal gifts of an individual singer.

Inspiration can also be through a dream. One of the most famous Eskimo
poems – the *Dead man's song* – is presented as if by the dead man himself,
but 'dreamed by one who is alive', by the poet Paulinaoq. This interpretation of the genesis of songs is strongly held by the Toda of southern India:
Emeneau includes a whole section of 'Songs dreamed' in his collection. In
one case a woman 'dreamed' her song in which two dead men speak. In
another a man was said to have dreamed a poem about a mother lamenting
her forced departure from her child (she had died when her baby was only
one month old, and the dreamer's wife was caring for the child). The
dreamer awoke from his dream before the song was finished; but, though
it was the middle of the night, he roused everyone to hear him sing the
34-line song

O my child!
O child that does not know how to talk! O child that does not
  know the places!...
The child that I bore is crying...
I have sat, forsaking my child. I have sat, forsaking my buffaloes.

(Emeneau, 1971, pp. 582–3)

Any understanding of the effect of this song as it was sung and of the nature
of poetic composition as understood by the Toda must take account of the
assumption that songs can on occasion be 'dreamt' and can provide a
channel of communication with the dead.

Dreams are also thought significant for poetry among the Australian
Aborigines of Arnhem Land. Here the so-called 'gossip songs' by contemporary oral poets are composed and delivered on the understanding that
'the songman merely repeats songs given to him in dreams by his personal
spirit familiar' – even though in practice a good songman is naturally 'alert
to all the gossip and song potential for miles around' (Berndt, 1973, pp.
48–9; 1964, p. 318). The sacred Arnhem Land song cycles, too, are believed
to come originally from the mythical time of the 'Eternal Dreaming', and
the poet is seen as in direct contact with the ancestral spirits in dream: it

is from them that he 'receives' the words and rhythms. 'The songs are the echo of those first sung by the Ancestral Beings: the spirit of the echo goes on through timeless space, and when we sing, we take up the echo and make sound' (Berndt, 1952, p. 62). It is partly because of this interpretation that performance can have the effect that Berndt describes.

> The songs, since they 'belong' to the divine Beings, give the ritual an atmosphere of reality, in the sense of veracity, and a deep consciousness of affiliation and continuity with these Beings themselves. Sacred songs, sung on the ceremonial ground by hereditary leaders, in conjunction with ritual and dancing, and in the presence of religious symbols or emblems, vividly reflect and re-inspire the religious emotions of all who hear them.
>
> (ibid. p. 62)

Inspiration does not always come from outside the poet. Sometimes his own powers are stressed; 'not all men can make songs', as the Hopi poet Koianimptiwa pointed out (Curtis, 1907, p. 484). This is clear in the case of the Dinka of the southern Sudan. They see the composition of poetry as something rather akin to lying (i.e. making fictions). A man is a 'liar' (*alueeth*), though in a less derogatory sense of the word than usual, if he is distinguished in singing or dancing or any aesthetic field:

> Every young man and woman is considered an *alueeth* by virtue of preoccupation with aesthetic values, and such an evaluation is not really a criticism to the Dinka. It is a critical praise which the Dinka regard as a compliment on the lines of the expression 'It's too good to be true'.
> Composition of a song is seen in somewhat the same way. To compose a song is called 'to create' (*cak*); to tell a lie is to 'create words' (*cak wel*). *Cak* is also applied to creation by God. In all these meanings is a common denominator of making something which did not exist.
>
> (Deng, 1973, p. 84)

Consonant with this theory of poetic composition, the Dinka see their poems as closely connected to, and arising from, the particular circumstances of their origin. Songs are known to be based on events and to have been composed with the purpose of influencing people with regard to these events. Even when the owner himself does not compose his own song, but goes to an expert, it is still shaped to his purpose. He has to supply to the expert the

> detailed information about his situation and particularly the aspects he wants stressed. The glorious or glorified aspects of his lineal history, the relatives or friends he wants to praise and the reasons for doing so, the people he wants to criticize and the reasons for criticism are among the many details that are usually included in the background information.
>
> (Deng, 1973, p. 85)

The Dinka therefore see their songs not 'as abstract arrangements of words with a generalized meaning far removed from the particular circumstances of their origin' (p. 84) – a not uncommon view in modern English and American critical theory – but rather as something designed to bring about changes and play an effective part in social life.

> Songs everywhere constitute a form of communication which has its place in the social system, but among the Dinka their significance is more clearly marked in that they are based on actual, usually well-known events and are meant to influence people with regard to those events. This means that the owner whose interests are to be served by the songs, the facts giving rise to that song including the people involved, the objectives it seeks to attain whether overtly or subtly and whether directly or indirectly, all combine to give the song its functional force. This cannot be fully understood through the words alone whether spoken, sung, or, as is now possible, written. The words of the song, their metaphorical ingenuity, and their arrangement contribute to this force, but to appreciate the functional importance of the song, words must be combined with the melody, the rhythm, and the presentation of the song for a specific purpose.
>
> Lienhardt writes:
>
> When I used occasionally to read poetry and was asked what I was reading, I used to say I was reading songs; it was always asked then what *sort* of songs – prayers, war songs, courting songs, or songs for singing when accompanying a bull. Eventually I decided to call poems 'sitting songs' which at least suggested some sort of a purpose which they might serve...I had great difficulty, even with people whom I had accustomed to the idea, to convey that words of a song could be separated from its music, for everyone is not thinking of the 'meaning' of what he sings, a meaning which could be paraphrased in some way.
>
> (ibid. pp. 84–5)

Unless we appreciate this Dinka interpretation of the nature and purpose of poetry, we cannot understand how their songs can be so effective in bringing about change and affecting actions and relationships.

How far such local theories about poetic genres and purpose are accepted by *everyone* in a local audience is perhaps impossible to say in any given case. Certainly views about the nature of poetry itself, as well as taste for particular details, are liable to vary between individuals, and to change over time, and between generations differences make themselves felt. But it seems fair to suggest that even if not totally shared by everyone, local theories of the kind described by Deng for the Dinka or Babalọla for Yoruba *ijala* poems provide a more fruitful starting-point for the analyst interested in the role and effects of such poetry than assuming that it must necessarily be represented according to some model of poetry implicitly assumed by the foreign observer. Often enough the general framework is at least intelligible to most people present, while leaving room for shades of interpretation within it – as with the Fijian heroic poet Velema where the details may be queried, but not the underlying poetic theory of divine inspiration.

> Sceptics...suspect that the poet exaggerates the virtues of the heroes ...yet no one doubts the validity of his talent for literary rapport with the supernatural...the poet's ecstacy thus [for his listeners] determines the events of history...Natives at The-Place-of-Pandanus trust the ancestral communications of seers so perfectly that those who dispute of even recent history refer to them for solution. Through such communion forgotten genealogies of the last generation can be known again with certainty.
>
> (Quain, 1942, pp. 8–9)

In considering local evaluations of the success or failure of poetic compositions it is helpful to know of these underlying poetic theories, which may differ from our own. Thus the idea – held by the Dinka and many others – that music and presentation may be as important as 'meaning' implies a particular stress on criteria relating to performance and delivery rather than, as so often with written poetry, primarily on text and content. The local evaluation of a song among the Dinka must also take account of the purposive quality of Dinka songs: 'A good song should move the audience toward its objectives. A war song must arouse a warlike spirit and a dance song must excite the dancers. If the objective of the song is to win sympathy in a sad situation, both the words and the music should be effectively sad' (Deng, 1973, p. 93). Deng shows how these criteria influence the Dinka in their sense of what is or is not a good song (Deng, 1973, pp. 91ff) consonant with their view of the nature of poetry.

By contrast Yoruba hunters judge *ijala* songs more by what they conceive to be the 'accuracy' of the singer's words and the wisdom expressed in the song – since his words are assumed to have been directly taught him by the god Ogun – allied to the musical and performing ability with which he conveys the god's utterances effectively to his audience (Babalọla, 1966, pp. 50ff).

Judging the effect of a particular piece of oral poetry on an audience can thus never be a simple matter, even for someone with deep knowledge of local conventions. To understand the effect fully one would need to know the 'meaning' locally attached to the particular characteristics of the poem as well as to poetry generally, the mood of the audience, the social and historical background, the appreciation of certain modes of delivery, and so on. All too often these are aspects about which observers tell us little, while they hasten on to generalise about the over-all 'functions' of poetic forms in a particular society. Because it is difficult to assess exactly how a poem is being received, this omission is not altogether surprising. But it is worth saying again that for a full appreciation of the effect and context of poetry in any culture, some attention must be given not just to obvious topics like occasion, audience or performers, but also to local ideas about the genesis, purpose and meaning of poetry.

4 Some effects of oral poetry

This discussion of audiences and the effects which performances tend to have on them has concentrated on obvious points and situations. But these straightforward purposes and effects are the ones to consider first – and they often get forgotten in sociological theorising. It is only after considering these aspects that it is sensible to move on to more generalised or abstract speculation.

The main point to emerge is the variety of effects oral poetry can have – an obvious point, once stated, but easy to overlook, given the attraction of monolithic theories of the social functions of literature. The effect a piece of poetry is likely to have depends not on some absolute or permanent characteristic in the text itself, but on the circumstances in which it is delivered, the position of the poet, and perhaps above all on the nature and wishes of the audience. To class *We shall overcome* as a 'protest song' and assume that its 'function' is to effect a political purpose, ignores the fact that for some audiences and in some cases it may be primarily listened to for entertainment, or sung (by a participatory audience) just to while away the time or as a kind of 'work song' to accompany a march. The same poem delivered in different circumstances or to different audiences may well have a correspondingly different effect. We know, for instance, that the Ainu epic *Kutune Shirka* was recited sometimes at religious ceremonies and sometimes when time simply lay heavy on peoples' hands, like waiting for fish to bite or by the fire at home on a winter night (Waley, 1951, p. 235). The very same Hawaiian songs which were first used during the hardships and oppression of war-time as outlets for frustration and a channel for informal social protest, were after the war used for purely recreational purposes (Freeman, 1957), while in contemporary Britain the same song by immigrant Punjabis can be used both to 'set toes tapping from Southall to Smethwick' with its racy beat on festive occasions, and to express the bitterness of the solitary Asian wife left isolated in a strange land by her 'overtime' husband who works day and night

> I don't want your fridge, your colour TV.
> I'd rather have you at home with me.
> The nights are cold in this heartless land;
> My husband, God help me, is an overtime man.

(Mascarenhas, 1973)

This multi-purpose potential in poetry is more pervasive than usually supposed. Indeed, the same poem on the same occasion can play different roles for different parts of the audience. It is common for poetry to be used as a veil for hidden political purposes: thus Mau Mau songs in Kenya set to well-known hymn tunes played an important part in the political movement, where to the European establishment they seemed merely to express religious sentiments; while many Irish 'love songs' about Dark Rosaleen or Kathleen Na Houlihan convey a political rather than a sentimental message to some listeners. And for the Somali independence movement, Andrzejewski describes how the compressed imagery of the *balwo* love lyric was turned to use in the struggle for independence in the later 1950s.

> The cryptic diction of the *balwo* was well suited for the purpose: satire and invective could easily be hidden in an apparent love poem. In public, or even on the government-controlled radio, a poet could say with impunity:
>
> *Halyey nim uu haysto oo*
> *Hubkiisu hangool yahaan ahay.*
>
> I am a man who is assailed by a huge wolf
> And who has only a forked stick.
>
> If challenged by a suspicious censor he could say that the wolf represented his despair in love, while the sophisticated members of his audience would interpret the image as describing the defencelessness of the Somali nation in face of the military might of foreign powers.
>
> (Andrzejewski, 1967, p. 13)

This contextual and relativist approach to the analysis of the effects of oral poetry does not mean that one must never generalise about the functions likely to be fulfilled, only that in indicating general patterns one cannot count on establishing *absolute* truths or avoid the need, with particular poems or genres, to enquire in detail about context, performer and audience. Indeed there are some very common patterns, many of which cut across the classification in terms of audience given in an earlier section.

Oral poetry, for instance, frequently serves to uphold the *status quo* – even to act as the kind of 'mythical' or 'sociological charter' which Malinowski emphasised as one function of oral prose narrative (Malinowski, 1926, pp. 78–9, 121). Court bards strengthen the position of rulers, poets act as propagandists for authority, the accepted view of life is propagated in poetic composition and, when poets are an established group, their own power and interests are often fortified by their performances. The social order is also maintained through the performance of poetry in ceremonial settings, where established groups express solidarity and social obligation in song. But the same processes can equally have effects disruptive of the settled social order; for songs can equally well be used to pressurise authority or express and consolidate the views of minority and dissident groups. The likely effectiveness of such poetry is demonstrated by the frequency with which it has been discouraged or banned by government – from the Irish authorities' harassment of nationalist singers during the nineteenth century (Zimmerman, 1967, p. 51) to the Nigerian military rulers' banning of political songs in 1966.

One of the most widely occurring occasions for poetry and song is in relaxation after work. Working parties in fields or forests or factories commonly end their sessions with a period of singing: this is documented from all over the world, from Sotho or Limba cultivators to Tatar hunters or the relaxed singing as groups of people travel home after the serious business of watching a football match. Beneath all cultural differences one underlying theme and purpose in these occasions is surely recreational. It constitutes both an 'act of sociability' (as Malinowski put it) and a means of recreation after work.

Other commonly found effects of performances of oral poetry include rituals of healing; ventilating disputes (either intensifying or resolving them); exerting social sanctions against offenders or outsiders; communicating in an oblique but comprehensible form truth which could not be expressed in more ordinary ways; providing for the articulation of man's imaginative creativity; realising a desire to grasp and express the world in beautiful words; adding solemnity and public validation to ceremonial occasions; providing comfort and some means of social action for the bereaved or oppressed...

But as soon as one embarks on a list it becomes obvious that it could go on endlessly. The main point about the effects of oral poetry is the infinite range of possibilities – as wide as the 'effects' of 'communication' itself – and no list, even of common patterns, could be definitive. According to the context in which it is delivered (and the prime elements in this are the performer and the audience) oral poetry can be used to reconcile, divide, maintain established authority or undermine it, propagandise, innovate, conserve, cajole, entrance, scandalise, attack, soothe – or a hundred other things. To judge which, if any, of these are in play it is essential not to begin from an abstract analysis of first principles, but from a consideration of the occasion and, above all, of the audience and of its reception and understanding of the performance.

8
Poetry and society

The last chapter may seem like a mere list of possible functions and effects, with little analysis of the more difficult areas. But it is important to look at these down-to-earth questions first, before considering more abstruse ones, and to bear them in mind when approaching the monolithic theories that appear in 'the sociology of literature'. These more general theories are the subject of this chapter.

1 The link between poetic and social institutions

It seems obvious that the content and context of literature, and the way literary activity is organised are closely correlated with the institutions of the society in which it is situated. This emerges from any consideration of function and contexts, for these relate to specific social groupings in any society, and to its social occasions and activities.

It is clear too that the organisation of poetic activity plays a wider part in society, over and above the particular groups and occasions on which it is practised, and without the participants necessarily including this among their conscious intentions. There are a number of ways in which this can be approached.

The existence of specialist or expert poets, for one thing, is a part of the division of labour in that society, and when there is a distinct class of influential poets this provides one powerful group in society and perhaps a channel for mobility. Again, poetic practice may be connected with the patterns of economic exchange. Poetry can provide one means for an expert performer to supplement his basic livelihood with minor gifts or even substantial payments; or for a professional to depend wholly on his art in a society which has the economic resources to support a practitioner of this kind.

Poetry and its performance can also be seen as a way in which a heritage of artistic performance (and of social values and ideas) is passed on from one generation to another – with changes and development, no doubt, but providing a basic continuity of artistic form and outlook between generations. This is so whether the artistic process includes relatively specialist art-forms (like the heroic epic tradition in Yugoslavia and Central Asia or the witty *qene* short poem in Ethiopia), or when it comprises the less differentiated but still conventionally formulated oral art of cultures with less marked divisions between specialist and everyday performer.

The continuity of cultural tradition may extend, too, over space as well as time. In large and otherwise diverse countries and regions, the activities of poets have not infrequently played an important part in creating or maintaining cultural unity. This is so in the large and heterogeneous region of West African savannah in which travelling Mande-speaking minstrels have contributed to a certain cultural unity. In Ethiopia, the wandering *azmari* poets helped to create poetic uniformity among otherwise heterogeneous groups (Chadwick, III, 1940, p. 525) while in early Ireland the poets 'were the only national institution...in the absence of towns or any centralized political system' (Green in Dillon, 1954, p. 85). This type of cultural influence has been noted in many other areas, from the territories of mediaeval Europe traversed by travelling minstrels to the widespread poetic culture of China and Tibet, and any analysis of social relationships throughout the area would have to include the effects of this poetic activity.

Even a brief list like this of probable connections between poetic activity and the general functioning of society shows that both the links between poetic activity and the society in which it takes place, and its over-all functions in that society can be of far-reaching importance. One can neither understand the organisation of literary activity in isolation from its social setting, nor grasp the functioning of the society without reference to the poetic activity which takes place among its members.

So much is easy to say: to go on and give a precise formulation is more difficult. To say that there is a relationship between 'society' and 'poetry', and that neither can be fully understood without reference to the other, is too general to be meaningful – even though it is the kind of point an analyst of oral poetry will want to make, particularly in the face of accounts which treat oral poetry as mere 'texts' without reference to their social settings and significance, or which ignore the part played by literature in the general functioning of society.

One way of trying to grasp the precise relationship is to avoid the more *general* propositions, and instead to analyse the realisation of oral poetry in a specific society at a given time. This is the kind of analysis which gives meaning to generalities.

This sort of study has not been as common as one might suppose. Researchers with a primarily literary interest have tended to concentrate on stylistic and textual matters and taken little interest in the *social* organisation of poetry or its wider effects, while sociologists and anthropologists have often gone for analysis of the overtly political and officially recognised groupings rather than the activities of poets: when poetry has been considered it has often been relegated to some neat pre-determined category. Even the accounts that are available tend to concentrate on certain aspects – not surprisingly, since oral poetry has an infinite range of ramifications, not all of which can be encapsulated in a single account.

But there are some illuminating accounts, and brief reference to two or three may be useful to the reader who wants to follow up more detailed treatments of the ways in which poetic activity and its results can be seen to fit into society.

One of the first instances to come to mind is that of the Somali of the Horn of Africa. It is not accident that they have been referred to frequently, for Somali poetry in its social background is among the more fully analysed cases of oral literature. In the various works by Johnson, Lewis, Mumin, and, above all, Andrzejewski, the historical, cultural and political setting is fully analysed, showing the roles it plays both in the 'traditional' nomadic and rural setting and in the modern urban context of entertainment, politics and 'revolution', by word of mouth, radio and dramatic performance to enthusiastic audiences. A very different treatment of the role of poetry within a small closed setting is Jackson's brilliant account (1972) of Negro songs in Texas prisons, from which the description of Johnnie Smith was drawn in chapter 6. Again, there is Strehlow's detailed and impressive analysis (1971) of the style and setting of Aranda and Loritja poetry in Central Australia and the relation of these poems to totemic ceremonies as well as to more informal occasions.

2 Does one type of poetry always go with a particular form of society? 'Heroic age', 'ballad society' and 'oral culture'

Specific cases provide the kind of insights impossible to achieve through generalities, and are clearly to be pursued in their own right. In the end it is only through such specific studies that we can understand the detailed ways in which poetry actually functions within society.

Many analysts however are not content with descriptions of specific historical cases, but are interested in wider patterns. This is a typically sociological tendency: to try to find general relationships and types, rather than resting satisfied with the unique case. It is natural too to speculate that certain kinds of poetry – heroic epic for instance – may fit especially well with a certain type of social order and to wish to try to construct typologies of this kind. Indeed this is not just a recent question. Attempts to connect type of poetry and stage of society were consistent with the romantic and evolutionist interests of many nineteenth-century thinkers. And Victor Hugo probably epitomises fairly well one general approach to the subject when he writes in his *Preface to Cromwell* (1827): 'To sum up hurriedly the facts that we have noted thus far, poetry has three periods, each of which corresponds to an epoch of civilization: the ode, the epic, and the drama. Primitive times are lyrical, ancient times epical, modern times dramatic' (Quoted in Anderson and Warnock, 1967, p. 335).

There have been more recent attempts to discover such wider patterns, and to try to relate certain types of society to certain types of poetry and poetic activity. Among these are the theories concerning the relationship of heroic poetry and 'heroic age' societies as put forward by the Chadwicks, the postulation of the typical 'ballad society' by a number of ballad scholars, and the type of discussion of 'oral culture' fostered by the work of McLuhan and others.

The view of H. M. Chadwick that heroic epic most naturally and commonly goes with a 'heroic' type of society is perhaps the most immediately appealing. It was first proposed in *The Heroic Age*, first published in 1912, and was then taken up in joint publications by him and his wife Nora Chadwick and later by C. M. Bowra.

Chadwick points out the basic similarities in a number of the poems usually classed together as 'epic'. He prefers the term 'heroic poem' and points to the basic similarity in such poems as the *Iliad*, the *Odyssey* and early Teutonic epic. Parallel forms were also noted among the Mongols, Tatars, Finns, Tamil, Serbs and many others. These poems resemble each other not only in being narrative and designed primarily for entertainment, but also because of a basic likeness in outlook. There is a concentration on the adventures of human beings who act as heroes, fired by the longing for fame and glory. 'The outstanding feature is a pronounced individual interest, both as shown by the poet or narrator, and as attributed to the characters themselves' (Chadwick, III, 1940, p. 727). Chadwick claims, further, that 'the resemblances in the poems are due primarily to resemblances in the ages to which they relate and to which they ultimately owe their origin' (Chadwick, 1926, p. viii). The society in which this epic arises is, he suggests, characterised by an aristocratic and military ethos, itself reinforced by the existence of court minstrels who praise the dominant warrior princes. This is 'the heroic age'. Many societies have had a 'heroic age' – a period in which the splendid deeds of heroes eclipsed all that came later. But in different societies this heroic stage came at different epochs. For the Greeks it was set far back, around and after the fall of Troy, for Russians in the glorious age of Vladimir Monomakh in the twelfth century, for the Southern Serbs in the period before the Turkish destruction of the old Serbian kingdom at Kosovo in 1389, and so on (Chadwick, III, 1940, pp. 727ff; Bowra, 1957, p. 3). It was from these 'similar social and political conditions' that the widely found parallelisms in epic poetry arose (Chadwicks, I, 1932, p. xiii).

For the Chadwicks, the primary evidence on which this theory rested was to be found in the poems themselves. It is significant that it is often unclear in their discussion of the 'heroic age' whether this term refers to the period in which the poems were composed, or to the society actually depicted in the poems. The reason for this is that though they occasionally distinguish between them, the Chadwicks regard them as basically one and the same. Their view is that the poems were primarily composed as celebratory accounts of the deeds of contemporary warrior princes and heroes: as such, they assume, the poems give a more or less exact picture of current conditions. For an 'accurate description of the Heroic Age' one should therefore look at its literature (Chadwick, III, 1940, p. 731).

If one accepts these two assumptions the Chadwicks' connection between heroic poetry and the 'heroic' stage of society looks *prima facie* uncontestable. But serious doubts arise.

First, the kind of poetry widely regarded as 'heroic' or 'epic' does not *just* arise in the situation envisaged as natural by the Chadwicks. The poems of twentieth-century Yugoslav minstrels do not celebrate the deeds of warlike contemporaries, but tell the adventures of a long-vanished, glorious and largely imaginary past to local audiences who had gathered in a neighbour's house in the rural village or in coffee shops in town. And yet, as Lord and Parry have argued, these epic poems are as 'authentic' and original as any epic text from the classical past. If this can happen now how can we be certain that, for past epic, only one context was the typical and natural one?

The second difficulty lies in the Chadwicks' implicit acceptance of the reflection theory of literature – the idea that the minstrel gives an accurate picture of the world around him. This is extremely doubtful. May he not be equally likely to select and distort or magnify what he sees? or not to compose directly about what he sees, but to draw on a world of imagination coloured by literary motif and convention as well as by his personal experience? Depicting a heroic society and a heroic ethos in poetry does not mean that this is the historical reality of the society in which the poet *himself* lives and works.

Once this *necessary* link is questioned between content of poem and society in which it is composed, the whole theory becomes more doubtful. Which of the two is being talked about – poetic image or historical reality – is often ambiguous, and trying to resolve the ambiguity either dissolves the theory or else proves it untenable in certain respects. For it is not true that it is only in the aristocratic and warrior-dominated period described by the Chadwicks that heroic poetry arises (unless the definition of 'heroic' becomes circular – which is an evident danger). Similarly, warlike and aristocratic societies may flourish without necessarily producing the kind of epic poetry postulated by the Chadwicks – witness the stress on panegyric rather than narrative poetry in a number of earlier African kingdoms.

The whole concept of a 'heroic age' tends to dissolve, both when one questions the assumption that the evidence and justification for it can be found in the poem itself, and also when one looks more closely at the terms in which the Chadwicks characterise it. It is seen as 'essentially a barbaric period', coming between the stages of 'primitive' and of 'civilized' times. The terminology reflects the evolutionist models of the nineteenth and early twentieth centuries. But these simple models of development of society have been increasingly under fire as the complexity, even the messiness, of historical development are more fully realised. When the concept of broad evolutionary stages of society itself comes into question, much of the plausibility of the 'heroic stage' tends to vanish. One is left asking whether there is evidence that societies in which epic poetry has flourished (or does flourish) were all at a roughly identical stage of development? The doubts must be intensified by more recent embellishments of the idea of a 'heroic age'. I am thinking primarily of Bowra's mystical delineation of it as 'a crucial and dramatic stage in the emergence of the individual from the mass', and his contrast between the heroic society and those societies which never reached that stage but 'stayed congealed in a world of tribal terrors and tabus' and of 'theocratic absolutism' (Bowra, 1957, pp. 8 and 28). Even the Chadwicks' more moderately stated theory must remain doubtful until backed by evidence which does not depend on assumptions based on the simple evolutionary sequence of development – or on circular definitions.

I may seem to be dismissing an important and appealing theory very cursorily. And I do not think that it can in the end stand up to analysis. Nevertheless it was a richly productive theory and stimulated much further work. It was, for once, a *comparative* theory and – even before the 'oral-formulaic' approach – led outwards from conventional studies of classical literature to other European literature and then to oral literature throughout the world. It was the impetus of this theory which led, eventually, to the magnificent and unparalleled three-volume work on *The Growth of Literature* which occupied so many years of research by the Chadwicks. They state this genesis explicitly in the Preface to the first volume published in 1932.

> Twenty years ago in *The Heroic Age* one of the authors called attention to many striking analogies between ancient Teutonic and Greek heroic poetry, and endeavoured to show that these were due to parallel development, arising from similar social and political conditions. Subsequent study convinced him that this parallel development between the two literatures was by no means limited to the category or genre in question...
>
> About nine or ten years ago both authors began to take the work seriously in hand. By this time we had realised that in order to obtain a sound basis for such comparative study it was necessary to make a detailed examination of other literatures, both ancient and back-

ward. But in the course of the next two or three years we became more interested in the general aspect of the problem than in its special application to ancient Teutonic and Greek literature. Hence the work has changed its character and grown to much larger dimensions than was at first intended.

(Chadwick, I, 1932, p. xiii)

The Chadwicks themselves in the end had some doubts of the validity of their initial theory, and modern evidence and analysis have cast further doubts, but this in no way diminishes the intellectual stimulus their work has provided to the comparative study of literature. It will remain one of the classic theories in the field and continues to stimulate scholars.

Another attempt to relate type of poetry to type of society is found in the efforts of a number of scholars to delineate the kind of society in which ballads typically arise – the 'ballad society'. Its nature has been characterised in slightly different ways, but recurrent elements are its supposed isolation, its homogeneity, and its reliance on oral culture. The typical background of European ballads is envisaged, for instance, as a 'small, stable and self-sufficient' community (Entwistle, 1951, p. 7) based on localised governments and norms, 'self-centred and self-sufficient, attached to their own soil by instinctive patriotism' (ibid. 1951, p. 7). Lack of writing is also important – 'the *sine qua non* of traditional ballad societies was their non-literacy' (Buchan, 1972, p. 17). For Hendron, similarly, the 'generic characteristics' of a typical 'folksinger' (of which the ballad singer is taken to be the prime example) are that '(1) he lives in a rural or isolated region which (2) shuts him off from prolonged schooling and contact with industrialized urban civilization, so that (3) his cultural training is oral rather than visual' (Hendron, 1961, p. 7). On one view the ballads were originally aristocratic and later went 'down the social scale, as the tastes of the upper classes changed and drew further away from those of the peasantry', so that 'the traditional ballad became mainly a peasant art' (Hodgart, 1950, p. 138); while for others the 'typical' ballad society is primarily 'communal' and 'co-operative' all along (as in Buchan, 1972, chapter 5). But there is general agreement that 'the ballad society' is typically a 'folk' and isolated one, based on oral transmission, and that ballads essentially and typically belong 'to the whole people' (Hodgart, 1950, p. 138).

The localised, non-literate and basically homogeneous qualities of this ballad society are envisaged not only as the 'typical' setting for the creation and performance of ballads but, by some analysts, as pre-conditions of their existence – 'necessary for the ballads' survival' (Hodgart, 1950, p. 138). This is seen as a parallel to the other conditions (those of 'the heroic society') necessary for heroic poetry.

> The ballad community is essentially mediaeval, in contrast not only to modern but to pre-mediaeval society like that of the wandering

Germanic peoples. The latter had their own distinctive kind of poetry, the heroic epic, which is national in that it is about the leaders of the whole people; whereas the ballad is local, and deals only with the affairs of a small, static group.

(Hodgart, 1950, p. 131)

In this kind of approach, ballads are seen as essentially dependent on a certain set of social conditions for their origin or survival – and the relationship between ballads and their 'homogeneous agricultural and feudal environment' can be assumed 'in view of the dependence of literature on social environment' (Housman, 1952, p. 43).

It is worth remembering the background to this concept of the 'ballad society'. It is an attempt to give more precise formulation to the accepted connection between 'society' and poetry, and gains apparent backing from the cluster of ideas about the 'folk society' discussed (and queried) earlier. It also appears to command considerable support from the empirical evidence. In historical terms, what are classified as 'European ballads' did indeed emerge into notice 'after the great migrations and crusades have subsided, and medieval man has settled down to cultivate his own acre', as Entwistle has it (1951, p. 91). Similarities have been noted in a wide range of mediaeval societies ranging from the Danish society commented on by Olrik to the North-East and Border areas of Scotland from the fourteenth to the eighteenth centuries described by Buchan (1972, chapter 3). The theories based on the evidence have been given support by the discovery of existing (or recent) cultures in which 'traditional' ballads have survived, arguably by oral means, and which seem to show the same characteristics as the mediaeval societies in which the ballad first grew up. There are, for instance, the dance-ballads documented in the nineteenth century from the remote Faroe Islands (Kershaw, 1921), or what appeared to be ballads recorded in the far north of Russian or the Serbian mountains. Even more striking support seemed to be provided by the research of Sharp and others in the Southern Highlands of the United States, the Southern Appalachian Mountains. Here ballads flourished early this century, and the social context presented by Sharp seemed to constitute a typical 'ballad society' isolated from urban civilisation, nearly self-supporting, illiterate and sharing a common cultural heritage of song. Maud Karpeles describes her view of this society, when she and Sharp visited it in 1916–18.

> The mountain regions of North Carolina, Tennessee, Virginia, and Kentucky are inhabited by people whose ancestors left the British Isles some two hundred years previously. Until recently they had been more or less cut off from the rest of the world on account of the mountainous nature of the country. Fifty years ago, when we were there, there were few roads: just rough tracks over the mountains or alongside the rivers, or even at times in the river-bed itself. The

mountain people lived in small, more or less self-contained communities, for the most part in primitive log-cabins. They scratched
the soil and provided for their own subsistence. Few could read or
write, but they had a fine inherited culture and this was nowhere more
apparent than in their songs: folk songs of British origin. Everyone
sang them, old and young alike, and they sang little else. In fact,
throughout our stay in the mountains we never heard a bad tune,
except occasionally when we were staying at a missionary settlement.

(Karpeles, 1973, pp. 96–7)

In the light of this evidence, it seemed reasonable to speak of the typical
'ballad society', and to go on to postulate causal links between the conditions
pertaining to this type of society and the type of literary genre known as
the ballad.

But the matter is more complicated than appears. It is questionable, for
instance, how far the postulated characteristics are really applicable to all
the societies in which ballads have arisen or have been in circulation. *Are*
they so isolated and so cut off from the influence of written literature, for
instance? The model in the minds of many proponents of these theories
is that of 'pure oral tradition', separate and independent from written
forms: the written ballads when they do obtrude themselves, are regarded
as 'interference' (Hodgart, 1950, p. 138) or as exerting a 'detrimental
influence upon the words of the folk-ballad' and 'vastly inferior to the
genuine peasant song' (Sharp, 1972, pp. 125–6). But, as we saw in chapter
5, this model of separation between the 'pure' and 'genuine' 'traditional
ballad', and written or broadside forms may appeal to the romantic, but
does not accord with the facts of distribution and transmission. Written and
oral forms interact and overlap, and – above all with ballads – any attempt
at a clear-cut distinction between the 'traditional' 'oral' ballad and the
broadside and written ballads quickly breaks down. 'Isolation' and 'self-
sufficiency' too are very relative terms – highly appropriate to the romantic's model of 'folk society', but not easy to apply unambiguously to actual
historical periods. *Were* the mediaeval communities in which ballads are first
noted so isolated culturally? What about the effects of wandering minstrels,
of the church, of travelling merchants or of popular protest movements?
Again, one's faith in the 'isolation' of the Appalachian mountain villages
is slightly shaken when one realises that, even in Sharp's time, there were
schools, hotels and sizeable towns as well as missionaries in the area; and
recent American scholars have suggested that Sharp's view of isolation was
much exaggerated. The clear outlines initially demarcating the 'ballad
society' from others begin to become blurred when one considers them in
detail, and 'ballad societies' are no longer so easily distinguishable.

A further difficulty lies in the ambiguity of the relationship posited
between the existence of ballads and the society in which they are circulated.

Merely speaking of 'a ballad society' may sound unexceptionable. But to ask about possible causal relationships immediately brings difficulty. Is a 'ballad society' of the kind described a necessary condition for the existence of ballads? If so, (apart from the ambiguities in the concept itself) how is one to explain the existence of what have been described as 'ballads' in mediaeval China, or of urban broadside ballads, or the popularity of 'ballads' in contexts of all kinds today, urban and commercial as well as amateur and rural? Is it that a society of the type envisaged (supposing this to be clearly distinguishable) is a sufficient condition for the emergence and circulation of ballads? This seems even less tenable, for there have been many groups (in Africa and elsewhere) that romantics would claim to be self-evidently parallel to their traditional 'ballad societies'[1] where ballads in the general sense of 'a narrative song in which the action is focused on a single episode' (to take Karpeles's definition, 1973, p. 39) are *not* particularly significant.

One way round these difficulties is a more rigorous definition of the term 'ballad'. After all, many kinds of song and poem have been broadly classed under this term, some very different from others, and sometimes including what in other contexts writers call 'heroic poetry' or even 'lyric'. Some ballad scholars have tried, by implication at least, to narrow the term through their insistence that they are concerned only with 'traditional' and 'genuine', or perhaps only with 'mediaeval' ballads, and that their theories apply only to them. This certainly makes the possible relationship more specific (if less interesting), but only too often results in tautology. If *only* those 'ballads' and those 'societies' are to count which fit with the pre-defined model (non-literate, 'folk', and 'isolated'), then the theory becomes circular and can tell us nothing of interest about real relationships.

The attractive theory of a relationship between a particular type of society and a particular genre of poetry turns out to be less promising than it seemed at first sight. Its initial attraction lies largely in its ambiguity, and once one tries to resolve this it turns out to be either tautologous or, at best, doubtful (when not positively wrong) as to the facts.

This is worth emphasising, since this kind of theory, postulating a general relationship between type of poetry and social setting, is just the sort that is, rightly, bound to attract interest. It has been popular among ballad scholars, and has been influential. But, though further research on specific aspects of its factual suggestions may be useful, the assumption that it is necessarily proven can be misleading. This is especially so when the theory is used as a basis for historical speculation about what 'would naturally' happen or 'must have been so' in a period for which historical evidence is lacking or not easily accessible. That this is a temptation today

---

[1] This is not to say that such societies did in fact correspond with the romantic 'folk culture' envisaged by such theorists, any more than the Appalachian Mountain once did.

as in the earlier days of ballad scholarship is shown by Buchan's interesting analysis of ballads in North-East Scotland. In his discussion of the social background of the earlier period, his approach is speculative, resting on the *theory* of a 'ballad society' rather than direct factual evidence.

> The social patterns that obtained in the rural Northeast from the mid-fourteenth to the mid-eighteenth centuries undoubtedly provided an atmosphere conducive to the singing of traditional tales...conditions in labour and living where an oral culture would naturally thrive...such a community as the toun, unlettered, comparatively isolated and self-reliant, living and working co-operatively, would provide an eminently suitable environment for a sturdy oral tradition. An oral culture would thrive in the communal environment, because the processes of oral transmission depend upon corporate activity.
>
> (Buchan 1972, pp. 18, 26)

When reading apparently confident assertions of this kind, it is well to remember that causal connections between the efflorescence of ballads and particular patterns of social organisation are not proved. If anything, the contrary seems to be the case. In other words, insofar as they are a distinct literary genre, ballads, like other forms of literature, seem to be relatively free-floating rather than definitively linked to one form of social organisation – 'dependent on the social environment' as Housman had it – and they provide a literary form which people can, if they choose, adapt to many different purposes and contexts.

Besides the attempt to relate types of society to literary genres in terms like the 'heroic age' and 'ballad society' – both related to earlier evolutionary approaches – there have been a few interesting attempts to correlate specific literary phenomena with particular types of society or of political organisation. Lomax, for instance, has suggested that acephaly in singing correlates with a well-integrated social organisation, such as the Australian – a suggestion that Greenway, for one, would dispute, citing the significantly 'individualistic' nature of much singing in Australia (Greenway, 1964, p. 175) – or, again, that the style and mood of local singing bears some constant relationship to the treatment of women and the over-all sexual mores of a society (Lomax, 1959). Among these theories one deserves greater attention and must be treated in some detail. This is the theory particularly associated with Marshall McLuhan, about the significance of 'oral culture' and its differentiation from the 'visual' culture of the written word.

McLuhan's basic theory postulates a crucial difference between the world of 'typographic man', whose universe depends on the visual written word, and that of 'oral' or 'auditory man', which includes both the culture of non-literate peoples, untouched by writing, and the 'post-literate' world, in which once again 'oral modes' flourish. In the view of McLuhan and his associates, crucial factors both in social organisation and man's psychical make-up and perceptions, have to do with the technology of communications. The presence or absence of writing is, apparently, the single most important factor for the development of cultural and psychological forms, and to this can be linked the whole range of social and economic institutions that we associate with modern civilisation.

> Until WRITING was invented, we lived in acoustic space, where all backward peoples still live: boundless, directionless, horizonless, the dark of the mind, the world of emotion, primordial intuition, mafia-ridden...A goose quill put an end to talk, abolished mystery, gave us enclosed space and towns, brought roads and armies and bureaucracies. It was the basic metaphor with which the cycle of CIVILIZA-TION began, the step from the dark into the light of the mind.
>
> (McLuhan, 1970, pp. 13–14)

These views – emotive and ambiguous as they often are – have recently had a considerable vogue, and it may seem an irrelevant pandering to fashion to bring them in here. But it is often not realised that McLuhan's stance in *The Gutenberg Galaxy*, where he formulates his views about 'typographic man', was directly influenced by Lord and Parry's studies of oral literature among the Yugoslav minstrels. McLuhan makes this clear at the outset of *The Gutenberg Galaxy*, where he opens his 'Prologue' with the following words:

> The present volume is in many respects complementary to *The Singer of Tales* by Albert B. Lord. Professor Lord has continued the work of Milman Parry, whose Homeric studies had led him to consider how oral and written poetry naturally followed diverse patterns and functions. Convinced that the poems of Homer were oral compositions, Parry 'set himself the task of proving incontrovertibly if it were possible, the oral character of the poems, and to that end he turned to the study of the Yugoslav epics'. His study of these modern epics was, he explained, 'to fix with exactness the *form* of oral story poetry...Its method was to observe singers working in a thriving tradition of unlettered song and see how the form of their songs hangs upon their having to learn and practice their art without reading and writing'.
>
> Professor Lord's book, like the studies of Milman Parry, is quite natural and appropriate to our electric age, as *The Gutenberg Galaxy* may help to explain. We are today as far into the electric age as the Elizabethans had advanced into the typographical and mechanical age. And we are experiencing the same confusions and indecisions which they had felt when living simultaneously in two contrasted forms of society and experience. Whereas the Elizabethans were poised between medieval corporate experience and modern indi-

vidualism, we reverse their pattern by confronting an electric technology which would seem to render individualism obsolete and the
corporate interdependence mandatory.

Patrick Cruttwell had devoted an entire study (*The Shakespearean
Moment*) to the artistic strategies born of the Elizabethan experience
of living in a divided world that was dissolving and resolving at the
same time. We, too, live at such a moment of interplay of contrasted
cultures, and *The Gutenberg Galaxy* is intended to trace the ways in
which the *forms* of experience and of mental outlook and expression
have been modified, first by the phonetic alphabet and then by
printing. The enterprise which Milman Parry undertook with reference to the contrasted *forms* of oral and written poetry is here
extended to the *forms* of thought and the organization of experience
in society and politics.

(McLuhan, 1967, p. 1)

Some of McLuhan's stimulus was thus derived from the claims in *The
Singer of Tales* about the oral nature of Yugoslav rural culture and the
special way in which 'oral composition' took place, in a mode – according
to Parry and Lord – essentially different from that characteristic of written
composition. For this reason alone, McLuhan's theory is worth some attention and re-appraisal in the light of recent assessments of the work of Parry
and Lord.

Moreover it is of interest to students of oral poetry to consider how far
the postulates of McLuhan and others as to the nature of 'oral culture' are
valid: for, if they are, oral poetry must be seen as arising from, and existing
in, the context of that culture. Finally, this theory (or group of theories)
is worth considering as yet another attempt to sketch out a relationship
between poetry and society – in this case between poetry and a certain
configuration of cultural and psychological realities.

McLuhan's view of 'literate man' and his culture is of a mechanised,
hyper-individualistic and narrowly bureaucratic form of association. In
contrast to what he regards as the more emotionally integrated and warmly
co-operative world of oral culture, the focus is overwhelmingly on *one* of
the senses only: the visual one. Man is 'typographic man' – detached, aloof,
over-specialised and cut off from the kind of psychic and emotional unity
possible in an 'oral' culture. In non-literate culture, by contrast, man is
whole and integrated, closely and emotionally involved with the group of
which he forms part, and living in a homogeneous and stable community,
rather than the 'visual or civilized and fragmented world' of modern urban
life. The increasingly oral nature of modern culture, with its emphasis on
oral modes, for instance in jazz and the non-written media of radio and
television, brings some of the same consequences. 'Electronic man' has
regained the emotional involvement and wholeness of the older 'tribal'
man, and once again all his senses are in play. 'In post-literate acoustic

space...we have regained our sensorial WHOLENESS' says McLuhan (1970, p. 16); so we can be 'retribalised' and give up the 'aloof and dissociated role of the literate Westerner' so long imposed on us by the limiting and dryly academic medium of print (1967, p. 12).

> An increase in visual component in any society creates specialism, alienation, fragmentation, civilization, etc. The decrease in the same, as via TV, creates involvement, tribalization, visceral awareness, etc...We begin again to structure the primordial feelings and emotions from which 3000 years of literacy divorced us. We begin again to live a myth.
>
> (McLuhan, 1970, pp. 33, 17)

Though McLuhan and his followers write largely in terms of 'man' – 'tribal man', 'typographic man', 'electronic man' and so on – it is clear that certain assumptions are made about the nature of the society at large in which such men exist. 'Oral culture', it seems, involves a warm, closely-knit, non-individualistic and communal society, in which 'rationality' has little play, and action and decisions are taken on a 'corporate' basis within 'the web of kinship' (1967, pp. 88ff). Literate culture on the other hand implies an emphasis on bureaucracy with its 'rational' norms, on large-scale organisation, and on the power of the written word over people's lives.

This kind of approach (at least in part) has also, predictably, been taken up with enthusiasm by a number of those preoccupied with sketching out the 'folk society' and the workings of 'folk tradition' and so on. David Buchan in his recent book on *The Ballad and the Folk* asserts the importance of *The Gutenberg Galaxy* for the study of oral literature, and goes on to speak in terms of 'the oral mind' and the conditions in which 'an oral culture would naturally thrive' (Buchan, 1972, pp. 2, 276, 18). McLuhan, it seems, has much to say to some students of oral poetry and its social context.

This is only a brief sketch of the main lines of McLuhan's theory – full understanding of this and associated approaches would involve a more detailed account of his writing, and also that of scholars like H. A. Innis or W. J. Ong (for a fuller account of aspects of this approach see Finnegan, 1975). But enough has been said to show the relevance of the approach as at least a background to the study of oral literature.

In some respects, this general approach has been valuable. It has helped to intensify the current questioning of print as *the* purveyor of 'proper' culture, and to encourage study of other forms – not only the oral literature of far-off and non-literate peoples but also the oral forms conveyed here and now by word of mouth, radio, television, tape recorder and so forth. The establishment of such forms as a proper area for study, and the awareness of parallels between the so-called 'primitive' and the contemporary industrial world have not been due to McLuhan alone. But he has been adept at taking up such points – along with some of the emotive overtones that so commend themselves to romantics – and giving them a popular appeal to a wider public.

Useful too is the insistence that there are various modes of apprehending reality, and that it is mistaken to regard writing as self-evidently the 'best'. McLuhan and others have helped to remind us that writing may have its drawbacks (and so, he might have added, have oral media) and that it can be misleading to apply the criteria of written literature to oral forms.

Much in the approach (or the movement) propagated by McLuhan and his followers has therefore been to the good. But, as will be clear from the main lines of argument earlier in this book, I have many doubts about its validity or even – in the end – its usefulness.

The ambiguities and emotive style of McLuhan's writings have been pointed out elsewhere (e.g. Miller, 1971; Finnegan, 1975), and need not be pursued here. It is relevant to take up those main points from his and similar writings which, despite the lack of rigorous argument and clarification, do relate to the study of oral poetry.

The first is that there is something called 'oral culture' and typified in 'acoustic' or 'auditory man' which is essentially to be differentiated from a culture in which writing is the pre-eminent mode of communication and man is 'typographic man'.

> Civilization is built on literacy because literacy is a uniform processing of a culture by a visual sense extended in space and time by the alphabet. In tribal cultures, experience is arranged by a dominant auditory sense-life that represses visual values. The auditory sense, unlike the cool and neutral eye, is hyper-esthetic and delicate and all-inclusive. Oral cultures act and react at the same time. Phonetic culture endows men with the means of repressing their feelings and emotions when engaged in action. To act without reacting, without involvement, is the peculiar advantage of Western literate man.
>
> (McLuhan, 1967, p. 96)

But is this radical divide between 'oral' and 'written' modes, 'oral' and 'visual' cultures, intelligible and valid? In the initial excitement stirred up by the apparent 'discovery' by Parry and Lord of the special form taken by oral composition and published in *The Singer of Tales*, it must have seemed so. Lord stresses the incompatibility of 'oral' and 'written' composition, and concludes that once a minstrel takes in the concept of written composition he loses his oral ability (see quotation on p. 160). Furthermore, he and Parry had apparently discovered the secret of this special oral procedure: composition in the process of performance, using the 'oral-formulaic' style – a style which itself, according to strict Parry–Lord theorists, was an infallible sign of 'oral composition'.

It was explained in chapter 3 that this initial acceptance of the Lord–Parry research was too categorical. By now many students of the subject have become sceptical about claims that a formulaic style is a dependable sign of oral composition, and there are also indications that 'oral composition' need not always be on the Yugoslav model (joint composition-performance) and that oral and written modes may not really be incompatible after all (see above chapters 3 and 5). In fact, the distinction between 'oral' and 'written' is now realised to be far less sharp than was once thought, at any rate in the context of literature. And if *that* line has become blurred, it is surely much harder than it must initially have seemed to McLuhan to make the clear differentiation between 'oral' and 'visual' cultures, with all that, in his argument, flows from it.

A second related question is whether what McLuhan would term an 'oral culture' necessarily has the postulated characteristics at all. For McLuhan and others, the world of the Zulu or the Eskimo is presumably a typically 'oral' one, in which written literature has been relatively recent and the traditional forms of communication dependent on 'oral' not 'visual' means. But it is hard to recognise McLuhan's 'oral culture' in these societies. Consider, on the one hand, the aristocratic and aggressive ethos of the Zulu, resulting in the effective empire-building of the great Zulu king Shaka through his innovation of the short stabbing spear – or consider on the other the deeply personal meditative poetry of the Eskimo poet, composed in long hours of poetic effort, pacing outside in solitude. These are just a few of the relevant factors, in two societies. A full refutation would inevitably fill a book; it must suffice to say that anyone acquainted with research on societies of this kind is likely to find laughably over-simplified and off the mark such generalising comments as 'tribal cultures cannot entertain the possibility of the individual or of the separate citizen' or their 'tribal trance of resonating word magic' (McLuhan, 1967, p. 94) or 'the boundless, directionless, horizonless...dark of the mind' of non-literate culture (1970, p. 13).

This basic divide between our modern industrial society – mechanised, rational, individual and literate – and the primitive 'them', dominated by magic, communal norms and oral communication, and somehow mystically closer to nature than ourselves – this distinction has had great popularity with sociologists (often via the technical-sounding concepts of *Gesellschaft* and *Gemeinschaft* and others) as well as with romantics who like to dream of the vanished world of integrated emotion and natural feeling which we have lost. This is an old distinction that McLuhan has latched onto – but its antiquity does not make it a good one (even when it is embellished with the extension of a post-industrial reversion to the 'primitive'), and the plenitude of facts that are now known about the complexity and variety of cultures throughout the world, through space and time, makes such simplified generalisations both unhelpful and misleading. Primarily non-literate cultures – to concentrate on them – are not all characterised by the qualities McLuhan attributes to his tribal and auditory culture, and to assume them as necessary properties of some postulated 'oral culture' can only mislead those interested in an objective analysis of oral literature and its detailed social context.

These attempts to relate oral literature (or certain types of oral literature) to particular types of society have all turned out to be unacceptable as they stand. But the question they have been concerned with has been a rational one: can one draw up any causal relationship (or even common correlation) between type of society and type of literature (or perhaps type of organisa-tion of literary activity)? Theories about the 'heroic age', the 'ballad society' or 'oral culture' have proved unsatisfactory. But the question still remains, and doubtless further attempts will be made in the future to suggest other answers.

In the meantime, I have no hopeful over-all theory to venture myself. Certain positive points do, however, emerge from this critical examination of earlier theories.

The first and most important point is the strikingly free-floating nature of literature, the way the same 'poem' or the same genre can play very different roles in different circumstances, and can be changed *or* developed *or* held static according to the manifold intentions of the people concerned at any one time. This was also the main point to emerge from the discussion of functions and contexts in the last chapter. It is reaffirmed here, as the major recurrent reason for rejecting earlier theories: that literature is too flexible (and man too ready to adapt it to his needs) to be directly and closely determined by the societal forms of the culture in which it is being used. Related to social forms, and used in accordance with current social conventions, it surely is; but rigidly and directly bound by any one 'type of society' or 'social environment' it certainly is not.

This free-floating nature of literary forms leads our attention to the part played by the geographical diffusion over space and time of particular literary genres. The whole notion of 'diffusion' has been out of fashion in anthropology and sociology in recent years, to be replaced by concepts such as the function of a literary genre in an actual society or social situation, and – at the extreme – by the idea of the self-contained 'tribal' or 'traditional' society. Certainly over-stress on the diffusion of literary forms can be misleading, particularly if it is presented as diffusion to passive populations who have no hand in distributive and creative pro-cesses, or where the search up the chain of descent to a remote historical origin is assumed to be more interesting than the local meaning or use or active reinterpretation of a given form. The underplaying of diffusion as a relevant concept may also be reasonable in certain areas. Functionally-defined poems like love songs, dirges or wedding songs have such a wide incidence that they can be regarded as a near-universal aspect of human culture, with no need to postulate specific historical connections between their occurrence in areas as far apart as the Eskimo north, Southern Africa and Fiji. But now that the amount of contact and communication between even the most rural and 'primitive' peoples is more fully recognised, along with the much wider effect of literacy than used to be supposed, it makes sense once again to raise questions of the possible diffusion of genres and styles of performance. This is clearly appropriate for the European ballad form, and it has been suggested for the epic: 'the ultimate sources' are 'the same for the Greek epic as for the rest of Western Europe' (see Carpenter, 1958, p. 18). At the very least the ballad and epic seem to be associated with a wide European culture area, in the same way perhaps that Alan Lomax has demarcated wide culture areas in respect of musical styles (Lomax, 1959). For certain forms at least, it is still worth pondering Nora Chadwick's assessment, based on her long and sympathetic study of oral literatures all over the world: 'From the great centres of civilization...like ripples made by pebbles cast into a pond, the waves of culture spread outwards from the great cultures of the past – Mesopotamia, Egypt, Etruria, Greece, China; and again in more recent periods – Rome, Persia, Arabia, India, Turkestan' (Chadwick, 1942, p. xiv).

This capacity of literature to be used in a wide variety of human situations, historical periods and geographical settings makes it difficult to envisage *any* very generalised theory about the relationship between type of society and type of literature. This is the second main point to emerge from this discussion of earlier theories. It may be that all one can hope for are on the one hand fairly general (and therefore vague) comments about recurrent patterns, and on the other detailed analyses of particular situations and relationships, drawn up in a more modest framework. The general comments are perhaps useful as initial parameters or even hints about where to look – the likelihood, for instance, that a society with greater division of labour and economic resources is better able to give scope for the development of specialist poets and provision of leisure for their performances (a point well made long ago by the Chadwicks[1]) or that oral poets are likely (but not certain) to respond to changing economic and political conditions, if only because the interests and opportunities of their audiences are liable to change. Beyond this, it is perhaps better to try to build up understanding of social and literary interrelationships through detailed studies like those of Andrzejewski and Johnson on the Somali, Deng on the Dinka or Strehlow on the Central Australian Aborigines, rather than continuing to search for high-level theories linking type of society with type of literature. At any rate, it is clear that such theories

---

[1] But one which does not necessarily imply anything about the quality of poetry or the general degree of poetic cultivation in societies with differing degrees of economic development.

cannot be simple ones, but will need to take account not only of certain apparently recurrent patterns, but also of the manifold ways in which man makes use of literature, and the inventiveness and imagination of human beings.

3 Literature as the reflection and consequence of social forms

The difficulty of generalisation is even clearer when one moves on to consider some of the very general theories about the relationship of literature and society that have been postulated or implied within the sociology of literature. In each case one needs to insist that even if each high-lights certain facets of literature, no one theory gives a full picture of the great variety and complexity of literature and literary activity; and if applied rigidly can distort our understanding.

Many of these more general approaches envisage literature as basically dependent on its social environment: poetry following from, and affected by, 'society', as it were, rather than the other way round. In this light, literature is seen as primarily a reflection of the circumstances and norms of the society from which it springs, or the result of economic and techno-logical conditions.

This 'reflection theory' of literature – implicit as often as explicit – has been influential. It is inherent in much of the speculation about 'ballad society' and 'heroic age'. From the writing on these topics it becomes clear that the 'evidence' often adduced to lend support to the claimed relation-ship between the society and its literature often depends on the *assumption* that the literature directly reflects the society in which it arose. In his chapter on 'Some ballad communities' Hodgart, for instance, moves be-tween the picture of society depicted in ballads and the actual community in which the ballads were composed – 'such was the community which some of the ballads describe and by which some were produced' (Hodgart, 1950, p. 137) – and it is not always clear to the reader which he is discussing. Of course, if the ballads can be assumed to reflect the social conditions in which they arose, there is no need to make the distinction. The same assumption is implicit in much other writing about 'ballad societies' as well as in Chadwick's description of 'the heroic age'. Chadwick in his first book argues from the parallel of the Teutonic 'heroic age' (where there is some historical support for the picture depicted in the poetry) to that of the Greek 'heroic age' where he suggests that Homer gives an accurate account of contem-porary society: 'We possess no evidence which affords us grounds for doubting that the [Homeric] poems give an equally faithful reflection of conditions and ideas which prevailed in real life' (1926, p. 432). Because of this assumption one is never quite sure in the Chadwicks' writings whether the 'heroic age' is, so to speak, in the poetry or in actual historical fact – and of course if the reflection theory *is* correct it comes to the same thing.

As soon as one states it explicitly it is clear that in any literal and direct way the reflection theory cannot hold. The exact forms of housing or food or love or leadership, or the amount of wealth, power or heroism belonging to various individuals or groups depicted by a poet in the literature he composes need not reflect an exact correspondence with those of everyday life around him. As soon as one considers the matter directly, it is obvious that any writer selects from the world known to him, and does this according to his own personal philosophy and perceptions and making use of the literary conventions of his culture and/or his particular group within that culture. The notion of direct and literal reflection of current conditions does not work for oral any more than for written literature. The glorious heroes and sumptuous courts in the epics sung by Avdo Mededović and other Yugoslav minstrels bear little resemblance to conditions in rural Yugoslavia in the 1930s. The references to horses in nineteenth-century Ob Ugrian poetry have poetic significance even though the poets and audience did not own horses, and the lords, beautiful ladies and 'lily-white hands' in the songs Sharp collected in the Southern Appalachian Mountains are literary, not social, realities. What comes into poetry may reflect certain aspects of society and express ideas and reactions which are of concern to people at the time – but to take literary forms as representing a direct and full reflection, or as a *direct* source of social history can only be misleading. If one wants definite information, in other words, about the social conditions in which a poet composes and performs – whether it is the world of Homer, of ballad singers or of the Beatles – one must have evidence over and above what can be found in the poetry.

If the simple and direct kind of reflection presupposed in some writing will not do, this does not mean that the idea of literature as reflection is worthless. On the contrary, all literature in an indirect and subtle way must reflect the society in which it exists. Provided the complex and selective nature of this relationship is recognised, we have a useful reminder that a poet is, after all, a product of his own culture, rather than the free untrammelled genius of romantic theory. Ian Watt sums up the position so well that it is worth quoting his remarks at some length, and extending his comments to apply to oral poetry as well as the written literature which is his prime concern

> There is a rather misleading simplicity about the word 'reflects'. In some senses all writing cannot but be a 'reflection' of society, since it contains many elements which are socially derived. Language, to begin with, is a social product; and most writing – certainly most literature – is related to some established tradition or model of expression. More specifically, literary works usually reflect various sur-

face features of the life of a society. Yet although the clothes and meals and customs described are rarely invented, they may not be those current at the time of writing; and since this is often true of more important matters, literature cannot be assumed to be necessarily a reliable reflection of the society of any specific period...

Literary genres often reflect the social attitudes of the particular group which produced them, rather than that of the society which their content overtly portrays. Pastoral poetry, for example, does not tell us much about the economy or institutions of the Sicilian shepherds whose lives it pretends to describe, but it does reveal the taste for a fashionable kind of escape which arose in the later days of Greece and Rome among certain urban and leisured audiences. The influences of the author's particular social orientation in distorting his picture of social reality may not be conscious, but it is always present to some degree. Most of the court literature of the past made the nobles much more noble and the rustics much more rustic than they were in reality; while in the last hundred years the various radical, socialist, and communist movements have produced proletarian fiction in which the picture of the worker is a good deal more heroic or tragic than would probably be substantiated by objective sociological investigation.

Even the kinds of writing which aim at the most literal and detailed description of their society are far from being sociologically reliable mirror images of reality; for, quite apart from the influences of the social group, the author's own individual temperament and his personal ideology play a compelling, though usually unconscious, role...

Literature, then, reflects society, but it usually does so with various degrees of indirectness and selectivity. The particular 'society' which it reflects is often equally difficult to determine; we hardly know, for instance, how far Homer describes the period of the Trojan War, and how far his own.

(Watt, 1964, pp. 306–8)

This general caution also applies to social norms. It is tempting to take clear statements in literature about, say, the importance of heroism or of love, or the general ethos pervading some genre of poetry, as a true reflection of the moral code held or even followed by members of a society. This view is all the more appealing when we lack other detailed sources about people's behaviour and views, or as part of a theory about literature's role in social control.

But this simple reflection of social norms in literature applies no better to oral than to written literature – where its falsity as a general assumption is well recognised. Certainly, some oral poetry represents certain moral views or a general ethos which is widely acceptable and followed in a society, and certain kinds of poetry are sometimes, in non-literate or in literate contexts, used by elders to inculcate certain values into youth: didactic song riddles in Makua initiation rites in East Africa, for instance, or the way Homer was taught in classical Greek schools as an earnest of their cultural heritage, or the use of religious hymns and chants all over the world. But equally literature can also express the views of minority or divergent groups within the society at large, or convey ideas pleasing in a literary context but not necessarily acceptable in everyday life. Such examples are by no means uncommon – even in what used to be mistakenly regarded as the 'homogeneous' and 'communal' context of 'primitive society' – as will be clear from the examples cited earlier (chapters 6 and 7). It is also clear in such instances as the Bagre religious poetry (sometimes known as the Bagre myth) of the Ghanaian Lodagaa people, where the views about God expressed in the poetry of this group are notably different from those of Lodagaa society at large: 'the whole myth of Bagre is very much more theocentric...than is the experience of everyday religion' (Goody, 1972, p. 30). Another striking instance can be found in the anti-saint literature of the Somali, which challenges the over-devoutness of the orthodox and established religion of the area (Andrzejewski in Shils, forthcoming) or in the poetry of minority groups or sub-cultures, or rebels against age and authority all over the world. All in all, though the social norms of any established 'community' may be reflected in a complex way in their literature, it is likely to be in an indirect and subtle fashion. Literature as such does not provide any crude basis for neatly deducing a society's group norms and ideals.

The general idea that types of literature and of literary activity are likely to follow from the nature of the society in which they occur, and be influenced by it, has also taken the form of trying to draw over-all connections between the general economic and technological development of a society and the literature which might be said to 'result'.

It seems, on the face of it, a common-sense idea that a society with little economic or material development is likely, equally, to have a poorly developed literature. This idea is supported, too, by the fact that a society with surplus economic resources and developed division of labour is more likely to foster the development of a professional category of poet (i.e. one dependent more or less solely on the practice of his art for economic livelihood) and perhaps of a distinctive 'leisured' class with the propensity for entertainment by specific genres of literature. It may seem sensible to go on to assume that poetic development in a wider sense is correlated with economic development.

It is perhaps a surprise to discover that – even in the most down-to-earth ways – this equation does not hold. 'Economic development' is not a clearly measurable concept, but in most equations of this sort it is usually assumed to be clear enough – with modern urban industrial economies and, to a lesser degree, rich agricultural societies coming near the top. And yet poetry often flourishes strikingly in pastoral societies, where people have few material possessions, minimal division of labour and little economic surplus in any obvious sense. The Somali nomadic wanderers in the semi-desert stretches of Northern Somalia are famous as a 'nation of poets' while the mobile cattle-herding Dinka of the Southern Sudan, with their simple material culture and limited raw material have created in their poems rich allusions and images woven around the beauty of their cattle (Lienhardt, 1963; Deng, 1973). Many similar examples could be cited. Indeed it has been suggested that far from being a hindrance to poetry, the absence of material technology among such peoples who must perforce travel light may even encourage them to turn their energies to literary creativity. Hunting and gathering peoples, commonly regarded as low in the scale of economic development, can show great literary talent and sustained interest in the cultivation of poetry. The poems of the Eskimo, for instance, deserve to be widely known for their deeply meditative, ironic and personal insight, a poetic development in no way inhibited by the harsh material conditions and limited economic resources with which they have traditionally had to contend. The Australian Aborigines were once regarded as the most 'primitive' of mankind – a judgement partly founded on their poverty and (apparently) meagre technology – and yet it is among one of these groups (the Arnhem Landers) that some of the most symbolically complex of poetic cycles have been composed and performed: among them the great Djanggawal song cycle recorded and translated by R. Berndt (1952). It is clear that poetry can flourish and can reach a high level of conscious art without the existence of complex economic and technological organisation or, indeed, the presence of kings or specialised religious and political institutions.

As soon as the question is considered directly, it becomes clear that, as Kirk puts it, 'it is an obvious fallacy that poetry can only flourish in comfortable or luxurious surroundings' (Kirk, 1965, p. 60). But unconscious assumptions connecting material and poetic development have often influenced assertions about a people's poetry or lack of it, so that one encounters the not uncommon idea that the Homeric epics 'could not have been' composed in the early Greek 'Dark Ages', or the common expectation that the cultivation of poetry is unlikely to be found among people living in slums or in 'backward' colonial areas. It has been a matter of constant surprise to collectors and (even more) to local 'knowledgeable' people to find that in many a poor and despised near-by community oral literature was flourishing – the poor whites of the Southern Appalachian Mountains, the seventeenth-century Irish 'vagabonds and rymers...', Zulu labour migrants in the urban areas of South Africa or Negro prisoners in American jails. The prejudice which connects poor material conditions with lack of artistic achievement dies hard. But it must be clear to a dispassionate enquirer that in the light of the evidence now available from all over the world, any generalised attempt to postulate a direct correlation of economic with poetic development would be simple-minded. The Chadwicks state the matter with due caution when they conclude at the end of their massive account of 'the growth of literature' that 'intellectual progress would seem to be not wholly governed by material civilisation' (Chadwick, III, 1940, p. 900).

Some of the impetus towards making this correlation has come from earlier evolutionist theories, which sought (in many cases) to place societies in a single ascending ladder of development. According to such views – based often on speculation, or wishful thinking, rather than evidence – it was 'obvious' that certain types of literary development went with certain earlier stages of society and that cultures gradually moved up a scale of increasing complexity in all respects. Bowra, for instance, draws a direct connection in terms of evolutionary stages, between 'Palaeolithic conditions' and both ancient and recent 'Palaeolithic song' which is necessarily 'simple', 'emotional' and 'primitive'.

> If we try to construct the history of early song, we are by the nature of things prevented from finding any materials for it. This means that we must reshape the problem and ask whether there is not some method of enquiry which is not historical in the sense that it explores the past, but may none the less throw some light on song at its most primitive stages. We may look at those songs available to us which are primitive not only in the sense that they are less organized and elaborated than modern songs but are also the products of conditions in many respects close to those of the Late Palaeolithic Age and reflect the outlook of societies which live in a primaeval simplicity. Such songs contain in an undifferentiated and unspecialized form elements which more advanced poetry contains in much more differentiated and more specialized forms. They may not resemble the lost songs, if any, of the historical Stone Age, but they are products of savage societies which still eke out a precarious existence in some parts of the world by the same means and in much the same conditions as Late Palaeolithic man. They reveal what human beings, living in the most elementary conditions, do to make words rhythmical and memorable and different from the parlance of every day. They represent a stage in the evolutionary development of song before it has branched into many later varieties and while it is still closely connected with certain urgent human needs, which call for it as a means of expression but are confined to the lowest level of subsistence known to us. Though we can discover nothing about historical Palaeolithic song, we can examine living primitive song, which is born from what are in most respects Palaeolithic conditions and bears many marks of them.
>
> (Bowra, 1962, pp. 15–16)

Similar assumptions of a corresponding evolutionary series of stages in poetry and economic development are made in the analyses of Mackenzie (1911), who suggests the dance, then the dance-song, as the most primitive and early forms, with poetry followed only later by prose narrations, and the line of development characterised by increasing economic and poetic complexity as one moves up the evolutionary scale of 'material and psychical stages'.

This kind of analysis sounds neat and scientific, as well as fitting with the popular assumption that in all societies poetry emerges at an earlier stage than prose, but it is as well to remember that there is no evidence for it in the early prehistoric stages: this part is pure speculation. In so far as there is evidence about recent non-industrial societies, it provides many counter-instances to the supposed lines of development envisaged.

It is as well to be clear about the doubtful nature of a number of these assumptions, for though few people would wish to postulate economic and technological institutions as a basis for predicting poetic development in a literate industrial society, the continuing influence of evolutionist assumptions has made this line sometimes appear better-founded than it really is in the case of non-industrial societies. So it must be asserted clearly that the evidence we now have suggests no straight line of development correlating economic, poetic and chronological stages.

In the various approaches which tend to see literature as in a sense the *consequence* of social conditions, and affected by them, the danger lies not in entertaining them as suggestive ideas, but in trying to apply them in a simple and literal-minded way. The idea of evolutionary stages is perhaps no longer a helpful concept, but there is much to be learned from approaches which see literature as in a general sense reflecting society; it is here that sociologists have made an important contribution in querying some of the more established romantic interpretations. As Albrecht puts it,

> the reflection theory has done valuable service in challenging older insights and established traditions. It has directed attention to the social and cultural characteristics of literature in addition to its more narrowly formal aspects. It has emphasized the conception of artists as agents of social forces rather than as individual geniuses or great men with inventive imaginations. It has provided social and historical modes of analysis as alternatives to exclusively biographical and aesthetic approaches and offered concepts of cultural relativism in place of absolutist aesthetic principles and social determinism in place of artistic individualism.
>
> (Albrecht, 1954, p. 431)

4 Literature as social action

A different approach to the relationship between literature and society is to take the first as the active and initiating factor. For literature can be influential in its own right, as a mode of applying pressure rather than merely a result or epiphenomenon of social institutions.

This is a long-accepted approach and is obviously illuminating in many contexts. It is also particularly worth stressing in the case of *oral* literature. For earlier preconceptions about non-literate (and 'primitive') societies as 'communal', 'unchanging', 'non-individualistic' 'bound to tradition' and 'homogeneous' have tended to lead to the unquestioning assumption that literature can play only a passive role in such societies.

It is here that the usefulness of looking first at the position of poets (chapter 6) and at some of the detailed functions and contexts of oral poetry (as in chapter 7) comes out most clearly. Oral – like written – poetry can be used to bring about a variety of effects on the individuals, social groups, and social institutions with which it is involved. It can be used to influence people's ideas, introduce (or combat) change, uphold *or* challenge the political order – and a whole range of other possibilities.

Much of chapter 7 implicitly exemplified how one can regard literature as potentially *active* (depending on the purposes and understandings of those involved). This approach will not be further elaborated here, but this does not imply that I think it of less importance than the approaches to the relation of poetry and society discussed earlier. On the contrary, I think it a crucially important way of regarding literature (and literary activity), and that it is unfortunate that it has so generally been underplayed in the analysis of oral poetry.

But this approach – like others – ceases to be illuminating when stated only at a high level of abstraction. Pinpointing these more general approaches can be useful if it helps us to understand possible assumptions and preconceptions underlying – perhaps implicitly – assertions we make about literature as a social phenomenon, or pointing us to illuminating aspects of the subject not always considered, such as the active role sometimes taken by oral poetry. But any search to try to establish some definitive abstract theory – or even 'theoretical framework' – at the general macro-level of 'Society' is less likely to illuminate literature as a social phenomenon.

To gain further understanding perhaps one must stop trying to relate the two vague entities 'Literature' and 'Society' and try instead to understand literature *in* society, rather than as opposed to society. To do this one often needs to engage in detailed study of such micro-social institutions as the nature of audiences and patrons, the modes by which poets become socialised and trained in their craft, the complementary and in one sense identical processes by which individuality and tradition have full play in any given literature. Once more Ian Watt expresses this well.

> Although there is an age-old divergence between those who see man as essentially a social being, and those who insist on his individual uniqueness, the force of the contradiction begins to disappear the moment a writer puts pen to paper: as W. B. Yeats put it, 'art is the social act of a solitary man.'

It is a social act, however, of a very special kind, and one which reminds us that 'literature and society' can be a misleading phrase in yet another way, because it suggests a more absolute distinction between the two terms than is actually the case. If only because, in one perfectly valid sense, literature *is* its own society: it is the subtlest and the most enduring means which man has devised for communicating with his fellows.

(Watt, 1964, p. 313)

Perhaps even to speak of 'literature' in general terms can be misleading, whether or not it is opposed to another supposed entity termed 'society'. For what is interesting and significant is not, most often, some thing called 'literature' but rather what people do: the ways they act within a literary context, the social conventions connected with literary activity which they observe or manipulate, the different uses to which they can put literary formulations – literature, in fact, conceived as social action by *people* rather than as a static entity in its own right.

Here too one needs to remember that it is not just the words of a poem that may be significant, but the wider question of who actually *controls* the activity of poetry. It is not just poetry, but power over poetry that often concerns people. Thus in Hawaii the person or family to whom it was dedicated owned the poem and took steps to control its distribution. 'Others were not allowed to use them, except to repeat them in honour of the owner. It was just as much criticized, just as serious a crime as plagiarism is in European literature' (Pukui, 1949, p. 255). In Polynesia praise poems were social assets belonging to particular families, and in some cases 'the claim of an heir to rank depends upon his power to reproduce, letter perfect, his family chants and his "name song", composed to celebrate his birth' (Beckwith, 1919, p. 28). A somewhat similar case is the way the Arnhem Land Aborigines regard the right to have 'access to the dream-spirits manifested in the stories' as the significant point about the ownership of a song (Berndt, 1970, p. 588). Control over poets and poetry has been a constant preoccupation of those in authority through the ages. This attempt to gain power over poetry, rather than just to compose or enjoy it, is easy to miss if one insists on staying with the abstract formulation of 'Poetry' on the one hand and its relation to 'Society' on the other.

The final point I would like to stress is the inability of any of the general theories to give a *comprehensive* account of literature. One may gain insight from a theory into this or that aspect of literature in society, but to take any of them as *the* definitive explanation or description or delimitation of literature can only close one's mind to the rich variety of ways in which people have formulated their ideas and feelings and insights in the form of literature and in which the composition, distribution and functioning of literature can take place.

The concluding point, then, is the infinitely rich variability of oral poetry and its uses – as well as a final plea that, while the sociologist must (rightly) insist on the significance of the social context of literature and search for the recurrent patterns that manifest themselves in socially organised literary activity, he should also remember the role of literature as the medium for the creative imagination of man. The sociologist as well as the literary student would do well to look again at the question Richard Hoggart raises at the end of his essay on 'Literature and society' and ponder his answer.

> Why *should* men try to 'recreate' their personal and social world? Why should they – as well as analysing it, probing it, generalizing about it, taking it to pieces, finding its component parts – have felt moved to 'make it again'?
>
> One reason seems to be that men do it not so as to effect anything but, so to speak, for its own sake; because they feel wonder and awe about the nature and terms of their life; and because they feel amusement, irony and pride at man's attempts to cope.
>
> Another reason seems to be the wish to be in touch with others. Literature implies an audience: perhaps not a very large audience, perhaps an audience that is 'fit though few' – but always an audience. It assumes the possibility and the worthwhileness of communication with other human beings. Without having to say so explicitly, it says at the back of its mind: we are not alone; though we may be 'poor, bare, forked animals', we can try and hope to get in touch. And this, though it may not at first glance seem to have much to tell the student of society, has a significance for him which he would neglect to his enormous cost.
>
> (Hoggart, 1966, pp. 247–8)

Concluding comment

I have no general theoretical conclusion to present as conclusion to this book. The aim has been to provide a short guide to the study of oral poetry and its controversies, and not to set up a model of my own. Nevertheless there are some remarks to make briefly in this concluding comment.

First, a main point in this discussion has been the denial of a clear-cut differentiation between oral and written literature. Throughout the book I have rejected the suggestion that there is something peculiar to 'oral poetry' which radically distinguishes it from written poetry in nature, composition, style, social context, or function. This may seem a very negative conclusion. It may also appear perverse that, while rejecting the concept of 'oral poetry' as an entirely separate category, I should nonetheless have chosen to write a book about it: and then spent much of it explaining away my title.

But the position is not totally self-contradictory or negative. The rejection of errors – or what seem to me errors – can have its uses; and dubious generalisations about 'oral poetry' have long held sway. To bring some doubts into the open is essential as part of the search after truth and also to combat the idea, still prevalent, that there is some deep and fundamental chasm between those of us who are 'modern', industrial and literate and the supposedly far-different world of non-literate, 'traditional' or 'develop-ing' peoples. Getting rid of this particular model of literature – and of society – will help us, I believe, to understand the continued strength of oral poetry in a world which (for that matter) still contains much illiteracy, and also to recognise its appearance even in the most highly 'literate' and industrial settings as a normal and valued manifestation of human artistic expression and activity.

And then, the suggestion that the oral/written distinction, so far as it exists, is more like a continuum (or perhaps a complex set of continuums) than a sharp break between two separate categories does not mean that it is foolish to concentrate on one end of this continuum rather than the other. In practice, poetry which falls towards the oral end has often been neglected in studies of literature, and a comparative book primarily devoted to the topic is certainly overdue. It is not a contradiction to focus on this aspect, while at the same time insisting that there is no sharp and absolute break between oral and written forms of poetry.

There is much to learn from concentration on the oral side of poetry. In particular, the element of *performance*, of oral presentation, is of such obvious and leading significance in oral poetry that, paradoxically, it raises the question whether this element is not also of more real importance in the literature we classify as 'written' than we often realise. Is there not an auditory ring in most poetry? is reading aloud, declaiming aloud, not in practice an important part of our culture? how many people only appreciate poetry through the *eye*? is 'literature' not something more than a visually apprehended text? I suggest that something can be learned about written literature by considering the 'oral performance' element in oral poetry.

Although I am not trying to put forward one model of 'society' or of 'literature' in this book, I have to admit that whether through the findings of the subject itself or from my own preconceptions in studying it, the picture that I derive from this study of oral poetry is of man as an active, imaginative and thinking being – and not as the product of 'social structure', the arena for unconscious urges, or the result of deep cognitive and symbolic mental structures which are in a sense beyond his power to affect. Literature is, and expresses, people doing things, and making choices. It is not the blind result of superorganic laws – those of 'oral style' or 'oral tradition' or whatever – which pre-determine people's activities or operate only at the abstract level of some impersonal 'social function' or 'reflection of society'. It was an individual – not an unthinking social force or literary law – who chose to use poetry to mourn her husband killed in the building of the Great Wall of China, and it is other individuals who chose to repeat it:

> With flowers blooming and birds singing,
> Spring is here calling us to visit friends far and near.
> Other women are accompanied by their husbands and sons,
> Poor me, I shall go to the wall where my husband's bones bear.
> Great Wall! Great Wall! If you can save us from enemies,
> Why not save first our dear ones?
>
> (Wang in Dundes, 1965, p. 311)

If literature is essentially people acting, it does not follow that we look for the a-social and untrammelled poet, outside and beyond society, or that we must follow the romantic theorists in interpreting poetry as something belonging to 'nature' as opposed to 'society', the product of free and unconscious 'natural' impulses. For in poetic institutions as in any other, people act within a social context, following the social conventions that they both use and create.

'People doing things' does not just refer to the outward and observable acts by which people organise poetic activity or use poetry to achieve political power, economic reward and cooperation, religious satisfaction, aesthetic pleasure – or the other roles already mentioned. There is also a sense in which they use it to 'create' the world around them. Poets and performers of lament songs or praise poems create and re-order the situation through their poetic expression, just as Texas prisoners transformed their environment by their songs. The imagery and symbolism in poetry and the whole view of the world conveyed there mediates peoples' experience of that world – creates it according to its own image. For the people involved, the nature of the world *is* what they create and picture it to be in their poetry. For the Hawaiians, their perception of the world around them is partly created by poetic images like that of Hawaii as 'the cluster of islands floating on the sea' just as for the Gilbertese islanders part of the essence of chiefship is created as well as expressed in their song

> That man came shouting, 'I am a chief.'
> Certainly he looks lazy enough for the title;
> He also has the appetite of a king's son,
> And a very royal waddle.
> But he shouts, 'I am a chief';
> Therefore I know he is not one.
>
> (Grimble, 1957, p. 206)

Similarly the Ibo poet's and listener's experience of beauty – and of the place of women and of love and of the beauties of nature and many other things – is in part shaped and created by poems like the *Praise of a beautiful lady* translated by Romanus Egudu.

> Young lady, you are:
> A mirror that must not go out in the sun
> A child that must not be touched by dew
> One that is dressed up in hair
> A lamp with which people find their way
> Moon that shines bright
> An eagle feather worn by a husband
> A straight line drawn by God.
>
> (Egudu and Nwoga, 1973, p. 20)

Here again, what is involved is not the passive repetition of externally determined words – artistic or ritual or utilitarian or whatever – but people actively moulding the world around them: the world of symbols which, ultimately, constitutes the world we experience and live in. It is through poetry – not exclusively, certainly, but surely pre-eminently – that people create and recreate that world.

This view of man – and this particular emphasis in sociological analysis – is not *forced* upon one by the study of poetry; even though it is a subject which does, I hold, tend to incline one to that approach. What is certain, however, is that to ignore the existence of this huge wealth of oral poetry throughout the world, in the present as well as the past, is to miss one of the great sources and products of man's imaginative and reflecting and dramatic faculties – of those things which mark him out as a human and a social animal. If this very preliminary introduction leads anyone on to study particular instances of oral poetry in more depth, or even to notice the oral poetry and literary activity around him with more understanding – then this book will have served its purpose.

References

(*Note*. This list is confined to works which are directly referred to in the text. It is *not* intended as a full or systematic bibliography of oral poetry.)

Abrahams, R. D. 1970a. Creativity, individuality, and the traditional singer, *Studies in the Literary Imagination*, 3, 1.

(ed.) 1970b. *A singer and her songs. Almeda Riddle's book of ballads.* Louisiana State University Press, Baton Rouge.

Abrahams, R. D. and Foss, G. 1968. *Anglo-American folksong style.* Prentice-Hall, Englewood Cliffs, New Jersey.

Abrams, M. H. 1958. *The mirror and the lamp: romantic theory and the critical tradition.* Norton and Co., New York.

Adali-Mortty, G. Ewe poetry, in Beier 1967.

Albrecht, M. C. 1954. The relationship of literature and society, *American Journal of Sociology*, 59.

Alexander, M. (trans.). 1966. *The earliest English poems.* Penguin, Harmondsworth.

1973. *Beowulf.* Penguin, Harmondsworth.

Andersen, J. C. 1928. *Myths and legends of the Polynesians.* Harrap, London.

Anderson, G. K. and Warnock, R. (eds.) 1967. *Tradition and revolt.* Revised ed. Scott Foresman and Co., Glenview, Illinois.

Andrzejewski, B. W. 1963. Poetry in Somali society, *New Society*, 1, 25 (21 March).

1967. The art of the miniature in Somali poetry, *African Language Review*, 6.

The veneration of Muslim saints and its impact on oral literature in Somali, in Shils (forthcoming).

Andrzejewski, B. W. and Innes, G. 1972. Reflections on African oral literature, *African Language Review*, 10.

Andrzejewski, B. W. and Lewis, I. M. 1964. *Somali poetry. An introduction.* Clarendon Press, Oxford.

Anyumba, H. O. 1964. The nyatiti lament songs, *East Africa past and present*, Présence africaine, Paris.

Arya, S. P. 1961. Folk-songs and social structure, *Indian Journal of Social Research*, 2, 2.

Austerlitz, R. 1958. *Ob-Ugric metrics. The metrical structure of Ostyak and Vogul folk-poetry.* FF Communications, No. 174, Helsinki.

Babalọla, S. A. 1966. *The content and form of Yoruba ijala.* Clarendon Press, Oxford.

Baissac, C. 1888. *Le folk-lore de l'île-Maurice*. Les littératures populaires de toutes les nations, 27, Paris.

Barnes, N. 1932. American Indian verse. Characteristics of style, *Bulletin of the University of Kansas, Humanistic Studies*, 2, 4.

1925. *American Indian love lyrics*. Macmillan, New York.

Bartlett, F. C. 1920. Some experiments on the reproduction of folk stories, *Folklore*, 31, reprinted in Dundes 1965.

Bascom, W. R. 1954. Four functions of folklore, *Journal of American Folklore*, 67.

Bawden, C. Mongolian poetry in Finnegan 1976.

Bayard, S. P. 1953. The materials of folklore, *Journal of American Folklore*, 66.

Becker, H. S. 1974. Art as collective action, *American Sociological Review*, 39.

Beckwith, M. W. 1919. *The Hawaiian romance of Laieikawai*. 33rd annual report of Bureau of American Ethnology.

1951. *The Kumulipo. A Hawaiian creation chant*. Chicago University Press, Chicago.

Beier, H. U. 1956. Yoruba vocal music, *African Music*, 1, 3.

1960. Transition without tears, *Encounter*, 15, 4.

(ed.). 1967. *Introduction to African literature*. Longmans, London.

(ed.). 1970. *Yoruba poetry. An anthology of traditional poems*. Cambridge University Press, Cambridge.

Beier, H. U. and Gbadamosi, B. (eds.). *The moon cannot fight. Yoruba children's poems*. Mbari publications, Ibadan, n.d.

Ben-Amos, D. Toward a definition of folklore in context, in Paredes and Bauman 1972.

Benson, L. D. 1966. The literary character of Anglo-Saxon formulaic poetry, *Publications of the modern language association*, 81.

Berndt, C. H. and R. M. 1973. *The Barbarians*. Penguin, Harmondsworth.

Berndt, R. M. 1952. *Djanggawul. An aboriginal religious cult of North-Eastern Arnhem Land*. Routledge and Kegan Paul, London.

Berndt, R. M. and C. H. 1964. *The world of the first Australians*. Angus and Robertson, London.

1970. Time for relaxation, in S. A. Wurm and D. C. Laycock (eds.), *Pacific linguistic studies in honour of Arthur Capell*, Australian National University, Sydney.

Best, E. 1923. *The Maori school of learning*. Dominion Museum Monograph 6, Wellington.

1924. *The Maori as he was*. Dominion Museum, Wellington (3rd impression, 1952).

Boas, F. 1925. Stylistic aspects of primitive literature, *Journal of American Folk-lore*, 38.

Boswell, G. W. and Reaver, J. R. 1969. *Fundamentals of folk literature*. Anthropological Publications, Oosterhout, 1969.

Bottomore, T. B. and Rubel, M. 1963. *Karl Marx. Selected writings*. Penguin, Harmondsworth.

Bown, L. and Crowder, M. (eds.). 1964. *Proceedings of the first international congress of Africanists*. Longmans, London.

Bowra, C. M. 1957. *The meaning of a heroic age*. Earl Grey Memorial Lecture, 37, Andrew Reid and Co., Newcastle upon Tyne.

1962. *Primitive song*. Mentor Books, New York.

1966. *Heroic poetry*. Macmillan, London.

Brewster, P. G. 1953. *The two sisters*. FF Communications, 62, No. 147, Helsinki.

Bronson, B. H. 1969. *The ballad as song*. University of California Press, Berkeley and Los Angeles.

Brown, J. 1763. *A dissertation on the rise, union, and power, the progressions, separations, and corruptions, of poetry and music*. London.

Buchan, D. 1972. *The ballad and the folk*. Routledge and Kegan Paul, London.

Buck, P. H. 1938. *Ethnology of Mangareva*. Bernice P. Bishop Museum Bulletin, 157.

Carpenter, R. 1958. *Folk tale, fiction and saga in the Homeric epics*. University of California Press, Berkeley and Los Angeles.

Carrington, J. F. 1949. *Talking drums of Africa*. Carey Kingsgate Press, London.

Chadwick, H. M. 1926. *The heroic age*. Cambridge University Press.

Chadwick, H. M. and N. K. 1932, 1936, 1940. *The growth of literature*. 3 vols. Cambridge University Press.

Chadwick, N. K. 1942. *Poetry and prophecy*. Cambridge University Press.

Chadwick, N. K. and Zhirmunsky, V. 1969. *Oral epics of Central Asia*. Cambridge University Press.

Chang, Y. R. 1956. Tone, intonation, singsong, chanting, recitative, tonal composition, and atonal composition in Chinese, in M. Halle *et al.* (eds.), *For Roman Jakobson*, Mouton, The Hague.

Child, F. J. (ed.). 1957. *The English and Scottish popular ballads*. 5 vols. The Folklore Press, New York (reprint of 1882 edition).

Clanricarde. 1722. *Memoirs of the Right Honourable the Marquis of Clanricarde*. London.

Coffin, T. P. 1950. *The British traditional ballad in North America*. American Folklore Society, Philadelphia.

Cohn, N. 1946. *Gold Khan*. Secker and Warburg, London.

Comparetti, D. 1898. *The traditional poetry of the Finns*. Longmans, Green and Co., London.

Cook, P. A. W. 1931. History and *Izibongo* of the Swazi chiefs, *Bantu Studies*, 5.

Cope, T. (ed.). 1968. *Izibongo. Zulu praise-poems*. Clarendon Press, Oxford.

Cray, E. 1967. 'Barbara Allen': cheap print and reprint, in D. K. Wilgus (ed.), *Folklore international*, Folklore Associates, Hatboro, Penns.

Crosby, R. 1936. Oral delivery in the Middle Ages, *Speculum*, 11.

Culley, R. C. 1967. *Oral formulaic language in the Biblical psalms*. University of Toronto Press, Toronto.

Curschmann, M. 1967. Oral poetry in mediaeval English, French, and German literature: some notes on recent research, *Speculum*, 42.

Curtis, N. 1907. *The Indians' book*. Harper and Bros., New York and London.

Cushing, G. F. 1970. Songs and tales of the Ob Ugrians, unpub. lecture at School of Oriental and African Studies, University of London.

Dadie, B. B. 1964. Folklore and literature, in Bown and Crowder.

Damane, M. and Sanders, P. B. (eds.). 1974. *Lithoko. Sotho praise-poems.* Clarendon Press, Oxford.

Delargy, J. H. 1945. The Gaelic story-teller, *Proceedings of the British Academy*, 31.

Deng, F. M. 1973. *The Dinka and their songs.* Clarendon Press, Oxford.

Denisoff, R. G. 1960. Songs of persuasion. A sociological analysis of urban propaganda songs, *Journal of American Folklore*, 79.

Dillon, M. 1947. The archaism of Irish tradition, *Proceedings of the British Academy*, 33.

(ed.). 1954. *Early Irish society.* Radio Eireann, Dublin.

Diop, B. 1966. *Tales of Amadou Koumba.* Eng. trans., Oxford University Press, London.

Doleželová-Velingerová, M. and Crump, J. I. (trans.) 1971. *Ballad of the hidden dragon (Liu Chih-yüan chu-kung-tiao).* Clarendon Press, Oxford.

Dorson, R. M. 1963. Current folklore theories, *Current Anthropology*, 4.

(ed.). 1972. *African folklore.* Indiana University Press, Bloomington and London.

Dronke, P. 1968. *The medieval lyric.* Hutchinson, London.

Duggan, J. J. 1973. *The song of Roland. Formulaic style and poetic craft.* University of California Press, Berkeley and London.

Dundes, A. (ed.). 1965. *The study of folklore.* Prentice-Hall, Englewood Cliffs, N.J.

Edmonson, M. S. 1971. *Lore. An introduction to the science of folklore and literature.* Holt, Rinehart and Winston, New York.

Egudu, R. and Nwoga, D. 1973. *Igbo traditional verse.* Heinemann, London.

Elwin, V. and Hivale, S. 1944. *Folk-songs of the Maikal Hills.* Oxford University Press, London.

Emeneau, M. B. 1958. Oral poets of South India – the Todas, *Journal of American Folklore*, 71, reprinted in Hymes 1964.

1966. Style and meaning in an oral literature, *Language*, 42.

1971. *Toda songs.* Clarendon Press, Oxford.

Emerson, N. B. 1909. *Unwritten literature of Hawaii. The sacred songs of the hula.* Bureau of American Ethnology, Bulletin, 38, Washington.

Entwistle, W. J. 1951. *European balladry.* Clarendon Press, Oxford.

Finnegan, R. 1970. *Oral literature in Africa.* Clarendon Press, Oxford.

1974a. How oral is oral literature? *Bulletin of the School of Oriental and African Studies*, 37.

1974b. Can there be an unbiased sociology of literature? *International Journal of Comparative Sociology*, 15.

1975. Communication and technology (D101:8). Open University Press, Milton Keynes.

(forthcoming). Oral literature and tradition, in E. Shils (ed.), *Tradition.* Duckworth, London.

(ed.). 1977. *Penguin anthology of oral poetry.* Penguin, Harmondsworth.

Fitzgerald, R. (trans.). 1965. *The Odyssey.* Panther Books, London.

Fletcher, A. C. 1900. *Indian story and song from North America.* Small Maynard and Co., Boston.

Fortune, R. *Sorcerers of Dobu.* Dutton and Co., New York.

Frazer, J. G. 1918. *Folk-lore in the Old Testament.* 3 vols. Macmillan, London.

Freeman, L. C. 1957. The changing functions of a folksong, *Journal of American Folklore,* 70.

Freuchen, D. (ed.). 1962. *Peter Freuchen's book of the Eskimos.* Barker, London.

Friedman, A. B. 1961. The formulaic improvisation theory of ballad tradition – a counterstatement, *Journal of American Folklore,* 74.

Fry, D. K. 1967. Old English formulas and systems, *English Studies,* 48.

Gerould, G. H. 1932. *The ballad of tradition.* Clarendon Press, Oxford.

Glassie, H., Ives, E. D. and Szwed, J. F. [1970]. *Folksongs and their makers.* Bowling Green University Popular Press, Bowling Green, Ohio.

Gomme, G. L. 1885. The science of folk-lore, *Folk-lore Journal,* 3.

Gonda, J. 1959. *Stylistic repetition in the Veda.* N.V. Noord-Hollandsche Uitgevers Maatschappij, Amsterdam.

Goody, J. (ed.). 1968. *Literacy in traditional societies.* Cambridge University Press.

1972. *The myth of Bagre.* Clarendon Press, Oxford.

Grainger, P. 1908. Impress of personality on traditional singing, *Journal of the Folk-Song Society,* 3, 12.

Graña, C. 1971. *Fact and symbol. Essays in the sociology of art and literature.* Oxford University Press, New York.

Grant, E. W. 1927/9. The Izibongo of the Zulu chiefs, *Bantu Studies,* 3.

Gray, B. 1971. Repetition in oral literature, *Journal of American Folklore,* 84.

Green, M. M. 1964. *Igbo village affairs.* 2nd ed., Cass and Co., London.

Greene, D. M. 1957. The lady and the dragoon: a broadside ballad in oral tradition, *Journal of American Foklore,* 70.

Greenway, J. 1953. *American folksongs of protest.* University of Pennsylvania Press, Philadelphia.

1964. *Literature among the primitives.* Folk Associates, Hatboro, Pennsylvania.

Grimble, A. F. 1957. *Return to the islands.* Murray, London.

Gummere, F. B. 1897. The ballad and communal poetry, *Harvard Studies and Notes in Philology,* 5, reprinted in Leach and Coffin, 1961.

Hadas, M. 1954. *Ancilla to classical reading.* Columbia University Press, New York.

Harries, L. 1962. *Swahili poetry.* Clarendon Press, Oxford.

Hatto, A. T. 1970. *Shamanism and epic poetry in Northern Asia.* School of Oriental and African Studies, University of London.

Hendron, J. W. 1954. The scholar and the ballad-singer, *Southern Folklore Quarterly,* 18, reprinted in Leach and Coffin, 1961.

Hiskett, M. 1964–5. The 'Song of Bagauda': a Hausa king list and homily in verse, *Bulletin of School of Oriental and African Studies,* 27–8.

Hivale, S. and Elwin, V. 1935. *Songs of the forest. The folk poetry of the Gonds.* Allen and Unwin, London.

Hodgart, M. J. C. 1950. *The ballads.* Hutchinson, London.

Hodgart, M. (ed.). 1971. *The Faber book of ballads.* Faber and Faber, London.

Hoebel, E. A. 1972. *The law of primitive man.* Atheneum, New York.

Hogg, J. 1834. *The domestic manners and private life of Sir Walter Scott.* Glasgow.

Hoggart, R. 1966. Literature and society, in N. Mackenzie (ed.), *A guide to the social sciences.* Weidenfeld and Nicolson, London.

Hollo, A. (ed.). 1964. *Negro verse.* Vista books, London.

Holloway, J. 1970. The later English broadside ballads...three articles, *The Listener*, 83, May and June.

Housman, J. E. (ed.). 1952. *British popular ballads.* Harrap, London.

Hymes, D. (ed.). 1964. *Language in culture and society.* Harper and Row, New York.

Innes, G. 1973. Stability and change in griots' narrations, *African Language Studies*, 14.
  1974. *Sunjata. Three Mandinka versions.* School of Oriental and African Studies, London.

Jackson, B. (ed.). 1972. *Wake up dead man: Afro-American worksongs from Texas prisons.* Harvard University Press, Cambridge, Mass.

Jacobs, M. 1966. A look ahead in oral literature research, *Journal of American Folklore*, 79.

Johnson, J. W. 1971. The development of the genre *heello* in modern Somali poetry. M. Phil. thesis, University of London.

Johnston, H. A. S. 1966. *A selection of Hausa stories.* Clarendon Press, Oxford.

Jones, A. M. 1943. *African music.* Rhodes-Livingstone Museum Occasional Papers, 2.

Jones, J. H. 1961. Commonplace and memorization in the oral tradition of English and Scottish popular ballads, *Journal of American Folklore*, 74.

Jones, P. T. H. 1959–60. Puhiwahine – Maori poetess, *Te Ao Hou*, 28–31.

Jousse, M. 1925. Le style oral rythmique et mnémotechnique chez les verbo-moteurs, *Archives de philosophie*, 2, 4.

Kagame, A. 1951. *La poésie dynastique au Rwanda.* Institut Royal Colonial Belge, Bruxelles.

Kailasapathy, K. 1968. *Tamil heroic poetry.* Clarendon Press, Oxford.

Karpeles, M. 1967. *Cecil Sharp. His life and work.* Routledge and Kegan Paul, London.
  1973. *An introduction to English folk song.* Oxford University Press, London.

Kershaw, N. 1921. *Stories and ballads of the far past.* Cambridge University Press.

Kettle, A. 1970. The artist and society (A100:4). Open University Press, Bletchley.

Kirk, G. S. 1965. *Homer and the epic.* Cambridge University Press.

Knott, E. 1922. *The bardic poems of Tadhg Dall Ó Huiginn*, Vol. 1, Irish Texts Society, Vol. 22, (1920).

Knott, E. and Murphy, G. 1967. *Early Irish literature.* Routledge and Kegan Paul, London.

Korson, G. 1943. *Coal dust on the fiddle. Songs and stories of the bituminous industry.* University of Pennsylvania Press, Philadelphia.

Lang, D. M. (ed.). 1971. *Guide to Eastern literatures.* Weidenfeld and Nicolson, London.
Laṣebikan, E. L. 1955. Tone in Yoruba poetry, *Odu,* 2.
Last, M. The traditional Muslim intellectual in Hausaland: the background, in Shils, forthcoming.
Lathrop, F. C. 1957. Commercial parlor-ballad to folksong, *Journal of American Folklore,* 70.
Lattimore, R. (trans.). 1951. *The Iliad of Homer.* Routledge and Kegan Paul, London.
Laws, G. M. 1957. *American balladry from British broadsides. A guide for students and collectors of traditional song.* American Folklore Society, Philadelphia.
Laydevant, F. 1930. La poésie chez les Basutos, *Africa,* 3.
Leach, M. (ed.). 1949. *Standard dictionary of folklore, mythology and legend.* Funk and Wagnalls, New York.
Leach, MacE. 1957. Folksong and ballad – a new emphasis, *Journal of American Folklore,* 70.
Leach, MacE. and Coffin, T. P. (eds.). 1961. *The critics and the ballad.* Southern Illinois University Press, Carbondale.
Leakey, L. S. B. 1954. *Defeating Mau Mau.* Methuen, London.
Lemert, E. M. 1967. *Human deviance, social problems, and social control.* Prentice-Hall, Englewood Cliffs, N.J.
Lestrade, G. P. 1937. Traditional literature, in I. Schapera (ed.), *The Bantu-speaking tribes of South Africa.* Routledge, London.
Lewis, C. S. 1942. *A preface to Paradise Lost.* Oxford University Press, London.
Lienhardt, G. 1963. The Dinka of the Nile Basin, *The Listener,* 69.
Lloyd, A. L. 1952. *Come all ye bold miners. Ballads and songs of the coalfields.* Lawrence and Wishart, London.
    1967. *Folk song in England.* Lawrence and Wishart, London.
Lomax, A. 1959. Folk song style, *American Anthropologist,* 61.
Lord, A. B. 1956. Avdo Međedović, Guslar, in A. B. Lord (ed.), *Slavic folklore. A symposium.* American Folklore Society, Philadelphia.
Lord, A. B. 1965. Oral poetry, in A. Preminger (ed.), *Encyclopedia of poetry and poetics.* Princeton University Press, Princeton, New Jersey.
    1968a. *The singer of tales.* Atheneum, New York, 1968 (1st pub. 1960).
    1968b. Homer as an oral poet, *Harvard Studies in Classical Philology,* 72.
Lovejoy, A. O. 1948. *Essays in the history of ideas.* Johns Hopkins Press, Baltimore.
Luomala, K. 1955. *Voices on the wind. Polynesian myths and chants.* Bishop Museum Press, Honolulu.

Mabogunje, A. 1958. The Yoruba home, *Odu,* 5.
MacCormick, D. 1969. ed. J. L. Campbell, *Hebridean folksongs. A collection of waulking songs.* Clarendon Press, Oxford, 1969.
MacKenzie, A. S. 1911. *The evolution of literature.* John Murray, London.

McLuhan, M. 1962. *The Gutenberg galaxy*. Routledge and Kegan Paul, London.
   1967. *Understanding media: the extensions of man*. Sphere Books, London.
   1970. *Counterblast*. Rapp and Whiting, London.

McMillan, D. J. 1964. A survey of theories concerning the oral transmission of the traditional ballad, *Southern Folklore Quarterly*, 28.

McNeill, I. 1963. The meter of the Hittite epic, *Journal of Anatolian Studies*, 13.

Macrae, N. 1975. Pacific Century, 1975–2075?, *The Economist*, Vol. 254, No. 6854, 4 Jan.

Magoun, F. P. 1953. Oral-formulaic character of Anglo-Saxon narrative poetry, *Speculum*, 28, reprinted in Nicholson, 1971.

Malinowski, B. 1926. *Myth in primitive psychology*. Kegan Paul, Trench, Trubner and Co., London.

Malo, D. (trans. N. B. Emerson). 1903. *Hawaiian antiquities*. Hawaiian Gazette, Honolulu.

Marshall, J. J. 1931. *Popular rhymes and sayings of Ireland*. Second ed., Tyrone Printing Co., Dungannon.

Mascarenhas, A. 1973. An Indian overtime lament, *Sunday Times*, Oct. 21.

Merriam, A. P. 1954. Song texts of the Bashi, *African Music*, 1, 1.

Miller, J. 1971. *McLuhan*. Fontana, London.

Miner, E. 1968. *Introduction to Japanese court poetry*. Stanford University Press, Stanford.

Mitcalfe, B. 1961. *Poetry of the Maori*. Paul's Book Arcade, Hamilton and Auckland.

Mofokeng, S. M. 1945. Notes and annotations of the praise-poems of certain chiefs and the structure of praise-poems in Southern Sotho, unpub. dissertation for honours (Bantu Studies), University of the Witwatersrand.
   1955. The development of leading figures in animal tales in Africa, unpub. doctoral thesis, University of the Witwatersrand.

Moore, J. R. 1916. The influence of transmission on the English ballads, *Modern Language Review*, 11.

Morris, C. 1972. *Medieval media. Mass communication in the making of Europe. An inaugural lecture*. University of Southampton.

Mulford, D. C. 1964. *The Northern Rhodesia general election 1962*. Oxford University Press, Nairobi.

Mumin, Hassan Sheikh (trans. B. W. Andrzejewski). 1974. *Shabeelnaagood. Leopard among the women. A Somali play*. Oxford University Press, London.

Murko, M. 1929. *La poésie populaire épique en Yougoslavie au début de XXe siècle*. Travaux publiés par l'Institut d'études slaves, No. 10, Paris.

Musil, A. 1928. *The manners and customs of the Rwala Bedouins*. American Geographical Society, New York.

Nagler, M. N. 1967. Towards a generative view of the oral formula, *Transactions of the American Philological Association*, 98.

Nettl, B. 1956. *Music in primitive culture*. Harvard University Press, Cambridge, Mass.

Nichols, S. G. 1961. *Formulaic diction and thematic composition in the Chanson de Roland*. University of North Carolina, Studies in the Romance Languages and Literatures, 36, Chapel Hill.

Nicholson, L. E. (ed.). 1971. *An anthology of Beowulf criticism*. University of Notre Dame Press, Notre Dame.

Nisbet, R. A. 1970. *The sociological tradition*. Heinemann, London.

Nketia, J. H. K. 1955. *Funeral dirges of the Akan people*. Achimota.

1962. *African music in Ghana. A survey of traditional forms*. Longmans, Accra.

1963. *Drumming in Akan communities of Ghana*. Nelson, Edinburgh.

Non-art of the ballad, The, 1971. *Times Literary Supplement* 3638, 19 November.

Norris, H. T. 1968. *S̲h̲inqīṭī folk literature and song*. Clarendon Press, Oxford.

Notopoulos, J. A. 1964. Studies in early Greek oral poetry, *Harvard Studies in Classical Philology*, 68.

Odum, H. W. and Johnson, G. B. 1926. *Negro workaday songs*. University of North Carolina Press, Chapel Hill.

Olrik, A. 1965. Epic laws of folk narrative, translated in Dundes 1965.

Opie, I. and P. 1967. *The lore and language of schoolchildren*. Clarendon Press, Oxford.

(eds.). 1955. *The Oxford dictionary of nursery rhymes*. Clarendon Press, Oxford.

Opland, J. 1971. 'Scop' and 'imbongi' – Anglo-Saxon and Bantu oral poets, *English Studies in Africa*, 14.

Opland, J. 1974. Praise poems as historical sources, in C. Saunders and R. Derricourt (eds.), *Beyond the Cape Frontier: studies in the history of the Transkei and Ciskei*. Longman, London.

Ortutay, G. 1959. Principles of oral transmission in folk culture, *Acta Ethnographica*, 8.

Paden, J. N. 1965. A survey of Kano Hausa poetry, *Kano Studies*, 1.

Paredes, A. 1964. Some aspects of folk poetry, *Texas Studies in Literature and Language*, 6.

Paredes, A. and Bauman, R. (eds.). 1972. *Toward new perspectives in folklore*. American Folklore Society, University of Texas Press, Austin and London.

Paredes, A. and Stekert, E. J. (eds.). 1971. *The urban experience and folk tradition*. American Folklore Society, University of Texas Press, Austin and London.

Parry, M. 1930, 1932. Studies in the epic technique of oral verse-making. 1. Homer and Homeric style. 2. The Homeric language as the language of an oral poetry, *Harvard Studies in Classical Philology*, 41, 43.

Parry, M. and Lord, A. B. 1954. *Serbocroatian heroic songs. I. Novi Pazar: English translations*. Harvard University Press and Serbian Academy of Sciences, Cambridge, Mass., and Belgrade.

p'Bitek, O. 1974. *Horn of my love*. Heinemann, London.

Phillpotts, B. S. 1931. *Edda and saga*. Butterworth, London.

Phillips, N. 1975. Personal communication.

Pinto, V. de Sola and Rodway, A. E. (eds.). 1965. *The common muse. Popular British ballad poetry from the fifteenth to the twentieth century.* Penguin, Harmondsworth.

Pukui, M. K. 1949. Songs (meles) of old Ka'u, Hawaii, *Journal of American Folklore*, 62.

Quain, B. H. 1942. *The flight of the chiefs. Epic poetry of Fiji.* J. J. Augustin, New York.

Rasmussen, K. 1927. *Across Arctic America. Narrative of the Fifth Thule Expedition.* Putnam, New York.

    1931. *The Netsilik Eskimos. Social life and spiritual culture.* Report of the Fifth Thule Expedition 1921–4, Vol. 8, 1/2, Gyldendalske Boghandel, Copenhagen.

    1932. *Intellectual culture of the Copper Eskimos.* Report of the Fifth Thule Expedition 1921–24, Vol. 9, Gyldendalske Boghandel, Copenhagen.

Rhodes, W. 1962. Music as an agent of political expression, *African Studies Bulletin*, 5, 2.

Roberts, H. H. and Jenness, D. 1925. *Songs of the Copper Eskimos.* Report of the Canadian Arctic Expedition, Vol. 14, Ottawa.

Rogers, H. L. 1966. The crypto-psychological character of the oral formula, *English Studies*, 47.

Rollins, H. 1919. The black-letter broadside ballad, *Modern Language Association of America*, Baltimore.

Rose, E. 1961. *A history of German literature.* Owen, London.

Rosenberg, B. A. 1970a. The formulaic quality of spontaneous sermons, *Journal of American Folklore*, 83.

    1970b. *The art of the American folk preacher.* Oxford University Press, New York.

Ross, J. 1959. Formulaic composition in Gaelic oral literature, *Modern Philology*, 57.

Rothenberg, J. (ed.). 1969. *Technicians of the Sacred.* Doubleday, New York.

Russo, J. Is 'oral' or 'aural' composition the cause of Homer's formulaic style?, in Stolz and Shannon, 1976.

Sandars, N. K. 1971. *The epic of Gilgamesh.* Penguin, Harmondsworth.

Schachter, R. 1958. French Guinea's RDA folk-songs, *West African Review*, 29.

Scott, W. 1802. *Minstrelsy of the Scottish Borders*, 2 vols., Kelso. (Also later edition, ed. T. F. Henderson, Blackwood, Edinburgh and London, 1902).

Sharp, C. J. 1932. *English folk-songs from the Southern Appalachians.* 2 vols. Oxford University Press, London.

    1972. *English folk song. Some conclusions.* 4th edition (ed. M. Karpeles), EP Publishing, East Ardsley, Wakefield, 1972.

Sharp, C. J. and Karpeles, M. 1968. *Eighty English folk songs from the Southern Appalachians.* Faber and Faber, London.

Shils, E. (ed.). Forthcoming. *Tradition*. Proceedings of a seminar series at University College, London, 1972, Duckworth, London.

Smith, M. G. 1957. The social functions and meaning of Hausa praise-singing, *Africa*, 27.

Smith, N. C. (ed.). 1905. *Wordsworth's literary criticism*. Frowde, London.

Sokolov, Y. M. 1950. *Russian folklore*. Trans. C. R. Smith, Macmillan, New York.

Staal, J. F. 1961. *Nambudiri Veda recitation*. Mouton, 's-Gravenhage.

Stanford, W. B. 1967. *The sound of Greek*. University of California Press, Berkeley and Los Angeles.

Stein, R. A. 1959. *Recherches sur l'épopée et le barde au Tibet*. Presses universitaires de France, Paris.

Stekert, E. J. 1965. Two voices of tradition: the influence of personality and collecting environment upon the songs of two traditional folk singers, unpub. doctoral dissertation, University of Pennsylvania.

Stern, T. 1957. Drum and whistle 'languages': an analysis of speech surrogates, *American Anthropologist*, 59.

Stolz, B. A. and Shannon, R. S. (eds.). 1976. *Oral literature and the formula*. Center for Coördination of Ancient and Modern Studies, University of Michigan.

Strehlow, T. G. H. 1971. *Songs of Central Australia*. Angus and Robertson, Sydney.

Subotić, D. 1932. *Yugoslav popular ballads. Their origin and development*. Cambridge University Press.

Sümer, F., Uysal, A. E. and Walker, W. S. (trans. and ed.). 1972. *The book of Dede Korkut. A Turkish epic*. University of Texas Press, Austin and London.

Taylor, A. 1931. '*Edward*' and '*Sven i Rosengård*'. *A study in the dissemination of a ballad*. University of Chicago Press, Chicago.

Tedlock, D. 1972. *Finding the center. Narrative poetry of the Zuni Indians*. Dial Press, New York.

Thalbitzer, W. 1923. *The Amassilik Eskimo. Vol. 2. Language and folklore*. Meddelelser om Grønland, Bd. 40.

Thompson, S. 1955–8. *Motif index of folk literature*. Revised edition. 6 vols. Rosenkilde and Bagger, Copenhagen.

Thoms, W. 1846. Letter, in *The Athenaeum*, No. 982, Aug. 22.

Thomson, D. 1974. *An introduction to Gaelic poetry*. Gollancz, London.

The Times, Report of presidential address to Anthropology section on oral tradition, British Association, 1971.

Titiev, M. 1949. *Social singing among the Mapuche*. Anthropological Papers, University of Michigan, 2. Ann Arbor.

Tracey, H. T. 1933. *Songs from the kraals of Southern Rhodesia*. Salisbury.
    1948. *Chopi musicians. Their music, poetry, and instruments*. Oxford University Press, London.

Trask, W. T. (ed.). 1969. *The unwritten song. Poetry of the primitive and traditional peoples of the world*. 2 vols. Jonathan Cape, London.

Turville-Petre, E. O. G. 1953. *Origins of Icelandic literature*. Clarendon Press, Oxford.

Utley, F. L. 1961. Folk literature: an operational definition, *Journal of American Folklore*, 74, reprinted in Dundes 1965.

Waley, A. 1951. Kutune Shirka. The Ainu epic, *Botteghe oscure*, 7.

Walton, E. L. 1930. Navajo song patterning, *Journal of American Folklore*, 43.

Wang, B. 1935. Folksongs as regulators of politics, *Sociology and Social Research*, 20, reprinted in Dundes 1965.

Watt, I. 1964. Literature and society, in R. N. Wilson (ed.), *The arts in society*. Prentice-Hall, Englewood Cliffs.

Watts, A. C. 1969. *The lyre and the harp. A comparative reconsideration of oral tradition in Homer and Old English epic poetry*. Yale University Press, New Haven.

West, J. O. 1967. Jack Thorp and John Lomax: oral or written transmission? *Western Folklore*, 26.

Whallon, W. 1969. *Formula, character, and context. Studies in Homeric, Old English, and Old Testament poetry*. Harvard University Press, Cambridge, Mass.

Whiteley, W. H. (ed.). 1964a. *A selection of African Prose. 1. Traditional oral texts*. Clarendon Press, Oxford.

   1964b. Problems of a lingua franca: Swahili and the trade-unions, *Journal of African Languages*, 3/3.

Wilgus, D. K. 1959. *Anglo-American folksong scholarship since 1898*. Rutgers University Press, New Brunswick.

   1965. An introduction to the study of hillbilly music, *Journal of American Folklore*, 78.

   1971. Country-Western music and the urban hillbilly, in Paredes and Stekert 1971.

   1973. The text is the thing, *Journal of American Folklore*, 86.

Wilkinson, R. J. 1924. *Malay literature*. FMS Government Press, Kuala Lumpur.

Wilkinson, R. J. and Winstedt, R. O. (collectors). 1957. *Pantun Mělayu*. 3rd edition. Malaya Publishing House, Singapore.

Williams, J. E. C. 1971. The court poet in medieval Ireland, *Proceedings of the British Academy*, 57.

Williams, R. Vaughan. 1934. *National music*. Oxford University Press, London.

Winner, T. G. 1958. *The oral art and literature of the Kazakhs of Russian Central Asia*. Duke University Press, Durham, N.C.

Winternitz, M. 1927, 1933. *A history of Indian literature*. Trans. S. Ketkar, 2 vols., University of Calcutta, Calcutta.

Wolf, J. Q. 1967. Folksingers and the re-creation of folksong, *Western Folklore*, 26.

Wright, D. (trans.). 1957. *Beowulf: a prose translation*. Penguin, Harmondsworth.

Zimmermann, G.-D. 1967. *Songs of Irish rebellion. Political street ballads and rebel songs 1780–1900*. Figgis, Dublin.

Index

Titles of relatively long poems (e.g. ballads and epics) are included, but not those of short lyrics. A brief explanation is usually attached for the less familiar genres, titles or poets listed in the index.